Understanding Social Problems

Understanding Social Problems

Issues in Social Policy

Edited by

Margaret May
London Guildhall University

Robert Page
University of Leicester

Edward Brunsdon
London Guildhall University

BLACKWELL
Publishers

Copyright © Blackwell Publishers Ltd 2001
Editorial matter and arrangement copyright © Margaret May, Robert Page and Edward Brunsdon 2001
Chapter 9 copyright © Paul Spicker 2001

First published 2001

2 4 6 8 10 9 7 5 3 1

Blackwell Publishers Ltd
108 Cowley Road
Oxford OX4 1JF
UK

Blackwell Publishers Inc.
350 Main Street
Malden, Massachusetts 02148
USA

British Library Cataloguing in Publication Data

A CIP catalogue record for this book is available from the British Library.

Library of Congress Cataloging-in-Publication Data

Understanding social problems : issues in social policy / edited by
Margaret May, Robert Page, Edward Brunsdon.
      p.   cm.
Includes bibliographical references and index.
   ISBN 0–631–22029–1—ISBN 0–631–22030–5 (pbk.)
   1. Social problems—Great Britain.   2. Great Britain—Social policy.
I. May, Margaret.   II. Page, Robert M.   III. Brunsdon, Edward.
   HN390 .U53   2001
   361.6′1′0941—dc21
                                                         00-009971

Typeset in 10½ on 12½ pt Times
by Best-set Typesetter Ltd., Hong Kong
Printed in Great Britain by TJ International, Padstow, Cornwall

This book is printed on acid-free paper.

Contents

Figures

Tables

About the Contributors

John Baldock is Reader in Social Policy at the University of Kent at Canterbury. His main research and teaching interests concern the ageing of the population in industrial societies and the provision of care services for older people. He has also published widely on the personal social services. His recent writing has focused on cultural issues and ageing; for example 'Social Services and Contrary Cultures', in P. Chamberlayne et al. (eds), *Welfare and Culture in Europe* (1999), as well as more general studies of social policy, including co-editing (with N. Manning et al.) the text *Social Policy* (1999).

Edward Brunsdon is a Principal Lecturer in Social Policy at London Guildhall University, where he teaches and researches British and comparative social policy and welfare management. His main research interests are commercial and occupational welfare in the UK and Europe, on which he is currently preparing a study for the Open University Press. His recent publications include studies of social care management (with M. May) in S. Horton and D. Farnham, *Public Management in Britain* (1999), and of occupational and commercial welfare in R. Page and R. Silburn (eds), *British Social Welfare in the Twentieth Century* (1999).

John Clarke is Professor of Social Policy at the Open University. Drawing on a background in cultural studies, his interests have centred on the political, ideological and organizational conflicts around social welfare. Much of his recent work has addressed the impact of managerialism on the remaking of welfare systems: *The Managerial State* (1997), co-authored with J. Newman; *New Managerialism, New Welfare?* (2000), co-edited with S. Gewirtz and E. McLaughlin. He has also researched and written on US culture and politics (including *New Times and Old Enemies: Essays on Cultural Studies and America* (1991)).

Dee Cook is Professor of Social Policy and Director of the Regional Research Institute at the University of Wolverhampton, where she teaches social policy and criminal justice. She previously lectured in criminology at Keele University. In an earlier life she worked for the Inland Revenue, the Department of Health and Social Security and later in an advice centre. Her academic research and publications have focused on: comparative analyses of tax and social security fraud; racism, citizenship and exclusion; crime and locality; welfare to work; community safety policies. Her current research centres on the relations between criminal justice and social policies under New Labour.

Hartley Dean is Professor of Social Policy at the University of Luton. His principal interests lie in the fields of poverty, welfare rights and citizenship, but he has recently undertaken research involving the economic survival strategies of marginalized groups. His publications include: *Social Security and Social Control* (1991); *Dependency Culture: The Explosion of a Myth* (with P. Taylor-Gooby) (1992); *Welfare, Law and Citizenship* (1996); *Poverty, Riches and Social Citizenship* (with M. Melrose) (1999); *Begging Questions: Street-level Economic Activity and Social Policy Failure* (ed.) (1999).

David Donnison is Professor Emeritus in the University of Glasgow's Department of Urban Studies and a Visiting Professor in the Warwick Business School. He has worked in many neighbourhood projects and was previously chairman of the Supplementary Benefits Commission, Director of the Centre for Environmental Studies and Professor of Social Administration at LSE. He has published extensively on social policy, and his books include: *Policies for a Just Society* (1998); *Long-term Unemployment in Northern Ireland* (1996); *Politics of Poverty* (1982).

Bob Franklin is Professor of Media Communications in the Department of Sociological Studies at the University of Sheffield. He co-edits *Journalism Studies*. His recent publications include: *Social Policy, the Media and Misrepresentation* (1999); *Hard Pressed: National Newspaper Reporting of Social Work* (1998); *Making the Local News: Local Journalism in Context* (1998); *Newszak and News Media* (1997); *The Handbook of Children's Rights* (1995). His main teaching is currently in the area of political communications, especially censorship and government news management, and the media's coverage of social policy.

Arthur Gould is Reader in Swedish Social Policy at the Department of Social Sciences at Loughborough University, where he teaches a range of policy units. He has published many articles and books about Swedish social policy and drug issues. He is currently writing a book on Sweden in the 1990s and an article on feminism and prostitution in Sweden. His recent publications include a study of Swedish social policy for the *Journal of European Social Policy*, 1998 Vol 9, and A drug-free Europe: Sweden on the offensive, *Druglink*, Vol 14 No 2.

Meg Huby comes from a background in the environmental and natural sciences but now lectures in the Department of Social Policy & Social Work at the University of York, where she teaches on social welfare and environmental issues. Her current research focuses mainly on social aspects of environmental policy, but she is also interested in methodological issues; both are reflected in her recent study *Social Policy and the Environment* (1998).

Helen Jones is a Senior Lecturer in the Department of Social Policy and Politics at Goldsmiths College, University of London, where she teaches undergraduate and postgraduate social policy and history courses. Her main research interests are gender and health history in twentieth-century Britain and the politics surrounding current social policies. Her publications include: *Health and Society in Twentieth-Century Britain* (1994); *Women in British Public Life, 1914–1950* (2000).

David Kelleher is a Senior Research Fellow at London Guildhall University, where he has taught on undergraduate and post-graduate courses and is at present engaged on a study of the Irish in England. He has previously studied and written about Bangladeshi people with diabetes and made a cross-cultural study of people with chronic pain. His publications include: *Researching Cultural Differences in Health* (ed. with S. Hillier) (1999); *Challenging Medicine* (ed. with J. Gabe and G. Williams) (1994).

Jane Lewis is the Barnett Professor of Social Policy at the University of Oxford. Her main interests have been gender, welfare and the family, on which she has published widely. Her most recent publications include: *Gender, Social Care and Welfare State Restructuring* (ed.) (1999) with K. Kiernan and H. Land, *Lone Motherhood in Twentieth Century Britain* (1998). She is currently working on a study of marriage and cohabitation, to be published in 2001, and a critical text on the family.

Mark Liddiard is a Lecturer in Social Policy at the University of Kent, where he has worked on a variety of research projects. He has a particular interest in qualitative methodologies. He is co-author, with Susan Hutson, of *Youth Homelessness: The Construction of a Social Issue* (1994). More recently he has focused specifically on cultural policy issues, and has published on museums, art subsidies and the impact of the mass media on public attitudes and on policy-makers. He is currently working on a book about historical exclusion in museums, titled *Making Histories of Sexuality and Gender* (2001).

Susanne MacGregor is Professor of Social Policy at Middlesex University, London. Her recent research activities have included directing a study of two East London estates as part of a Joseph Rowntree Foundation area regeneration programme and a study of community development approaches to drugs prevention for the Home Office. Her teaching and research interests are the politics of social policy, poverty and social exclusion, urban and community development, and substance use studies, on which she was published widely. Her most recent publications include *Social Issues and Party Politics* (ed. with H. Jones) (1998).

Eugene McLaughlin is a Senior Lecturer in Criminology and Social Policy at the Open University. He has written widely on the politics of policing and race in contemporary Britain. Among his books are: *Out of Order? Policing Black People* (co-edited with E. Cashmore) (1991); *Community, Policing and Accountability* (1994); *New Managerialism, New Welfare* (co-edited with J. Clarke and S. Gewirtz) (2000).

Margaret May is a Principal Lecturer in Social Policy at London Guildhall University, where she teaches and researches British and comparative social policy and welfare management. Her main research interests are commercial and occupational welfare in the UK and Europe, on which she has written widely (with E. Brunsdon). She is a past editor of the *Social Policy Review* and co-editor (with P. Alcock and A. Erskine) of: *The Student's Companion to Social Policy* (1998); *The Encyclopaedia of Social Policy* (2000).

Karim Murji lectures at the Open University, Milton Keynes. His main interests are racial and ethnic divisions and crime and policing, on both of which he has researched extensively.

Robert Page is a Reader in Social Policy in the School of Social Work at the University of Leicester. He is the author of two books: *Stigma* (1984); *Altruism and the Welfare State* (1996). Also he has jointly edited a number of other volumes including: *Social Welfare in Transition* (1994) (with J. Ferris); *Modern Thinkers on Welfare* (1995) (with V. George); *British Social Welfare in the 20th Century* (1999) (with R. Silburn). He is a member of the editorial board of the *Journal of Social Policy* and of *Benefits* (a specialist social security journal). He acts as reviews editor for both journals.

Nigel Parton is Professor in Child Care and Director of the Centre for Applied Childhood Studies in the School of Human and Health Sciences at the University of Huddersfield. He is co-editor of *Children and Society*, and his recent books include: *Child Protection: Risk and the Moral Order* (1997) (with D. Thorpe and C. Wattam); *Child Sexual Abuse: Listening, Hearing and Validating the Experiences of Children* (2000) (with C. Wattam); *Constructive Social Work: Towards A New Practice* (2000) (with P. O'Byrne). His main teaching is currently in the areas of social theory, social work, child protection and child welfare, on social work and multidisciplinary health and social work courses.

Pauline Prior is a Lecturer in Social Policy at the Queen's University of Belfast. Her research is mainly into mental health policy, including gender, law and history, but it also includes work on the use of general health services. She teaches social policy, with specific courses on policies for health and personal social services. Her publications include: *Mental Health and Politics in Northern Ireland* (1993); *Gender and Mental Health* (1999).

Lorraine Radford is a Reader in Social Policy at the University of Surrey, Roehampton, where she teaches courses on women and social policy, and social policy and social change. Her main research interests have been in the area of domestic violence, its impact upon children, and gender and crime. Her recent publications include: *Domestic Violence: A National Survey of Court Welfare and Family Mediation Practice* (1997) (with M. Hester and C. Pearson); *Unreasonable Fears* (1999) (with S. Sayer). In 1998 she helped co-author a report on domestic violence for the British Medical Association: *Domestic Violence a Health Care Issue.*

Karen Rowlingson is a Lecturer in Social Research in the Department of Social and Policy Sciences at the University of Bath, where she teaches on social policy and social security. She has carried out research on: family finances, credit, debt and wealth; the growth of lone parenthood; disability, benefits and work; benefit fraud. She has published widely in these areas. Her most recent publications include: *Social Security in Britain* (1999) (with S. McKay); *Fate, Hope and Insecurity: Future Orientation and Forward Planning* (2000).

Paul Spicker is a Senior Lecturer in Social Policy at the University of Dundee. He has written widely on social policy, including studies of poverty, social security and social care, including: *Poverty and Social Security* (1993); *Social Policy: Themes and Approaches* (1995); *The Welfare State: A General Theory* (2000). His research has included studies of benefit delivery systems, the care of old people, psychiatric patients, housing management and anti-poverty strategies.

Guide to the Book

The study of social problems is a principal theme in both undergraduate programmes in social policy and professional courses in health and social care. Social problem investigation also features prominently in the project work that forms a central element of assessment in many applied social studies programmes. It is with these interests in mind that this book has been designed. In particular it aims to provide students with:

- a starting point from which to explore the issues raised in particular chapters and the distinctive concerns of social policy analysts;
- the information bases for developing project proposals, preparing for other assignments and participating in group discussions and team activities.

It can be used both as a course text and as a basis for a student's independent work, and, while it is aimed primarily at those interested in social policy, students of other social sciences will also find much of value in the contributions.

Each chapter, written by an author with an established research record in a particular field, is designed to be read both separately and alongside others addressing related questions. We suggest that, when preparing their own work, students should explore these other chapters as well as the areas of particular interest to them, and also consider the issues posed in the first section. Tutors and students using it as a general text will find it most helpful to discuss the contributions to part one first before addressing the other chapters.

We have tried to ensure consistency: so each chapter discusses the changing perspectives on the nature and scale of different social problems in recent decades, changes in governmental and societal responses to them and current concerns and policy options. However, in a volume with so many contributors, students will inevitably find differences of emphasis as well as of style. In reading them we hope they will become aware of the diverse political and ideological traditions on which the discipline of social policy draws and the varying ways in which the study of social problems has been approached. We hope this encounter will persuade them to explore further and read more widely. To this end each chapter is supported by a set of 'issues to consider', which can be used either individually or for group work, and a guide to further reading and web-based sources.

This book arose from discussions with our students and with colleagues teaching courses on social problems and supervising projects at other institutions. We should like to thank them for their support with this venture and all the contributors for their patience and co-operation with our various editorial requests. We should also like to express our gratitude to Adam Smith for his help with copy-editing and to Sarah Falkus of Blackwell for all her advice and support throughout this project.

Margaret May, Robert Page and Edward Brunsdon

Social Problems in Social Policy: An Introduction

Margaret May, Robert Page and Edward Brunsdon

Given the frequency with which social problems are discussed in the social policy literature it is surprising to find so few recent texts devoted directly to discussing this area. Though there are a wealth of American studies, their approach does not always lend itself easily to the exploration of current concerns in the UK. Moreover, the changing landscape of both the discipline of social policy and its subject matter, social policies, mean that the available British texts are increasingly historical in focus (Butterworth and Weir, 1972; Fitzgerald, Halmos, Muncie and Zeldin, 1977; Manning, 1985).

The absence of specialist publications should not, however, be taken as indicative of a lack of interest in social problems. Indeed, the exploration of social problems has always been an integral part of the study of social policy and many publications from the 1940s to the early 1970s had a strong social problem focus. Like the discipline in general most had a marked practical orientation, a characteristic symbolized by its base in teaching and research in social administration and the relative neglect of theoretical issues. Consideration of these and more reflective discussions of social problems were much more likely to be found in the sociological literature.

The growth in specialist social policy publishing from about the mid-1970s did not, however, lead to a marked increase in the range of titles on social problems. It is difficult to ascertain why this was exactly, but Manning's compilation (1985) offers one clue. This text, like many of the period, aimed to move away from what were regarded as the narrow preoccupations of social administration and build on the theoretical insights emerging from sociology and other disciplines. The study of social policy was to be taken in a new direction. Instead of empiricism and prescription – the fundamental characteristics of social administration – there was to be a greater emphasis on theory and differing explanations of welfare developments. As the editor's preface made clear:

We have aimed, therefore, to address the political and economic conflicts which shape the emergence of social problems generally, and in particular areas; and we have tried to set aside some of the conventional limits of social administration, both in terms of the range of social problems examined, and in terms of the theoretical concepts brought to bear in their analysis. (Manning, 1985, p. vii)

Out went poverty and homelessness; in came violence against women, race and crisis management. References to state theory, Marxism, cultural studies and the sociology of science displaced discussions of administrative reformism.

A similar shift to a more theoretical approach to social policy characterized many contemporary publications, opening up new questions and challenging previous understandings. Commonly held assumptions about the benevolent role and purpose of state welfare were subjected to critical review; research into the structuring of welfare systems in capitalist societies was reinvigorated and their operation challenged by feminist and anti-racist writers and disability campaigners. Traditional accounts of social problems were also questioned as analysts began to explore the processes by which social issues came to pro-minence and the ways in which social problems were 'created' rather than 'discovered'.

While enriching the discipline, this 'sociological turn' also led to fears that some of the strengths of the traditional approach, not least in finding practical solutions to the problems of the day, might be jettisoned too quickly. Indeed, for Glennerster (1988) the decision to change the name of the Social Adminis-tration Association to the Social Policy Association in 1987 was symptomatic of a growing preference within the subject to study ever more obscure forms of theory rather than deal with the practical problems affecting people's lives.

More recently, however, there has been something of a *rapprochement* between more theoretically inclined analysts and those who, holding fast to the discipline's normative roots, favour a more practical orientation to the study of social policy. This tendency is reflected in this book, its contributors showing a willingness to use the strengths of both approaches as the occasion demands and considering both changing perceptions of social problems and changing responses to them.

Reflecting these developments, *Understanding Social Problems* is divided into four parts. Part one is devoted to the issue of studying social problems. It opens with Clarke's review of the way social problems have been approached from a sociological perspective, looking at both what he terms the realist/natu-ralistic and nominalist/constructionist perspectives and their implications. Page then charts the distinctive way in which social problems have been explored in the field of social policy and administration.

Part two, the largest part, with four sections, contains informative contribu-tions on family issues, poverty and social exclusion, health and community con-cerns. In the first of these sections Lewis draws attention to the pattern of family change and the situation of lone parents, who continue to be seen by policy makers and others as problematic. Baldock considers the issue of caring and dependency in relation to the dimensions of age and disability, and Radford explores the issues of domestic violence. Donnison opens the second section with a broad reflection on the changing nature of poverty, while Rowlingson tackles the issue of child poverty, which has come to prominence once more as a result of the Blair government's pledge to eradicate it within twenty years. Liddiard considers another important form of social exclusion, homelessness. Finally in this section Spicker addresses the underlying issue of the distribution of income and wealth.

Health inequalities, which have figured prominently on the public agenda since the publication of the Black Report in 1980 (Department of Health and Social Security, 1980) are considered by Jones in the third section, on health, which also includes contributions from Prior on mental health and Kelleher on problematic identities. The concluding section in this part focuses on community problems. MacGregor explores the broad question of the problematic community; Cook tackles the issue of safe neighbourhoods; Gould focuses on drugs and drug abuse.

The growing interest in the way the media reports social problems is reflected in part three. Franklin and Parton consider the way in which the reporting of child abuse has come to prominence during the past thirty years, and Dean explores the different ways in which welfare fraud and white-collar crime are reported. In the final chapter in this section McLaughlin and Murji examine how the media portrays racist violence.

In part four, the focus moves to emerging or re-emerging social problems. The boundaries of social policy have never been fixed or immutable. Indeed, in his influential study entitled *The New Social Policy*, Cahill (1994) argues that attention needs to be focused on issues such as communicating, viewing, travelling, shopping and playing rather than on more traditional concerns. Analysts such as Ferris (1991) and George and Wilding (1999) have also attempted to ensure that environmental issues receive attention within social policy. Some commentators may be reluctant to move in such directions. But debates about the protection afforded to both consumers and the natural environment were central to the policy discourse in the nineteenth and early parts of the twentieth centuries and are, once again, attracting increasing attention. Meanwhile, the fragmentation of state welfare provision has led to a parallel revival of interest in issues of regulation and quality control. These issues are taken up in Huby's study of food as a social problem and in May's review of the thorny issue of regulation and how it might be used, in Goodin's classic phrase (1985), to 'protect the vulnerable'.

As Erskine (1998) observes, researching social problems is one route into the study of social policy. It is a route that highlights policy analysts' concerns with welfare and the essentially contested, normative nature of the discipline. In developing this volume we have, therefore, not attempted to make any groundbreaking theoretical advance or to make the case for a move away from traditional to new social problems. Rather we have aimed to provide a user-friendly guide, which we hope will both encourage readers to explore the issues encountered when studying social problems in social policy and further enrich the social policy literature.

References

Butterworth, E. and Weir, D. (eds) 1972: *Social Problems of Modern Britain*. London: Fontana.

Cahill, M. 1994: *The New Social Policy*. Oxford: Blackwell.

Department of Health and Social Security 1980: *Report of the Working Group on Inequalities in Health (The Black Report)*. London: HMSO.

Erskine, A. 1998: The approaches and methods of social policy. In P. Alcock, A. Erskine and M. May (eds) *The Student's Companion to Social Policy*. Oxford: Blackwell.

Ferris, J. 1991: Green politics and the future of welfare. In N. Manning (ed.), *Social Policy Review 1990–91*. Harlow: Longman.

Fitzgerald, M., Halmos, P., Muncie, J. and Zeldin, D. (eds) 1977: *Welfare in Action*. London: Routledge & Kegan Paul.

George, V. and Wilding, P. 1999: *Social Policy and the Sustainable Society*. London: Macmillan.

Glennerster, H. 1988: Requiem for the Social Administration Association. *Journal of Social Policy*, 17 (1), 83–4.

Goodin, R. 1985: *Protecting the Vulnerable*. Chicago: University of Chicago Press.

Manning, N. (ed.) 1985: *Social Problems and Welfare Ideology*. Aldershot: Gower.

Part One

Studying Social Problems

Chapter 1

Social Problems: Sociological Perspectives

John Clarke

Introduction

This chapter explores sociological approaches to the study of social problems. To do so, it:

- distinguishes between realist and constructionist perspectives in sociology;
- explores the contribution of the constructionist perspective to rethinking the study of social problems;
- considers the principal concepts and differences within the constructionist perspective;
- concludes by examining some theoretical and political challenges to the constructionist perspective.

Although there are many and diverse sociological approaches to the study of social problems, I want to suggest that they can be organized round a fairly basic distinction between two perspectives. The first – resting on what might be called a realist or naturalistic perspective – starts from the existence of social problems and attempts to explain how and why they occur. The second – based on what can be called a nominalist or constructionist perspective –starts from asking how some conditions come to be defined or construed as social problems. This distinction implies very different views of the social world and how it might work, and this chapter will explore these differences and their consequences for the study of social problems. The distinction is not unique to sociology, extending widely across the social sciences though taking different shapes in different disciplines. As Page's chapter makes clear, many of these general issues are to be found in social policy, which adds its own distinctive orientations and analyses. This chapter will, however, give rather more attention to the second – constructionist – perspective, not least because it connects with a wider set of current developments in the social and human sciences.

Realism: The Discovery, Explanation and Solution of Social Problems

Let us begin with the realist perspective. Here, the existence of social problems provides the starting point for the sociological enterprise. What sociology has to offer is the capacity to 'go behind' the problem and uncover its causes in social conditions. There is a difference between the perspective and sociological theories. The perspective is shared by a range of widely diverging theories (or forms of explanation). Indeed, any particular social problem is likely to be explained by a variety of different – and conflicting – sociological explanations. For example, the social problem of poverty, as Donnison's chapter demonstrates, may be explained as the result of:

- processes of subcultural formation (a 'culture of poverty');
- patterns of intergenerational socialization (a 'cycle of deprivation');
- geographical patterns of social and economic differentiation (producing poor areas, regions and so on);
- patterns of income distribution through the market and the state (creating relative poverty within a national distribution of income);
- the effect of class conflict within capitalist economies (the 'impoverishment' of the working class).

Each of these theories starts from the 'fact' of poverty as a social problem and seeks to discover or reveal the underlying causes – the processes, mechanisms or conditions – that give rise to the problem. This view of social problems and the task of the sociological enterprise reflects key features of sociology's nineteenth-century origins. Many sociologists sought to model the practice of sociology on developments in natural sciences, and this underpins the view of empirically observable phenomena (poverty, crime, deviant behaviour and so on) as objects whose underlying causes can be discovered.

At the same time, many sociologists saw the sociological enterprise as a practice that was closely allied with social reformism – providing the means by which knowledge about social conditions could be produced. Such knowledge would then contribute to the purposive improvement of the social conditions, processes or practices that had given rise to the problem. This concept of the intersection of social problems, social research and social reform has been the dominant one in Western sociology during the twentieth century (see Gouldner, 1970). Although this has been predominantly a reformist tradition, seeing social science as the servant of the state, some of its main elements were shared by more radical or critical theories, such as some versions of Marxism, which aimed to reveal different underlying causes in the 'real relations' of capitalist production.

The study of social problems has occupied a particularly significant place in the development of sociology in the United States, where it has formed a distinct sub-discipline or field of inquiry. This formation has its roots in the development of social research in the early twentieth century, with its strong commitment to exploring, explaining and remedying social problems in the pursuit of social improvement (see Page's chapter and the discussion in Manning, 1985). Concerned with the disruptions and disturbances associated with the intersection of urbanization and industrialization in US society, sociologists developed studies and analyses of a range of social problems such as poverty, crime, family breakdown, illicit drug use and immoral sexuality. The dominant explanations centred on processes of social disorganization and social pathology that, they claimed, produced deviations from or disruptions of the norms of American society. These approaches came under challenge in the 1950s and 1960s from other sociological approaches, which stressed both more structural causes and the significance of forms of cultural, social and political conflict. Subsequently, textbooks and collections on the study of social problems have tended to be organized round the contrast between different theories, perspectives and approaches. For example, Etzioni (1976) distinguished between consensus and structural-functionalist; conflict and alienation; symbolic interactionist, ethnomethodological and neo-conservative perspectives (the revival of pathology and disorganization models). The long-running reader edited by Rubington and Weinberg (first edition, 1971) contrasts five perspectives: social pathology; social disorganization; value conflict; deviant behaviour; labelling. The categories change, overlap and blur between different volumes but the process of the categorization of competing perspectives appears to be an inexorable feature of writing about the study of social problems (including this chapter). Within US sociology, social problems continue to be the focus of a thriving sub-discipline or field of study that has its own learned society (the Society for the Study of Social Problems) and its own journal (*Social Problems*). In Britain, the academic home of social problems has been less clearly defined – tending to be taken up in sociology, criminology and social policy.

An alternative way of distinguishing between theories of social problems within the realist perspective is to contrast the 'level of analysis' on which their explanations are focused. Many theories that seek to explain social problems operate at the level of the biological or psychological conditions that make some people behave badly – discovering the chromosome, gene or mental characteristic that separates the deviant from the normal. Such explanations tend to operate at an *individual* level of analysis, dealing with the particular characteristics of different and deviant individuals. Other explanations tend to focus on a *micro-social* level, dealing with patterns of interaction between specific individuals and groups (peer groups, dysfunctional families and so on). Beyond this, many sociological explanations have been developed at what may best be termed the *meso-social* level (that which falls between micro-social or social interaction level and whole societies or social structures – the macro-social level.). The meso-level is inhabited by explanations that focus on specific social patterns, social institutions and even geographical localities within a wider society. Examples might include subcultures, the role of families or cultural/ moral institutions, or specific places, such as slums, ghettos and other 'dangerous places' with which social problems are associated. Finally, some forms of sociological theorizing focus on the *macro-social* level, dealing with the character and consequences of social structures: forms of socio-economic division and the dynamics of oppression, inequality and domination.

The Construction of Social Problems

Box 1.1

For the most part, theories of social problems within the realist perspective share the view that social problems are objectively describable phenomena requiring explanation. There are some difficulties with this view of social problems – and these difficulties are raised by the alternative, constructionist, perspective in the social sciences. The central difficulties concern whether or not social problems have an objective, factual existence as phenomena for sociologists to investigate and explain. For example, is the existence of people without adequate accommodation the same thing as a social problem of homelessness? Is the existence of people without adequate means of subsistence the same as there being a social problem of poverty? In different social and historical circumstances these conditions have sometimes been identified as social problems. In other circumstances, they have been treated as private misfortunes. At other points, they have been considered the normal or natural state of affairs. The problem about social problems is that they are, in very important ways, matters of social definition. The naturalistic or realist perspective treats social problems as though they are given: they are phenomena on whose existence we can all agree. The constructionist perspective insists on the need to take a step back from this view and ask instead: who says this is a social problem – and what sort of social problem do they say it is?

The constructionist perspective draws on a very different sociological inheritance, one that treats society as a matrix of meaning. It accords a central role to the processes of constructing, producing and circulating meanings. Within this perspective, we cannot grasp reality (or empirical phenomena) in a direct and unmediated way. Reality is always mediated by meaning. Indeed, some of its proponents argue that what we experience is 'the social construction of reality' (Berger and Luckmann, 1967). How something (or someone) is named, identified and placed within a map of the social order has profound consequences for how we act towards it (or them). There cannot be social problems that are not the products of processes of social construction – naming, labelling, defining and mapping them into a place – through which we can make sense of them.

The crux of this argument was established by Becker (1963) in relation to sociological explanations of deviant behaviour. Such explanations attempted to account for the difference between those who behaved normally and those who behaved in a deviant way. Becker pointed to a number of problems with this approach. First, it assumed the accurate and unproblematic knowledge of who was normal and who was deviant. But, said Becker, the distinction is socially constructed. It involves the exercise of judgement by social actors, located in social institutions, applying social norms. Secondly, deviance is context-specific rather than universal. The behaviour that is viewed or classified as deviant varies between and even within societies, and between different historical periods. As a result, Becker argued, it is analytically and methodologically incorrect to pursue the explanation of deviance in terms of discovering the 'deviant characteristics' of the 'deviant person', when deviance is a product of a process of labelling some behaviours as deviant. In short, deviance is socially constructed:

> Social groups create deviance by making the rules whose infraction constitutes deviance, and by applying those rules to particular people and labelling them as outsiders. From this point of view, deviance is not a quality of the act a person commits, but rather a consequence of the application by others of rules and sanctions to an 'offender'. The deviant is one to whom that label has been successfully applied: deviant behaviour is behaviour that people so label. (Becker, 1963, p. 9)

This approach has been very influential in the realm of criminology and the sociology of deviance (see Muncie and McLaughlin, 1996), but it has been less widely developed in relation to social problems more generally (but see Bacchi, 1999; Saraga, 1998). Nevertheless, we can draw out some significant implications for the study of social problems. If we take poverty as a social problem, it is possible to see how the constructionist perspective might force us to reconsider how poverty becomes a social problem – and how it is treated as a social problem. Poverty (as it is conventionally understood as a social problem) is constructed round a binary distinction between 'normal' people (those who are not poor) and 'deviant' people (those who are poor). It involves the construction of normative boundaries (the continuing debate about what counts as being poor or, more accurately, definitions of what you have to lack to be counted as poor). Poverty is then 'produced' or 'constructed' by applying those normative distinctions to groups of people, marking some as poor. Much sociological (and social policy) energy has been expended on trying to determine what it is that makes some people poor (that is, deviant from the norm of being not poor). This constructionist perspective does not involve denying that people will, in practice, lack the means of subsistence – but that only some people, at some times, and in some places, will be defined or labelled as being in poverty.

Some things follow from this constructionist perspective on poverty. First, we can see that poverty is, at one level, a matter of definition. Social scientists disagree about how to define and measure it – but political and public debates also reflect the *contested* character of the issue, including arguments about whether poverty can really exist in some types of society. Second, we can see that how poverty is defined, constructed and responded to is the subject of wide social and historical variation (for example whether it is a social problem requiring the attention of public agencies). Third, we can see how the label is constructed and applied to particular individuals – in the UK primarily through the workings of the benefits system. Fourth, such practices reveal how what Becker called the labels of deviance shape how people are treated. To be officially categorized as poor or in need is to become vulnerable to official intervention, investigation and scrutiny. Fifth, looking at poverty in this way raises the question: what other definitions of this situation are not visible or not taken seriously? Constructing this pattern of access to material resources as poverty closes off other possible constructions. For example, there is a long radical tradition of trying to refuse the poverty label and replacing it with a structural analysis of inequality. Such a view suggests that there is not a binary distinction between the poor and not-poor but a structure through which resources are unequally distributed between different groups or classes (see Donnison's chapter). Poverty is, in such a view, not a matter of deviance from the social norm, but a necessary effect of the structure of ownership and the control of material resources (see, for example, Kincaid, 1973; Jones and Novak, 1999).

The Constructionist Perspective: Concepts and Conflicts

The basic constructionist view associated with Becker and others has been subjected to a wide range of criticisms, some of which have attempted to refute its claims, while others have tried to develop and enhance the approach. I shall come back to some of the arguments over whether constructionist perspectives provide an adequate way of studying the social world at the end of this chapter. For the moment, however, I wish to concentrate on the ways in which they have been developed that go beyond the early formulations. Most of these centre on three main aspects: the social context of social constructions, the conflictual or contested character of social constructions and the unstable or changeable character of social constructions. In particular, attempts to develop social constructionism have hinged around issues of power (Bacchi, 1999, pp. 50–64; Clarke and Cochrane, 1998). This interest in social constructionism and its potential development is part of the wider changes in the social sciences, in which the cluster of concerns about culture, meaning and language have come to occupy a more central place (Burr, 1996; Clarke, 1999). Social constructionism is one tributary that flows into this wider movement. The developments I want to highlight occur at the points where social constructionism intersects with two other currents in particular.

One key intersection has been the exploration of the relation between social construction and the Marxist concept of ideology. Ideological analysis adds two distinctive strands to the social constructionist perspective: a concern with processes of conflict, social division and power, and an attention to the question about which social constructions become dominant. There are many positions and theories about ideology. These have ranged from relatively simple views of dominant ideas reflecting the interests of dominant classes to more elaborate views of hegemonic struggles conducted in and through attempts to fix meanings, definitions and ideas of 'ways of life' derived from Gramsci's work. There is not space here to explore all the variations, so I want to draw out just two main issues.

The first is about the motivation or purpose of particular social constructions. As a perspective, social constructionism tends to be fairly agnostic about the relations between social forces, social interests and social constructions. Social constructionist studies have tended to focus on particular examples of social constructions (specific labels, specific social problems) and to deal with their particular contexts and consequences. There is no general theory about the relation between social structure and social construction. Marxist theories of ideologies offer one way of bridging this gap, by connecting a focus of power, conflict and social divisions to the rise and dominance of specific social constructions. To return to the example of poverty, a basic Marxist development of treating poverty as a social construction would be to point to the functions it performs for capitalist interests. So, poverty as a social construction conceals deeper structural relations of inequality. It deflects attention onto the problems and character of poor people. In the process, attention is deflected away from the wider structuring of the ownership of capital and the social, economic and political power associated with it. The effect is to provide an ideological concealment that helps to secure the continued survival of a capitalist system.

A more complex Marxist development might consider poverty the product of a set of conflicts and compromises between classes and other social groups. Struggles against inequality may have forced concessions and reforms from the dominant social groups, but these are nevertheless constructed as being matters of poverty rather than inequality. So the struggles of subordinate groups have an impact of political and ideological (or cultural) power. At the same time, however, dominant groups try to retain their dominance by accommodating or incorporating subordinate concerns while retaining the capacity to frame and limit such challenges. Because such conflicts are only ever temporarily resolved, the social constructions through which they are articulated remain open to new challenges, changes and contestations. So poverty is an established and dominant social construction (especially against contrary constructions which centre on structural inequality). But it is also the focus for attempts to change its meaning – sometimes towards a more individualist- or victim-blaming view (poor people have only themselves to blame) and sometimes towards a more structural view (poverty can be overcome only by equalizing wealth). Such

Marxist approaches (sometimes referred to as neo-Marxist) emphasize the contested process of social construction, stressing the ways in which social conflicts are represented in the realm of ideology. Ideology is significant for such analyses because it is where patterns of domination and subordination can be reproduced and secured – or resisted and challenged.

The second major line of development of social constructionism has been through its intersection with poststructuralist approaches to discourse (Bacchi, 1999; Burr, 1996). Discourse provides a focal concept for poststructuralism that draws attention to the ways in which forms of knowledge are socially produced and organized. Jaworski and Coupland (1999) have suggested that it may be the implied relation between language in use and social order that explains the attraction of discourse as a concept for social analysis: 'Discourse is language use relative to social, political and cultural formation – it is language reflecting social order but also language shaping social order, and shaping individuals' interaction with society. This is the key factor explaining why so many academic disciplines entertain the notion of discourse with such commitment' (Jaworski and Coupland, 1999, p. 3).

However, approaches centred on discourse tend to reject the Marxist conception of ideologies expressing or articulating social interests. Instead, they suggest that the intertwining of knowledge and power in specific discourses (such as the bio-medical discourse of health and illness or the discourse of poverty) produces social reality, rather than reflects it (see, *inter alia*, Bacchi, 1999; Dean, 1991; 1999; Rose, 1989). Discourses produce their 'realities' by becoming embodied in institutionalized arrangements and the social practices (actions) that sustain them. So, a discourse of poverty produces 'poor people': it names them; it describes them; it is embodied in institutions (from the Benefits Agency to popular journalism); it is carried in social practices that link poor people and other social agents. The discourse of poverty produces the minutiae of social arrangements through which poor people are to be discovered, identified and managed. There are forms to be filled in, interviews to be attended, home visits to be conducted, assessments to be completed and so on. Discourses produce specific sorts of 'subject': poor people; those who investigate poor people; those who manage, assist and control poor people; even those who are not-poor people. Each subject position implies certain ways of behaving and certain sets of powers to act. Agents of the poverty system are empowered to extract information about people's lives and circumstances; they are empowered to make judgements on, give advice to and even carry out surveillance on 'poor subjects'.

This concern with discourse derives in part from the work of Foucault, who was concerned to explore the dynamics of power and governmentality in modern societies in ways that went beyond (what he saw as) Marxism's instrumental view of the state and ideology as vehicles of class rule. This broadening of how power and knowledge are seen to work to produce forms of social order and discipline has been a powerful force in producing critical deconstructions of a range of dominant social knowledges. Some of these have involved challenges to 'expert' knowledges about 'social problems' – ranging from disability through homelessness to deviant sexualities (see, for example, Saraga, 1998; Mort, 1987; O'Brien and Penna, 1997). The engagement with discourse has also challenged other knowledges about categories of people and their relation to the social world – around axes of social differentiation of 'race', ethnicity, gender and nationality and how these might intersect with social policy and social problems (see, for example, Lewis, 1998; Saraga, 1998).

This distinction between ideology and discourse is a convenient one to help us draw out some distinctions between Marxist and poststructuralist sources for developing social constructionism as a perspective. Ideology points to processes of meaning making and meaning control that reflect or articulate existing social interests – the view that the dominant ideas in any society are ideas of the dominant class (or the ideas that serve the interests of the dominant class). Dominant ideologies work to subordinate or incorporate other social groups, reinforcing the other forms of economic, social and political subordination. Ideologies aim to naturalize and universalize the ideas that support the domination of a particular class or social group. They aim to legitimate particular views of how the world is (and should be), so that the power, interest and control of the dominant group is not challenged. In the simplest formulations, then, ideologies have two effects: to subordinate or incorporate non-dominant social groups and to legitimate and conceal the conditions that support the dominant social group's domination.

Discourse is directed more towards the production of knowledge and social reality (and to the constitution of subject positions and powers within it). Its practitioners are critical of the functionalist and instrumental view of ideas in the theory of ideology, suggesting that it reduces the realm of knowledge and power to the expression and pursuit of class interests. By contrast, discourse studies lay much less emphasis on the origin of ideas and more on their organization in systemic structures that define what can be known and said. Power, in this view, is not something to be protected and legitimated by ideology, but something that is produced and distributed through knowledge – not least in the ordering of who is allowed to 'know' and to 'say' things. For example, in relation to social problems, there is usually a hierarchy of knowledges (and of those who know things) that privileges 'expert' knowledge – produced by scientists, investigators and the like – over 'lay' knowledge. Poverty, in our society, is a subject that is publicly discussed by experts rather than by poor people. In contrast to the two main effects of ideologies, then, discourses have different consequences: they create and empower 'subjects' or 'agents' who can speak and act in specific ways; they produce and control the limits of the (legitimately) 'knowable' and 'sayable'. In a sense, these can be seen to invert the effects attributed to ideologies, replacing 'concealment' with the 'production' of knowledge and substituting forms of empowerment for the function of subordination.

Like all such distinctions, however, it is neither absolute, nor simple in practice. Discourse draws together many analytic approaches (see Jaworski and

Coupland, 1999). The concept has also been taken up by many who link it to more structuralist concerns with power, inequality and social divisions. This chapter is not particularly concerned to force an abstract tidiness on this richness of meanings and usages. Rather, the significant point is the vitality of the analyses of social problems and social policies that embody this attention to the contextual, contested and changeable nature of social constructions. They may draw on different theoretical resources; they may use different theoretical terminology, but they share an orientation to the importance of language, culture, meanings, knowledges, definitions and their social production (Clarke, 1999; 2000).

Challenges to the Constructionist Perspective

Nevertheless, this constructionist perspective is often subject to criticisms that challenge its value or appropriateness to the study of social problems. In this final part of the chapter, I want to consider two of these. They concern the supposed lack of substance and the supposed lack of any politics of social constructionism. First, social constructionism is seen to trivialize the reality of social problems – creating a sense that these issues are merely social constructions. It may be that the emphasis on language, meaning, imagery and so on involved in social constructionist analyses foregrounds what we are used to seeing as peripheral or epiphenomenal matters (compared with the gritty stuff of real life). But if we can only apprehend and act on real life through language, then social constructions matter profoundly.

Box 1.2

Constructions, ideologies and discourses become institutionalized. They become the 'taken for granted' wisdom about the way of the world and what can be done in it. They define the thinkable (and attempt to dismiss alternatives as unthinkable, utopian, politically motivated and the like). In the process, dominant constructions become 'solidified' – apparently immovable and irresistible ways of thinking and acting that sustain patterns of social arrangements. Dominant constructions of our time and place have insisted that a woman's place is in the home, that white people are naturally superior, that poor people are not to be trusted, and more. Each of them has been supported by knowledges, has been embedded in institutional arrangements and has been embodied in social practices that have attempted to make those truth claims come true in practice. Those solidifications – patterns of institutionalized habit and repetition – are not insubstantial; nor are they 'just words'.

Indeed, one might suggest that what a 'realist' perspective takes as social structures could be thought of as the effects of previous social constructions and their 'solidification'. A social constructionist perspective, however, insists that such solidity is still a social accomplishment – it is not natural, it is not universal, and it is not eternal. Social constructionism insists, abstractly, that all social constructions have the potential to be deconstructed and reconstructed – however inert and immovable they may appear. This is not the same as suggesting constructions can be changed easily or at will. What a constructionist perspective reveals is how the density and solidity of social reality has been constructed and how many layers of habit, everyday wisdom, institutionalized norms and forms of social power have been built up to keep things that way. But such conditions are always in need of being reproduced – they do not carry on without the expenditure of social energy. They may, then, be reproduced differently through conflict, contestation and challenge.

A rather different set of arguments surround the politics of social constructionism. One claim is that social constructionism is political, in that it is inherently radical and critical. There is no doubt that a social constructionist perspective will always have a sceptical or critical relation to existing social constructions – the act of revealing their 'constructed' character necessarily challenges any claim to truth. But this is a generic scepticism – it applies to all social constructions (not just dominant ones). It is a scepticism that may be felt more sharply by those who hold and are supported by dominant constructions (since they usually involve the strongest truth claims). But, in practice, social constructionism is politically agnostic – it is sceptical about all constructions, whether dominant or subordinate, hegemonic or counter-hegemonic.

This agnosticism gives rise to the second (and converse) argument about social constructionism – that it lacks politics. Its relativism – the view that there are always multiple and competing constructions – is sometimes considered a failure of political nerve or a withdrawal from politics. I think this is a more difficult issue, particularly where we have been used to seeing a close alignment between social analysis and political orientation. But I think treating social constructionism as a perspective – a way of looking at social reality – may help us make sense of a separation between perspective and politics. Knowing that there are multiple and competing social constructions does not seem to me to diminish the importance of politics.

On the contrary, taking social constructions seriously draws attention to their consequences for 'real lives' and implies – if not insists – that the choice between social constructions matters (see also Bacchi, 1999, pp. 199–207). Clearly, social problems command the attention of the social sciences in a number of ways – studies of their causes and conditions will continue to be pursued in economics, psychology, sociology and social policy. But social constructionism will also continue to question what sort of problem this is. Who says it is a problem? What sorts of solution are directed to this sort of problem? Social research needs this sceptical distance if it is not just to reproduce the dominant wisdom about social problems.

Issues to Consider

- What difference does it make to approach social problems from a constructionist rather than from a realist perspective?
- Take a contemporary social problem. Consider who gets to 'know' and 'speak' about it in public and political debate. Who does not? Are there differences between 'expert' and 'lay' knowledges? How are they treated? What sorts of expert and expert knowledge get to define the problem? Are there other views, approaches, explanations or knowledges that do not get heard or are marginalized?
- Can you think of any constructions of social problems that have become deeply institutionalized, so that we take them for granted?
- Can you think of any social problems whose constructions are profoundly contested by competing discourses?

Suggestions for Further Reading

Of the many American texts, Rubington and Weinberg's (1985) continues to be a classic introduction to the study of social problems and social policy within US sociology, emphasizing multiple perspectives. Muncie and McLaughlin's (1996) examines some of these issues in relation to the definition and explanation of crime and deviance, while Saraga (1998) develops a social constructionist approach to the intersection of social divisions and social policy. Bacchi (1999) provides a stimulating introduction to the poststructuralist critique of problem- and policy-centred approaches in the social sciences, presenting a 'what's the problem?' analysis that examines the conditions and processes through which problems and solutions are constructed.

References

Bacchi, C. 1999: *Women, Policy and Politics: the construction of policy problems*. London: Sage.

Becker, H. 1963: *Outsiders: Studies in the Sociology of Deviance*. New York: Free Press.

Berger, P. and Luckmann, T. 1967: *The Social Construction of Reality*. London: Penguin.

Burr, V. 1996: *An Introduction to Social Constructionism*. London: Routledge.

Clarke, J. 1999: Coming to terms with culture. In H. Dean and R. Woods (eds), *Social Policy Review 10*. London: Social Policy Association.

Clarke, J. 2000: The cultural turn in social policy. In J. Ryan et al. (eds), *Cultural Turns, Geographical Turns*. London: Longman.

Clarke, J. and Cochrane, A. 1998: The social construction of social problems. In E. Saraga (ed.), *Embodying the Social: constructions of difference*. London: Routledge/Open University.

Dean, M. 1991: *The Constitution of Poverty*. London: Routledge.

Dean, M. 1999: *Governmentality: Power and Rule in Modern Society*. London: Sage.

Etzioni, A. 1976: *Social Problems*. Englewood Cliffs: Prentice-Hall.

Gouldner, A. 1970: *The Coming Crisis of Western Sociology*. New York: Avon.

Jaworski, A. and Coupland, N. (eds) 1999: *The Discourse Reader*. London: Routledge.

Jones, C. and Novak, T. 1999: *Poverty, Welfare and the Disciplinary State*. London: Rouledge.

Kincaid, J. 1973: *Poverty and Equality in Britain*. London: Penguin Books.

Lewis, G. (ed.) 1998: *Framing Nation; Forming Welfare*. London: Routledge/Open University.

Manning, N. (ed.) 1985: *Social Problems and Welfare Ideology*. Aldershot: Gower.

Mort, F. 1987: *Dangerous Sexualities: medico-moral politics in England since 1830*. London: Routledge & Kegan Paul.

Muncie, J. and McLaughlin, E. (eds) 1996: *The Problem of Crime*. London: Sage/Open University.

O'Brien, M. and Penna, S. 1997: *Theorising Welfare*. London: Sage.

Rose, N. 1989: *Governing the Soul*. London: Routledge.

Rubington, E. and Weinberg, M. (eds) 1971: *The Study of Social Problems: Five Perspectives*. New York, London: Oxford University Press.

Rubington, E. and Weinberg, M. (eds) 1985: *The Study of Social Problems*. Oxford: Oxford University Press.

Saraga, E. (ed.) 1998: *Embodying the Social: constructions of difference*. London: Routledge/Open University.

Chapter 2

The Exploration of Social Problems in the Field of Social Policy

Robert Page

Introduction

This chapter will focus on the ways in which social problems have been addressed in the academic specialism known as social administration or, as it is now more commonly described, social policy. Although there have been frequent references to 'social problems' such as poverty, ill health and homelessness throughout the history of social policy in Britain (see Bruce, 1968; Fraser, 1984), there has been relatively little conceptual discussion of what is meant by this term or of the processes by which such phenomena become established within what Byrne (1999) has described as 'that strange academic entity "social policy"' (p. 4). The limited theoretical debate in the academic study of social policy springs largely from the emphasis on practical issues and the desire to bring about social change, which characterize this subject area (Wilding, 1983; Alcock, 1996; 1998; Erskine, 1998). In the case of 'social problems', it was generally assumed that the specialist in social policy would be sufficiently familiar with the broad concept, so that a detailed investigation of a particular problem could proceed without any unnecessary definitional diversions.

Indeed, those seeking a more reflective definitional discourse would have been better advised, as Clarke notes in the previous chapter, to consult the sociological literature. Here they would discover a wide range of books and articles (most notably from American scholars) focusing on the diverse conceptual approaches which sociologists have utilized in the study of social problems such as social pathology, social disorganization, value conflict and critical theory (see Merton and Nisbet, 1961; Rainwater, 1974; Rubington and Weinberg, 1985; Sullivan and Thompson, 1994; Jamrozik and Nocella, 1998).

The Coming of the Social Problem in the Field of Social Policy

The defining of any phenomenon as a social problem implies that this is an occurrence that requires some form of collective response rather than an individual resolution. In *The Sociological Imagination*, C. Wright Mills (1959) famously characterized this as the difference between a personal trouble and a public issue:

> When, in a city of 100,000, only one man is unemployed, that is his personal trouble, and for its relief we properly look to the character of the man, his skills, and his immediate opportunities. But when in a nation of 50 million employees, 15 million men are unemployed, that is an issue, and we may not hope to find its solution within the range of opportunities open to any one individual. (p. 8)

In general terms it can be argued that the history of social policy in Britain has been characterized by a gradual change from concern with personal troubles, which might be ameliorated by individual, familial or philanthropic endeavour, to an emphasis on public issues, which require a more extensive and systematic collective response. Such an observation should not, as Titmuss (1974) and Baker (1979) among others have noted, lead us to assume that this change in emphasis indicates a developing humanitarianism. The recognition of a particular phenomenon as problematic can be a prelude to negative forms of social action. For example, some highly repressive collective measures were introduced in Tudor England to deal with the growing problem of unemployment (Beier, 1974; de Schweinitz, 1961). Similarly, many of the mental deficiency measures introduced in the early decades of the twentieth century were, as King (1999) has recently reminded us, both illiberal and inhumane.

Of course, the identification of a social problem does not mean that there will be widespread agreement about its extent, cause or resolution. For instance, the approach adopted by the Charity Organisation Society (COS) to the problem of poverty in late-nineteenth-century England was not shared by other social reformers of the period. The COS, which was established in 1869, rejected the idea that the growing problem of poverty was the result of an inequitable economic and social system. This organization held fast to the belief that it was possible for citizens of good character to become self-reliant provided they received appropriate advice and support rather than indiscriminate forms of financial relief. Believing that a more scientific approach to philanthropy was required, the COS established a number of autonomous district committees to deliberate on the merits or otherwise of claims for assistance and ensure that those in need were directed towards appropriate voluntary providers. Although the COS was not opposed to social reform in principle, it considered that the development of a more extensive poor relief role for the state would undermine self-advancement and lead to the undesirable development of social 'rights' (Humphreys, 1995).

From the latter part of the nineteenth century the individualistic approach to poverty came under increasing challenge from various quarters. In particular, the pioneering studies of Booth and Rowntree served to discredit the assumption that poverty resulted from some form of character defect. These researchers found that poverty was more closely associated with the vagaries of the trade cycle, sickness and old age. This emphasis on structural factors certainly struck a chord with leading Liberal and Fabian thinkers of the time. For example the New Liberal thinker Hobhouse favoured the development of public hospitals, libraries and parks as well as the introduction of old age pensions and increased levels of employment protection. For Hobhouse, such measures would increase individual self-realization and create a more altruistic society (see Dennis and Halsey, 1988).

Sidney Webb, the most influential Fabian thinker of the period, believed that the rising level of poverty was caused by the inefficiencies of capitalism. For Webb social ownership, economic planning and greater degrees of intervention by local and central government were needed to counter the level of deprivation arising from unemployment, sickness and old age. Unlike those influenced by Marxist ideas, Webb and his fellow Fabians believed that it was possible to use the existing machinery of the state for socialist purposes. Although Webb acknowledged that one of the prerequisites for a successful assault on poverty was the election of a sympathetic government, he believed that the expert administrator would act as the driving force for reform. As Sullivan (1999) notes: 'This one-time civil servant, who was to become a Labour MP, had been fascinated in his early life by positivist philosophical thought. Positivism's belief in a well-ordered and harmonious society guided by an educated elite appealed to this lower middle-class civil servant *manqué*' (p. 110).

Although the influence of Fabianism is easier to detect in post-1945 British social policy, it is undoubtedly the case that from the late nineteenth century onwards there was a greater willingness to look to the state to resolve the social problems of an industrial age. The Liberal administrations of Campbell-Bannerman (1906–8) and Asquith (1908–15), which introduced a wide range of measures, including school meals, old age pensions and national insurance, in an effort to resolve some of the pressing problems of the age, provide a notable example in this regard (Hay, 1983). Again, it is important to recognize that the impetus for these measures was not necessarily humanitarian. Many of the Liberal reforms were introduced in order to shore up Britain's precarious position as a major economic and military power. The provision of services such as subsidized school meals and basic medical treatment was intended to enable poorer children to become the workers and soldiers of tomorrow. Measures of this kind not only served to secure national prosperity but also helped to maintain social stability by damping down working-class unrest.

The idea that it was both possible and desirable for the government to tackle some of the pressing social problems of the age certainly took hold in the early decades of the twentieth century, most notably during the First World War (Pugh, 1993; Thane, 1982). However, state welfare did not fully come of age until the outbreak of the Second World War. Between 1939 and 1945 social policy initiatives far exceeded the level of interventionism seen during the previous conflict, not least because of the sheer scale of the demands thrown up by 'total war', such as the evacuation of mothers and children and the establishment of emergency medical services (Titmuss, 1950).

During periods of hostilities the issue of postwar 'reconstruction' tends to come to the surface, not least in order to boost morale. From the middle of 1940 it is possible to detect a growing interest in the rebuilding of British society in newspaper editorials, popular magazines and in other influential publications such as Temple's (1942) *Christianity and the Social Order*. However, it was the publication of Beveridge's report on Social Insurance (Social Insurance and Allied Services, 1942) that was to prove decisive in ensuring that reconstruction was highlighted in official circles. His concerted attack on the five giants of want, disease, idleness, ignorance and squalor struck a chord with a war-weary public who did not want to see a return to prewar forms of deprivation. Although Beveridge's proposals did not represent a revolutionary departure from the prewar situation, the promise of a compulsory, contributory social insurance scheme provided the public with further evidence that the major social problems of the age, such as poverty, could be countered by purposeful government intervention.

There were also important developments in education, health and family support. The Education Act of 1944 provided working-class children with enhanced life chances by making academic achievement rather than ability to pay the principal criterion for secondary schooling. The raising of the school leaving age to fifteen also ensured that all children would receive a minimum of four years post-primary education. Although progress was slower with health care, the increased level of central direction during wartime convinced many interested parties of the benefits of a more planned service. The coalition government announced its support for a free and comprehensive hospital service as early as 1941, though the initial plans formulated by Ernest Brown (Minister of Health in the wartime coalition government) and Henry Willink (Minister of Health in the postwar caretaker Conservative government) failed to attract sufficient political support (Willcocks, 1967). In contrast, the long-running campaign for family allowances did end in success. Again, it can be argued that the impact of war, which had led to an increased concern about the future well-being of children, was decisive in this case. However, Macnicol (1980) cautions against such an interpretation, arguing that the introduction of family allowances had become more acceptable to the wartime government mainly because payments of this kind could underpin work incentives and labour mobility and dampen down expectations about the introduction of a minimum wage.

Although the coalition government had shown a willingness to wrestle with some important social problems of the age, it was the Attlee governments of 1945–51 that were credited with conducting a full-scale assault on the five giants. Despite the precarious nature of Britain's economic position, the Labour government was able not only to honour its commitment to full employment but also to press ahead with some major social reforms. For example, Labour was committed to introduce universal social security, and its 1946 National Insurance Act represented a decisive shift in this direction. Although the adoption of the contributory principle meant that the form of protection (means-tested national assistance) afforded to those with inadequate cover was less generous, the establishment of a minimum income standard for all was a significant step forward (Sullivan, 1996).

Labour's record on the housing front was rather more mixed. Faced with a severely depleted housing stock as a result of enemy bombing, Labour succeeded in building only one million homes by 1951 compared with a target of four or five million. This shortfall has been linked to Bevan's unwillingness to accept a trade off between quality and quantity and to his administrative oversights, such as the issue of too many house building licences at a time when labour and materials were short, which led to slow completion rates (Francis, 1997). However, given the adverse economic conditions of the period, Bevan's achievements should not be under estimated. As Jefferys (1992, p. 61) notes: 'Bevan's house-building programme meant that affordable, decent accommodation was, as never before, within the reach of thousands of lower-income families.'

Bevan's and indeed Labour's greatest postwar achievement was the establishment of the National Health Service, which Hennessy (1992, p. 132) considers to be the 'nearest Britain has ever come to institutionalising altruism'. Recognizing that only a unified hospital system could provide an acceptable standard of 'free' health care for all, Bevan succeeded in pushing through a skilfully devised nationalization scheme which met with the approval of the consultants. His plans for primary health care proved more contentious, and the introduction of the NHS was secured only after the GPs were finally reassured that Labour had no plans to introduce a salaried service. Although some have argued that Bevan's achievements in health care have been exaggerated (Klein, 1995), it remains the case that this reform ensured that high quality medical care at the time of need became available to the great majority of people.

Social Problems and Social Policy since 1950

Although, as we have seen, the precise reasons for the development of state welfare in the twentieth century remain a matter of continuing debate (Baldwin, 1990), it is clear that many of the post-1945 reforms were underpinned, like a number of earlier measures, by the assumption that social problems were likely to result more from some form of structural malfunction rather than from individual behaviour. Crucially, it was believed that Keynesian economic policies and benevolent forms of state welfarism could remedy these structural impediments. Indeed, Rowntree suggested that the postwar Labour government's commitment to full employment, coupled with their social security reforms, had led to the virtual elimination of poverty in York by 1950 (Rowntree and Lavers, 1951).

The idea that the establishment of the welfare state would be sufficient to ensure that social problems would gradually fade away certainly took root in postwar Britain (see Abel-Smith and Titmuss, 1987). According to some commentators, the fledgling academic subject of social administration contributed to the reinforcement of this viewpoint (Williams, 1989). Certainly, the idea that social problems could be resolved by carefully conducted empirical studies and the subsequent introduction of appropriate policy instruments permeated the growing academic discipline of social administration (Mishra, 1977). There was a belief that methodological advances would enable policy makers to be provided with ever more accurate assessments of the causes of social problems. Indeed, one was often left with the impression that the only barrier to the elimination of social problems would be a lack of political will or the 'technical inefficiency of some public agencies' (Lee and Raban, 1988, p. 50). Although, some of the leading figures in the subject were acutely aware that the post-1945 welfare state had neither abolished poverty (Abel-Smith and Townsend, 1965) nor had been of exclusive benefit to the working class (Abel-Smith and Titmuss, 1987), their faith in the potential of state reform was seen by some later commentators as misplaced (Taylor-Gooby and Dale, 1985).

It should also be noted that the growing acceptance of the view that state intervention could counter the structural causes of social problems created the space for more individualistic explanations to resurface in relation to remaining areas of public concern in the post-1945 period. For example, the fact that certain groups, such as 'problem families', continued to display severe deprivation despite the introduction of state welfare services led a revitalized Eugenics Society to argue that this continuing deprivation resulted from an underlying ineducability (Macnicol, 1999).

The Challenge to Traditional Social Administration

While the positive aspects of the 'traditional' social administration approach (Wilding, 1983), such as a willingness to challenge dominant ideas by means of empirical evidence and a genuine desire to improve the quality of life of poor and dispossessed people, should not be overlooked, it is important to recognize some important shortcomings – not least the atheoretical base of the subject. The lack of theorizing within the subject left it vulnerable to the charge that it had failed to recognize the underlying causes of social problems because of an implicit unwillingness to challenge the structural inequalities thrown up by capitalism. Indeed, by the end of the 1960s social administration, like the welfare state with which it was inextricably linked, came under attack from both feminists and neo-Marxists for this very reason. Instead of ameliorating social problems in a capitalist society, state welfare was now being portrayed as contributing to such phenomena. Neo-Marxist commentators drew attention to the inability of the welfare state to tackle such problems as poverty and unemployment because of the vital part both played in the maintenance of a capitalist society. They argued that the NHS was created to ensure that workers' episodes of illness were minimized and that the prime purpose of state education was to ensure that capitalist work habits, values and aspirations were instilled in the young. Similarly, the main purpose of the social security system was not perceived to be the eradication of want but, rather, to limit periods of idleness. Those who were unwilling or unable to perform their respective roles in society were to be subjected to surveillance or control by 'soft cops', such as social workers and probation officers, or, when necessary, by more punitive law enforcement agencies.

According to feminists, the welfare state operated on traditional patriarchal lines in relation to the roles of men and women in the family and the operation of a male-breadwinner social security system. They drew attention to the fact that women's experiences in areas such as education and health were inferior in many respects to those of men. They also highlighted the fact that even those women who had gained some measure of independence through paid work were still to be found in forms of employment which failed to match the status and rewards enjoyed by men (Wilson, 1977; Charles, 2000).

In addition, other crities argued that the 'welfarist' approach to social problems failed to or meet the needs and aspirations of a wide range of marginal groups, ranging from people with physical and mental disabilities to members of ethnic minorities.

The New Right and Social Problems

Although the challenges of neo-Marxism and feminism served to undermine public confidence in the ability of the welfare state to tackle social problems, it did not lead to demands for a more radical form of egalitarianism. On the contrary, the apparent decline in support for the welfare state enabled a broad coalition of New Right theorists to portray this institution as problematic in its own right (Barry, 1999). These commentators argued that it had become economically inefficient and socially disruptive. Economically, the rising cost of the welfare state was linked to a decline in the economic performance of the nation. It was argued that scarce economic resources were being sucked into the 'unproductive' public sphere at rates that were beginning to undermine the profitability of the 'productive' private sector.

As for social disruption, British commentators such as Willetts (1992), Marsland (1996) and Skidelsky (1998), joined forces with American counterparts such as Murray (1984; 1990) and Mead (1986) to highlight the way in which the operation of the welfare state was creating social problems by providing incentives for behaviour which damaged the individual, the family and the wider community.

The notion of an underclass (see Macnicol, 1987; Mann, 1992) was resurrected by Murray (1994) to explain why a growing minority of poorer citizens were willing to subsist on benefits rather than avail themselves of work and training opportunities. According to Murray a culture of dependency had been allowed to take root in the lower echelons of society owing to the availability of generous welfare benefits. Crucially, this culture was being transmitted to a new generation who, like their parents before them, were eschewing the values of work, self-reliance and individual responsibility, with all the negative consequences this was deemed to have for the wider society. Murray expressed particularly concern about the growth of one particular constituent part of the underclass – lone mothers. 'The key to an underclass is not the individual instance but a situation in which a very large proportion of an entire population lacks fathers, and this is far more common in poor communities than in rich ones' (Murray, 1990, p. 13).

Under the Conservative governments of both Thatcher (1979–90) and Major (1990–7) various attempts were made to tackle the 'culture of dependency'. In the case of social security a number of measures were introduced to reduce both current and prospective forms of dependence. These ranged from cuts in benefit entitlement to the introduction of the Job Seekers Allowance, the Social Fund, Incapacity Benefit and the Child Support Agency. It was envisaged that such measures would eventually reduce citizens' expectations of state support.

Although the various Conservative reforms had little effect on total welfare state spending (Glennerster and Hills, 1998), their 'cultural' impact should not be underestimated. The main achievement of contemporary Conservatism was to persuade growing numbers of citizens about the virtues of individualism and the free market and to engender more sceptical ideas about the role of collectivism in modern society. As a result, a problem such as unemployment was now deemed to require lower rather than higher rates of income tax, deregulation rather than regulation and entrepreneurialism rather than state interventionism. Poverty was once again linked with individual failings or inappropriate lifestyle choices rather than with structural factors.

New Labour and Social Problems

The return to power of the Labour Party in 1997 might have led some to expect a return to a more structural approach to social problems. However, New Labour's desire to distinguish itself from traditional forms of social democracy and democratic socialism (Labour Party, 1997) has inevitably led it to reconsider its approach to both the cause and the resolution of contemporary social problems.

In terms of causes, New Labour recognizes that economic and social change will continue to generate various forms of social problems. For example, it acknowledges that the pattern and duration of work has been transformed as a result of global economic developments. The change from a manufacturing to a service economy in the UK has led to a decline in the demand for traditional male manual work as well as to a reduction in the number of secure lifetime forms of employment in both the public and private sectors. In addition, the growth of female participation in the labour market has led to changed expectations concerning personal relations and the pattern of care. Crucially, however, New Labour believes that social problems can be created or exacerbated by various factors. For example, the priority that New Labour has accorded to 'welfare reform' stems in part from its belief that poorly functioning or outmoded state welfare services are actually a *cause* of social problems. As the leading proponent of New Labour's third way – Anthony Giddens – states, 'Even in its most developed forms, the welfare state was never an unalloyed good. All welfare states create problems of dependency, moral hazard, bureaucracy, interest-group formation and fraud' (Giddens, 2000, p. 33).

It is clear that New Labour believes that the inappropriate actions or inactions of individuals can cause social problems. Although commentators such as Field (1995; 1997), who served briefly as a New Labour Minister for Welfare Reform (1997–8), and Deacon (1999) have acknowledged the way in which the operation of the welfare state can give rise to dishonesty and dependency, they have also been keen to stress that citizens must be regarded as moral agents who should take some personal responsibility for their behaviour.

New Labour believes that the resolution of social problems requires a purposeful partnership between the government and the individual. The government is seen to have two key roles. First, it must pursue sound economic policies to create the conditions for steady growth and low levels of inflation and unemployment. Second, it must ensure that all citizens have sufficient opportunities to acquire the education, skills and training necessary if they are to prosper in a changing and uncertain labour market. As the first New Labour Chancellor Gordon Brown has stated, 'What people resent about Britain today is not that some people who have worked hard have done well. What angers people is that millions are denied the opportunity to realise their potential and are powerless to do so. It is this inequality that must be addressed' (Brown, 1999). To this end New Labour has introduced measures intended to create *Opportunity for All* (Department of Social Security, 1999). For example, it is recognized that too many children are forced to grow up in poverty with all the negative consequences this entails. To counter this problem efforts are being made to improve both the living standards of this group (enhanced income support and child benefit allowances; additional investment in housing; various health initiatives) and the level of educational opportunities (Sure Start and Education Action Zones). Also various measures have been introduced to reconnect disadvantaged adult groups to the labour market, such as the New Deals, the minimum wage, the National Childcare strategy, individual learning accounts, tax credits and reforms to the benefits system.

New Labour recognizes, however, that it also has a responsibility to provide adequate support for those unable to participate in the labour market. For instance, a minimum income guarantee, which is being increased in line with earnings, has been introduced for poorer pensioners. Moreover, from the end of 2000 all pensioner households will receive a winter fuel allowance (£150), and those aged 75 or over will receive a free television licence.

New Labour believes that citizens must also play a greater role in combating social problems. As Tony Blair (1998, pp. 3–4) has stated, 'For too long, the demand for rights from the state was separated from the duties of citizenship and the imperative for mutual responsibility on the part of individuals and institutions.' Accordingly, citizens are seen to have a duty to avail themselves of work and training opportunities and to behave in socially responsible ways. Those who fail to meet these expectations are likely to be penalized in various ways. Those who refuse to participate in some of the New Deal programmes without good cause may find that their benefits are temporarily withheld, while curfews may be imposed in areas where groups of young people cause a nuisance late at night.

It is also a belief of New Labour that civil society needs to be rejuvenated if social problems are to be tackled effectively. The idea that the state could single-handedly tackle such phenomena is now regarded as mistaken. A growth in voluntary activity at the local level is considered vital if social problems are to be prevented as well as ameliorated (Johnson, 1999). As Blair (1998, p. 4) notes, 'A key challenge of progressive politics is to use the state as an enabling force, protecting effective communities and voluntary organisations and encouraging their growth to tackle new needs, in partnership as appropriate'. This notion of partnership has emerged as a central theme in New Labour's approach to social problems. Social problems are now seen to be rooted in the complex interplay of market forces, undesirable forms of state intervention and inappropriate forms of individual behaviour, New Labour believes, not least because of its commitment to pragmatic policy making (Powell, 2000), that diverse solutions will prove more effective than the unitary approaches of the past.

The main weakness of New Labour's approach to social problems is the way in which 'broader questions of power, property and privilege' have been side-lined (Thompson, 1997, p. 226). There is a danger that the disadvantaged will be expected to adopt ever more 'responsible' attitudes to work, welfare and family formation in a period when the direct assault on the structural causes of social problems has been put on hold.

Social Problems and the Field of Social Policy: Where Next?

New Labour's approach to social problems and social policy, like those of previous administrations, presents a challenge to those who study social policy. Some might choose to ignore such developments, preferring to pursue a more theoretical approach to the subject in the hope that this might enhance the academic status, though not necessarily the relevance, of the subject. Others may respond by attempting to develop more sophisticated social research techniques that might provide New Labour with a more rational or informed guide to policy making. In contrast, there will be those who will wish to engage with New Labour's approach because of their commitment to the normative tradition within the study of social policy. Given that the study of social policy 'involves beliefs and taking sides about issues which social science cannot resolve' (Erskine, 1998, p. 14) it is inevitable that the assumptions New Labour makes concerning principles and practices will be subjected to critical appraisal. Is New Labour right, for instance, to assume the following: that citizens are motivated more by self-interest than altruism; that the state is as likely to be a cause of social problems as the market; that individuals should take more responsibility for meeting their own needs and resolving their own problems; that citizens' rights should be matched by obligations; that equality of opportunity is a more desirable goal than equality of outcome? Given that there are likely to be divergent viewpoints on these questions, it seems appropriate to conclude that there are likely to be as many debates about the construction, causes and remedies for social problems in this century as there were in previous eras.

Issues to Consider

- What are the main characteristics of social policy approaches to social problems?
- How accurate is it to suggest that there was a move from individual to structural explanations of social problems during the twentieth century?
- Can purposeful forms of state action solve social problems?
- Compare and contrast the approach to social problems advanced by the New Right and New Labour.

Suggestions for Further Reading

Alcock (1996), Alcock et al. (1998) and Bulmer et al. (1989) all provide informative introductions to the development of the academic study of social policy in the UK. Titmuss (1950) is an exemplar of the problem-oriented approach to social policy, highlighting the complexities and dilemmas involved in devising appropriate policies for a range of wartime issues. Manning (1985) provides a stimulating introduction to the attempts to provide a theoretically grounded approach to the study of social problems within the field of social policy. Marsland (1996) offers an impassioned and informative guide to New Right thinking on social policy and the causes of social problems in contemporary British society. Le Grand et al. (1992) provide a useful companion to this volume, focusing on the economic dimensions of social problems and social policy issues.

References

Abel-Smith, B. and Titmuss, K. (eds) 1987: *The Philosophy of Welfare*. London: Allen & Unwin.

Abel-Smith, B. and Townsend, P. 1965: *The Poor and the Poorest*. London: Bell & Sons.

Alcock, P. 1996: *Social Policy in Britain*. London: Macmillan.

Alcock, P. 1998: The discipline of social policy. In P. Alcock, A. Erskine and M. May (eds), *The Student's Companion to Social Policy*. Oxford: Blackwell.

Alcock, P., Erskine, A. and May, M. (eds) 1998: *The Student's Companion to Social Policy*. Oxford: Blackwell.

Baker, J. 1979: Social conscience and social policy. *Journal of Social Policy*, 8 (2), 177–206.

Baldwin, P. 1990: *The Politics of Social Solidarity*. Cambridge: Cambridge University Press.

Barry, N. 1999: Neoclassicism, the new right and British social welfare. In R. Page and R. Silburn (eds), *British Social Welfare in the Twentieth Century*. London: Macmillan.

Beier, A. 1974: Vagrants and the social order in Elizabethan England. *Past and Present*, 64 (August), 3–29.

Blair, T. 1998: *The Third Way: New Politics for the New Century*. London: Fabian Pamphlet no. 588, Fabian Society.

Brown, G. 1999: Equality – then and now. In D. Leonard (ed.), *Crosland and New Labour*. London: Macmillan.

Bruce, M. 1968: *The Coming of the Welfare State*. London: Batsford.

Bulmer, M., Lewis, J. and Piachand, D. (eds) 1989: *The Goals of Social Policy*. London: Unwin Hyman.

Byrne, D. 1999: *Social Exclusion*. Buckingham: Open University Press.

Charles, N. 2000: *Feminism, the State and Social Policy*. Basingstoke: Macmillan.

De Schweinitz, K. 1961: *England's Road to Social Security*. New York: Perpetua.

Deacon, A. 1999: The balance of rights and responsibilities within welfare reform. In R. Walker (ed.), *Ending Child Poverty: Popular Welfare for the 21ˢᵗ Century*. Bristol: Policy Press.

Dennis, N. and Halsey, A. 1988: *English Ethical Socialism*. Oxford: Clarendon Press.

Department of Social Security 1999: *Opportunity for All: Tackling Poverty and Social Exclusion*. Cmnd. 4555, London: Stationery Office.

Erskine, A. 1998: The approaches and methods of social policy. In P. Alcock, A. Erskine and M. May (eds), *The Student's Companion to Social Policy*. Oxford: Blackwell.

Field, F. 1995: *Making Welfare Work: Reconstructing Welfare for the Millennium*. London: Institute of Community Studies.

Field, F. 1997: *Reforming Welfare*. London: Social Market Foundation.

Francis, M. 1997: *Ideas and Policies under Labour 1945–1951*. Manchester: Manchester University Press.

Fraser, D. 1984: *The Evolution of the British Welfare State*, 2nd edn. London: Macmillan.

Giddens, A. 2000: *The Third Way and Its Critics*. Cambridge: Polity.

Glennerster, H. and Hills, J. (eds) 1998: *The State of Welfare*, 2nd edn. Oxford: Oxford University Press.

Hay, J. 1983: *The Origins of the Liberal Welfare Reforms 1906–14*, Revised edn. London: Macmillan.

Hennessy, P. 1992: *Never Again*. London: Vintage.

Humphreys, R. 1995: *Sin, Organized Charity and the Poor Law in Victorian England*. London: Macmillan.

Jamrozik, A. and Nocella, L. 1998: *The Sociology of Social Problems*. Cambridge: Cambridge University Press.

Jefferys, K. 1992: *The Attlee Governments 1945–51*. London: Longman.

Johnson, N. 1999: The personal social services and community care. In M. Powell (ed.), *New Labour, New Welfare State?* Bristol: Policy Press.

King, D. 1999: *In the Name of Liberalism: Illiberal Social Policy in the United States and Britain*. Oxford: Oxford University Press.

Klein, R. 1995: *The New Politics of the NHS*, 3rd edn. London: Longman.

Labour Party 1997: *New Labour: Because Britain Deserves Better*. London: Labour Party Election Manifesto.

Le Grand, J., Propper, C. and Robinson, R. 1992: *The Economics of Social Problems*. London: Macmillan.

Lee, P. and Raban, C. 1988: *Welfare Theory and Social Policy*. London: Sage.

Macnicol, J. 1980: *The Movement for Family Allowances, 1918–45: A Study in Social Policy Development*. London: Heinemann.

Macnicol, J. 1987: In pursuit of the underclass. *Journal of Social Policy*, 16 (3), 293–318.

Macnicol, J. 1999: From 'problem family' to 'underclass', 1945–95. In H. Fawcett and R. Lowe (eds), *Welfare Policy in Britain: The Road from 1945*. London: Macmillan.

Mann, K. 1992: *The Making of the English Underclass? The Social Division of Welfare and Labour*. Buckingham: Open University Press.

Manning, N. (ed.) 1985: *Social Problems and Welfare Ideology*. Aldershot: Gower.

Marsland, D. 1996: *Welfare or Welfare State?* London: Macmillan.

Mead, L. 1986: *Beyond Entitlement*. New York: Free Press.

Merton, R. and Nisbet, R. (eds) 1961: *Contemporary Social Problems*. New York: Harcourt Brace & World Inc.

Mishra, R. 1977: *Society and Social Policy*. London: Macmillan.

Murray, C. 1984: *Losing Ground*. New York: Basic Books.

Murray, C. 1990: *The Emerging British Underclass*. London: IEA.

Murray, C. 1994 *Underclass: The Crisis Deepens*. London: IEA.

Powell, M. 2000: New Labour and the third way in the British welfare state. *Critical Social Policy*, 20 (1), 39–60.

Pugh, M. 1993: *The Making of Modern British Politics*, 2nd edn. Oxford: Blackwell.

Rainwater, L. 1974: *Social Problems and Public Policy*. Chicago: Aldine.

Rowntree, B. and Lavers, G. 1951: *Poverty and the Welfare State*. London: Longmans, Green and Co.

Rubington, E. and Weinberg, M. (eds) 1985: *The Study of Social Problems*. Oxford: Oxford University Press.

Skidelsky, R. 1998: *Beyond the Welfare State*. London: Social Market Foundation.

Social Insurance and Allied Services 1942: *The Beveridge Report*. Cmnd. 4842, London: HMSO.

Sullivan, M. 1996: *The Development of the British Welfare State*. Hemel Hempstead: Prentice-Hall/Harvester Wheatsheaf.

Sullivan, M. 1999: Democratic socialism and social policy. In R. Page and R. Silburn (eds), *British Social Welfare in the Twentieth Century*. London: Macmillan.

Sullivan, T. and Thompson, K. 1994: *Introduction to Social Problems*, 3rd edn. New York: Macmillan.

Taylor-Gooby, P. and Dale, J. 1985: *Social Theory and Social Welfare*. London: Edward Arnold.

Temple, W. 1942: *Christianity and the Social Order*. London: Penguin.

Thane, P. 1982: *The Foundations of the British Welfare State*. London: Longman.

Thompson, W. 1997: *The Left in History*. London: Pluto.

Titmuss, R. 1950: *Problems of Social Policy*. London: HMSO.

Titmuss, R. 1974: *Social Policy: An Introduction*. London: Allen & Unwin.

Wilding, P. 1983: The evolution of social administration. In P. Bean and S. MacPherson (eds), *Approaches to Welfare*. London: Routledge.

Willcocks, A. 1967: *The Creation of the National Health Service*. London: Routledge & Kegan Paul.

Willetts, D. 1992: *Modern Conservatism*. Harmondsworth: Penguin.

Williams, F. 1989: *Social Policy: A Critical Introduction*. Cambridge: Polity.

Wilson, E. 1977: *Women and the Welfare State*. London: Tavistock.

Wright Mills, C. 1959: *The Sociological Imagination*. Oxford: Oxford University Press.

Part Two

Social Policy, Social Problems

The Family

Chapter 3

Family Change and Lone Parents as a Social Problem

Jane Lewis

Introduction: Family Change as a Social Problem

The statistics on family change in the last quarter of the twentieth century are dramatic. Over the space of a single generation the number of people marrying has halved, the number divorcing has trebled and the proportion of children born outside marriage has quadrupled (Scott et al., 1998; Newman and Smith, 1997). Attitudes have also changed, becoming less traditional on the issues of marriage, divorce, cohabitation and on the idea of working mothers. By the end of the 1980s, fewer than 50 per cent of 18–24 year-olds thought it necessary to marry before having children (Kiernan and Estaugh, 1993).

It has become tempting to write of the 'rise and decline' of marriage, given that marriage became virtually universal in the immediate postwar decades and seemingly much less popular in the closing years of the century. Such a judgement would be premature, but the broad trends associated with the decline of marriage and the rise of cohabitation fuelled a *fin de siècle* anxiety about the 'breakdown of the family'.

This surge of anxiety has been manifest, as Baldock and Radford show in the next two chapters, in a mounting concern about care in the family and in a renewed awareness of the family as a site of violence. This chapter:

- documents the rapid pace of family change, whereby sex has become separated from marriage and marriage from parenthood;
- examines the fear that men and women are becoming more individualistic and more selfish;
- identifies what commentators consider to be the drivers of family change, increasing male irresponsibility and female economic independence;
- considers policy approaches, particularly with regard to lone mother families.

Family Change and Lone Parents

Faced with dramatic and rapid family change, academics have tended to make a causal connection with the pursuit of a more selfish individualism. The fear is that men and women are less committed to each other and to other family members, especially their children. By the beginning of the twenty-first century the optimism of the family sociology of the late 1960s and early 1970s has given way to profound pessimism. The influential American literature has stressed the importance of the pursuit of the commitment to 'personal growth' and 'moving on', whether for men who leave marriages and fail to maintain their families, or careerism on the part of women. Some policy makers and academics feared that the law had permitted or even encouraged certain forms of behaviour, which in turn contributed to family breakdown, for example by removing the idea of fault and therefore blame from the process of divorce (Cohen, 1987) and by giving lone mother families the wherewithal to subsist on state benefits (Murray, 1984).

Since the early 1990s family breakdown and family policy have been at the very top of the political agenda, but have led to something close to moral panic only in the English-speaking countries. In many other European countries there is much more concern about the falling birth rate than about the change in family structure. The anxiety in Britain and the United States in particular has centred on what happens to children after divorce or with unmarried mothers. Academic opinion is far from united on this issue. The most recent thorough review of the literature on children of parents who divorce has concluded that they are more likely to be in poverty and to be poorer when they are adults, to perform less well in school, to leave home when they are young, to become sexually active early and to have health and behavioural problems (Rodgers and Pryor, 1998). However, research has tended not to see family breakdown as a process beginning with conflict and poor parent–child relationships that may benefit from early intervention and support. While the successful socialization of children is probably the main source of anxiety for policy makers, adult behaviour is necessarily also a focus of concern. What are the implications for the broader society if women and children can live autonomously without men? To what extent is the greater economic and sexual autonomy of women causing family change? And what about male irresponsibility? Men's position as husbands and fathers was problematized at the beginning of the twentieth century, when it was felt that their obligation to maintain their families was the only sure way of maintaining work incentives (Bosanquet, 1906). But, under the influence of theories of maternal deprivation, the role of men in the family took a distinctly back seat in mid-century. As we enter the twenty-first century fears have again been raised about what happens to young men in particular if they are not tied into families. May they not become a threat to the social order? (Dench, 1994).

The issues raised by family change are social but also moral, which is why they are so controversial. As Wilson (1976) pointed out, the family has tended to be viewed as both bedrock and fragile. As the fundamental mediating institution in society, its health has always been under the microscope to some extent. Policy makers have always had a set of assumptions about how the family should look and about the roles that its members should play. The most fundamental idea underpinning family policies in the UK since the early twentieth century has been the male-breadwinner model, in which men as husbands and fathers are expected to take primary responsibility for earning and women as wives and mothers primary responsibility for caring for husbands, children and adult dependants. The ideal two-parent, male-breadwinner family was an 'ought'; the social reality – the 'is' – was always different, although in some historical periods it matched the ideal more closely than in others. More families came closer to resembling the idea in the 1950s and early 1960s than at any other time in the century. In this sense, these postwar decades deserve to be seen as aberrant rather than as the norm. However, it is important to remember that the postwar welfare settlement was constructed on the assumption of full-time, male employment and stable families. This helps to explain why the rapid change in family structure is such a major issue.

Even though policy makers have had a clear idea of the kind of family they would like to promote, family policy has been far from simple. In the first place, in the British context it has tended to be implicit rather than explicit (Land and Parker, 1978). The absence of public childcare provision, for example, reflected the strong belief that looking after children, whether in terms of maintenance or care, was a private, family responsibility. This contrasts with the position in most continental European countries, where governments have explicitly accepted the responsibility of reconciling paid work and unpaid caring work. Second, while assumptions about the 'ought' of family life have been strong, state policies have in practice been Janus-faced. Governments may not have welcomed the increasing numbers of lone parent families, but they have nevertheless allowed them the wherewithal to subsist. It should be noted that this does not amount to saying that the provision of welfare benefits has caused the rapid increase in lone motherhood (a point I return to later). However, governments have both condemned what they tend to view as deviant behaviour and at the same time permitted it to exist.

Academics and policy makers have expressed concern about the growth of what they fear is selfish individualism: that somehow the changes manifested in the demographic statistics signify the atomization of society. What happened in the second half of the twentieth century was the erosion of prescription, whether legal, for example in the deregulation of divorce, or cultural and economic, for example in respect of the male-breadwinner model, which had to give way to a dual-earner model. It is far from clear whether the erosion of prescription resulted in more selfish individualism. Finch and Mason's (1993) influential research on family obligations showed that in the absence of external prescriptive frameworks people worked hard to negotiate caring relationships. Smart and Neale (1999) came up with similar findings in respect of divorcing couples, and Weeks et al. (1999) in respect of the negotiation of non-heterosexual relationships. The instinct of policy makers is often to reach back for familiar forms and prescriptions when faced with rapid change, but whether it is possible to put the clock back is another matter.

Behavioural Change

Anxieties about family breakdown tend to be derived more from the dramatic statistical evidence of family change than from knowledge of the changing nature of interaction within families. Behavioural change is real, albeit often misunderstood. Many would date the beginnings of family change to the 1960s, usually characterized as a permissive decade, not least because of the relaxation of the laws on divorce, abortion and homosexuality that took place at the end of the decade. This in turn prompts the conclusion that the liberalization of legislation which took place in that decade should be reversed. However, a closer examination of the statistics tells a more complicated story.

Looking at the postwar period, we may identify two important phases of change in what we might term the marriage system (Lewis and Kiernan, 1996). The evidence suggests that significantly more teenagers began to have sex in the late 1950s and 1960s (before the contraceptive pill became widely available). Table 3.1 shows that in the 1960s the increase in sex outside marriage resulted in a sharp rise in the extramarital birth rate; but the marital birth rate also increased.

What happened in the 1960s was a separation of sex and marriage. This made the decade significantly different from the war years, when the extramarital birth rate also rose sharply; but then marriages failed to take place because of death and other general wartime disruption. In the 1960s, more sexual activity at younger ages resulted in an increased pregnancy rate, but the majority of those women who got pregnant went on to shot-gun marriages. In 1969, after the passing of the abortion legislation, 55 per cent of extramarital conceptions were legitimized by marriage, 32 per cent resulted in illegitimate births, and 14 per cent were aborted. It may well be that the people who contracted shot-gun marriages went on to divorce, but at the time the fact that most people married made it seem as though there was little fundamental change in the marriage system. This view was further supported by the low divorce rate (table 3.2) during these years.

So it is not surprising that there was little panic about the family in the family sociology literature of the 1960s (e.g. Fletcher, 1966). Notwithstanding the separation of sex and marriage, it was possible for commentators to express confidence about the future of the traditional family in the context of the new sexual freedom.

From the beginning of the 1970s, the changes in marriage patterns were much more marked. Table 3.3 shows the decline in the first marriage rate and the rise in the age at first marriage. The divorce rate (table 3.2) rose dramatically in the 1970s, levelling off from the 1980s, while the extramarital birth rate rose steeply

Table 3.1 Marital and extramarital births, 1940–92

	Marital birth rate per 1,000 married women aged 15–44	Extramarital birth rate per 1,000 single, divorced and widowed women aged 15–44
1940	98.8	5.9
1945	103.9	16.1
1950	108.6	10.2
1955	103.7	10.3
1960	120.8	14.7
1965	126.9	21.2
1970	113.5	21.5
1975	85.5	17.4
1980	92.2	19.6
1985	87.8	26.7
1990	86.7	38.9
1995	82.7	39.6

Sources: Office of Population Censuses and Surveys (OPCS), *Birth Statistics: Historical Series 1837–1983*, table 3.2b and c, Series FM1 no. 13 (London: HMSO, 1987). OPCS, *Birth Statistics: Historical Series 1837–1983*, table 3.1, Series FM1 no. 22 (London: HMSO, 1995)

Table 3.2 Divorce rates per 1,000 married people

Year	Rate
1950	2.8
1960	2.0
1965	3.1
1970	4.7
1975	9.6
1980	12.0
1985	13.4
1990	13.0
1993	13.9

Sources: OPCS, *Marriage and Divorce Statistics 1837–1983*, Historical Series, FM2, no. 16, table 5.2 (London: HMSO, 1995); OPCS, *Marriage and Divorce Statistics 1837–1983*, table 2.1, FM2, no. 21 (London: HMSO, 1995)

in the 1980s and 1990s. Thus the last two decades of the twentieth century saw a new pattern: marriage became less popular among the never-married; marital birth rates declined; extramarital birth rates increased. These trends are inextricably linked to the growth in cohabitation (table 3.4).

Cohabitation was in all probability common at the beginning of the twentieth century, when divorce was very rare indeed. When separation allowances were provided for the first time for the wives of servicemen during the First World War, special provision had to be made for what were called 'unmarried

Table 3.3   First marriages, England and Wales

Year	All ages (000s)	Rate[a]	Mean age
Men			
1961	308.8	74.9	25.6
1971	343.6	82.3	24.6
1981	259.1	51.7	25.4
1985	253.3	46.6	26.0
1991	222.8	37.0	27.5
1995[b]	198.5	31.8	28.9
Women			
1961	312.3	83.0	23.1
1971	347.4	97.9	22.6
1981	263.4	64.0	23.1
1985	258.1	58.2	23.8
1991	224.8	46.9	25.5
1995[b]	198.5	40.1	26.9

[a] Per 1,000 single persons aged 16 and over
[b] Provisional
Sources: OPCS, Population Trends 47 (spring 1987) (HMSO);
Office for National Statistics, Population Trends 87 (spring 1997)
(Stationery Office)

Table 3.4   Women aged 18–49 cohabiting by legal marital status, Great Britain, %

Legal marital status[a]	1979		1981		1985		1991		1995	
Married	–		–		–		–		–	
Non-married										
single	8		9		14		23		26	
widowed	0	11	6	12	5	16	2	23	[8]	27
divorced	20		20		21		30		27	
separated	17		19		20		13		11	
All	3		3		5		9		10	

[a] Women describing themselves as separated were, strictly speaking, legally married; because women who are separated can cohabit, they have been included in the 'non-married' category
Source: Office for National Statistics, Living in Britain, 1995 General Household Survey, table 12.7
(Stationery Office) ©Crown Copyright 2000

wives' (Parker, 1990). Cohabitation probably reached its nadir in the 1950s and 1960s, when marriage was almost universal. Living together before marriage began in earnest in the 1970s. In the 1990s typically 70 per cent of never-married women who married had cohabited with their husbands, compared with 58 per cent of those marrying between 1985 and 1988, 33 per cent marrying between 1975 and 1979, and 6 per cent marrying between 1965 and 1969. Divorced women were very commonly cohabiting during the 1980s and 1990s. Cohabitation tends to be short-lived and childless, but by 1994 75 per cent of extramarital births were being jointly registered, and 58 per cent of these were by couples

Table 3.5 Distribution of types of lone-mother families with dependent children, 1971–1991, %[a]

	1971	1981	1986	1991
Single lone mothers	1.2	2.3	3.2	6.4
Separated lone mothers	2.5	2.3	2.6	3.6
Divorced lone mothers	1.9	4.4	5.6	6.3
Widowed lone mothers	1.9	1.7	1.1	1.2
All lone mothers	7.5	10.7	12.5	17.5

[a] The estimates are based on three-year averages, apart from 1991
Source: John Haskey, Trends in the numbers of one-parent families in Great Britain, *Population Trends*, 71 (spring 1993), Office for National Statistics © Crown Copyright 2000

living at the same address. However, the statistics on relationship breakdown show that cohabitation is even more unstable than marriage, four times more according to British Household Panel data (Ermisch and Francesconi, 1998).

The outcome of all the trends during the last quarter of the twentieth century was a large increase in the number of lone mother families (table 3.5).

During the 1960s, sex was separated from marriage. But during the 1980s and 1990s, marriage became separated from parenthood. This major change helps to explain the fact that academics and policy makers have become much more pessimistic about the family.

The Rise of Selfish Individualism?

Do these statistics amount to a rise in individualistic behaviour that is essentially selfish? American academics were the first to suggest that this was the case. Bellah et al. (1985, p. vii) opened their account of middle-American life with the statement 'We are concerned that this individualism may have grown cancerous.' They identified two forms of individualism: first, the utilitarian, which amounted to the traditional American desire to get ahead and to be self-reliant, and, second, the expressive, which emphasized self-expression and the sharing of feelings rather than material acquisition. The perception of Bellah et al. was that the values of the public sphere – the 'coolly manipulative style' (1985, p. 48) that is required to get ahead – were invading the private world of the family. Such an anxiety has a long history. The ideology of separate spheres, in which the ruthless competition that was thought necessary for the successful operation of the market was balanced by the haven of the family, where a woman would care for the male worker and also for those too weak to engage in the public sphere, was central to late-nineteenth- and early-twentieth-century classical liberalism. In Bellah et al.'s view, the contractual structure of commercial and bureaucratic life threatened to become an ideology for personal life.

Obligation and commitment would be replaced by an ideology of full, open and honest communication between self-actualizing individuals.

Fears about the growth of selfish individualism also became widespread in the UK. For example, in the course of the British parliamentary debates over the 1996 Family Law Act, Baroness Young said that 'for one party simply to decide to go off with another person . . . reflects the growing *self-first disease* which is debasing our society' (Hansard, Lords, 29 February 1996, c. 1638, my emphasis). Policy makers during the 1990s automatically assumed individualism to be the natural antithesis of interdependence (Smart and Neale, 1997).

However, this is not accepted by all commentators, especially not by those who focus more on changes in the nature of intimate relationships and on their meanings (e.g. Giddens, 1992). These writers agree that people have become more individual, but not that this necessarily entails greater selfishness. Rather, they tend to see a more complicated set of changes in values and obligations than those who focus on the behavioural outcomes of family change and then read motivation from them. Giddens has suggested that we have seen the emergence of the 'pure relationship', a social relationship entered into for its own sake and for what one can derive from it in terms of material, but more usually emotional, exchange. But while love has in this interpretation become contingent rather than 'for ever', it has also become more democratic. Recent empirical work on the obligation of family members to care for one another (Finch and Mason, 1993) and on the behaviour of divorcing couples (Smart and Neale, 1999) has offered evidence that while there is greater individualization, there is no reason to believe that this is also selfish or that people have abandoned their responsibility for making ethical choices. Rather, in the absence of the old prescriptive frameworks, people negotiate their commitments to one another.

Nevertheless, the balance of opinion has been towards unease at the idea that love may no longer be defined as a commitment to a choice, but rather as a continuing transaction and evaluation of rewards. Above all, there has been anxiety about the implied lack of permanence in such arrangements, especially in regard to the effects on children.

The Drivers of Family Change

There has been a tendency to identify these as individualistic and selfish behaviours.

Men's irresponsibility

By the early 1990s, the political debate had become dominated by those who stressed the irresponsibility and selfishness of men as well as of women. Michael Howard, then Home Secretary, said in a speech to the Conservative Political

Centre in 1993, 'If the state will house and pay for their children the duty on [young men] to get involved may seem removed from their shoulders . . . And since the state is educating, housing and feeding their children the nature of parental responsibility may seem less immediate' (Howard, 1993). The father's duty to maintain was argued not only because the role model it provided for children was important, but also because of fairness to the taxpayer:

> when a family breaks up, the husband's standard of living often rises whereas that of his wife and children falls, even below the poverty line. Taxpayers may then be left to support the first family, while the husband sets about forming another. This is wrong. A Father who can afford to support only one family ought to have only one. (*The Economist*, leader, 9 September 1995).

Such views stood in stark contrast to the attitudes expressed some twenty years earlier in the Report of the Royal Commission on One-Parent Families (Cmnd. 5629, 1974), which recognized the difficulty in a liberal democratic society of determining who had the right to procreate and, in the absence of any capacity to stop further reproduction by men, recommended that the state was bound to support the mothers and children they left behind.

The prime concern of political commentators about men's obligation to maintain their families was often allied with a more generalized concern on the political Right (Morgan, 1995), on the political Left (Halsey, 1993; Dennis and Erdos, 1992), among politicians (Hansard, Commons, 3 December 1993) and in the media (e.g. BBC *Panorama*, 20 September 1993) about an increase in male irresponsibility. All argued that the successful socialization of a child required the active involvement of two parents. Dennis and Erdos (1992) sought to trace the rise of the 'obnoxious Englishman' to family breakdown. Their chief concern was the effect of lone motherhood on the behaviour patterns of young men. Lone motherhood was in their view responsible for at best irresponsible and at worse criminal behaviour in the next male generation. In fact such convictions about the link between absent fathers and rising crime rates have not been tested for any large-scale British sample. Halsey (1993) believed that the traditional family is the 'tested arrangement' for safeguarding children's welfare and that 'only a post-Christian country' could believe otherwise. In his view, the greed and individualism engendered during the Thatcher years were largely responsible for the disintegration of the traditional family. Morgan (1995), while not blaming individualism, argued for more incentives, for example in the form of tax allowances, to encourage the formation of two-parent families.

The assumption behind much of this literature was that men are instinctively uncivilized, and that family responsibility was the only thing that ties them to communal living. Dench (1994, pp. 16–17) argued strongly that family responsibilities are an indispensable civilizing influence on men:

> If women go too far in pressing for symmetry, and in trying to change the rules of the game, men will simply decide not to play . . . If women now choose to . . . withdraw the notion that men's family role is important, then they are throwing away

their best trick. Feminism, in dismantling patriarchy, is simply reviving the under-lying greater natural freedom of men . . . Many women are now setting great store by the coming of New Man . . . the current attack on patriarchal conventions is surely promoting almost the exact opposite, namely a plague of feckless yobs, who leave all the real work to women and gravitate towards the margins of society where males naturally hang around unless culture gives them a reason to do otherwise. The family may be a myth, but it is a myth that works to make men tolerably useful.

In this interpretation, as much blame is attributed to women for undermining the traditional male role of breadwinner as to men. The influential journalist Phillips (1997) also concluded that it is the erosion of the male role that has created 'yobbish men'.

This kind of view has much in common with some feminist analysis (e.g. Ehrenreich, 1983) in so far as it diagnoses the problem in terms of male flight. Stacey (1990) has commented that young working-class men are not sure whether to regard one of their number who becomes a breadwinner as a hero or a chump. However, feminists differ profoundly from many of the academics and commentators who identify the problem as the erosion of the male role, and who seek to turn the clock back to something approaching the 1950s, with clearly segregated roles between men and women within families. The responsibility of being a breadwinner is considered vital to the wider society, to men's identity as social beings, and to the successful socialization of children. However, as American sociologists and demographers pointed out, the fall in male manual workers' earnings during the 1980s and 1990s made it impossible for many of them to act as breadwinners (e.g. Wilson, 1987). The UK evidence also shows the extent to which men's contribution to the family economy has diminished (Harkness et al., 1996). In other words, structural change may be as or more important a factor than male irresponsibility and selfishness.

The identification of male behaviour as problematic during the 1990s was new in the postwar period, although it had been common at the beginning of the twentieth century (Lewis, 1986). The fear in both historical periods was similar: given the opportunity, men would pursue their own selfish interests and ignore those of their families. Becker's (1981) work on a 'new home economics' argued that people marry when the utility expected from marriage is greater than it is if they remain single. Given that women desire children, they will look for a good male breadwinner. Men will look for a good housekeeper and carer. According to this theory, a rise in women's employment and an increase in their wages will threaten the stability of marriage, for it will no longer offer women unequivocal gains. However, Cohen's (1987) use of Becker's ideas put more emphasis on the possibilities for men's opportunistic behaviour. Cohen pointed out that investments in marriage are front-loaded for women because of child bearing. The relative decline in the value of women on the marriage market exposes them to the risk of the expropriation of their greater investment in marriage by their husbands. In Cohen's analysis, it was the introduction of no-fault divorce that permitted men to follow their 'natural' inclinations and behave opportunistically.

Thus the analysis of male behaviour has, like the literature from the early part of this century, tended to assume that men are naturally inclined to individualistic behaviour and that changes in the law have facilitated such behaviour. The main divergence is between the views of those who are ready to blame men for acting selfishly, and the views of those who are more likely to blame structural change or women for pushing men into such behaviour.

Women's economic independence

Women have also been seen to pursue a more individualistic course, which is sometimes construed as a search for self-fulfilment at the expense of other family members. Above all, women's changing participation in the labour market has been highlighted. This focus has a much longer history in the postwar period than the attention paid to male irresponsibility, and has been much more fully explored in a range of academic disciplines. As Oppenheimer (1994) has pointed out, the idea that women's increased economic independence has an effect on their marital behaviour is widespread, possibly because people with very different politics can accept it. Both Gilder (1987) in the US and Dench (1994) in Britain have seen the increase in adult women's participation in and attachment to the labour force as something that has stripped men of their traditional breadwinning role within the family, and they blame women for pursuing self-fulfilment in the form of a career at the expense of their families. But feminists are as likely to endorse a theory that stresses the importance of women's economic independence as are right-wing polemicists, while of course stressing women's right and/or need to work.

Neoclassical economists have suggested that as women's capacity to support themselves has increased, so they have been less willing to put up with unsatisfactory marriages (Becker et al., 1977). The fact that the majority of petitioners for divorce are female is taken as evidence of the growth in women's individualistic behaviour. However, there are many other explanations for the number of female petitioners. Men tend to react to breakdown with violence or by leaving the relationship, leaving women to seek divorce (Phillips, 1988). As the economically weaker partner, a woman will usually need to try to get the financial arrangements settled (Smart, 1982; Maclean, 1991). As Sorensen and McLanahan (1987) have demonstrated, women have in fact continued to be economically dependent because of short-time working and low pay.

Indeed, it is unlikely that greater independence in the form of earnings is in itself the primary impetus for women seeking divorce. Cherlin (1981) argued that the increase in women's employment was not a cause of the increase in divorce, but had made it easier. Beck and Beck Gernsheim (1995), who focus their attention more on meanings than on behaviour, have argued that, whereas mothers wholly dependent on men for economic support used to abandon their hopes, women who now have some means of supporting themselves can choose to abandon their marriages. De Singly (1996) suggests again that it is not paid employment *per se* that is responsible for women's greater readiness to consider divorce, but rather the awareness it creates of tensions within the marriage. The increase in female employment may thus be held to facilitate but not cause family breakdown, and this in turn has encouraged the search for explanations of family change beyond the economic.

It is unlikely that women abide solely by the dictates of economic rationality when making decisions about marriage, divorce and motherhood. Alternative value systems that give priority to emotional satisfaction and to care may be as important elements in the explanation of their behaviour in intimate relationships. Bellah et al. (1985) interpreted the desire for emotional satisfaction as selfish, but it may be the lack of interdependence, in the sense of emotional support, that triggers breakdown rather than the selfish pursuit of personal growth. It may also be that (possibly selfish) individualism is the outcome rather than the determinant of changes in economic and social behaviour. Many sociologists have noted what Burns and Scott (1994) have termed growing 'decomplementarity' between men and women. The basic premise of this theory of behaviour is that men and women have become more independent of each other. Oppenheimer (1994) has suggested something similar, positing a new collaborative model of marriage, which she argues has replaced the old specialization of men as breadwinners and women as housewives and carers. In this new form, marriage is based on the ability of each partner to make a contribution, unique or similar, and to pull his or her weight in the relationship.

Policy approaches

A major part of the debate about what has caused family change and the fear that it signifies more selfish behaviour has focused on the role of both public policy and the private law of the family. This again was argued first in the United States, where Murray (1984) in particular charged that the provision of welfare benefits had exacerbated the move towards individualism and away from familism; in other words, social provision caused family change by enabling women to lead an independent economic existence. This view made strong inroads into the policy debates in Britain and America. The notion that young unmarried mothers get pregnant in order to jump the queue for social housing, said openly at Conservative Party conferences during the early 1990s, was one way in which it was expressed. The more general fear about growing 'welfare dependency' grew stronger among politicians on both sides of the Atlantic during the 1980s and 1990s. However, both American and British research has effectively demolished the argument that there is a causal relation between social provision and family change (e.g. Ellwood and Bane, 1985; Ford et al., 1995). State benefits and access to social housing may facilitate the formation of lone mother families, but they do not cause it. The possibility of being able to achieve autonomous living via wages or benefits is crucial, but it is unlikely to be the only or even the decisive factor influencing behaviour.

Similarly, it is difficult to establish the part played by the law of divorce, say, in bringing about family change. Most social scientists have played down the effect of legal change when seeking explanations for the rising divorce rate. Rheinstein's (1972) comparative socio-legal study argued that marital break-down could be high even in the absence of divorce. In his comparative histori-cal study of divorce, Phillips (1988) also insisted that levels of marital breakdown have not been dependent on legal change.

However, faced with profound family change, policy makers tend to see their choices in dichotomous terms: either they try to put the clock back, or they rec-ognize the reality of social change and try to address it. There is evidence of both approaches in the policies of the 1990s.

Historically, policy makers in Britain have always experienced considerable difficulty in deciding how to treat lone mother families. Given the strong assumptions about how families should work, centred on a male breadwinner and a female carer, policy makers had to make up their minds how to define women with children and without men: as breadwinners or as carers. At the turn of the nineteenth century they were defined as breadwinners and were expected to support as many children as they could; the rest would be taken into the work-house. By the mid-twentieth century the pendulum had swung towards treating them as mothers, and under the postwar settlement those drawing social assis-tance were not obliged to register for work so long as they had children under 16. Only The Netherlands in continental Europe went as far in defining lone mothers as mothers for such a long period.

The policy approach began to change again as lone motherhood became an increasingly visible social problem (Kiernan et al., 1998). In 1979, families headed by lone mothers constituted 10 per cent of all families. By 1990, this pro-portion had nearly doubled, to 18 per cent. Expenditure on their benefits had also doubled in real terms and it was the increase in the proportion of lone parents on income support that attracted the government's attention. By the late 1980s only one out of three lone mothers were receiving regular mainte-nance from absent fathers, and 59 per cent were receiving state benefits. Sixty per cent of the children in families receiving income support were members of one-parent families. Margaret Thatcher took a growing interest in the demo-graphic trends and their consequences not only for public expenditure, but also for society as a whole. She wrote later:

> I became increasingly convinced during the last two or three years of my time in office that, although there were crucially important limits to what politicians could do in this area, we could only get to the roots of crime and much else besides by concentrating on strengthening the traditional family . . . all the evidence, statisti-cal and anecdotal, pointed to the breakdown of families as the starting point for a range of social ills. (Thatcher, 1995, pp. 628–9)

An acceptance of the idea that welfare benefits had played a part in causing an increase in lone mother families that was in itself harmful grew among Con-servative politicians during the late 1980s and 1990s.

The 1991 Child Support Act was designed to transfer the burden of support from the state to absent fathers. The legislation gave all biological fathers, unmarried and divorced, a persistent obligation to maintain their children. This legislation may be read as an attempt to re-establish the traditional responsibilities of men and women for children. It was clear that the father's responsibility to *provide* was supposed to take precedence over any responsibility he might have for *care*. The original child support formula (modified substantially in 1995) was subjected to severe criticism for its lack of regard to travelling expenses incurred by fathers who maintained contact with their children. The original formula also contained an element of support for the mother as carer. Nevertheless, the legislation also recognized that, given the changes in family structure, it was no longer possible to rely on the traditional roles attributed to husbands and wives. To that extent, the decision to treat all men and women in families as fathers and mothers represented a measure of recognition of the changed circumstances of many parents. This stands in contrast to the 1996 Family Law Act, which, while finally implementing a full no-fault divorce law, also explicitly sought to 'save marriage' by enforcing a twelve-month cooling off period.

When the child support legislation conspicuously failed in its aim to make absent fathers pay more and thereby reduce the amount paid out in benefits, the Conservative government began to emphasize the only remaining source of income for lone mothers, other than state benefits: the labour market. Conservative politicians had always found it difficult to decide whether or not it was appropriate for the mothers of small children to go out to work. Nevertheless, in 1996 the Department of Social Security announced both that no new claims for one-parent benefit would be accepted and that those newly claiming social assistance would no longer qualify for the special one-parent premium. Instead, it offered a new incentive to help lone mothers into paid employment, providing individual help with searching for jobs and training for work. The New Labour Government of 1997 confirmed these policies, although the 1998 Budget effectively restored the value of the benefit cuts to lone mother families. Lone mothers have been included in the government's welfare-to-work programme; as Lister (1998) has concluded, paid work is increasingly seen as *the* means to social inclusion. Britain's position near the bottom of the European childcare provision league tables has created enormous problems for lone mothers wishing to go out to work. The Labour Government has recognized this with its National Childcare Strategy, which will involve the expenditure of some £435 million for developing the infrastructure of childcare services over a five-year period (Department for Education and Employment, 1998). However, this money will go mainly to fund after-school care and is a modest amount given the lack of public provision in Britain.

The choice confronting governments – whether to recognize change or attempt to put the clock back – has by no means disappeared. Indeed, it is neatly encapsulated in the Labour government's Green Paper on the family and family policy. Entitled *Supporting Famil*ies (Home Office, 1998, my emphasis), it acknowledges the diversity of family forms that need support, while at the same time promoting marriage as the most desirable family form for children, a policy which also underpins the government's approach to 'family' education in schools.

Conclusion

Arguably, since the 1990s 'the family' has become the subject of explicit policy making in the UK for the first time in the postwar period. In most continental European countries governments have historically assumed a much greater responsibility for reconciling people's responsibilities to their families and to their workplaces. The welfare regimes of the Scandinavian countries also make very different assumptions about the roles of family members. All men and women are conceptualized as worker/parent citizens. For lone mothers this means that their needs are not categorized separately from those of married mothers. It also means that it is more possible for lone mothers to get income from wages and from the state, which, given their responsibility for paid and unpaid work, they need to be able to do. While the British government has moved towards a greater recognition of family issues, the framework within which it is acting leaves much to be desired, particularly in terms of the dichotomous choice that is still being made between treating lone mothers as workers and treating them as mothers. In practice the main problem faced by lone mothers is still poverty. This was recognized by the Finer Commission on One-Parent Families in 1974 (Cmnd. 5629), but it has been subordinated to the issue of 'welfare dependency' in the 1980s and 1990s. The fact remains, as Rowlingson emphasizes in her chapter, that between 1979 and 1991 the number of children living in households with less than half the average income trebled to 3.9 million. In 1974, 6.4 per cent of all under-16-year-olds relied on means-tested social assistance; by 1994 one-quarter did so. The rise for younger children was even greater, from 6.6 to 29.1 per cent (Hills, 1998).

Family change is strongly associated with the increase in poverty, because a family increasingly needs two earners. However, any attempt to provide disincentives to divorce are likely to be unpopular, and any attempts to treat married people markedly more favourably than unmarried, cohabiting people may also backfire, now that cohabitation is for most people a part of their adult experience. In its 1999 and 2000 Budgets, the Labour government began to recognize the polarization that has taken place in British society during the 1980s and 1990s and to prioritize the welfare of children. Greater investment in children may well be the key to curbing the extremely high incidence of young unmarried motherhood in Britain. Qualitative research has shown the extent to which motherhood represents the most available route into adulthood for many poor and badly educated young women (e.g. Phoenix, 1991). Divorce, the other main route into lone motherhood, seems unlikely to diminish greatly (even if it does not continue to rise), and ideally lone mothers need to be able to 'package income' from wages, from state benefits and from absent fathers. Unhappily, the botched implementation of the child support legislation has made it very difficult to extract money from this last source, which is a serious problem for the future. It is very unlikely that lone mothers will be able to earn enough to keep them and their children out of poverty. It is crucial that all three sources of income are recognized as important.

Issues to Consider

- 'What we are seeing is the breakdown of the family.' Do you agree?
- What role has the emergence of cohabitation played in family change over the past quarter of a century?
- How much evidence is there that selfish individualism is the main cause of family change?
- How have social policies treated lone mother families?
- What have been governments' approaches to family change over the last decade?

Suggestions for Further Reading

The Finer Report on One-Parent Families (Cmnd. 5629, 1974) was an extremely thorough and well-researched report. Appendix V provides an admirable history of the treatment of lone mother families. The best introduction to the demographic, historical and social policy aspects of family change is provided by Kiernan et al. (1998). Murray's (1984) polemical book was important on both sides of the Atlantic for raising the alarm about lone mother families and 'welfare dependency'. Newman and Smith (1997) provide a convenient compendium of statistics. Current trends can be explored through the Office of National Statistics website www.ons.gov.uk. Changes in government policy can be traced through www.open.gov.uk, and the women's unit www.cabinetoffice.gov.uk/womens-unit.

References

Beck, U. and Beck Gernsheim, E. 1995: *The Normal Chaos of Love*. Cambridge: Polity Press.

Becker, G. 1981: *A Treatise on the Family*. Cambridge, Mass.: Harvard University Press.

Becker, G., Landes, E. M. and Michael, R. T. 1977: An economic analysis of marital instability. *Journal of Political Economy*, 85 (61), 1141–87.

Bellah, R., Madsen, R., Sullivan, W., Swidler, A. and Tipton, S. 1985: *Habits of the Heart: Middle America Observed*. Berkeley: University of California Press.

Bosanquet, H. 1906: *The Family*. London: Macmillan.

Burns, A. and Scott, C. 1994: *Mother-headed Families and Why They Have Increased*. New Jersey: Lawrence Erlbaum.

Cherlin, A. 1981: *Marriage, Divorce and Remarriage*. Cambridge, Mass.: Harvard University Press.

Cmnd. 5629 1974: *Report of the Royal Commission on One-parent Families*. London: HMSO.

Cohen, L. 1987: Marriage, divorce, and quasi rents: or, 'I gave him the best years of my life'. *Journal of Legal Studies*, XVI (2), 267–304.

de Singly, F. 1996: *Modern Marriage and Its Cost to Women: A Sociological Look at Marriage in France* (translated from the French). London: Associated University Presses.

Dench, G. 1994: *The Frog, the Prince and the Problem of Men*. London: Neanderthal Books.

Dennis, N. and Erdos, G. 1992: *Families without Fatherhood*. London: IEA.

Department for Education and Employment / Department of Social Security. 1998: *Meeting the Childcare Challenge*. Cmnd. 3959. London: Stationery Office.

Ehrenreich, B. 1983: *The Hearts of Men: American Dreams and the Flight from Commitment*. London: Pluto Press.

Ellwood, D. and Bane, M. J. 1985: The impact of AFDC on family structure and living arrangements. In R. G. Ehrenberg (ed.), *Research in Labor Economics*, VII. Greenwich, Conn.: JAI Press.

Ermisch, J. and Francesconi, M. 1998: *Cohabitation in Great Britain: Not for Long, but Here to Stay*. Working Paper 98-1. University of Essex: ESRC Research Centre on Micro-Social Change.

Finch, J. and Mason, J. 1993: *Negotiating Family Responsibilities*. London: Tavistock/Routledge.

Fletcher, R. 1966: *The Family and Marriage in Britain*. Harmondsworth: Penguin.

Ford, R., Marsh, A. and McKay, S. 1995: *Change in Lone Parenthood*. Department of Social Security Research Report, no. 40. London: HMSO.

Giddens, A. 1992: *Human Societies: An Introductory Reader in Sociology*. Cambridge: Polity Press.

Gilder, G. 1987: The collapse of the American family. *The Public Interest*, Fall, 20–5.

Halsey, A. H. 1993: Changes in the family. *Children and Society*, 7 (2), 125–36.

Harkness, S., Machin, S. and Waldfogel, J. 1996: Women's pay and family incomes in Britain, 1979–1991. In J. Hills (ed.), *New Inequalities: The Changing Distribution of Income and Wealth in the UK*. Cambridge: Cambridge University Press.

Hills, J. 1998: *Thatcherism, New Labour and the Welfare State*. London: LSE, CASE Paper 13.

Home Office 1998: *Supporting Families*. London: Home Office.

Howard, M. 1993: *Picking up the Pieces*. Mimeo, Conservative Political Centre.

Kiernan, K. and Estaugh, V. 1993: *Cohabitation: Extra-Marital Childbearing and Social Policy*. London: Family Policy Studies Centre.

Kiernan, K., Land, H. and Lewis, J. 1998: *Lone Mother Families in Twentieth Century Britain*. Oxford: Oxford University Press.

Land, H. and Parker, R. 1978: Family policy in Britain: the hidden dimensions. In A. Kahn and S. Kamerman (eds), *Family Policy in Fourteen Countries*. New York: Columbia University Press.

Lewis, J. (ed.) 1986: *Labour and Love: Women's Experience of Home and Family, 1850–1940*. Oxford: Blackwell.

Lewis, J. and Kiernan, K. 1996: The boundaries between marriage, nonmarriage, and parenthood: changes in behaviour and policy in postwar Britain. *Journal of Family History*, 21 (3), 372–87.

Lister, R. 1998: From equality to social inclusion: new labour and the welfare state. *Critical Social Policy*, 18 (2), 215–25.

Maclean, M. 1991: *Surviving Divorce: Women's Resources after Separation*. London: Macmillan.

Morgan, P. 1995: *Farewell to the Family: Policy and Family Breakdown in Britain and the USA*. London: IEA.

Murray, C. 1984: *Losing Ground: American Social Policy 1950–1980*. New York: Basic Books.

Newman, P. and Smith, A. 1997: *Social Focus on Families*. London: Stationery Office.

Oppenheimer, V. K. 1994: Women's rising employment and the future of the family in industrialised societies. *Population and Development Review*, 20 (2), 293–342.

Parker, S. 1990: *Informal Marriage, Cohabitation and the Law, 1750–1989*. London: Macmillan.

Phillips, M. 1997: *The Sex Change State*. London: Social Market Foundation.

Phillips, R. 1988: *Putting Asunder: A History of Divorce in Western Society*. Cambridge: Cambridge University Press.

Phoenix, A. 1991: *Young Mothers*. Cambridge: Cambridge University Press.

Rheinstein, M. 1972: *Marriage, Stability, Divorce and the Law*. Chicago: University of Chicago Press.

Rodgers, B. and Pryor, J. 1998: *Divorce and Separation: The Outcomes for Children*. York: Joseph Rowntree Foundation.

Scott, J., Braun, M. and Alwin, D. 1998: Partner, parent, worker: family and gender roles. In *British Social Attitudes Survey, 15th Report*. Aldershot: Dartmouth.

Smart, C. 1982: Justice and divorce: the way forward? *Family Law*, 1982, 135–7.

Smart, C. and Neale, B. 1997: Wishful thinking and harmful tinkering? Sociological reflections on family policy. *Journal of Social Policy*, 26 (3), 301–21.

Smart, C. and Neale, B. 1999: *Family Fragments*. Cambridge: Polity Press.

Sorensen, A. and McLanahan, S. 1987: Married women's economic dependency, 1940–1980. *American Journal of Sociology*, 93 (3), 659–87.

Stacey, J. 1990: *Brave New Families: Stories of Domestic Upheaval in Late Twentieth Century America*. New York: Basic Books.

Thatcher, M. 1995: *The Downing Street Years*. London: HarperCollins.

Weeks, J., Donovan, C. and Heaphy, B. 1999: Everyday experiments: narratives of non-heterosexual relationships. In B. Silva and C. Smart (eds), *The New Family*. London: Sage.

Wilson, E. 1976: *Women and the Welfare State*. London: Tavistock.

Wilson, W. J. 1987: *The Truly Disadvantaged: The Inner City, the Underclass and Public Policy*. Chicago: Chicago University Press.

Chapter 4

Caring and Dependency: Age and Disability

John Baldock

Introduction: Dependency and Age, a Classic Social Problem?

> Old age will come to increasing numbers of the population and this should be seen as a natural part of life and not as a burden
>
> Sutherland, With Respect to Old Age, p. 5

Dependence on others at some points in life is a natural and inevitable condition. All of us experienced dependency as infants, many of us need support during our lives at times of illness or disability, and almost all of us will require help because of the limitations that age brings. However, it is only the frailty and dependency of old age that has regularly come to be seen as a social problem. The needs of young children and of healthy but disabled adults, while understood as both personal and social issues, are not generally portrayed as major social problems. It is the dependencies of old age on which this chapter will focus.

Old age has come to represent all the classic characteristics of a social problem (see the chapters by Clarke and Page). Concern about the growing proportion of older people in the population has tended to rise and fall, to wax and wane as a social issue, being ignored at some times and rising to a crescendo of debate at others; in its presentation there is a persistent tension between the observable evidence and perceptions of the 'problem'; it has become a site of conflict between substantial social interests, especially between the citizen, the family and the state. In particular, the needs of older people have frequently been presented as an unfair burden on others and thus as something deserving of public attention and social policy remedies.

For example, a report of a conference held in Cambridge in 1988 on 'intergenerational equity' opens with the following warning:

The rapid ageing of the populations of all industrial countries over the next forty years will be an economic and social transformation of vastly greater magnitude than the 1970s oil price shock or the 1980s recession. . . . This process of population ageing is likely to have a profound impact on many established social customs and institutions such as the pattern of work and retirement, the functioning of welfare systems, and the nature of family relationships . . . This demographic shift and its attendant social and economic problems must lead us to question . . . the principles of our social institutions (Johnson et al., 1989, p. 1)

Among the concerns of those who perceive the ageing of populations as a problem the following are frequently mentioned:

- that the growing proportion and unforeseen longevity of the retired population will put an unacceptable burden on pension systems, especially those funded out of current taxation;
- that because the numbers of the oldest old people, those over 75 or 80, are growing fastest there will be exceptional demands for social care from dependent older people, which the state and the family may find difficult to meet;
- that each succeeding generation of older people tends to be more demanding of income and services than the previous one and that that will particularly apply to the 'baby-boomer' generation, who have become accustomed to high and rising standards of living – it is sometimes suggested that this postwar generation has been particularly selfish, exploiting those coming before and after it (Evandrou, 1997);
- that the family, the traditional source of care for older people, will be less willing and less able to meet care needs than before, because of greater family instability and change due to divorce and single parenthood (see Lewis's chapter), and because the values that support family obligations to care are becoming less strong;
- that women, the main providers of social care from within the family, will be less able and willing to carry out the care tasks they traditionally have because their participation in paid work will leave them with less time to care and because fewer will accept the social norms that have hitherto defined family care as a woman's duty.

All these arguments raise both matters of fact – are these changes really happening in the ways portrayed? – and questions about values and perceptions – do they amount to extra burdens and problems, particularly unacceptable ones? They also imply sharp social divisions of interest between different social groups and institutions about how far each should meet the perceived burden: between retired older people and working people; between the state, the family, the voluntary sector and the market; and even between different classes of older people, particularly between those who have saved to meet the exigencies of old age and those who have not.

The main aim of this chapter is to compare what we know about age and dependency, that is to say what careful research has discovered, with the images and social constructions of the issue that are part of its status as a social problem. As other chapters also demonstrate, it is families, particularly women as informal carers, that are often detrimentally affected when policy choices are turned into social problems. This chapter describes how

- age has come and gone as a social problem, despite a relatively unchanging 'reality';
- state-provided help gets most of the attention, but does least of the care work;
- dependency itself is a complex mixture of what people need, what they expect and what is expected of them;
- suggested solutions are often more unwelcome than the social problems themselves.

How Demographic Ageing Came to Be a Social Problem

The fundamental processes that have produced demographic ageing in many societies, particularly industrial ones, are well known. They are well summed up in the title of an excellent account of the mechanisms, *Fewer Babies, Longer Lives* (Ermisch, 1990). Women are having fewer children, and people are living longer; it is less understood why and for how long birth rates will continue to fall and to what extent and why more people can expect to live longer. It is broadly accepted that economic growth and higher living standards have played the main role, and that medical interventions, despite their economic and personal importance, have been relatively unimportant in extending average life expectancy. However, the trends involved can change quite abruptly, disrupting forecasts. In Scandinavia in the 1990s birth rates tended to climb from their postwar lows, while in some industrial societies, such as parts of the former Soviet Union, death rates started to rise again for some social groups. None the less, increases in longevity seem to be well established in industrial societies. Over the last half century life expectancy has been growing by about two years for every decade (Office of Population, Censuses and Surveys, 1989). There is increasing evidence that old people are becoming healthier and less dependent at any given age. It is also clear that the perceptions that make ageing a social problem are often less based on fact and more dependent on cultural and political factors: a generalized fear of being old within youth-orientated consumer societies; the increasing resistance of taxpayers to support the non-working population; and possibly a decline in people's willingness to both give and receive informal care from within the family and the community.

The construction of old age as a social problem came as part of the price of progress and of the welfare state. During the first half of the twentieth century, which was dominated by two world wars, economic recession and high levels of unemployment, surprisingly little attention was paid to the fact that the UK population over 65 grew, by 150 per cent, to over five million (OPCS, 1989). Before the Second World War the needs of disabled people were considered almost entirely a private and family matter, not a social one. For example, the 1930 version of the much amended Poor Law stated: 'It should be the duty of a father, mother, grandmother, husband or child, of a poor, blind, lame or impotent person . . . to relieve and maintain that person.' The state would help only if the family did not have the means to assist, and then the solution was still the workhouse, or Public Assistance Institution as it was then called. In that period, Townsend and Wedderburn point out (1965, p. 10) that 'very little information on the problems of the aged living at home or receiving treatment and care in hospitals or other institutions was published. It is an extraordinary fact [that] . . . suddenly, in the late forties and fifties, or so it may seem to the historian of the spoken or written word, the problems of old age were discovered.'

The idea that an ageing population is a problem was implicit in the plans for postwar reconstruction. In 1942 the Beveridge Report, while essentially remembered as a progressive document, considered the changing age composition of the population and discussed how increasing numbers of 'non-productive' old people might become a burden on the working members of the community. It sought a positive solution by suggesting that many people should extend their working lives. 'There is no reason to doubt the power of large numbers of people to go on working with advantage to the community . . . after reaching the minimum pensionable age of 65 for men and 60 for women' (Beveridge, 1942, p. 99). But integral to this 'solution' was a view that dependence in old age was undesirable.

Box 4.1: The institutional care solution

In 1944 the Nuffield Foundation asked Seebohm Rowntree to 'gather as complete information as possible with regard to the various problems – individual, social and medical – associated with ageing and old age' (Rowntree, 1947, p. 1). Rowntree's report suggested what, in today's terms, was a novel solution to becoming a burden to one's family:

Many cases have been encountered . . . of old people maintaining a hopeless struggle against adversity in order to cling to the last vestiges of independence . . . If sufficient Homes can be provided, and if the homelike atmosphere found in some of them is introduced to all Homes, many old people will prefer no doubt to enter them rather than to continue living in unsatisfactory conditions in private homes. This will lessen the need for extensive plans of home help, home nursing, visiting, and home meals services for old people who would be better off in a Home or Institution. (Rowntree, 1947, p. 96)

The postwar welfare state was not planned with older people in mind so the ways in which their needs have come to dominate it have been seen as problems. Beveridge's social security system was designed mainly to protect workers and their families at times of illness and unemployment. It would take forty years to build up rights to a basic pension under the scheme and in the mean time Beveridge argued that state pensions should be provided only to those below a means-tested poverty threshold (Beveridge, 1942, p. 99). Instead the government introduced the universal old age pension for all from 1948, but at a level lower than Beveridge recommended. From then on the state retirement pension, which people received by right if they had paid the appropriate contributions while in work, would often be worth less than a means-tested minimum social assistance income. One consequence has been that for the past half-century between a quarter and a third of all retired people have been forced into dependence on state charity. British old people became 'a problem'. Provision for them dominated the social security budget. Similarly the National Health Service was constructed as an acute service for all ages. Its provision of long-term geriatric care has been steadily reduced, and the resulting preponderance of older people in acute wards is often described as a problem of 'bed-blocking'.

Even within local authority social care services, policies providing for older people have been marginal or residual concerns despite the large proportion of resources consumed. The 1948 National Assistance Act gave local authorities the main responsibility for providing and overseeing services for older people, and the 1970 Local Authority Social Services Act effectively transferred this to the local Social Services Departments. However, from the 1950s to the 1980s the central concerns of the social work profession were to do with children and families: protecting children from poverty and abuse and seeking solutions to juvenile delinquency, a recognized 'social problem' in the 1960s when the difficulties of older people remained largely invisible. There appears to be a limit to the number of social problems public debate can cope with at any one time. The needs of older people first began to be noticed as part of the 'rediscovery of poverty' in the 1960s (Townsend and Wedderburn, 1965; Atkinson, 1969). It was found that retired people were by far the largest group among the poor – those living at state assistance levels or below. In the years that followed, although new pension schemes were introduced from time to time (graduated retirement pensions in 1966, the state earnings related pension in 1978, personal pensions in 1988), these have had little impact on poverty among older people (Walker, 1990). For a time during the 1980s the financial needs of the old were overshadowed by those of the unemployed. In the 1990s the 'problem' reappeared, but now in a new guise: it was the care needs of the very old that began to preoccupy governments.

In an extraordinary way in the 1990s the care of frail elderly people became a central social policy concern in all major industrial nations. From Scandinavia, across Western Europe to the United States, and in Japan, Korea and Australia, committees of inquiry were set up to advise governments about tackling the care needs of older people. In many cases substantial legislation followed, setting up new methods for financing and providing social care (OECD, 1996). For example, in 1990 the British government passed the NHS and Community Care Act, which required a more systematic assessment of older people's needs and the targeting of state help on the most needy. In 1994 the German parliament enacted a new universal system of social care insurance, providing services or cash in lieu for those who passed incapacity tests. In 1990 Japan embarked on the Gold Plan, a ten-year strategy to improve the health and welfare services for older people in their own homes, largely funded by the state. Coupled with these spasms of inquiry and legislation was the 'discovery' of informal care. Governments came to notice and accept that most help for dependent old people was provided by their families, and that women did most of the work.

Who Cares for Dependent Older People?

Old people who live on their own are the ones most likely to receive help from public employees such as community nurses, health visitors, social workers, homehelps and care assistants. Table 4.1 shows the usual source of help received by older people living on their own and unable to do the basic tasks of daily living. It is clear that even for this group the main sources of help remain informal carers: relatives and to a lesser extent neighbours and friends.

The first comprehensive study of informal care in Great Britain showed that there were more than six million people at any one time providing significant assistance to another adult or to a disabled child (Green, 1988). These numbers were broadly confirmed by repeat surveys in 1990 and 1995 (Office of Population, Censuses and Surveys, 1992; Rowlands, 1998). There was an apparent increase in the number of carers in the 1990 survey, to 6.8 million, and an analysis suggested that this was because media attention and the high profile of carer pressure groups in the debates about community care had 'sensitised people about caring' and enabled them to identify themselves as carers (Parker and Lawton, 1994, p. 4). This is an example of how public issues can change perceptions. People more marginally involved in care, particularly men, were drawn into identifying themselves as carers. The image and idea of a carer had become clearer to people. However, the survey data on informal care also showed that most 'heavy' caring, more than twenty hours a week, was done by women and that women were more likely to be the main carers (Rowlands, 1998, tables 24, 36). In addition, over a quarter of all caring was carried out by people over 65 and nearly half of these cared for more than fifty hours a week, most commonly for their spouses (Rowlands, 1998, tables 23, 24). This leads to the almost paradoxical conclusion that one of the key solutions to the problem of growing numbers of older people needing help will indeed be that there are also growing numbers of older people available to do the care work.

It has become very clear that informal carers are the 'low-cost' linchpin of the care system. One study estimated the value of their unpaid work at £27 billion in the UK in 1995, based on an assumed hourly rate of £7 (Laing,

Table 4.1 People aged 65 and over living alone: help with tasks, Great Britain, 1994

Usual source of help	Bathing and washing %	Domestic tasks including cooking %	Walking outside the house %
Relative	46	59	67
Friend/neighbour	3	24	26
Voluntary worker	1	1	0
NHS or personal social services	45	19	6
Paid help	2	26	0
Other	3	2	1

Source: General Household Survey 1994, Office for National Statistics, © Crown Copyright 2000

1996). This is a rough estimate, but telling compared with the just over £3 billion spent by the NHS and local authorities on non-residential care in the same period. The 1990 NHS and Community Care Act required local authorities to consider the needs of family carers, and the Carers (Recognition and Services) Act 1995 gave them an entitlement to have their needs assessed. However, much of the evidence points to their receiving less not more help in recent years. Between 1985 and 1995 the proportion of carers living in the same household as a main dependent who reported regular visits from a doctor fell from 13 to 8 per cent. The proportion reporting no regular visitor at all from state or voluntary services rose from 69 to 75 per cent (Rowlands, 1998, table 38). Commenting on these figures, Parker suggests that it 'is perhaps not so surprising when recent policy has put so much emphasis on enabling older people – many of whom live alone and may have no carer – to stay out of long-stay care settings' (Rowlands, 1998, p. 47). The targeting of older people who live on their own has meant most carers get less support. The problems of care and dependency in old age are full of such trade-offs. The nature of the 'social problem' and its possible solutions varies according to whose interests or perspectives are being considered. Gains for some are often losses for others.

How Much Dependency Will There Be?

Uncertainty about the future size of a phenomenon is often a key to its becoming a social problem. It is difficult to estimate how much care the older people of the future will need. Most forecasts assume that what are called age-specific rates of dependency will remain the same; that is to say, for example, that the proportion of people over 80 who need help to go out of doors or to climb stairs will remain the same as it is currently. If we couple this assumption with predictions of substantial increases in the number of very old people, a large future problem of dependency is constructed. However, there is growing evidence that people are not only living longer but that more of them are remaining healthy and independent for longer.

The General Household Survey is one based on respondents' judgements of their own abilities, rather than on those of a doctor or some other professional. So it is possible that the apparent improvements in mobility that are reported by people over 85 are a reflection of a growing unwillingness to admit to physical limitations. There is evidence that older people feel it is illegitimate, even immoral, to give in to the effects of old age (Williams, 1990; Hepworth, 1995). In a society in which being old is not a source of respect and in which youth, fitness and autonomy are particularly valued, it is possible that some of the age-specific 'improvements' in health and ability are in part a reflection of new attitudes and values rather than real changes. However, the measures of mobility used in table 4.2 are fairly clear-cut indications of what people can and cannot do. They are good measures of the changing need for help, whatever the reasons for the changes. There is evidence suggesting that while there will be more old people in the future, and particularly more very old people, it does not necessarily follow that the total need for care will rise.

Box 4.2: Age-specific dependency rates

Small annual changes in future age-specific dependency rates can imply very large variations in the numbers of people who will need care. The Royal Commission on Long Term Care, which reported in 1999 (Sutherland, 1999), considered three scenarios for age-specific dependency rates: staying as they were in 1995 (the baseline case); rising by 1 per cent per year; falling by 1 per cent per year. These assumptions had considerable effects on the predicted number of people who might need care in Britain in the future.

The baseline case forecast 3.27 million older people with dependency in 2031, compared with only 2.27 million if age-specific rates fall by 1 per cent per year, and 4.68 million if they rise by 1 per cent per year (Wittenberg et al., 1998, p. 116). These differences have huge implications for the costs of care and the number of carers who may be needed. Some experts believe that current fears may be very exaggerated because they underestimate the degree to which extra life-expectancy will also mean extra years of healthy *non*-dependent life. This was the possibility suggested by two of the advisors to the Royal Commission:

> Empirical evidence on trends in disability from the UK supports the view that health expectancy is indeed rising, at least at severe levels of disability. On this evidence, it is by no means impossible that the numbers of people needing intensive long-term care will stay the same as at present, even though the population ages. On the other hand, at milder levels of disability there appears to be no such improvement. (Bebbington and Bone, 1998, p. 1)

Table 4.2 People aged 85 and over with mobility difficulties, Great Britain

	1980 %	1985 %	1991 %	1994 %	1996 %
Unable to					
walk out of doors	48	47	44	37	37
get around the house	10	6	6	3	4
get in and out of bed	10	7	7	4	4

Note: The survey is of people living at home, not of people in institutions
Source: General Household Survey 1996, Office for National Statistics, © Crown Copyright 2000

Table 4.3 People aged 75 and over who have reported health difficulties, Great Britain

	1972 %	1981 %	1985 %	1991 %	1996 %
Activity restricted in last 14 days	13	19	21	21	24
Consulted GP in last 14 days	20	19	20	19	22

Note: The survey is of people living at home, not of people in institutions
Source: General Household Survey 1996, Office for National Statistics, © Crown Copyright 2000

Milder forms of disability tend to be even more a matter of perceptions than observable inabilities to do specific activities. Paradoxically, if people are asked whether their health has in some way restricted their activities recently then an increasing proportion of older people seem to think it has, and an increasing proportion are likely to consult their doctors.

Taken together tables 4.2 and 4.3 reflect that ill-health and even dependency are essentially social constructions, that is to say they are matters of perception and involve comparing one's situation with some expectation of normality. What is normal may change as a society comes to expect higher levels of activity and well-being in old age. (The chapters by Clarke, Donnison, Jones and Prior give other examples of changing constructions of normality.) Thus, while older people at a particular age may be becoming healthier, judged by their abilities, more of them may feel less fit, or they may feel they are entitled to help to do the things older people of the generation before did not expect to do. Medical and lay definitions of ill-health and disability are different, but neither kind is necessarily more valid than the other. Thus, while older people's need for care and assistance may in some objective sense be falling, their expectations of help may rise. Like social problems, issues of care and dependency in old age are matters of myth and values rather than of science and facts. The 'social problem' may get worse despite the benefits of social policy responses which seek to reduce it.

Dementia and Fears of Dementia

If the needs of older people are a social problem, then dementia is its most acute manifestation. When people are asked what they fear most about growing older many will mention the prospect of becoming confused and forgetful, and the possibility of dementia (British Gas, 1991). In fact their fears are not entirely logical. Many people with dementia, including those suffering from Alzheimer's disease, do not appear to suffer greatly from their disorder, though they may suffer from the responses of those around them: the condition is often more disturbing to others. It is depression and loneliness that old people complain of more. Discussions about dementia frequently exhibit the characteristics of a social problem discourse, even of a form of moral panic. For example, in 1982 a fairly careful assessment of the issues produced by the NHS Health Advisory Service received much media attention, largely because of its title, *The Rising Tide* (Health Advisory Service, 1982). The report extrapolated from many varied estimates of mental illness and dementia in older people and predicted a 'flood likely to overwhelm the entire health system' (HAS, 1982, p. 1).

Those who have studied and worked with older people with dementia do not necessarily reject the figures and forecasts that lie behind the predictions of a growing social problem. Kitwood, one of the most thoughtful commentators, wrote:

> The rising tide of dementia is of . . . the quiet kind. For many years now prevalence has been slowly but steadily increasing, and this is likely to continue for many years to come . . . The scale of the problem is immense. In the UK alone, most estimates suggest that the total number of people affected is between half and one million . . . Its presence will have profound and lasting effects – for good or ill – on the entire pattern of our economic, political and social life. (Kitwood, 1997, p. 1)

However, the whole thrust of Kitwood's contribution was to argue that perceptions of dementia as a threat and burden to the rest of society prevent progress to solutions that are humane and effective. Frequently people with dementia are understood only within a standard medical paradigm which sees them as senile and assumes that nothing can be done beyond meeting their basic physical needs. They are no longer considered fully human or persons. This is the image that Kitwood described as 'dementia as a death that leaves the body

---

Box 4.3: Dementia in old age

There is a tendency in the media and in popular debate about the issue to treat dementia as if it were an absolute condition which one either has or does not have. In fact, it is a matter of degree, and a great deal of room for misunderstanding, exaggeration and prejudice exists. The American Psychiatric Association (1980) provides widely accepted definitions that distinguish between mild dementia ('work and social activities are significantly impaired but the capacity for independent living remains'), moderate dementia ('independent living is hazardous and some degree of support is necessary') and severe dementia ('activities of daily living are so impaired that continuous support is required; for example the person is unable to maintain minimal personal hygiene, is largely incoherent or mute').

behind' (1997, p. 3). It is a myth that leaves family carers without appropriate support and often with none.

It is the family, not the health service or social services, that largely cares for older people with mental disabilities. Beds for 'psychogeriatrics' in hospitals have been dramatically reduced over the past twenty years, though outpatient attendances have risen. Many residential and nursing homes are less willing to accept people with mental and behaviour difficulties. Most such old people are cared for in the community. Extrapolations from the OPCS disability surveys of the British population estimated that of 322,000 people aged over 65 with 'advanced cognitive impairment' (scoring 7 or over on the OPCS scales) 47 per cent lived in private households with others, 13 per cent lived on their own, 7 per cent were in NHS hospitals, and 33 per cent were in residential or nursing homes (Kavanagh et al., 1995, pp. 128–30). People with dementia are more likely than those with physical disabilities to be living with carers, most commonly a spouse or a child. As a recent study of community care reports:

> Spouse carers along with other close family carers, are a particularly important source of assistance for users with cognitive impairment or behavioural disorder (CI/BD). [In our study] 48% of carers of users with CI/BD are the sons or daughters of the user, and 36% are spouses. Less close family members account for only 4% ... This is consistent with the hierarchy of caregiving described by some writers. The nature of the assistance required means that friends and neighbours are rarely identified as the carers of cognitively impaired users. (Bauld et al., 2000, pp. 85–6)

The same study showed that in 1994 and 1995 households caring for older people with mental illness were on average getting more support from statutory services: from social services to a value of £115 a week compared with £81 a week for physically disabled users; from the NHS to a value of £37 a week compared with £35 a week (Bauld et al., 2000, tables 8.12 and 8.14). To a large extent these differences were due to the costs of offering occasional respite care to relieve carers. But this funding is not spread among all those households looking after older people with mental illness. The OPCS study showed that many received very little public help (see Table 4.4). It does not seem unreasonable to draw the conclusion that there are large numbers of carers supporting severely mentally ill older people in the community at any one time, and that a substantial proportion do so unaided by social or health services to any significant degree. One study in the 1980s concluded that over a third of the carers involved were so stressed that they probably needed psychiatric help themselves (Levin et al., 1989).

Conclusion

Social problems often emerge where none of the major institutions in society is prepared to take responsibility for social reform. All the various parties can then

Table 4.4 People aged 65 and over with advanced cognitive impairment in private households receiving services during the past year, Great Britain, 1986, %

Service	%
Psychiatrist	12
Community nurse	36
Health visitor	12
Meals on wheels	8
Home help	24
Social worker	14
GP	91
Respite care	11

Source: Martin et al., 1989

blame each other, and even the victims of the problem: in this case the frail older people themselves. Consequently, when a solution is suggested it is rarely greeted with acclaim, especially by those on whom responsibility would fall. The fate of the 1999 report of the Royal Commission on Long Term Care (Sutherland, 1999) is an example of this. The setting up of a royal commission is often the response of a government confronted by a social problem. In December 1997 Sir Stewart Sutherland's commission was given the job of examining 'the short and long term options for a sustainable system of funding of Long Term Care for elderly people, both in their own homes and in other settings' (Sutherland, 1999, p. ix). The commission's report was very clear in both its findings and its suggested solutions. It concluded not merely that 'on this analysis the current system is failing' but that 'no amount of statistics or cool analysis can take away the human despair which individuals feel when confronted with the system as it is' (para. 4.46). In order to resolve this, the commission's first and main recommendation was equally blunt: 'Personal care should be available after an assessment, according to need and paid for from general taxation' (p. xix). This is a radical solution, which seeks to give a need for social care the same status as a need for medical treatment. The royal commission's central suggestion is that the costs of providing formal care for older people should be borne by the state and the taxpayer in much the same way as the National Health Service provides free medical care. At the time of writing the government had yet to respond to the commission's report. Students of social problems will know that it is most unlikely to accept its main recommendation, whether right or wrong. While a social issue remains a social problem there is generally conflict about who is to blame, who ought to take remedial action and who should pay the costs. Most of the parties to these conflicts may find it more comfortable to live with the social problem than risk the responsibilities that come with a solution.

Issues to Consider

- Society has always contained older people who need help. Why have their needs only sometimes been considered a social problem?
- What factors may lead to a reduction in family care and what sorts of social policy may be needed in response?
- Social problems often emerge when there is uncertainty or disagreement about the facts of a social issue. Is this true of social care in old age?
- Why is dementia so alarming to people? Examine what evidence you can find about the nature and prevalence of dementia among older people. Does it amount to a social problem?
- Obtain a copy of the report of the Royal Commission on Long Term Care. Find out what the government's response was to the recommendations. How far does a social problems perspective allow one to understand this response?

Suggestions for Further Reading

The most comprehensive and accessible analysis of care and dependency for older people is to be found in the report by Sutherland (1999). The Office for National Statistics' annual publication *Social Trends* will usually contain data on the population and circumstances of older people; data are also available through the Office for National Statistics website www. statistics.gov.uk. Useful information and fact sheets can be downloaded from the Age Concern website www.ace.org.uk. In the government the Department of Heath is responsible for issues to do with caring and dependency and its website usually contains useful information and links: www.doh.gov.uk. Still one of the best and most comprehensive accounts of the social needs of older people is that by Tinker (1992), while Walker and Naegele (1999) provide interesting descriptions of how the 'social problems' of age are dealt with in different European countries. On a different level, but equally challenging, Forster (1990) is a brilliant and moving account of dependency and old age, and Kitwood's (1997) thoughtful and humane understanding of dementia also makes for salutary reading.

References

American Psychiatric Association 1980: *Diagnostic and Statistical Manual of Mental Disorders*, 3rd edn. Washington DC: APA.

Atkinson, A. B. 1969: *Poverty in Britain and the Reform of Social Security*. London: Cambridge University Press.

Bauld, L., Chesterman, J., Davies, B., Judge, K. and Mangalore, R. 2000: *Caring for Older People: An Assessment of Community Care in the 1990s*. Aldershot: Arena, Ashgate Publishing.

Bebbington, A. and Bone, B. 1998: *Healthy Life Expectancy and Long Term Care*, Personal Social Services Research Unit Discussion Paper no. 1426. Canterbury: University of Kent.

Beveridge, W. 1942: *Social Insurance and Allied Services*, Cmnd. 6404. London: HMSO.

British Gas 1991: *The British Gas Report on Attitudes to Ageing*. London: British Gas.

Ermisch, J. 1990: *Fewer Babies, Longer Lives, Policy Implications of Current Demographic Trends*. York: Joseph Rowntree Foundation in association with the Simon Population Trust.

Evandrou, M. (ed.) 1997: *Baby Boomers – Ageing in the 21st Century*. London: Age Concern Books.

Forster, M. 1990: *Have the Men Had Enough?* London: Penguin.

Green, H. 1988: *General Household Survey 1985: Informal Carers*. London: HMSO.

Health Advisory Service 1982: *The Rising Tide: Developing Services for Mental Illness in Old Age*. London: HMSO.

Hepworth, M. 1995: Positive ageing: what is the message? In R. Brunton, R. Burrows and S. Nettleton (eds), *The Sociology of Health Promotion: Critical Analyses of Consumption, Life-style and Risk*. London: Routledge.

Johnson, P., Conrad, C. and Thomson, D. 1989: Introduction. In P. Johnson, C. Conrad and D. Thomson (eds), *Workers Versus Pensioners: Intergenerational Justice and an Ageing World*. Manchester and New York: Manchester University Press.

Kavanagh, S., Schneider, J., Knapp, M., Beecham, J. and Netten, A. 1995: Elderly people with dementia: costs, effectiveness and balance of care. In M. Knapp (ed.), *The Economic Evaluation of Mental Health Care*. Aldershot: Arena, Ashgate Publishing.

Kitwood, T. 1997: *Dementia Reconsidered: The Person Comes First*. Buckingham: Open University Press.

Laing, W. 1996: *Care of Elderly People: Market Survey 1996*. London: Laing and Buisson.

Levin, E., Sinclair, I. and Gorbach, P. 1989: *Families, Services and Confusion in Old Age*. Aldershot: Gower.

Martin, J., White, A. and Maltzer, H. 1989: *Disabled Adults: Services, Transport and Employment*, OPCS Surveys of Disability in Great Britain, Report no. 4. London: HMSO.

OECD 1996: *Caring for Frail Elderly People: Policies in Evolution*, Social Policy Studies no. 19. Paris: OECD Publications Service.

Office for National Statistics 1996: *Living in Britain: Results from the 1994 General Household Survey*. London: Stationery Office.

Office for National Statistics 1998: *Living in Britain: Results from the 1996 General Household Survey*. London: Stationery Office.

Office of Population, Censuses and Surveys 1989: *Mortality Statistics*, Series DH1, no 22. London: HMSO.

Office of Population, Censuses and Surveys 1992: *General Household Survey: Carers in 1990*, OPCS Monitor SS92/2. London: HMSO.

Parker, G. and Lawton, D. 1994: *Different Types of Care, Different Types of Carer: Evidence from the General Household Survey*. London: HMSO.

Rowlands, O. 1998: *Informal Carers*. An independent study carried out by the Office of National Statistics on behalf of the Department of Health as part of the 1995 General Household Survey. London: Stationery Office.

Rowntree, B. 1947: *Old People*. Report of a Survey Committee on the Problems of Ageing and the Care of Old People, for the Nuffield Foundation. Oxford: Oxford University Press.

Sutherland, S. 1999: *With Respect to Old Age: Long Term Care – Rights and Responsibilities*. A Report by the Royal Commission on Long Term Care. London: Stationery Office.

Tinker, A. 1992: *Elderly People in Modern Society*, 3rd edn. London: Longman.

Townsend, P. and Wedderburn, D. 1965: *The Aged in the Welfare State*. London: Bell & Sons.

Walker, A. 1990: Poverty and inequality in old age. In J. Bond and P. Coleman (eds), *Ageing in Society: An Introduction to Social Gerontology*. Aldershot: Sage.

Walker, A. and Naegele, G. (eds) 1999: *The Politics of Old Age in Europe*. Buckingham: Open University Press.

Williams, R. 1990: *A Protestant Legacy: Attitudes to Illness and Death Amongst Older Aberdonians*. Oxford: Clarendon Press.

Wittenberg, R., Pickard, L., Comas-Herrera, A., Davies, B. and Darton, B. 1998: *Demand for Long-Term Care: Projections of Long-Term Care Finance for Elderly People*. Canterbury: Personal Social Services Research Unit at the University of Kent.

Chapter 5

Domestic Violence

Lorraine Radford

Introduction

The term 'domestic violence' is used most frequently to refer to men's physical, sexual or psychological violence to women in the context of a heterosexual relationship. Recent estimates suggest that between a quarter and a third of women report having experienced domestic violence during their lives, between 1 in 9 and 1 in 10 women experiencing it within the past year (ESRC, 1998). In the nineteenth century concerns about husbands' 'cruelty' or 'brutality' were central to debates on welfare and family law reform (Gordon, 1989; May, 1978), but from the 1920s the problem virtually disappeared from public discourse. In the UK and in the USA, domestic violence emerged again as a social problem with the rebirth of feminism in the 1970s.

Building on Lewis's and Baldock's discussions of the widespread anxiety about the state of the 'family' and its caring capacity, this chapter charts the changing recognition of domestic violence as a social problem in the period from the 1970s to the late 1990s. It focuses on four questions:

- How has the problem of domestic violence been defined and approached by academics and practitioners since the 1970s?
- Why did domestic violence re-emerge as a social problem at this time?
- How has the problem of domestic violence been represented in policy debates, and what have been the proposed solutions?
- What possibilities exist for preventing domestic violence in the future?

Thinking about Violence

As other contributors to this volume also argue, how we define a problem affects how we think about its solution. There is no consensus over the definition, extent and impact of domestic violence. Even the language used to refer to it varies, from the use of gender-neutral terms, such as 'spousal violence' or 'partner abuse', to terms which are gender-specific, such as 'woman battering', or terms like 'family violence' or 'wife abuse', which suggest that violence occurs in the context of a particular relationship. In the UK, 'domestic violence' is now the most widely used term, but in the USA 'family violence' and 'spouse abuse' are frequently used as well. Variations in the language used to refer to a problem can reflect broader conceptual and ideological differences, as the issues posed in Box 5.1 illustrate. The box provides two lists of potentially abusive acts, adapted from different research studies on domestic violence. One is based on questions asked during research on 'spousal violence', the other is based on questions asked in research on domestic violence to women.

Legal definitions of violence and assault cover the unjustified use of physical force by the offender and the harm caused to the victim. The behaviour included in the spousal violence list in the box covers solely acts of physical force without reference to the context, intent or harm to the victim. If when thinking about violence we include reference to the context, intent and harm, we may decide to include some of the acts from the domestic violence list. Some acts, such as a slap, can vary considerably in terms of the injuries caused. Whether or not a person requires medical help may indicate the harm caused. The acts included in the domestic violence list cover a broader range of abusive behaviour – physical, sexual and psychological violence, bullying and controlling behaviour. These reflect both a broader definition of violence and a recognition of the intimate context in which abuse takes place. The acts included in the domestic

Box 5.1: Kinds of violence

How do the two lists differ? What aspects of abusive behaviour are included or excluded from these two lists?

Acts of spousal violence[a]	Domestic violence to women[b]
Threw something at spouse	Punched with fists
Pushed, shoved, grabbed spouse	Beat so badly medical help needed
Slapped spouse	Frightened partner
Kicked, bit, or hit spouse with fist	Acted like bully
Beat up spouse	Forced sex
Choked spouse	Ordered partner around
Threatened spouse with knife or gun	Would not let partner get a job
Used knife or gun on spouse	Partner jealous and suspicious

[a]Adapted from Gelles and Straus, 1988
[b]Adapted from Dominy and Radford, 1996

Box 5.2: Dominant discourses

Ideology	Intervention
Psychopathological	
Emphasis upon health problems, characteristics of the victim, addictive personalities and abnormal behaviour	Treatment for depression, alcohol, drugs, physiological disorders
Popular among therapists and health and social workers	Therapy to improve perpetrator's self-esteem and victim's addiction to violence
Systemic	
Emphasis on how couple or family interactions create the problem through communication failures, caused by high frustration levels and poor resources	Couple counselling or family therapy
Popular among therapists, counsellors, social workers and probation officers	
Social Learning / Family Violence	
Emphasis on cycle of violence from parent to child, learned behaviour, stress factors, conflict and violence in society	Tackling of violent society Breaking cycle of violence through role models for youth, assertiveness training, anger management, stress reduction
Popular with family violence researchers, social workers and probation officers	
Feminist	
Emphasis on violence against women, power and control, political, cultural and social issues	Direct provision of services, e.g. refuges 'by and for' women
Women as 'appropriate victims'	Self-help, empowerment
Popular with feminists and violence-against-women researchers	Political campaign for social change
Pro-feminist	
Emphasis on violence and masculinity; use of feminist model to inform intervention with men	Promotion of men's responsibility to change through prevention
Popular with feminists, pro-feminists, violence-against-women researchers and men's programme workers	Re-education and inter-agency working

violence list emphasize violence and control in the context of a gendered power relationship.

As with other 'social problems', the ideological perspectives on violence and abuse vary as the definitions do. Widely different remedies are supported, from therapeutic interventions and treatment to re-education projects and public awareness campaigns. The dominant discourses on domestic violence and the main policy options associated with them are set out in Box 5.2. It shows how some perspectives view violence in individual terms, as deviant behaviour, stemming from an illness or from drink-induced disorders (Gayford, 1978). For others it is a result of relationship difficulties, the result of a couple's poor communication skills aggravated by stresses within the family, or a pattern of abusive behaviour passed on through successive generations in a family (Pizzey, 1974). Other discourses point towards structural factors, such as patriarchy, male power and women's oppression (Dobash and Dobash, 1980) or the social construction of masculinity and violence against women (Newburn and Stanko, 1995). The preferred policies and interventions similarly vary from treatment or therapy for individuals or couples to practical help, prevention work and an emphasis on the broader social context in which domestic violence occurs.

The first three approaches can also sometimes favour policies of non-intervention. In the psychopathological discourse non-intervention may be urged to encourage a victim to change her behaviour. The systemic discourse may favour non-intervention because saving a family is considered more important than preventing violence. Or it may be reasoned that violence will cease if the family members can work together towards harmony. In the social learning / family violence discourse, intervention may be seen as fruitless if the cycle of violence persists anyway.

All these dominant discourses have been apparent in the history of the UK debates on domestic violence policy. The next section will show how there have been tensions and contradictions between these discourses, especially over the balance to be struck between saving families and protecting women from domestic violence.

A 'Hidden Crime'

There was little public discussion about domestic violence in the 1960s, although women frequently came to magistrates' courts to ask for separation or bind-over orders because of cruelty by their husbands (Smart, 1984). At the time, knowledge about domestic violence came mostly from clinical practice, with the very small number of abusers who came to the attention of the courts or psychiatry, or from social workers' case work with 'troubled families' (Mullender, 1996).

Throughout the 1950s and early 1960s the 'male-breadwinner' model of family life, in which men earned the pay packet to support homemaking wives, dominated family law and social policy, even though a rising divorce rate meant that single parenting by women was on the increase (see Lewis's chapter). Writings by feminists such as Betty Friedan highlighted the growing dissatisfaction of middle-class women with the homemaking role (Friedan, 1963), and by the mid-1970s women who worked solely as homemakers were in a minority anyway, as women's participation in paid employment in most OECD countries expanded rapidly. Economic activity rates for women with young children grew from 24 per cent in 1961 to 39 per cent in 1971 and 47 per cent in 1973, most of the growth being in part-time work (Fox-Harding, 1997). These increased opportunities for women's employment were not, however, matched by an expansion in childcare provisions or a sharing of unpaid domestic labour and care work between men and women (Coote and Campbell, 1987). In comparison with men, women had very poor pay and employment rights.

The 'discovery' of domestic violence as a social problem in the 1970s was linked to growing activity in the feminist movement. The 1970s also saw the start of a decline in interest in traditional class-based politics and the rise of more identity- and lifestyle-based 'new social movements', such as environmentalism, the peace movement, gay and lesbian rights and feminism. The new social movements were diverse in their politics and organization, but they shared an emphasis on direct action to bring about social change. In the 1970s feminism nurtured the principles of self-help, experience sharing and services collectively provided by and for women. In women's groups and women's centres across the country, feminism created the conditions in which women could speak out and share their experiences of family life, poor pay, inadequate childcare and abuse. Poor pay and working conditions, childcare, opportunities for education and training, health care and violence became the key concerns of 1970s feminism.

In 1972 Erin Pizzey opened a women's centre, which, famously, became the first safe house or refuge for women leaving violent men. Pizzey would probably identify herself more as a domestic violence campaigner than as a feminist, although her activities in the 1970s were initially inspired by, and fired inspiration into, the feminist movement. The refuge in Chiswick attracted a lot of media interest, particularly when court proceedings for overcrowding were initiated by the local council. The demand from women for a safe place to stay seemed to be endless. Operating an open door policy, at one stage the small terraced house was accommodating about 150 women and children. Other refuges were subsequently set up across the country by women's groups, and together these formed the National Women's Aid Federation (NWAF) in 1974.

The impact of domestic violence on heterosexual women, especially mothers under the age of 40, became the main focus of early interventions and public policy. The abuses of older women, lesbian women and women with disabilities were scarcely considered then and have mostly remained neglected issues. Women without children had a difficult time finding support, refuge and accommodation (Binney et al., 1988). Black and minority-group women were assumed to have the same needs as white women and to be equally able to use the services provided for them.

In the media and in policy debates domestic violence was represented as a 'hidden crime', the extent of which was yet to be realized. In 1973 Jack Ashley MP announced to the House of Commons that there were as many as 16,000 abused women making calls to the police each year, but official crime records did not reflect anything like this level of need (Hansard, 1973). In 1975, the Bedfordshire police also claimed that many more women affected by domestic violence attempted to use the law than appeared in official crime figures. Only about one-quarter of the 288 cases of domestic violence recorded by the Bedfordshire force proceeded to prosecution, and one-third of those that did were then either discharged or 'otherwise dealt with' (House of Commons Select Committee, 1975). For instance, an extensive research study of police and court records, started in 1974 in Scotland, found that 25 per cent of all the assaults known to the police and courts were assaults by husbands on wives (Dobash and Dobash, 1980).

Parallel with the discovery of 'battered babies' in the 1960s, the term 'battered women' was coined and widely used to refer to women who experienced domestic violence. Women's testimonies in the media and in research studies highlighted the brutality of the physical abuse involved: 'A month ago he threw scalding water over me, leaving a scar on my right arm . . . Two weeks ago he hit me full in the face because I went to my home town for the day. My lip was badly cut' (Pizzey, 1974, p. 35). And 'He once used a stick, he hit me once with a fibreglass fishing pole, six feet long' (Dobash and Dobash, 1997, p. 267).

In 1975 the government set up a select committee to investigate violence in marriage and to make recommendations for change. Its concerns reflected the issues highlighted by the media – domestic violence was more prevalent than it appeared, it was severe, it threatened the welfare of the future generation, and the state had a part to play in making a response quickly (Dobash and Dobash, 1992). A separate committee was set up to look at violence to children. The impact that domestic violence had on children figured greatly in the committee's discussions but barely at all in the policy outcomes. The Chiswick refuge and the NWAF-affiliated refuges gave extensive evidence. There were fundamental differences between the ways they represented the problem of domestic violence. NWAF rooted its understanding of domestic violence within an analysis of patriarchy, gender and power, seeing the abuse of women as linked to their general position in society, and emphasized law reform, better practical help and more refuge services. The Chiswick refuge argued that domestic violence stemmed from deviancy in the family, alcohol abuse, mental illness and from past experiences of living in a violent home as a child (Pizzey, 1974); it was very keen to promote the need for therapeutic care to break the cycle of violence and to stop children following the examples of their parents and growing into abusers or victims. Both refuges, however, similarly stressed the need for women to leave abusive men.

The 'Exit Discourse'

The radical implications of supporting women and children to lead violence-free lives have not been endorsed by social policy. The 'exit discourse' has dominated policy activity on domestic violence in recent years (Bacchi, 1999). A common response to domestic violence, it is based on asking the question, 'why doesn't the woman just leave?' Before outlining the policy trends since the Select Committee Report (HCSC, 1975) it is worth closely examining this question and the assumptions on which it is founded. Pause a while to consider the following questions:

- What practical and emotional difficulties may a woman face when leaving a violent partner?
- What assumptions are made about the nature of domestic violence when asking 'Why doesn't she just leave?'

Women may face a number of practical and emotional difficulties when separating from their violent partners. The difficulties are summarized in Box 5.3:

Box 5.3: Reasons why it is difficult to separate from an abusive partner

- The perpetrator will not let her go.
- The woman believes there is no way out and nobody cares.
- She fears for her life should she leave.
- She feels that it is all her fault.
- She is isolated from her family and friends.
- She fears 'losing' her children or being considered an unfit mother.
- She has nowhere to go.
- She is in love with the perpetrator and hopes he will change.
- The perpetrator threatens or attempts to commit suicide if she goes.

The exit discourse frames the problem of domestic violence in terms of women's *reluctance* to leave, implying that most refuse to walk away from the abuse. Most women who experience domestic violence do in fact separate from their abusers, although not all of them will be successful on the first attempt, because separation is not an easy process (Kirkwood, 1993). Leaving may not be the final solution, because violence often continues and may even escalate after a separation (Hester and Radford, 1996a). Women are at greater risk of homicide at the point of or shortly after separation (Daly and Wilson, 1988). Asking why a woman does not leave also centres attention on her behaviour and choices rather than on the perpetrator's responsibility to stop the violence or an agency's responsibility to act.

An Emergency Problem

Most of the Select Committee's recommendations focused on helping women separate quickly from their abusers in emergencies or crises. Local authorities were urged to sympathetically consider applications for refuge funding. Refuges were recommended initially on the basis of one family place per 10,000 of the population, although this standard has never been achieved. Major changes in the family law and homelessness policy followed the report. The Domestic Violence and Matrimonial Proceedings Act 1976 enabled spouses or cohabitants to apply to court for an order prohibiting violence and 'molestation' and for the right to occupy the matrimonial home and to exclude their violent partners. The Act gave the courts new powers to make these orders very quickly and the police powers to arrest. Previously a woman had to start proceedings for divorce or damages to get an order for protection, while under the new law a woman could get an injunction within a few hours, sometimes without the ex-partner being present in court (*ex parte* orders). In addition, the Housing Homeless Persons Act 1977 allowed local authorities to consider homeless those who had left home because of domestic violence. The new housing law further stressed the importance of keeping parents and children together. Previously women made homeless owing to domestic violence could lose their children into local authority care (Hague and Wilson, 1996).

The emphasis within social policy on the crisis or emergency problem caused by domestic violence meant that women had to appear to be in dire straits before approaching an agency for help in the first place. This had a rationing effect on resources, limiting refuge provision to temporary accommodation and injunctive 'protection' to three months. It also limited demand, as an unknown number of women rejected help, preferring to deal with things themselves. As many as two out of three women may not contact another agency and will draw on their own resources and strengths, or rely on informal networks for support (Dominy and Radford, 1996). The refuge movement had always highlighted non-directive methods of working and maximizing women's ability to make their own decisions. Within statutory agencies the approach was directive, channelling women into one course of action, such as obtaining an injunction. The directive approach contributed to the judgement of women who returned to live with their abusers or 'failed' to separate from them. Women who did not leave would be judged by agency workers in 'helping' professions to be either 'hooked on abuse' or so damaged by it as to be unable to make a rational decision.

Domestic Violence is a Crime

Research carried out in the mid-1980s showed that, despite the new legal provisions, often agencies such as the police continued to be reluctant to take domestic violence seriously or to intervene in domestic disputes. Edwards's

(1989) research into the London metropolitan police found that the problem was both the attitude of the police and their frustration over the difficulty of making meaningful interventions. Many officers failed to record, charge and arrest perpetrators, because they believed that the women would not want to press charges or would later withdraw their complaints and would not proceed to prosecution. Policing issues came to dominate policy options in the 1980s. Feminists argued that domestic violence was a crime that should be treated just as seriously as other crimes of violence. The problem was not women's reluctance to get help but the agencies' reluctance to get involved. The Conservative government's commitment to law and order issues in the context of social welfare privatization meant that a crime control response was much favoured.

News from the USA of the early findings about the deterrent effects of arrests on domestic violence spread quickly to the UK and also had an influence on policing policy at the highest levels (Mullender, 1996). Guidance was issued to the police in London in 1986, urging the better recording of incidents and the use of a more pro-arrest stance. A specially important new development in the UK was the establishment of police domestic violence units. The first was set up in London in 1987, and by 1989 further units has been established in West Yorkshire, Manchester and Birmingham, spreading to most of the country by the early 1990s (Hester and Radford, 1996b). Domestic violence units were staffed largely by female officers with a remit to respond sensitively to and provide appropriate advice and support for women who experienced domestic violence (Home Affairs Committee, 1993). In 1990, in a concerted attempt to improve the police response, the Home Office issued a circular (Circular 60/90) to all police forces in England and Wales (Home Office, 1990).

The police's response to the circular varied across the country, and research in 1995 showed that some forces had made considerable progress, but others little (Grace, 1995). Throughout the 1980s and 1990s the arrest rate for domestic violence offenders remained low, with prosecution rates lower still (Hoyle, 1998). The appropriateness of relying mostly upon a police response to domestic violence was questioned by some researchers. Black feminists for instance have been critical of this emphasis on policing, pointing out the difficulties black women may have turning to the police for protection (Mama, 1989).

In the 1990s conflict between the government's commitment to 'preserve the family' for the sake of the children and the growing need to respond to pressure to protect the rights of women to be free from violence and abuse came to the fore. In the UK, as in many other Western nations, a 'father deprivation' discourse came to dominate debates on the family. Lone mothering was ideologically reconstructed as inept and harmful to children. In social welfare policy, concerns about child poverty and the increased dependence of lone mothers on state benefits fuelled the growth of a moral panic about single mothers breeding an 'underclass' of delinquent youths and irresponsible men (Mann and Roseneill, 1994; see too Lewis's chapter). The idea that 'families need fathers' became prevalent in courts' decisions on childcare arrangements after divorce and separation. A child's right to know a non-resident parent and have contact with him was increasingly viewed in terms of the mother's responsibility to ensure contact happens (Hester and Radford, 1996a). A mother who does not support her child's right to contact with the father risks being labelled selfish or implacably hostile by the courts, and may face imprisonment (Radford and Sayer, 1999). The efforts of agencies such as the refuges, the police and housing departments have been undermined by 'family saving' policies which aim to encourage fathers' involvement in the care and support of their children.

Community Intervention

From the 1990s government documents have stated that domestic violence is a complex problem involving many different agencies in a community (Home Affairs Committee, 1993). This multi-agency approach started with the presumption that no extra resources would be provided for work against domestic violence, but that agencies could improve the services they offered with more effective and cooperative methods of working. Multi-agency projects grew in number to about 200 by 1999 (Cabinet Office, 1999). Multi-agency methods of working are seen to be the way forward in the present government's publication *Living Without Fear* (Cabinet Office, 1999). This 'joined up thinking' approach has become a dominant feature of New Labour social policy and has resulted in a growth in community responses to other social problems, such as crime and ill-health (see the chapters by MacGregor, Cook, and Jones). *Living Without Fear* offers guidance and does not refer to the standards of service survivors of domestic violence can expect.

The multi-agency approach in the UK draws heavily on two assumptions: that agencies' responses need to be coordinated to provide services more efficiently, and that women affected by domestic violence need encouragement to come forward for help. The approach has depended largely on the goodwill, rather than the legal responsibility, of agencies to work in a multi-agency way or to share resources, training and information. The 'forum' model of working has dominated multi-agency working. In it, representatives from a range of statutory and voluntary services meet to negotiate, consult and make collective decisions. The agencies involved and the methods of working in domestic violence forums vary from area to area (Hague et al., 1996). Unlike the projects in the USA, where there has been an emphasis on facilitating criminal justice interventions, domestic violence forums in the UK have stressed coordinating a range of services (Holder, 1999). Some projects offer mostly mutual support and networking opportunities for the agencies' employees. Others emphasize multi-agency 'intervention' to provide services to protect women from violence and prevent it from happening in the future. Prevention work in some projects has included establishing re-education programmes for the perpetrators of domestic violence. With adequate support services and commitment to the safety of women, some of these projects compare favourably with the responses of the traditional criminal justice system (Burton et al., 1998).

Some multi-agency initiatives on domestic violence are very innovative. Many have broadened their responses from simply criminal justice to include the support available from social services and health-care workers. Concerns about community safety (see Cook's chapter) have enabled some projects to develop with a broader focus on the prevention of violence against women, and this is the vision for all forums recommended in *Living Without Fear*. As yet however, few projects have broadened their focus to consider how best to support women and encourage them to build on their own strengths, resources and networks of support (Holder, 1999).

A Women's Issue?

This brief history of social policies since the 1970s shows that there have been some significant changes in the approach to domestic violence as a social problem. There has been a trend away from emphasizing a woman's own responsibility to solve the problem, or protect herself, towards a view that domestic violence is an unacceptable crime, which all agencies should try to prevent. The context in which domestic violence takes place is now considered a more important factor, and, increasingly, the gendered nature of the crime has been stressed. The gendering of domestic violence, as part of the broader problem of violence against women, has occurred, however, alongside a reconstruction of fathering and parental responsibilities, especially concerning separation and divorce, away from the absent male breadwinner towards the father who stays involved. 'Violent men' and 'fathers' have been created as two separate beings. Feminist critics have argued that one persistent feature of domestic violence policy has been the representation of domestic violence as a women's issue rather than as a problem for men (Dobash and Dobash, 1999). Reconsidering domestic violence as a problem for men would involve asking a different set of questions in debates about public policy, the family, sexuality and crime. The limits on thinking imposed by the 'exit discourse', in which women are blamed for not doing enough to help themselves, might be overcome if it became possible to ask instead questions about men's responsibilities to help create safe and violence-free relationships.

Issues to Consider

- What are the implications for social policy of viewing domestic violence as a problem for men? Consider this question with reference to the existing research literature on: the response of the criminal justice system; violence prevention work with men; public education and work with children and young people; health care; family court welfare; multi-agency work to combat violence against women.
- Dealing with discrimination within the criminal justice system in relation to crimes of violence is a major challenge for those concerned with building a fairer society. This issue has been raised in this chapter but not addressed in any depth. What steps should we need to take to ensure that an increased emphasis on men's responsibility for violence did not lead to more discrimination against families marginalized by poverty, their ethnicity or their culture?
- How is the effectiveness of a policy on domestic violence assessed? What criteria for success do you consider most relevant?

Suggestions for Further Reading

Gordon (1989) looks at the history of family violence as a social problem from the nineteenth to the twentieth century in the USA and in England, and should be read alongside Dobash and Dobash (1992), which provides an account of the recent history of domestic violence as a social problem as well as an eloquent critique of therapeutic interventions. Hague and Malos (1998) provide an up-to-date reader on domestic violence and social policy in Britain. Richie (1996) looks at the imprisonment of battered women who kill and gives the best account to date of the interplay between race, gender and poverty in the social construction of domestic violence. Mullender (1996) provides a very readable and comprehensive account of changing policy and practice with reference to social and probation work, while Stanko (1990) considers how men and women negotiate personal safety in the course of their everyday lives. A good resource for research on domestic violence in Britain is the Domestic Violence Data Source website at www.domesticviolencedata.org.uk – this includes links to other sites. Up-to-date information can also be obtained from the Zero Tolerance Charitable Trust (25 Rutland Street, Edinburgh EH1 2AE).

References

Bacchi, C. 1999: *Women, Policy and Politics: The Construction of Policy Problems.* London: Sage.

Binney, V., Harkell, G. and Nixon, J. 1988: *Leaving Violent Men.* Bristol: Women's Aid Federation.

Burton, S., Regan, L. and Kelly, L. 1998: *Supporting Women and Challenging Men: Lessons from the Domestic Violence Intervention Project*. Bristol: Policy Press.

Cabinet Office 1999: *Living Without Fear*. London: Home Office / Women's Unit.

Coote, A. and Campbell, B. 1987: *Sweet Freedom: The Struggle For Women's Liberation*. Oxford: Blackwell.

Daly, M. and Wilson, M. 1988: *Homicide*. New York: Aldane De Gruyter.

Dobash, R. and Dobash, R. 1980: *Violence Against Wives*. Sussex: Open Books.

Dobash, R. and Dobash, R. 1992: *Women, Violence and Social Change*. London: Routledge.

Dobash, R. and Dobash, R. 1997: Violence against women. In L. O'Toole and J. Schiffman (eds), *Gender Violence: Inter-disciplinary Perspectives*. New York: New York University Press.

Dobash, R. and Dobash, R. (eds) 1999: *Re-thinking Violence Against Women*. London: Sage.

Dominy, N. and Radford, L. 1996: *Domestic Violence In Surrey: Towards an Effective Inter-agency Response*. Roehampton: Surrey County Council / Roehampton Institute.

Edwards, S. 1989: *Policing Domestic Violence*. London: Sage.

ESRC 1998: *Taking Stock: What Do We Know About Violence?* Swindon: Economic and Social Research Council, Violence Research Programme.

Fox-Harding, L. 1997: *Perspectives in Child Care Policy*. London: Longman.

Friedan, B. 1963: *The Feminine Mystique*. New York: Dell.

Gayford, J. 1978: Ten types of battered wives. *Welfare Officer*, 1 (5), 9.

Gelles, R. and Straus, M. 1988: *Intimate Violence*. New York: Simon & Schuster.

Gordon, L. 1989: *Heroes of Their Own Lives: The History and Politics of Family Violence*. London: Virago.

Grace, S. 1995: *Policing Domestic Violence in the 1990s*, Home Office Research Study 139. London: Home Office.

Hague, G. and Malos, E. 1998: *Domestic Violence: Action for Change*, 2nd edn. Cheltenham: New Clarion Press.

Hague, G., Malos, E. and Deer, W. 1996: *Multi-agency Work and Domestic Violence*. Bristol: Policy Press.

Hague, G. and Wilson, C. 1996: *The Silenced Pain: Domestic Violence 1945–1970*. Bristol: Policy Press.

Hansard 1973: *Parliamentary Debates*, House of Commons, vol. 854, 20 June, 26 June WA 1142, WA 322, vol. 859, 4 July WA, 5 July 171 WA, vol. 850, 16 July 218.

Hester, M. and Radford, L. 1996a: *Domestic Violence and Child Contact Arrangements in England and Denmark*. Bristol: Policy Press.

Hester, M. and Radford, L. 1996b: In Hester, M., Kelly, L. and Radford, J. (eds), *Women, Violence and Male Power*. Milton Keynes: Open University Press.

Holder, R. 1999: Pick 'n' mix or replication: the politics and process of adaptation. In M. Shepard and E. Pence (eds), *Coordinating Community Responses to Domestic Violence: Lessons from Duluth and Beyond*. London: Sage.

Home Affairs Committee 1993: *Third Report: Domestic Violence*, vol. II. London: HMSO.

Home Office 1990: *Domestic Violence Circular 90*. London: Home Office.

House of Commons Select Committee 1975: *Report of the Select Committee on Violence in Marriage*, vol. 2, Report, Minutes of Evidence and Appendices, HC 553, II. London: HMSO.

Hoyle, C. 1998: *Negotiating Domestic Violence: Police, Criminal Justice and Victims*. Oxford: Oxford University Press.

Kirkwood, C. 1993: *Leaving Abusive Partners*. London: Sage.

Mama, A. 1989: *The Hidden Struggle: Violence to Women and the Voluntary and Statutory Agencies' Response*. London: London Race and Housing Group, republished 1996 by Whiting & Birch, London.

Mann, K. and Roseneill, S. 1994: Some mothers do 'ave 'em: backlash and the gender politics of the underclass debate. *Journal of Gender Studies*, 3 (3), 317.

May, M. 1978: Violence in the family: a historical perspective. In J. Martin (ed.), *Violence in the Family*. Chichester: Wiley.

Mullender, A. 1996: *Re-thinking Domestic Violence*. London: Routledge.

Newburn, T. and Stanko, E. (eds) 1995: *Men, Masculinities and Crime: Just Boys Doing Business*. London: Routledge.

Pizzey, E. 1974: *Scream Quietly or the Neighbours Will Hear*. London: IF Books.

Radford, L. and Sayer, S. 1999: *Unreasonable Fears*. Bristol: Women's Aid Federation England.

Richie, B. 1996: *Compelled to Crime*. London: Routledge.

Smart, C. 1984: *The Ties that Bind*. London: Routledge & Kegan Paul.

Stanko, E. 1990: *Everyday Violence*. London: Pluto.

Poverty and Social Exclusion

Chapter 6

The Changing Face of Poverty

David Donnison

Introduction

An Arab, writing nearly a thousand years ago, identified eight levels of poverty, giving each a different name. Starting with loss of savings and temporary deprivations due to drought or natural disaster, these descended through the stages at which a household has no food and then no possessions left that can be sold to buy it, and ended in total destitution (al' Abri, 1994). A recent British study produced a similar scale in a more scientific and democratic way. Mack and Lansley (1985) asked a representative sample of British people to identify things which 'you think [are] necessary, and which all adults should be able to afford and which they should not have to do without'. They then ranked households by the number of these necessities which they were unwillingly deprived of, and, finding that the proportion of households lacking these things rose steeply below certain levels of income, they were able to fix poverty lines for households of different sizes.

Every society has some concept of poverty. Indeed, such ideas help to create and define a society. Mack and Lansley found there was a high degree of agreement among the British about the necessities of life. Had they interviewed people from widely different countries or from Britain at widely different points in time there would have been no such agreement. At the core of poverty lies hardship. This is a more complicated idea than it may seem. It reflects assumptions about the things which are physically or psychologically intolerable to have to do without, and those will change from place to place and from time to time. It also suggests that things can and should be different.

I wish to thank Neil Trotter and Damian Killeen for their helpful comments on an earlier version of this chapter.

As Townsend said, any statement of a policy aimed to reduce deprivation 'contains an implicit explanation of its cause'; similarly explanations of deprivation contain an 'implicit prescription for policy' (cited in Coffield, 1980). Words describing poverty are action-oriented; this suggests that something should be done and poses questions about the behaviour of individuals, families and the wider society. This relation to action works both ways. When a society develops the economic and technical resources and the political and administrative capacity to cure diseases, to educate all its children and to replace its slum housing, then the untreated illness, unschooled children and bad housing that were previously considered normal become unacceptable and scandalous. There are times when discussion of these issues is led by research and the growth of knowledge about poverty, and times when the policy debate leads the discussion. Concepts of poverty are therefore inherently contentious because people disagree about what needs to be done.

The meanings of poverty and related words depend on the economy, the culture, the climate and other features of the society concerned, for these determine what it is shameful or painful to do without and what remedies may be available. Before the First World War, when electricity was still a luxury found only in the homes of the rich, poverty was defined by the lack of things like candles and coal. There are still societies living in that kind of way. But in Western countries today, where people depend so heavily on refrigerators, television sets, central heating and other things that work with electricity, to be without it has become a severe hardship.

Poverty is a changing phenomenon with meanings that can be fully grasped only as we gain an understanding of the society to be discussed. It is a relative concept, not a fixed or absolute one. Some have objected that this makes the whole idea too woolly and imprecise to be useful (Joseph and Sumption, 1979). Relative moral standards – a closely related idea – are treated with similar suspicion. It is true that such socially embedded concepts call for more investigation and harder thought before they can be well used. But when that work has been done we shall find that it is the relation of the idea to the lives of real people in real societies that gives it a hard edge with clearer meanings and clearer implications for action. To say that an idea or principle has to be interpreted within a social context does not mean that 'anything goes'. It means that you have some real evidence, which can be challenged and tested, to support the conclusions you draw from it.

This chapter therefore deals with words and ideas which are socially embedded, whose meanings change from place to place and from time to time, depending as they do upon the changing character of the societies to be discussed. It deals with concepts which imply or suggest requirements for action, and social action may in turn change their meaning, all of which makes them inherently contentious: a continuing source of argument and political debate.

How can a territory so slippery and provocative be best explored? The chapter divides this task into three steps, reviewing:

- the main concepts developed in social policy analyses of poverty;
- the principal influences on the 'poverty debate';
- their varying policy implications.

In evaluating the main concepts to be discussed – about a dozen of them – the chapter concludes that we are dealing with a family of related, overlapping ideas with usefully different meanings. There is no single, universally valid, right way of talking about poverty. While there may be no single core of meaning lying at the heart of this discourse, within a particular society some concepts and ideas will be more useful than others. They throw more light on the problems to be discussed and suggest more fruitful ways of addressing them. That emerges from a brief review of three sources of influence on the debate in Western societies, focusing on recent economic and social developments which have had an impact on poverty, the growth of public knowledge about these problems, and the changing climate of political opinion. This will help us to identify the concepts that are likely to be most helpful in this part of the world.

Since concepts of poverty always suggest action of some kind – that indeed is often their main purpose – the third section of this chapter turns to their practical implications. This obliges us to focus mainly on one society, and the UK has been chosen because it is most likely to interest readers of this book. The section provides a simplified model or 'story', which brings together the different processes under discussion and suggests how they interact. That leads to a brief conclusion which suggests that we may be approaching an important turning point in the debate, at which new questions are likely to become our central concern, issues also addressed in the other chapters in this section.

Concepts and Meanings

However poverty is defined, *unacceptable hardships* lie at its core. These hardships, which can be of many different kinds, are unacceptable in two senses. The speaker feels them to be intolerably *painful* or shameful, and believes them to be *unnecessary*: the world could be organized in ways that would reduce and perhaps eliminate them. A problem implies that there must be solutions: no solution – no problem. Two other things usually follow. The speaker has some ideas about the causes of the hardships, and about the action that would help to put things right.

The words people use when talking about poverty reflect these links – backwards to causes and forwards to solutions. Their meanings often overlap. The same hardships experienced by the same people – those of a lone parent living on a low income in a poor neighbourhood, for example – could be described with different words. She could be needy, dependent or excluded. Although these words do not precisely explain the causes of or solutions for her plight they encourage people to seek them in different directions. Hence the contention they often provoke.

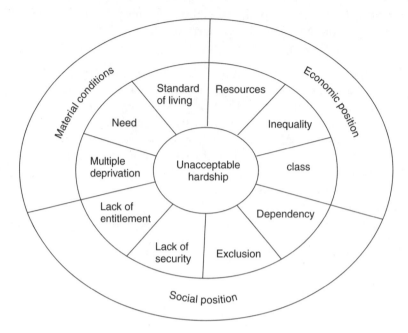

Figure 6.1 Family resemblances between different concepts of poverty. Reproduced with permission; adapted from Paul Spicker, 1999: Definitions of poverty. In D. Gordon and P. Spicker (eds), *The International Glossary on Poverty*. London: Zed Books

The terms used in such discussions and their implications for scholars have been reviewed by Walker (1995), Townsend (1993) and others. They have also been laid out in a useful international glossary, which concludes with an excellent review of this language by Spicker (1999). He summarizes what he calls the 'family resemblances between different concepts of poverty' in figure 6.1. I shall take Spicker's concepts in turn.

Three of them deal with material conditions:

- *Need* can be defined as a lack of basic necessities, some of which change over time and place (George and Wilding, 1976, pp. 132–5), or as suffering, or as an inability to participate fully in society arising from the lack of such necessities (Doyal and Gough, 1991), or in various other ways.
- *Standards of living* have often been calculated to produce a poverty line, below which people are defined as being in poverty. Such standards may be based on the costs of a diet and other essentials for physical efficiency (Rowntree, 1901; 1937), or on the minimum wage, or on benefit levels fixed, year by year, by the state (Abel-Smith and Townsend, 1965), or they may be calculated in other ways.

- The concept of *multiple deprivation* has been developed to distinguish those who suffer a long-lasting mixture of problems from those who briefly suffer one or two handicaps (such as students living temporarily on low incomes who may be able to return to their parents' homes when they need to). This concept has been widely used to identify whole neighbourhoods where many people are poor, and to explore the ways in which one problem – over-crowding for example – can complicate and exacerbate others – educational handicap or ill-health, for example (Gibb, 1998).

Three concepts deal with economic position:

- *Inadequate command over resources over time* is a concept devised to explore causes of poverty that may not be revealed by other measures: the plight of people in Third World countries who have no access to clean water or health services, for example (Dreze and Sen, 1989); or the situation of women in more prosperous societies who may have no control over their households' funds (Land, 1983).
- Comparisons with the non-poor are usually made or implied when people are described as being in poverty, so some have argued that *inequality* is the central problem, as Spicker emphasizes in his chapter in this volume (Tawney, 1964). Economists and statisticians have devised increasingly sophisticated ways to measure inequality, and the extent and 'depth' of the poverty of those at the bottom of the scale (Gordon and Spicker, 1999). All these measures are relative, in the sense that the situations of particular individuals are assessed in relation to those of others in the same society. This approach has been attacked by other social scientists, who have argued that it uses inequality (which may or may not be a problem) as a way of prolonging the debate about the altogether different issue of poverty (Dennis, 1997). Poverty, they point out, once it is conceived as an outcome of inequality, could be elimi-nated as easily by reducing the incomes of the rich as by raising those of the poor. That, some radicals have replied, is the point: questions have to be posed about a whole society, not only its poorest people.
- *Social class* is a concept for distinguishing different strata in a population according to their occupations and relationship to the means of production, or their culture and consumption patterns, or their status. It provides a method of social analysis, drawing attention to power relationships which underlie inequalities, and can help to explain why poverty arises and who is most likely to fall into it (Miliband, 1974). But the recurring attempts made to identify a separate 'underclass' of poor people have always failed. This term is the latest in a series of such terms which have recurred over two cen-turies – 'paupers', 'the undeserving poor', 'the social problem group', 'problem families', 'the culture of poverty' and 'the cycle of deprivation' are earlier examples. Clearly the more affluent people in Western societies have a psychological and political need to see the poor as a separate class of people who may, in some sense, be responsible for their own problems. But

research has always demonstrated that, while poverty may be explained with the help of class concepts (Macnicol, 1987), it cannot be defined in these terms.

Four concepts describe poverty in terms of social position:

- *Lack of entitlements* has, like class, been another concept used to remind us that poverty cannot be explained by basic scarcities of food, shelter and other things that people need; it arises from power structures which exclude some people from these goods (Dreze and Sen, 1989). Poverty, viewed from this standpoint, arises from a lack of enforceable rights.
- *Dependency on the state's social benefits* – particularly those distributed through means tests – has been used as a definition of poverty by researchers seeking publicly approved measuring rods of income which can provide poverty lines for households of different kinds (Townsend, 1979). It has also been used by critics on the right – many of them American – to stress the inadequacy and irresponsibility of the poor, parasitic on hard-working citizens, and to suggest that such benefits tempt people into poverty and trap them there (Murray, 1984).
- *Insecurity* and vulnerability have been identified as key features of poverty (Streeten, 1995), and that usefully reminds us that economic and social changes expose people to risks that some are ill-equipped to bear. Subsistence farmers, for example, who, with borrowed money, switch their output to cash crops in a fluctuating world market, may gain income at the cost of security. In more advanced economies the number of workers in insecure jobs may be much greater than the number who are unemployed, and the effects on their domestic lives almost as damaging (Paugam, 1995).
- *Social exclusion* is a term, originating in France, that has been adopted by the European Union, partly because it incorporated within the one concept all the sources of hardship – lack of income and education, prolonged unemployment, living in unpopular neighbourhoods, the discrimination suffered by women and ethnic minorities, and so on – and partly because it enabled the Union to bring into its discussions countries like Germany and Britain, whose governments denied they had any poverty: a nice example of the way in which the language of poverty debate is shaped both by research and by public education, and by politics and policies. Exclusion is too vague a term for precise measurement, but it has certain advantages. It provides a flexible and changing definition of poverty by locating the discussion within particular societies from whose changing resources and opportunities people are excluded, and it reminds us that we are dealing with a process, not a category of people – a process, moreover, in which we may all be involved, whether as excluded or as excluders. In the European Union this is now the main term used in discussions about poverty. It is interpreted in many different ways. But that may have advantages too: by keeping the debate about

meanings, causes and solutions open, policy makers and their advisors will be encouraged to keep thinking.

Spicker warns us that each of the terms arranged in the circle shown in figure 6.1 has several meanings – many of them further explored in his Glossary. Although they are logically distinct concepts, the meaning of each tends to overlap with the meanings of its neighbours. However, several of those placed on opposite sides of the circle (standard of living and dependency, for example) are entirely different in their meanings and implications. There is no single, core meaning, unless you take that to be 'hardship' – a term which poses as many questions as it answers. The words in Spicker's circle should be thought of, not as near misses around some target that will eventually be hit, but as usefully different concepts which throw light on different aspects of the problem and suggest different solutions.

The Debate Moves On

When we deal with action-oriented concepts it is not sufficient to distinguish and pin down different meanings, as if they were some kind of butterfly collection. The terms and their meanings are constantly being reshaped by changing economic and social conditions, by growing knowledge and public education, and by the developing agendas of government and politics. To understand where the debate is going we should look to all three of these influences. That calls for a serious work of history. Here there is space for no more than a brief outline of some of the points that would be explored in such a history.

Economic and social conditions

Developments throughout the industrial world reflect the growing unification of a world economy in which knowledge, goods and capital are increasingly mobile across national frontiers, and in which the advance of information technology and control systems and the scope for massive economies of scale are bringing about a dramatic concentration of production in a greatly reduced number of plants. These processes have many other features. There has for a very long time been a continuing reduction in the proportion of people's lives that is devoted to paid work – through extended education and training early in life, shorter working hours and longer holidays during their working years, and earlier retirement and greater life expectancy at the end of life. Hitherto, that reduction has been roughly paid for by increases in productivity which have enabled a smaller workforce to support more dependants and keep living standards rising. But in recent years increases in productivity have overtaken the voluntary withdrawal of workers from the labour force, making many people – mainly middle-aged men – unwillingly redundant (Campbell, 1999). Meanwhile, the growing number of women remaining in the labour force throughout their lives or returning to it very soon after bearing children has further reduced opportunities for men (Marris, 1996, pp. 36–9).

Together, these and other more local changes – the completion of postwar reconstruction, for example – have halted what had for some two centuries been a slow but steadily growing equalization of opportunities, incomes and wealth in the more developed economies. Starting about 1972 with the first oil shocks, that equalization was checked and then reversed, slowly at first, but – in Britain and some other countries – much more rapidly during the 1980s. In the 1990s the growth of poverty and inequality seems to have been checked, and possibly reversed, but it is too early to say how far that will go (Hills et al., 1999; Howarth et al., 1998). There are large numbers of people who now 'earn their poverty' in jobs that are low-paid and often insecure: 'the working poor'.

In Britain it is clear that the levels of poverty and long-term unemployment – much of it in the form of withdrawal from the labour force into sickness, disability or early retirement – were by the end of the 1980s far higher than those of previous decades. Children, young people and those who care for them are the main groups swelling the numbers in poverty. Inequality was growing faster than in any other country of the European Union (Joseph Rowntree Foundation, 1995). Those making up the growing numbers in poverty fell mainly into three roughly equal groups: the families of low-paid workers, lone parents and unemployed people. They were increasingly concentrated in particular cities – particularly those at the core of the old industrial conurbations (Glasgow, Newcastle upon Tyne, Liverpool and Manchester) and in the abandoned coalfields. Within towns there were also growing concentrations of poverty in particular neighbourhoods. More affluent people were likewise concentrating in other cities and neighbourhoods. The growing division of Britain was to be seen not only in the distribution of income and wealth: it could increasingly be seen on the ground, and many people feared we were heading for an American situation in which whole areas of stricken cities would be abandoned to dereliction and lawlessness.

Public knowledge

After a slow start, the public awareness of these matters has greatly extended and deepened. The Conservative government that came to power in 1979 abolished the standing Royal Commission on the Distribution of Income and Wealth, cut down its communications with the poverty lobby and let it be known that it regarded poverty as a Third World phenomenon only – *and* it reduced its aid to Third World countries. But, thanks very largely to the Rowntree Foundation and other independent funders of research, the few academics determined to monitor economic and social trends were able to do revealing research, based on the government's own data, and to publish it in widely read forms (Hills et al., 1999; Joseph Rowntree Foundation, 1995; Essen and Wedge,

1982; Bradshaw, 1990; Stitt and Grant, 1993). Broader discussions of the history of the debate also continued to appear (Vincent, 1991).

Central to the debate on poverty at the point when Margaret Thatcher came to power in 1979 was the argument between those who advocated a *relative definition* of poverty (Townsend, 1979) and those who insisted on *absolute measures* (Joseph and Sumption, 1979; Dennis, 1997). The relativists insisted that each generation reinvents poverty in new forms by creating new necessities that condemn those deprived of these things to new kinds of hardship. The absolutists insisted that poverty be defined in a fixed, unchanging fashion so that rising incomes would eventually lift everyone out of it. By the 1990s that argument was effectively over: poverty under either definition was increasing.

It was also becoming clearer that, no matter how sophisticated the measures devised, there is no clear-cut poverty line dividing the poor from the non-poor. Each measure ranks people in somewhat different ways, and people frequently move back and forth across any line that is drawn. The good news is that many of those in poverty this year will be doing better next year – but rarely *much* better. The bad news is that many of those slightly above any poverty line fear, with good reason, that they will fall below it next year. This fuzziness of poverty measures should be regarded, not as a problem but as a finding, giving us a clearer picture of reality. Meanwhile, the hardships of those in poverty are real. For males, suicide rates are much higher among those who are out of work. When homes are repossessed, families often break up and their lives are changed for the worse.

Research of this kind, though it uses massively greater data than its predecessors and more powerful statistical techniques, follows in an old and respected British tradition (Booth, 1882–97; Rowntree, 1901; 1941; Rowntree and Lavers, 1951), originating in local surveys of particular cities and now operating on a national scale with data provided by the state.

Altogether new ideas emerged from another tradition of British research into poverty and its effects, particularly strong in Scotland, which was developed by doctors concerned with public health. In Britain during the 1980s this work was carried forward by a few resolute people, Wilkinson and Marmot prominent among them (Marmot and Wilkinson, 1999; Marmot et al., 1991; Wilkinson, 1996). It had been known for many years that poor people were more likely to fall sick and die early than richer people, and that the distribution of medical services tends to follow an inverse care law, devoting fewer and poorer resources to the communities that most need them. The new message coming from this quarter – now reinforced by research in many other countries – was that in the industrialized countries of the world, health and life expectancy are related not to living standards, national product or rates of economic growth but to the distribution of incomes (see too Jones's chapter). Comparisons between states in the USA produced the same results. Life expectancies in countries, like Japan, which were growing more equal advanced faster than in countries, like Britain, which were growing more unequal. The deficit in life expectations found in the more unequal societies is not confined to poor people. People with incomes reaching up to the 60th percentile from the bottom – three-fifths of the population – suffer some of these effects. (The Inland Revenue might consider inscribing tax returns with the warning that 'Inequality damages your health'.)

Correlations do not explain anything; they call for explanations, and it is too early to reach final conclusions about the meaning of these. It seems likely that in the richer countries of the world health and happiness depend less on income or medical care than on a mixture of related factors, which include security of work, income, personal relationships, trust in neighbours and in authority, the prevalence of caring relationships towards other members of society and hope for the future – all of which tend to be related to the distribution of income. Some people have described these characteristics of a society as its 'social capital'.

These findings have profound implications. They demolish the love affair with economic growth, which was a worldwide political driving force throughout the twentieth century. Growth contributes to human welfare only if it enhances social capital and has equalizing effects. If, as in many parts of the world during recent years, it destroys social capital and increases inequality, growth is likely to be damaging – and not only to the most excluded or poverty-stricken people. There are important links to be forged here with the environmental debate (see Huby's chapter).

Meanwhile, other work is throwing fresh light on the scope for reducing poverty. Despite the work of social reformers, many people used to regard a large measure of poverty as unavoidable. 'The poor ye always have with you' was the text often used to clinch that argument. But recent studies have shown that the massive powers of the modern state for taxation, the provision of benefits and the promotion and regulation of the economy make it one of the principal forces creating or reducing poverty. Doyal and Gough (1991), in a ground-breaking work, have made comparisons within groups of countries at different stages of economic development that show which of them have been most successful in meeting a wide range of human needs. Their findings demonstrate that public policy makes big differences. Likewise, Hills (et al.) (1996) has shown that the sharp trend towards greater inequality in Britain in the years after 1985 was not matched in other European countries. The difference was to a large extent due to our government's policies for taxation and benefits. China, the reports of various international agencies show, is making great progress towards the reduction of poverty, thanks to policies designed to ensure that the rapid growth of its economy is used to achieve that (Gordon and Spicker, 1999, pp. 25–7).

These demonstrations of the important parts that governments play in creating or solving the problem deal with the national scale of action. But much of the action required has to be taken locally, and here too there is growing evidence of the importance of urban policies and civic leadership (Judd and Parkinson, 1990; *Urban Studies*, 1999). The great cities of Canada, economically and socially similar to those, such as Cleveland and Detroit, just across the American border, do not suffer the same degrees of poverty, squalor and social breakdown, and that must be largely due to public policies and a political culture which have more successfully built social capital.

The reasons why growth does not necessarily reduce poverty – why it does not 'trickle down' to the poorest, and why 'a rising tide does *not* lift all boats' (to quote the catch-phrases of the 1980s) – are also becoming clearer. Every generation turns some of the luxuries of its predecessors into necessities, reinventing poverty in new forms for those deprived of these things. Households cut off from their electricity supply, which was once a luxury, are now in serious trouble. Households whose rural grandparents were happy to fetch water from the well and knew nothing of water-borne sanitation cannot survive in a densely built urban society without a reliable water supply. Already, in some remote rural areas of the Scottish Highlands, where the local shops, schools, doctors and other services have closed or moved to distant towns, a motor car is becoming a necessity (Carstairs and Morris, 1991). Even if some of a rising national income is directed to poorer neighbourhoods through an increase in social security benefits, most of that money promptly flows out again to buy things produced elsewhere. In richer neighbourhoods an extra pound is often recycled through local shops, pubs, garages and tradesmen, enriching others on the way. Growth must be equalizing – between people and between neighbourhoods – if it is not to have these destructive effects.

Politics and policy

In many parts of Europe policy makers are beginning to respond to these changed conditions and to the growing public understanding of their effects. Programmes for the reduction of poverty are being more purposefully developed in these countries, and more sustained efforts are being made to give poor people a recognized place in consultative and planning bodies.

The UK, a late starter in this race, is also beginning to take these problems more seriously. The Social Exclusion Unit set up in Whitehall in 1997 may be most significant for symbolic reasons. Its first priorities seem to be concerned more with the effects of poverty than with its fundamental causes, but its existence advertises that the prime minister, to whom it reports, gives high priority to the initiative. Meanwhile, decisions to raise minimum wages, add tax credits for low-paid workers and assistance with the costs of child care and increase benefits for children will lift many low-paid workers out of poverty and may help unemployed people to extricate themselves from the 'poverty traps' that were preventing them from returning to work. The prime minister, the chancellor and the secretary of state for social security have all made bold claims that poverty will be reduced. Meanwhile some of the academics who worked on poverty research during the long years when it was unfashionable to do so have become government advisors.

Little noticed, but with great potential significance, is the fact that a British government is again talking openly about poverty, and for the first time using the definitions adopted by the European Union to report the number of people now in poverty and the scale of its intentions for the future. These measures define any household with less than half the average income for similar households in the same country as in poverty. This is clearly a measure of inequality; and that must eventually have implications for wage differentials, taxes and social benefits.

The argument does not stop there. A society committed to achieve greater equality has to treat all its people with equal respect, and this requires its decision makers to listen to those who experience a problem before deciding what to do about it. 'Top-down' styles of decision making have to give way to a community-based approach – representative democracy must become participatory democracy – enabling tenants to participate in managing their housing, patients to be involved in decisions about their treatment, pupils and their parents to play a part in shaping the development of their schools, and workers to gain more equal treatment from their employers.

The Scots are already working on the implications of this change in our perceptions of our central social problems. They set up a Social Inclusion Unit in response to Whitehall's Social Exclusion Unit, and senior ministers in the new Scottish government are responsible for a broad programme of measures to reduce poverty. The Social Inclusion Unit works in consultation with a network of community groups. Meanwhile members of the parliament formed a Social Inclusion Committee as one of their first collective acts, holding meetings, open to those experiencing poverty, in various parts of Scotland.

Underlying a growing European interest in social exclusion and unemployment are developments at the grass roots of politics which all serious politicians must be aware of. As unemployment rose all across the European Union, so did the vote of neo-Fascist parties in France, Germany, Austria, Italy and elsewhere, often with associated racist violence directed against immigrants, gypsies and refugees. Britain has so far been spared this but has long had, in Northern Ireland, its own problems of violence arising from communal conflict in areas of heavy unemployment and poverty. Political leaders in Europe must recognize that the legitimacy of their regimes and of the whole European project will be threatened if they cannot rebuild social capital within their societies.

Anti-poverty Policies: The British Case

It may be useful to gain some familiarity with a dozen terms used in discussions about poverty, and to study others ('structural dependency', 'transmitted deprivation', 'indigence', 'destitution' and many more) covered in the Glossary referred to above. But to stop there may only produce confusion. To gain a better understanding of poverty, its causes and remedies we need to bring these concepts together and use them to construct a theory – or, more simply, a story – about the processes which exclude and impoverish people. That can only be

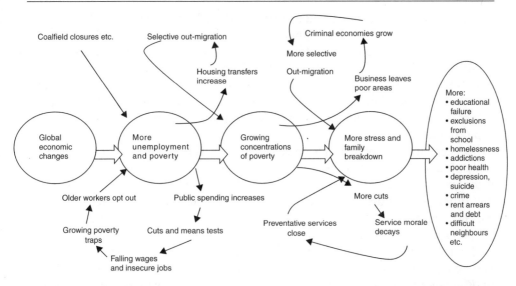

Figure 6.2 The causes and effects of poverty. Reproduced with permission; adapted from Paul Spicker 1999: Definitions of poverty. In D. Gordon and P. Spicker (eds), *The International Glossary on Poverty*. London: Zed Books

done for particular places. In China the crucial threshold beyond which people fall into a poverty trap is crossed when their stores of corn and sweet potatoes fall to a level that prevents them from rearing a pig. Without the pig they lose their 'main sources of cash for farm inputs and children's schooling . . . manure for crops . . . chemical fertilisers and insecticides' (Gordon and Spicker, 1999, p. 27). In each country the story will be different.

Here it will be most useful to take the British case, and to focus particularly on the cities and neighbourhoods with the heaviest concentrations of poverty. The story that follows has strong and weak links in it: to bring so many factors together compels some speculation. It may be wisest to regard it as a series of linked hypotheses, some of which are already well proven. Figure 6.2 summarizes the paragraphs that follow and shows the links between the processes described.

World-wide economic changes, coupled with local events like the closure of pits and defence industries, have brought about a massive loss of jobs – mainly for men with manual skills – which has been heavily concentrated in old industrial centres and closed coalfields. Glasgow lost more than half its jobs in manufacturing industries during the 1980s. Liverpool, Belfast, Manchester, Newcastle upon Tyne and other core cities of our older conurbations have fared much the same. The main response of workers to this disaster has been to move to other places. But the people who go tend to be the younger, better qualified, two-parent families. That selective emigration still continues, leaving behind it increasingly impoverished places, inhabited increasingly by the elderly, the less skilled and lone parents (Turok, 1999).

As populations of the stricken towns decline, housing space is freed and it becomes easier for those left behind to move. Families that used to wait twenty years for a transfer to a better council house find they can quickly move out of the least popular places. They are replaced by those who have nowhere else to go. Some are squatters and others use their addresses only as 'giro drops'. Some blocks of housing become 'transit camps', where people no longer know their neighbours or care about them (as MacGregor shows in her chapter). Social capital unravels.

Thus urban neighbourhoods are sifted and stratified, some becoming increasingly affluent while others become increasingly poor. There are council estates where more than half the households with children have only one adult in them, and other neighbourhoods where nearly every household has at least one car. Business withers in the poorer areas; banks, building societies and the better shops move out. The local secondary school – which may be one of the few remaining centres of order and courtesy outside people's homes – also closes, and youngsters have to take long bus journeys to schools in distant neighbourhoods, where they are regarded with hostility by local children. Truancy increases. Concentrations of deprivation grow larger.

In places where the legitimate economy collapses illicit economies develop. Some of these activities would be welcome in richer neighbourhoods, but they are criminalized in poorer places by social security regulations which require people living on social assistance benefits to be available for full-time work. Other activities would be criminal anywhere: burglary, extortionate money-lending, drug dealing, protection rackets and their operators' battles for territory. These criminalize young people and reinforce social polarization by hastening the exodus of those who are able to escape to safer streets.

The growing costs which these stresses impose on the state – particularly in social benefits – lead central government to search for ways to save money. Cities with declining populations lose grant income from the central government and council tax revenues. Cuts follow in housing expenditure, in social benefits and in many branches of local government. Cities trying to get their unemployed people into work find that the reductions they have to make in their own staff are among the main causes of unemployment. More people are compelled to seek means-tested benefits. Further cuts in local spending close down preventive family and youth support services, reduce support for teachers in hard-pressed schools and add a further twist to the vicious spiral. Many of Scotland's poorest places have suffered further from the abolition of the regions and the loss of resources which used to be transferred – particularly by Strathclyde – to areas selected for priority treatment.

Meanwhile the legislation protecting workers has been dismantled and, thanks to the high unemployment of the 1980s and early 1990s, wages and working conditions at the bottom of the labour market have been driven down. Twenty years ago it was exceedingly rare for anyone to get more money from social security benefits than he or she could earn from a job. But the decline in wages and the growing insecurity of jobs at the bottom of the labour market, the increase in rents and the spread of means-tested benefits – housing benefit in particular – all combine to make this kind of poverty trap much more common today. They help to explain why a huge proportion of our older workers have opted out of the labour market altogether into early retirement, sickness and disability.

Thus poverty, originating from the loss of jobs, sets off side effects which concentrate vulnerable families in places where it is most difficult to survive. The growing stresses they experience lead more of them to break up (Webster, 1999; see too Lewis's chapter). That produces poorer health, poorer performance in schools, more rent arrears, more trouble between neighbours, more homeless youngsters, more crime, more suicides, and so on. I am not suggesting that in a prosperous, equal society there would be no problems of this kind, but it is clear that all of them are strongly linked to the growth of poverty and inequality. We shall not make much progress in solving any of them unless we first achieve a decisive reversal of these destructive trends.

Some of the factors driving this process are now being reversed: unemployment has been falling; low-paid workers with children should be getting significant increases in their incomes; child care should be getting a little easier to find and pay for. But for unemployed or disabled people who are unable to get a job little has changed.

Conclusion

This story suggests many conclusions. Here there is space to touch only on the most important. The long list of social problems which attract so much attention from politicians and the media – the exclusion of children from school, homelessness and suicides among young people, drug addictions, ill-health, theft, violence, and trouble between neighbours – should be seen as the outcome of more fundamental economic changes and the damage they have done to the most deprived neighbourhoods and the families that live in them. We shall not get far if we tackle these symptoms and fail to address their fundamental causes. The people involved in the problems listed at the right-hand side of figure 6.2 need help; but a society that wants to reduce the number of people who get into these difficulties must unpick the process from the start, concentrating its main efforts at the left-hand side of the figure.

Important developments now unfolding on a national scale are already getting people back to work and may be reducing poverty, but there have long been growing differences between places where unemployment is low and falling – places such as Oxford city and county, where less than 2 per cent of the labour force is out of work, and Swindon, where workers are bused in from South Wales to keep the expanding factories going – and those that have borne the brunt of the collapse in Britain's manufacturing and mining industries and attract few jobs that can be done by the victims of that disaster – places such as

Glasgow, where 27 per cent of the households with dependent children have only one adult, and 37 per cent of them have no one in a paid job. There can be no standard, nation-wide prescription for action; each place will need careful study if a plan that matches its needs is to be put together.

The people who experience the problems to be tackled must be involved in preparing a response to them. Theirs is not the only voice that must be listened to, but they have knowledge and a political right to be heard that no one else can claim. Many of the mistakes made in the past would have been avoided if that voice had been listened to seriously.

Unravelling and reversing these complex processes will take a long time and cost a lot of money. But it can be done. It will call for imaginative civic leadership at local as well as at national and international levels. Many local civic leaders will not belong to the parties holding power in Westminster or the Scottish, Welsh and Northern Ireland assemblies. Therefore, no one party can solve these problems: cross-party alliances of people and politicians determined to reduce poverty will be needed.

As in all debates about important issues of social policy, the questions posed and the concepts used in debates about poverty are shaped partly by changing circumstances and growing knowledge, but also by the changing political agendas of the societies concerned. Major shifts in policy often come about, not when the old questions are finally answered, but when new questions are asked. After many years of research and public debate on the question whether the death penalty deterred people from killing each other there came a point, around 1963, when a new question was increasingly heard: whether it deters people or not, is capital punishment a tolerable feature of a civilized society? Two years later the death penalty was abolished. The debate still continues, but it is clear that this is now the question that has to be addressed by those seeking to reimpose the death penalty. Likewise, after years of research which gave Britain the world's most sophisticated prediction tests for allocating children to different kinds of secondary school at the age of eleven, people began – most insistently in the late 1960s – to ask whether selection at the age of eleven was what the nation needed. Kuhn (1970) made a similar point in his study of the development of knowledge in the natural sciences: there too, questions are not resolved but reformulated. Those who continue to research the old questions are not conclusively refuted; they simply drop out of the literature as younger scientists turn to explore the new questions.

I believe a point of this kind is being reached in the debate about this central area of social policy. Researchers now devising ever more precise and sophisticated measures of poverty should raise their eyes to spot the new question coming over the horizon of history. It deals with inequalities – not only of income, wealth, living standards and opportunities, but also of power, respect, rights and duties. If we listen to the people who experience poverty, that is what they will tell us. The answers to this question affect all of us, not only the poorest members of our societies. It is a question closely related to the other big issue to be tackled in the coming century – the sustainability of our lifestyle and environment.

Issues to Consider

- Draw up a list of necessities which you think everyone should have. Or look at the one produced by Mack and Lansley in *Poor Britain* (1985). In twenty years time, what new items are likely to appear on this list? What kinds of people are likely to be deprived of these new necessities? What could be done to prevent that?
- Choose a town you know well and take a walk round it. Is it becoming a more or a less equal place than it used to be? What evidence would you seek to check your first impressions? Should the local authority assemble such evidence and publish it regularly? What problems might such a publication make for them? What advantages would it have?
- Macnicol's study (1987, quoted above) showed that in each generation middle-class people invent new words and phrases – 'paupers', 'the social problem group', 'the underclass' were among those I quoted – which suggest that poor people are a distinct group, partly responsible for their own plight. Do you consider that view justified? If not, why do such words and phrases constantly recur? Can you spot the next words now emerging to replace those that have been discredited?
- I pointed out that money received by people living in poor neighbourhoods tends to flow out again quickly to buy goods and services produced elsewhere, while much of the money going into richer neighbourhoods circulates locally, enriching others before it moves on. Why does this happen? What could be done to help poorer neighbourhoods gain more from their local incomes?
- 'Poverty', 'need', 'exclusion', 'powerlessness' and other words used to describe the problems we have discussed are all pretty dreary: a real turn-off, many feel. Can you devise concepts and terms more likely to arrest attention and mobilize support? 'Fair shares for all' and 'One Nation' were, half a century ago, the slogans of the Labour and Conservative parties. Can we do better?
- If, some day, this country succeeds in resolving all the problems discussed in this chapter and becomes a free, equal and affluent society, what problems should we then turn to as the main focus of political concern and social research?

Suggestions for Further Reading

Rowntree's (1901) classic study, which transformed public debate about poverty, is still worth reading, and provides an interesting example of the way a social researcher devised definitions and methods that were designed to convince his middle-class readers. Doyal and Gough's (1991) much translated study is also of lasting interest. Whether or not you accept their attempt to demonstrate that 'need' has a basic, universal meaning that gives authority to policy prescriptions, it is well worth reading, as are the findings of the Joseph Rowntree Foundation (1995), *Inquiry into Income and Wealth*. Coming near the end of a period when the British government had sought to suppress any public discussion about poverty, it placed the issue squarely on the political agenda and is another example of the power that can be exercised by good social research. Marmot and Wilkinson's (1999) eminently readable report explores the links between poverty, equality and health and is again useful for many of the other chapters in this volume. Gordon and Spicker (1999) provide an indispensable guide to the terms and concepts used in discussions about poverty and references to most of the authors who write about it. Spicker's final chapter is a masterly review of the subject and is an essential source, worth consulting before any examination that is likely to deal with the issue! I am reluctant to recommend my own book, Donnison (1998), but people should not study poverty without considering what can be done about it, and what they themselves can do – not only if they were to become prime minister, but as local citizens. This is one of the few books aimed at the general public; it tries to answer those questions, as does Alcock et al. (1995), which provides a brief but stimulating coverage of current debates. You will also find a mass of information on the web sites listed at the end of chapter 9.

References

al' Abri, Al Farqir fil Alam 1994: *Poverty in the Arab World*, background paper for the World Summit for Social Development, ESCWA Poverty Eradication Series (in Arabic), quoted in D. Gordon and P. Spicker (eds) 1999: *The International Glossary on Poverty*. London: Zed Books.

Abel-Smith, B. and Townsend, P. 1965: *The Poor and the Poorest*. London: Bell.

Alcock, P., Craig, G., Dalgleish, K. and Pearson, S. 1995: *Combating Local Poverty*. Luton: Local Government Management Board.

Booth, C. 1882–97: *Life and Labour of the People in London*. London: Williams & Northgate.

Bradshaw, J. 1990: *Child Poverty and Deprivation in the United Kingdom*. London: National Children's Bureau.

Campbell, N. 1999: *The Decline of Employment Among Older People in Britain*, CASE Paper no. 19. London: London School of Economics.

Carstairs, V. and Morris, R. 1991: *Deprivation and Health in Scotland*. Aberdeen: Aberdeen University Press.

Coffield, F. 1980: *A Cycle of Deprivation? A Case Study of Four Families*. London: Heinemann Educational.

Dennis, N. 1997: *The Invention of Permanent Poverty*. London: IEA.

Donnison, D. 1998: *Policies for a Just Society*. London: Macmillan.

Doyal, L. and Gough, I. 1991: *A Theory of Human Need*. London: Macmillan.

Dreze, J. and Sen, A. 1989: *Hunger and Public Action*. Oxford: Clarendon Press.

Essen, J. and Wedge, P. 1982: *Continuities in Childhood Disadvantage*. London: Heinemann.

George, G. and Wilding, P. 1976: *Ideology and Social Welfare*. London: Routledge & Kegan Paul.

Gibb, K. 1998: *Revising the Scottish Area Deprivation Index*. Edinburgh: Scottish Office.

Gordon, D. and Spicker, P. (eds) 1999: *The International Glossary on Poverty*. London: Zed Books.

Hills, J. (ed.) 1996: *New Inequalities*. Cambridge: Cambridge University Press.

Hills, J. et al. 1999: *Persistent Poverty and Lifetime Inequality: The Evidence*, CASE Report no. 5. London: London School of Economics.

Howarth, C. et al. 1998: *Monitoring Poverty and Social Exclusion: Labour's Inheritance*. York: Joseph Rowntree Foundation.

Joseph, K. and Sumption, J. 1979: *Equality*. London: John Murray.

Joseph Rowntree Foundation 1995: *Inquiry into Income and Wealth*, vols 1 and 2. York: Joseph Rowntree Foundation.

Judd, D. and Parkinson, P. (eds) 1990: *Leadership and Urban Regeneration: Cities in North America and Europe*. London: Sage.

Kuhn, T. 1970: *The Structure of Scientific Revolutions*, 2nd edn. Chicago: Chicago University Press.

Land, H. 1983: Poverty and gender: the distribution of resources within the family. In M. Brown (ed.), *The Structure of Disadvantage*. London: Heinemann.

Mack, J. and Lansley, S. 1985: *Poor Britain*. London: Allen & Unwin.

Macnicol, J. 1987: In pursuit of the underclass. *Journal of Social Policy*, 16 (3), 293–318.

Marmot, M. and Wilkinson, R. (eds) 1999: *Social Determinants of Health*. Oxford: Oxford University Press.

Marmot, M. et al. 1991: Health inequalities among British civil servants: the Whitehall II study. *Lancet*, 337, 1387–93.

Marris, R. 1996: *How to Save the Underclass*. London: Macmillan.

Miliband, R. 1974: Politics and poverty. In D. Wedderburn (ed.), *Poverty, Inequality and Class Structure*. Cambridge: Cambridge University Press.

Murray, C. 1984: *Losing Ground: America's Social Policy, 1950–1980*. New York: Basic Books.

Paugam, S. 1995: The spiral of precariousness: a multidimensional approach to the process of disqualification in France. In G. Room (ed.), *Beyond the Threshold*. Bristol: Policy Press.

Rowntree, S. 1901: *Poverty: A Study of Town Life*. London: Macmillan.

Rowntree, S. 1937: *The Human Needs of Labour*, revised edn. London: Longmans Green.

Rowntree, S. 1941: *Poverty and Progress*. London: Longmans Green.

Rowntree, S. and Lavers, G. R. 1951: *Poverty and the Welfare State*. London: Longmans Green.

Spicker, P. 1999: Definitions of poverty: eleven clusters of meaning. In D. Gordon and P. Spicker (eds), *The International Glossary on Poverty*. London: Zed Books.

Stitt, S. and Grant, D. 1993: *Poverty: Rowntree Revisited*. Aldershot: Avebury.

Streeten, P. 1995: The poverty agenda and the ILO. In G. Rodgers (ed.), *New Approaches to Poverty Analysis and Poverty*. Geneva: International Labour Office.

Tawney, R. 1964: *Equality*. London: Allen & Unwin.

Townsend, P. 1979: *Poverty in the United Kingdom*. Harmondsworth: Penguin.

Townsend, P. 1993: *The International Analysis of Poverty*. Hemel Hempstead: Harvester Wheatsheaf.

Turok, I. 1999: Urban Labour Markets. The causes and consequence of change. *Urban Studies*, 36 (5/6), 893–915.

Urban Studies, Competitive cities. 36 (5/6), May 1999.

Vincent, D. 1991: *Poor Citizens: The State and the Poor in Twentieth-century Britain*. London: Longman.

Walker, R. 1995: The dynamics of poverty. In G. Room (ed.), *Beyond the Threshold*. Bristol: Policy Press.

Webster, D. 1999: *Social Inclusion Strategy in the Context of Urban Renewal: A Research-based Perspective*, Paper for Conference on 'Local Authorities and Social Exclusion', 3 July.

Wilkinson, R. 1996: *Unhealthy Societies*. London: Routledge.

Chapter 7

Child Poverty and the Policy Response

Karen Rowlingson

Our historic aim will be for ours to be the first generation to end child poverty, and it will take a generation. It is a twenty year mission but I believe it can be done

Blair, *Beveridge Lecture*, 1999

Introduction

The Prime Minister is not the only one in the Labour government committed to raising children's living standards. In July 1999, the Chancellor of the Exchequer, Gordon Brown, in his speech to the Sure Start conference, described child poverty as 'a scar on the soul of Britain'. Moreover, the government has not only introduced a number of policies and initiatives to achieve its 'historic aim', but also produced a paper which outlines how progress towards this aim can be evaluated (Department of Social Security, 1999). In the light of these recent initiatives, this chapter:

- places the government's recent pledge in a historical context;
- assesses the changing incidence and scale of child poverty;
- considers the consequences of child poverty and outlines the main policy instruments that have been used to reduce it.

The 'Problem' of Child Poverty

Child poverty is not a new issue. At the beginning of the twentieth century Rowntree (1901) highlighted the link between poverty and families with children. Partly in response to this, Beveridge recommended the introduction of family allowances in his 1942 report. The postwar welfare state settlement was expected to eradicate hardship, and it certainly reduced the number and proportion of poor children in Britain (Bradshaw, 1990), but in the 1960s and 1970s a number of studies found that poverty had not been completely eliminated. One such study (Townsend, 1979) found that children in unskilled manual working-class households had a 77 per cent chance of being poor, and this rose to 93 per cent when there were three or more children in the family. A pressure group, the Child Poverty Action Group (CPAG), was established in 1965 to fight childhood deprivation and campaign for its reduction.

The continuing existence of child poverty may seem reason in itself for governments to consider it a 'social problem', but this has not necessarily been the case hitherto. During the 1980s and early 1990s (at the very time when child poverty was increasing), successive Conservative governments argued that poverty no longer existed in Britain. Moreover, the very word 'poverty' was effectively banned from government publications. Poverty is, therefore, as Donnison's chapter also emphasizes, a highly politicized issue. Certain factions on the right of the political spectrum refuse to acknowledge its existence. In addition, while other groups on the right recognize its existence, they see poverty less as a social problem than as a problem of individual idleness and fecklessness.

The politicized nature of policy towards poverty means that the pledge to end child poverty could occur only after the election of a left-leaning government. This was a necessary but not sufficient condition for child poverty to become seen as a social problem. The two other conditions were: evidence about the staggering increase in child poverty over the 1980s and early 1990s; and an increasing awareness of the detrimental effects of child poverty.

Changing Incidence and Scale of Child Poverty

As Donnison highlights in the preceding chapter, there is no agreement on the conceptualization of poverty. Consequently, there is no single indicator of what can be used to measure its incidence. This chapter therefore draws on a range of measures to track the changing incidence and scale of child poverty in recent decades. But whatever indicator we use, it is clear that child poverty grew substantially in the 1980s and 1990s.

Table 7.1 illustrates the phenomenal rise in child poverty. In 1968, one child in ten lived in relative poverty. By this we mean that one child in ten lived in households with less than half average income (with child defined as a dependent child aged under 17, or under 19 and in full-time education). By the mid-1990s, this one child in ten had increased to one child in three (Gregg et al., 1999). Moreover, despite a fall in the number of families with children, the number of children living in households with below half average income had risen from 1.3 million in 1968 to 4.3 million in 1995–6.

The number of children living in relative poverty has therefore more than tripled in the past thirty years. Absolute measures of poverty also show that, while general living standards have risen, children have not shared in any increasing prosperity. In 1979, 10 per cent of children were living in households with below half average income (after housing costs). By 1995–6, a total of

Table 7.1   Children in poverty after housing costs, %

Year	%
1968	10.0
1973	12.4
1979	12.6
1984	19.1
1990	29.8
1993	32.5
1995–6	32.9

Source: Gregg et al., 1999

13 per cent of children were living in households with below the half average income in 1979 terms. Thus 3 per cent more children (which equates to 300,000) were worse off in absolute terms during a period when average income rose by 44 per cent (Adelman and Bradshaw, 1999).

Another way to measure poverty is to look at expenditure rather than income. Taking an expenditure-based measure of poverty we see that, over the past three decades, the bottom fifth of the population spent no more on children's items such as toys, children's clothing, shoes, fresh fruit and vegetables. Increasing poverty is therefore having a real impact on the living standards of children, and excluding the poorest from the rising standards of living which are enjoyed by the majority (Gregg et al., 1999).

There was a general increase in poverty during the 1980s and early 1990s affecting many sectors of the population, but families with children have experienced much greater increases in poverty than other groups. The poverty rate for children rose 21 per cent from 1968 to 1995–6 compared with a rise of 10 per cent for childless households (Gregg et al., 1999). Lone parents have overtaken pensioners as the group with the lowest average income.

Figures that tell us how many children are in poverty do not tell us how deep that poverty is. Another measure, called the poverty gap, gives us some idea of the intensity of poverty. An analysis of the Family Resources Survey by Adelman and Bradshaw (1999) shows that the children who are most likely to suffer poverty are least likely to suffer it intensely. For example, those in lone parent families or in families on means-tested benefits, such as income support, are very likely to suffer poverty but have a relatively small poverty gap. Thus while those children in families on income support are in poverty, the social security benefit does appear to be acting as a safety net by reducing the amount of deprivation they might otherwise experience. It is important, however, to avoid concluding from this that income support is set at a reasonable level. A study by Oldfield and Yu (1993) found that, for a family of two adults and two children under 11, an extra £34 a week was needed on top of income support rates to bring its income up to a modest level in 1993.

Another important aspect of poverty is its dynamic nature. Like adults, children move in and out of poverty. Hill and Jenkins (2001) have analysed the

---

Box 7.1: Factors associated with child poverty

- living in a lone parent family;
- living with cohabiting parents;
- living with young parents;
- living in a large family (particularly a family with three or more children);
- living in a household with no earner;
- living in a family on means-tested benefits;
- being Pakistani or Bangladeshi;
- living with a head of household who has a long-standing illness;
- living in rented accommodation;
- living in a rural area (before housing costs).

British Household Panel Survey (BHPS) from 1991 to 1996 to investigate the dynamic nature of child poverty. They found that 46 per cent of pre-school children were poor in at least one of the six years; about a fifth (21 per cent) were poor in at least half of the six years and 2.4 per cent were poor in all six years. Further research is still needed before we can say whether long spells of childhood poverty should be more or less of a concern than frequent moves in and out of poverty.

It is clear that the recent increase in child poverty is a peculiarly British phenomenon. The 1994 European Community Household Panel Survey revealed that the UK had the highest child poverty rates of nine EU countries in 1993 (Eurostat, 1997). The USA and Russia have higher rates of child poverty, but the rate of *increase* in Britain is unmatched (Adelman and Bradshaw, 1999).

So far this chapter has considered the extent of child poverty. But which children are poor? An analysis of the 1994–5 Family Resources Survey (FRS) by Adelman and Bradshaw (1999) shows that there are many factors associated with child poverty. I list them in Box 7.1.

Tables 7.2 and 7.3 illustrate some of these relationships. Table 7.2 shows how far the marital status of parents is an important factor. Families cannot be simply divided into those with two parents and those with a lone parent. It is clear that the relationship between the parents, whether they are married or cohabiting, is also important. Table 7.3 illustrates the relationships between child poverty and ethnicity, Pakistani and Bangladeshi families facing staggeringly high poverty rates.

A multivariate analysis shows that, when we control for other factors, lone parenthood itself is not an important factor – it is the economic status of the lone parent that is the most important variable. This can also be illustrated through a bivariate analysis, as is shown in table 7.4. Other important independent factors related to child poverty are ethnicity and large family size.

Table 7.2   Children in poverty after housing costs, by marital status, %

Parent(s)	%
Married	23.5
Living as a couple	49.5
Single or never married	61.7
Widowed	44.1
Separated	60.9
Divorced	54.2

Source: Adelman and Bradshaw, 1999

Table 7.3   Children in poverty after housing costs, by ethnicity, 1995–6, %

Ethnic group	%
White	30.6
Black Caribbean	39.7
Black African	54.7
Indian	30.8
Pakistani	78.9
Bangladeshi	81.1

Source: Adelman and Bradshaw, 1999

Table 7.4   Children in poverty, after housing costs, in different family types, 1995–6, %

Family type	%
All children	32.9
Couple working	17.3
Couple not working	88.7
Lone parent working	31.2
Lone parent not working	89.1

Source: Gregg et al., 1999

An analysis of the Households Below Average Income statistics (HBAI) by Adelman and Bradshaw (1999) shows that poverty has increased fastest among children in two groups: those with no full-time working parent and those living with a lone parent. The proportion in poverty with a full-time working parent has decreased (but this is not the case for children of self-employed parents).

Consequences

Child poverty has increased dramatically over the past thirty years, but this on its own does not explain why it has become such an important policy issue. The

---

Box 7.2: Factors correlated with child poverty

- Poor health (infant mortality, childhood death, mental health problems, poor diets).
- Poor cognitive development, low self-esteem.
- Poor education: less likely to stay on at school past 16, more likely to lack qualifications and lack literacy and numeracy skills.
- Poor employment prospects, low wages, unemployment.
- Behavioural problems, truancy, offending, drug and alcohol use.
- Child abuse and neglect, experience of domestic violence.
- Poor housing conditions, homelessness.
- Parent becoming a lone parent.

---

explanation lies in the consequences of child poverty. Hill and Tisdall (1997) quote a number of studies that have investigated the impact of poverty on children and their families. These (along with Gregg et al.'s more recent study (1999)) have highlighted the factors in box 7.2 as being correlated with child poverty.

Concern therefore focuses on four main issues: health, employment prospects, early childbearing for young women, criminal careers for young men. Poverty also reduces children's abilities to participate in consumption, and their consequent exclusion from participation is a crucial aspect of contemporary society.

Thus, the problem of child poverty is often seen in terms of its effects on individual children. It is also seen to be an issue about the long-term future of society. We frequently consider children an investment in the future – poor children are therefore seen as poor investments in the future. There is also a moral and sometimes religious dimension to the fight against poverty generally and to child poverty in particular. Summing this perspective, Bradshaw (1990) observes that the well-being of children should be of prime concern to any society. Not only is it indicative of the society's moral worth, but also children are 'the resources for its national future', its 'human capital'.

Another perspective is to consider the indirect social effects of the consequences of child poverty. For example, if child poverty eventually leads to offending, other members of society will become 'victims' of child poverty. And if child poverty eventually leads to lone parenthood and unemployment, other members of society will have to pay higher taxes towards the benefits for these groups. Thus, the consequences of child poverty touch us all.

Main Explanations

The negative consequences of child poverty are clear. But what causes it in the first place? Explanations operate on a number of levels. The most direct cause is a lack of resources, and one of the most obvious and common factors is a lack of parental employment. Children in 'unemployed benefit units' are over five times more likely than others to be poor, after we control for other factors (Adelman and Bradshaw, 1999). This begs the question: why are parents jobless? The answer to this question depends on ideological perspectives. A structural/demand-side perspective would focus on the barriers to employment such as the lack of suitable jobs, discrimination and so on. An individualistic/supply-side perspective would focus on the inadequacies of individuals in finding and staying in employment (see too the chapters by Page, Clarke and Donnison).

A further question also arises: why does joblessness result in poverty? The answer to this question would open up a different debate about the adequacy of benefit levels. Researchers have employed a range of sophisticated methods to argue that income support rates are woefully inadequate to meet the needs of families with children (Oldfield and Yu, 1993). If the government were really committed to reducing child poverty, surely it would merely need to raise benefit levels to an adequate level. However, this simple (but costly) solution would then reduce incentives to (paid) work. Incentives could be retained, however, through some form of basic income or negative income tax scheme, and, as we shall see, the Chancellor does seem to be working towards some version of the latter.

Although a lack of resources is generally seen to be the main cause of child poverty, it is also possible that poverty is caused by an inappropriate *use* of resources, or fecklessness, as it is sometimes called. Perhaps parents are spending too much on themselves to the detriment of their children. There is little evidence to support this argument. Middleton et al. (1994) found that one-half of the parents defined as poor had children who were not poor because the parents were going without items considered essential for adults, to make sure that their children were not deprived of items considered to be essential for *them*.

Another factor that can initially explain child poverty is ethnicity. But the relationship between ethnicity and child poverty is a complex one. Pakistani and Bangladeshi families have particularly high rates of child poverty; but their typically large family sizes and low rates of employment are likely to be important, rather than ethnicity itself.

Family type is another important factor. Lone parent families are among the very poorest of all family types, and yet, as I argue above, lone parenthood itself is perhaps not as important as the economic status of the lone parent. The role of cohabitation is perhaps surprising and difficult to understand. Unlike lone parenthood, cohabitation does not disappear as an important factor once other factors, such as economic status, are controlled for (Adelman and Bradshaw, 1999).

Government Responses

The Prime Minister's recent pledge to end child poverty is particularly striking given that the word poverty had been all but officially banned between 1979 and 1997. But if we take a longer-term perspective, there have been numerous attempts by various governments to raise children's living standards.

The introduction of family allowances in 1946 (replaced by child benefit in 1979) was intended to tackle the problem of child poverty. More recently, there has been a considerable discussion about whether child benefit should be taxed or means- or affluence-tested. One of the main arguments in favour of child benefit is that it is payable to the mother. Research suggests that shifting money 'from the wallet to the purse' means that more finds its way to the children. But it is only recently that the idea of giving money directly to dependent children has been contemplated. This has been introduced in a pilot form with the trials of Educational Maintenance Allowance, which is a means-tested benefit for 16–18 year-olds who stay in education. Child benefit could similarly be a child's right rather than a payment to parents to offset the financial costs of having a child.

In more recent years, governments have sought to raise children's living standards by increasing the incentives to their parents to find paid work. Financial incentives to work have long been considered an issue for large families, as the benefit system has paid out more to them, while employers pay the same wage regardless of the sizes of their employees' families. Thus, people with large families have been more likely to better off on benefit. In an attempt to tackle this problem, a Conservative government introduced Family Income Supplement (FIS) in 1971, and another Conservative government introduced family credit in 1988. While the words 'child poverty' were not mentioned at this time, the government was nevertheless aware of the disincentives to work which faced families with children. These benefits topped up the wages of parents working full-time in an attempt to ensure that they would be better off in work. The Labour government is continuing with this broad policy approach with the introduction of working families' tax credit (WFTC). Introduced in October 1999–2000, this now guarantees a minimum income of over £200 a week for a family obtaining full-time work. Payment of WFTC is through the wage packet, and it thus entails a shift from the purse back to the wallet (and therefore potentially from the child to the father).

The growth in lone parenthood in the 1970s and 1980s, and lone parents' levels of poverty, prompted governments to consider how their incomes could be increased. This has drawn attention to the way in which non-resident parents should contribute to the upkeep of their children. The 1991 Child Support Act radically overhauled the previous system and became one of the most controversial social policies of the decade. Many lone parent families failed to benefit from the changes, and many non-resident parents were expected to pay more. Once again the emphasis was on the adults in the families rather than on the children. Major reforms of the system were introduced in the late 1990s but the jury is still out as to whether these reforms will be enough to legitimize the system among parents and to deliver positive outcomes for children.

Current Issues and Policy Options

In the recent past a number of policies have been introduced to help raise the living standards of children. The pledge to end child poverty in the next twenty years, however, involves such a Herculean task (given the scale of the problem) that the government has recognized the need to tackle the fundamental causes of poverty from a wide range of angles. In current government-speak, it is taking a 'joined-up' approach. This involves policies on work, taxation, social security, education and special interventions for those in greatest need (Department of Social Security, 1999).

In education, the government is seeking to achieve the following:

• an increase in the proportion of children reaching particular numeracy and literacy levels by the time they are 11;
• a reduction in the proportion of truancies and exclusions from school;
• an increase in the proportion of 19-year-olds with at least a level-two qualification.

Targeted interventions to help families with young children include the Sure Start programme, which aims to promote the physical, social and emotional development of young children (up to the age of 3) in some of the poorest families. The government has allocated £540 million to establish 250 local programmes, which will be run by partnerships of local authority social services departments, local voluntary organizations and local parents. It is yet to be seen whether parents will consider the programme a helpful support or an unwanted intervention. The government hopes that Sure Start will improve children's educational outcomes and employment prospects as well as reduce the rates of offending and teenage pregnancy. Such outcomes, if they occur, will take many years to happen.

Measures in the 1998 and 1999 Budgets were intended to take 800,000 children out of poverty. The minimum wage, the 10p starting rate of income tax and cuts in national insurance targeted on the lowest paid have been focused on making work pay. There have also been record increases in child benefit and there will be a new children's tax credit from 2001. As I mentioned earlier, the government has also expressed a commitment to 'make work pay' through WFTC, and it is trying to encourage specific groups (for example lone parents) to enter the labour market with schemes such as the New Deals. In the longer term, it aims to 'create an integrated and seamless system of financial support for children' (HM Treasury, 1999). The main component of this system will be the integrated child credit, which is intended to bring together various strands of assistance, such as the working families' tax credit, the children's tax credit and income support.

Issues for Discussion

Much of the discussion so far has portrayed children as dependent on their parents. They are therefore considered a burden on parental resources, and a number of studies have assessed the costs of children to their parents (Oldfield and Yu, 1993; Middleton et al., 1994). Fewer studies, however, have looked into children's roles as workers and income generators. And only some have considered how parents are sometimes dependent on their children for emotional and sometimes physical support (for example in the form of care).

This last points leads us to the distribution of resources within families. While there have been many studies about the distribution of resources between members of a couple, few (apart from Middleton et al., 1994) have considered the distribution of resources between adults and children. Parents usually have full control over the resources in their families. It is assumed that parents (and mothers in particular) use resources in responsible ways as far as children are concerned, but this may not necessarily be the case, and this is why policy makers may consider giving some money direct to older children. Alternatively, we could consider giving children more material resources, such as free (or subsidized) meals, milk, school trips and holidays. Such in-kind benefits would ensure that children would be achieving a certain standard of living.

The assumptions we make about children affect the extent to which we consider child poverty a problem. Where poverty is concerned, children are often seen to be innocent victims or to be a burden on their parents' resources. But children can play a more active and positive role in families, and, in some ways, the emphasis on child poverty in particular, rather than on poverty in general, could be seen as patronizing towards children at the expense of other equally 'deserving' groups.

Issues to Consider

- Why has child poverty been prioritized over the poverty experienced by other groups, such as disabled and elderly people?
- What things do you think a child needs, that all children should be able to have, and which they should not have to do without? Compare your list with that used by Middleton et al. (1994, p. 49) and your responses to the questions posed at the end of Donnison's chapter.
- What are the main causes and consequences of child poverty?
- Critically assess the effectiveness of the main policy weapons used against child poverty.

Suggestions for Further Reading

Bradshaw (1990) is an excellent short guide to the rise in child poverty over the 1980s, covering its nature, causes and consequences. Bradshaw is currently working on a further analysis of the Family Resources Survey as part of an ESRC-funded project, *Poverty: the outcomes for children*. Middleton et al. (1994) reports the findings of another key study. Focusing on expenditure-based measures of poverty, it presents a wealth of information and a new 'consensual' approach to measuring child poverty. Gregg et al. (1999) provide an up-to-date and thorough analysis of two datasets – the Family Expenditure Survey and the National Child Development Study to explore the distribution of resources during childhood and the effects of childhood disadvantage in adulthood. A broader, more multi-disciplinary discussion of the issues addressed in this chapter and the previous one can be found in Hill and Tisdall (1997) and Daniel and Ivatts (1998), both of which provide useful overviews of the main findings and debates. These can be followed up through the web sites listed at the end of chapter 9. Further data can be obtained from the Office for National Statistics website: www.ons.gov.uk.

References

Adelman, L. and Bradshaw, J. 1999: *Children in Poverty in Britain: An Analysis of the Family Resources Survey 1994/95*, Paper prepared as part of the ESRC project *Poverty: the outcomes for children* in the Children 5–16 programme. York: York University and Social Policy Research Unit.

Bradshaw, J. 1990: *Child Poverty and Deprivation in the UK*. London: National Children's Bureau.

Daniel, P. and Ivatts, J. 1998: *Children and Social Policy*. Basingstoke: Macmillan.

Department of Social Security 1998: *New Ambitions for Our Country: A New Contract for Welfare*, the Green Paper on Welfare Reform. London: Stationery Office.

Department of Social Security 1999: *Opportunity for All: Tackling Poverty and Social Exclusion: Indicators of Success: Definitions, Data and Baseline Information*. London: Department of Social Security.

Eurostat 1997: Income distribution and poverty in the EU. *Statistics in Focus: Population and Social Conditions*, 6.

Gregg, P., Harkness, S. and Machin, S. 1999: *Child Development and Family Income*. York: Joseph Rowntree Foundation.

Hill, M. and Jenkins, S. 2001: Poverty amongst British children: chronic or transitory. In B. Bradbury, J. Micklewright and S. Jenkins (eds), *The Dynamics of Child Poverty in Industrialized Countries*. Cambridge: Cambridge University Press.

Hill, M. and Tisdall, K. 1997: *Children in Society*. Harlow: Longman.

HM Treasury 1999: *Supporting Children Through the Tax and Benefit System*. London: HM Treasury.

Middleton, S., Ashworth, K. and Braithwaite, I. 1994: *Small Fortunes: Spending on Children, Childhood Poverty and Parental Sacrifice*. York: Joseph Rowntree Foundation.

Oldfield, N. and Yu, A. 1993: *The Cost of a Child: Living Standards for the 1990s*. London: CPAG.

Rowntree, S. 1901: *Poverty: A Study of Town Life*. London: Macmillan.

Townsend, P. 1979: *Poverty in the United Kingdom*. Harmondsworth: Penguin.

Chapter 8

Homelessness

Mark Liddiard

Introduction

Homelessness is perhaps the most explicit of all social issues. It can certainly be viewed as the ultimate manifestation of social malaise in any society. Yet understanding it is far from straightforward. Even clarifying and defining the term homelessness is beset with difficulties, and this in turn has created innumerable obstacles for any agreed measurement or quantification of the problem. If academics and others cannot agree on what precisely homelessness is, then it is unsurprising that there is so little agreement about how much homelessness there is in society. Like all social problems, explanations have also been subject to extensive conjecture. Yet it is a compelling question – just how can we explain the existence of homelessness in a wealthy country, such as the UK, as we enter the twenty-first century? Again, all is far from clear. The only point of consensus is that homelessness is ultimately a complex and multi-causal social problem. The importance of government policy in explaining homelessness, from housing policy to labour market and benefit policy, has been hotly contested. Certainly, many issues appear to be closely related to the problem, such as mental illness and substance abuse, but the question is the degree to which such themes are causes of homelessness, or symptoms of a homeless experience? However, disagreements over the causes of social problems like homelessness are of more than intellectual interest. On the contrary, solutions to social problems depend heavily on their explanation. To resolve any social problem, one needs a good grasp of its causation. For this reason, solutions to homelessness are also hotly debated. None the less, the past decade has seen some interesting policy responses to homelessness in the UK.

This chapter seeks to explore four crucial areas of homelessness, all of which have important implications for understanding social problems more generally. It therefore looks in turn at:

- the problems of defining homelessness;
- measuring homelessness;
- explaining homelessness;
- resolving homelessness.

Defining Homelessness

What do we mean when we talk about homelessness? The immediate sense of the term, as regularly employed by the mass media and politicians, simplistically equates homelessness with 'rooflessness', or literally sleeping rough on the streets. This image of homelessness is certainly a potent and powerful one – the high visibility of homeless people on the street presents a tangible manifestation of a very public social problem, which can be difficult to ignore. However, just how accurate and comprehensive is such a definition? Equating homelessness with rooflessness may be straightforward and easy to understand, but just how well does this reflect the true scope of the problem? What about those who squat in empty buildings, sometimes without water and electricity? Are they homeless? They may have a roof over their heads, but if they have nowhere else to stay or call 'home', should they also be described as homeless? For this reason, homelessness is often defined more broadly than as rooflessness, and homeless people can also include those living in a range of unsatisfactory housing conditions, such as temporary hostels and bed and breakfast accommodation (B&Bs). Although these individuals may not lack a literal roof over their heads, the reality is that they may still lack a home and, in this sense, are homeless (Bramley, 1988).

This is the crux of the problem with defining homelessness – what do we mean when we talk about lacking a home? Rooflessness is clearly a more tangible concept to 'unpack' – by definition, it means lacking a roof over one's head. Homelessness, by contrast, is a more difficult concept – by definition, it implies lacking a home. But what precisely is a home? What do we mean when we talk about our home? However we respond to this question, one theme seems very clear – that a home implies much more than simply a physical shelter. In the words of Watson (1984, p. 60): 'A "house" is generally taken to be synonymous with a dwelling or a physical structure, whereas a "home" is not. A "home" implies a set of social relations, or a set of activities within a physical structure, whereas a "house" does not.'

Because the term home is such an ambiguous concept, one can define homelessness in a variety of ways. One can employ very narrow definitions of homelessness, which include only those sleeping rough. Yet one can justifiably define homelessness in a much broader sense, to include those living in a wide range of housing circumstances deemed to be unsatisfactory.

These difficulties with defining homelessness are not unique to this social problem. On the contrary, many social problems are inherently ambiguous concepts, which defy agreed definition. As other contributors to this volume show, many social problems are very open to definition, and the problem of homelessness is no exception. Why is this point so important? The lack of an agreed definition of homelessness is significant for a number of reasons, but is particularly crucial because of the impact it has on attempts to measure or quantify it.

Measuring Homelessness

Quantification is an important feature of any social problem. To have some sense of the size of a social problem is important, both for assessing its seriousness and extent, and also for considering the scale, cost and form of a potential intervention with a view to its resolution. To assess the impact of any particular policy, it is also necessary to judge whether the problem has increased or decreased. Trying to understand how much homelessness there is in a particular society at a given period in time is thus very important. However, the quantification of homelessness is beset with difficulties and problems, the most obvious of which is the very ambiguity of the term. If we cannot agree on what we mean by homelessness, how can we possibly agree on its extent? This point is absolutely crucial – the size of all social problems is inherently linked to the manner in which they are defined. This is precisely why so much debate about homelessness has taken place in something of a statistical void. However, this does not mean that we do not have figures and estimates about the size of homelessness in the UK. It simply means that when considering any figures, we must simultaneously consider how the term has been defined. Indeed, this is why definition is imbued with such significance in any consideration of social problems – because the manner in which one defines a social problem like homelessness determines the size and scale of that problem. In this way, definitions can be used strategically.

Box 8.1

Broad and all-encompassing definitions can be employed to enhance the size of a particular problem, and this in turn can attract attention and resources. Similarly, narrow and restrictive definitions can be employed, and this in turn can minimize the size of a problem such as homelessness. In this way, definitions of social problems can be used strategically by politicians, the mass media, pressure groups, voluntary agencies and others to influence their apparent size (Hutson and Liddiard, 1994).

The most common measure of homelessness has focused on the number of households accepted as homeless under homelessness legislation. The 1977 Housing (Homeless Persons) Act was the first measure to place responsibilities on local authorities to rehouse homeless families and individuals permanently.

This remained in force until the 1996 Housing Act modified the duties of local authorities towards the homeless (Lowe, 1998; Somerville, 1999). However, the criteria by which local authorities accept someone as homeless are complex and restrictive. In particular, one must establish a 'local connection', prove that one is not 'intentionally homeless' and show that one's situation is one of 'priority need' (Pleace et al., 1998). Despite these restrictive criteria, in 1995 English local authorities still accepted almost 121,000 households as 'statutorily homeless'. These statistics, however, refer only to those accepted as homeless. Just as many apply to local authorities to be accepted as homeless, yet are rejected under these criteria. They also refer to households, many of which are families with children, so the number of people concerned is much higher than this figure suggests. In this way, local authorities' figures on homelessness tell us fairly little about the number of people experiencing it. None the less, the numbers are still surprisingly large. In England alone, between 1984 and 1995, some 1.42 million households were accepted by local authorities as 'statutorily homeless'.

What these figures tell us almost nothing about, however, is the scale of single homelessness, because most single people are excluded from official homelessness figures (see Anderson, 1999). Here we have to rely instead on a variety of sources and on estimates of different kinds. One recent estimate from 1995, for example, included those living in hostels and squats and suggested that there were approximately 106,000 homeless people in London alone, including some 26,000 single homeless people (Pleace et al., 1998).

It is clear, therefore, that we have a variety of figures and estimates on the size of homelessness in the UK. Crucially, however, we must remember that they closely reflect the way homelessness has been defined. In this way, the ambiguous definition of homelessness represents a major obstacle to estimating the size of the problem.

Irrespective of these definitional issues, it is very clear that there are also a plethora of methodological problems with attempting to determine the number of people homeless at any point in time. First, it is difficult to locate and contact homeless people. Because of their lack of a fixed address, they may often be missed from conventional surveys. Even the 1991 Census, which specifically attempted to identify the number of homeless people on Census night, had problems locating them and was ridiculed for suggesting that no one was homeless in some large cities, such as Birmingham and Cardiff. There are also a large and transient number of homeless people who may be living on friends' floors or sofas because they have nowhere else to stay. Often, these individuals may not be in contact with any agencies and are thus effectively invisible – the so-called 'hidden homeless'. The elusive nature of the 'hidden homeless' and the difficulty of locating and counting them mean that the number of people affected by homelessness in this way is effectively unquantifiable.

There are also real problems with extrapolating figures and estimates over time and across geographical areas. The period of homelessness is an important point. Individuals move in and out of homelessness. Some may be homeless for just a day or two, while others may be homeless for much longer. Many more people will be affected by homelessness over the period of a year than will experience homelessness over the period of a week. Given that most counts of homeless people are simply snapshots taken at one particular time, extrapolating from these to determine the extent of homelessness over a longer period of time is inherently problematic. Similarly, many studies of homelessness focus on the experiences of large urban areas, particularly London. Yet in a number of ways the homelessness of large cities, especially London, may be different from homelessness elsewhere. This means that extrapolating from findings based on one area to try to garner a regional or national picture of the problem may be flawed and sometimes misleading.

Explaining Homelessness

Like most social problems, we can understand and explain homelessness in a variety of different ways. Some observers have focused on particular policy issues, such as the housing and labour markets, and benefit issues when seeking to explain the existence and persistence of homelessness. Others have focused instead on issues reflecting individual or family pathology, and have identified the clear links between homelessness and family conflict, mental illness and crime. However, on one thing there is general agreement – that homelessness is not a simple problem with a single cause. On the contrary, homelessness is a complex phenomenon, with many causes. Given the heterogeneity of the homeless and the sheer diversity of their backgrounds and problems, this point is perhaps unsurprising.

Explaining homelessness, however, is important, because its resolution invariably depends on comprehending its causes. Certainly, there is a real sense in which homelessness in any society is necessarily contextual. It reflects the wider socio-economic context in which it takes place, and in the UK a number of factors have attracted particular attention in attempts to understand the causes of homelessness.

By implication, homelessness is a housing problem. For this reason, many attempts to understand the problem in the UK have focused on the operations of the housing market and the impact of recent housing policies. Over the past twenty-five years, the UK housing market has experienced a very significant transformation. Of most note has been the expansion in home ownership. At some 68 per cent of all housing in the UK, owner occupation is now very much the majority housing tenure. The problem, though, is the way access to home ownership effectively excludes people on low incomes. Traditionally, they have looked instead to local authority housing and to the private rented sector to meet their housing needs. However, a significant part of the expansion in home ownership was achieved through the sale of council houses, under the 1980 'Right to Buy' legislation. This has resulted in the sale of some 1.8 million council houses. This policy has raised many concerns, such as a shortage of affordable housing for low-income groups. Traditionally, the private rented sector has provided an important source of accommodation, particularly for young single people. However, in the UK, the amount of private rented accommodation gradually declined throughout the twentieth century and currently stands at less than 10 per cent of all housing stock. For low-income single people, therefore, housing options are inherently limited – they are financially excluded from home ownership, are usually excluded from access to local authority housing and compete for a limited supply of private rented and housing association stock. In this context, it is perhaps unsurprising that some people struggle to secure affordable housing. Nevertheless, it is important to remember that homelessness is much more than simply a housing problem. After all, most housing problems are ultimately problems of low income, unemployment and poverty.

Unemployment and benefit issues have been a focus for those exploring the causes of homelessness, particularly homelessness among young single people. High rates of youth unemployment have certainly been seen to be linked to the problem of youth homelessness. There is good evidence that young people are disproportionately affected by unemployment, and youth unemployment rates are consistently higher than the average. However, what is of most concern is not unemployment *per se*, but rather the very low income levels that unemployment implies. This in turn has led to concerns about benefits for the unemployed, especially for unemployed young people. In 1988, the government introduced a number of important changes to the benefit entitlement of unemployed people under the age of 25 (see Hutson and Liddiard, 1994). The introduction of income support in 1988 was particularly characterized by a movement from benefit entitlement based on need to entitlement based on age. These changes meant that an unemployed single person under 25 became entitled to just 80 per cent of the Income Support received by someone aged 25 or over. At the same time, someone aged under 18 became entitled to just 60 per cent of the adult rate – even if he or she had been in identical circumstances. In fact, later in 1988 the income support eligibility of unemployed 16- and 17-year-olds was removed altogether. They were expected instead to be in employment, in training or financially dependent on their parents. Coupled with continuing concerns about the eligibility criteria and administration of housing benefit, as well as the operation of the Social Fund, there has been some concern that the benefit system in the UK has been instrumental in creating a problem of youth homelessness, particularly for people under 18. If some unemployed young people are excluded from state financial support, it should not surprise us if they experience housing difficulties and ultimately homelessness.

Many commentaries on homelessness, however, have not focused on government policies as a causal factor. Rather, many explanations have focused instead on the homeless themselves, their backgrounds and their problems. Surveys have consistently shown that the family backgrounds of many homeless people have been characterized by conflict and abuse, and severe family conflict often causes homeless people to leave home, whether by choice or by coercion (Smith, 1999; Evans, 1999). A background of abuse – physical, sexual and emotional – also seems to characterize many homeless populations (Hendessi, 1992). The importance of these points is evidently open to conjecture, but familial support – financial and otherwise – has been shown to be crucial in the successful negotiation of independence for young people (Hutson and Jenkins, 1989).

The fact that care leavers are disproportionately represented among the homeless simultaneously raises questions about the impact of having little or no family support and the effectiveness of the care system. What does seem crystal clear, however, is the very close relation between homelessness and an experience of care. While just 1 per cent of the population have such an experience, among the homeless this rate is consistently more than 20 per cent (Hutson and Liddiard, 1994). The difficulty, of course, is interpretation. To explain why there is this close relation we need to focus on several issues, such as the troubled backgrounds of those taken into care, the impact of the care system and the inadequacies of support for young people when they have left care.

Difficulties of interpretation are an inherent feature of many debates about the causes of homelessness. After all, it is very clear that some issues – such as mental health problems and an involvement in the criminal justice system – have a close relation to homelessness. The problem is establishing just what the nature of this relation is. There is certainly little doubt that homeless people have more mental health problems than their housed contemporaries. A survey in 1991, for instance, showed that among single homeless people mental health problems were reported by 28 per cent of those in hostels and B&Bs, by 36 per cent of day centre users and by some 40 per cent of soup run users. These figures are striking when compared to the 5 per cent of the general population experiencing mental health problems (Bines, 1998).

Why is this the case? Does it reflect the problems of accessing accommodation by those with a history of mental health problems? There is evidence, for instance, that even homelessness hostels may exclude people with a history of psychological problems, as well as violent or sexual offenders (Liddiard and Hutson, 1991). Such problems also make it less likely that individuals will be able to maintain independent accommodation, at least without appropriate support. However, an alternative and equally credible interpretation is that homelessness is itself a cause of psychological problems. There is no doubt that homelessness is a stressful and demanding experience, which can initiate and compound mental illness. In this sense, the close relation between homelessness and mental health difficulties is not in question. Rather, the problem is how to interpret this relationship.

The relation between homelessness and crime is also open to interpretation. It does seem that homeless people are more likely to have had experience of the criminal justice system than their housed contemporaries. It is less clear what this fact reflects. Is it a cause of homelessness or again simply a symptom of the realities of homeless life? There is no question that finding work and accommodation if one has a criminal record can be difficult, and there is a strong relation between a period in custody and homelessness (Carlisle, 1998). However, the high likelihood of an involvement in the criminal justice system may be as much a symptom of the realities of a homeless existence as a cause.

In many ways, therefore, debates about the causes of homelessness are far from clear. The precise impact of government policy may be hotly contested and often difficult to determine. Yet, even when it is clear that there is a close relation between an issue like mental illness and homelessness, the precise nature of the relation is invariably open to conjecture. This point can be made about many of the themes and issues regularly employed in attempts to explain homelessness. Some of these, such as an involvement in alcohol or drug abuse, may have a high public profile, but it is always important to remember that the mass media are strongly attracted by such topics, which can often match media agendas (Liddiard and Hutson, 1998). The result is sometimes misleading, with ill-informed media coverage, giving disproportionate attention to those features of homelessness such as substance abuse and prostitution, that help to attract a large audience.

Resolving Homelessness

If there is considerable disagreement about the causes of homelessness, there are corresponding differences of opinion about how to resolve it. Given the heterogeneity of homeless people, it is evident that there is no single solution to the problem. On the contrary, because of the diversity of the homeless and their problems, it is apparent that there are many potential solutions. While some people have focused on housing policies and, particularly, changes in benefit legislation and entitlement as the keys to resolve the problem, the heterogeneity of the homeless demands a variety of responses. Thus, one area on which successive governments have focused over the past decade has been rough sleeping. In 1998, the Prime Minister, Tony Blair, in a foreword to a report by the Social Exclusion Unit on rough sleeping, said that 'The sight of a rough-sleeper bedding down for the night in a shop doorway or on a park bench is one of the most potent symbols of social exclusion in Britain today' (Social Exclusion Unit, 1998, p. 1). Few would disagree with this sentiment, but how has the New Labour government attempted to address the problem of homelessness and rough sleeping? One of the first measures of the government was to appoint a 'homelessness czar', whose job has been to coordinate efforts to reduce the number of people sleeping rough. The report by the Social Exclusion Unit estimated that there were some 2,000 people sleeping on the streets each night in England alone, which was estimated at some 10,000 in a year; London was deemed to have the most significant problem, with an average of 400 rough sleepers each night. The stated objective of the government has been to cut the number of rough sleepers by two-thirds by 2002.

In many respects, these moves by the New Labour government have been welcomed. In particular, the suggestion that not enough was being done to prevent people becoming homeless in the first place was encouraging. There have certainly been some interesting attempts to look at the problem of homelessness in a more preventive and holistic sense, with the establishment of programmes designed to try to stem the number of care leavers, ex-servicemen and ex-prisoners ending up on the streets. However, the government has also had to acknowledge that homeless people need a mixture of remedies for their problem. After all, both long-term and short-term strategies for dealing with homelessness have a role to play. This distinction particularly came to a head in November 1999, when the homelessness czar, Louise Casey, provoked fury when she said: 'with soup runs and other kinds of charity help, well-meaning people are spending money servicing the problem on the streets and keeping it there. Even the Big Issue is perpetuating the problem.' These comments were widely interpreted by many agencies and the mass media to imply that food and clothing handouts were making it too easy for rough sleepers. Many charities doing soup runs for homeless people felt that they were being criticized for prolonging the problem, rather than solving it.

Whatever the wisdom and intention of these comments, they certainly served to raise the public profile of a long-standing debate about tackling homelessness – getting the balance right between short-term and crisis intervention, and the provision of longer-term strategies for the permanent resettlement of homeless people. Evidently, there is a need for both forms of intervention, although charities are themselves divided about the appropriate balance. Shelter, for instance, had previously argued that the balance of intervention was wrong, with too much focus on emergency services. In contrast, the Salvation Army has defended its approach, saying that while it was working to get people off the streets permanently, conducting soup runs was a means of making first contact, with a view to establishing relationships with homeless people and determining how best to offer them assistance. Ultimately, perhaps, there is a need for more effective links between short-term assistance and more permanent solutions to ensure a more holistic and integrated approach to homelessness – something that has sometimes been notable by its absence (Oldman, 1998; Franklin, 1999). This is perhaps the key to resolving homelessness – recognizing the diversity of the problem, which in turn demands a diversity of responses.

The future approach of the government towards homelessness remains to be seen. In any event, many services for homeless people – particularly for homeless single people – are the prerogative of voluntary agencies and charities. Yet there is no doubt that the government has a crucial role to play in drawing public attention to the problem, offering resources and changing policies. However, the extent to which we are likely to see a resolution of homelessness in the UK is very much open to debate. There is certainly some concern at the government's apparent fixation with rough sleeping. Although this is the most visible manifestation of homelessness, it represents only a small part of the homelessness problem. Any comprehensive resolution of homelessness will ultimately have to address the problem of homelessness in its entirety.

Conclusion

It is difficult to encapsulate the complexities and nuances of homelessness in one brief chapter. It is ultimately a very public and visible social problem, simultaneously laden with ambiguity. How do we define homelessness? How much homelessness is there? How do we explain it? How should we tackle it? These are all questions that lie at the heart of any discussion of the subject. Yet there are few simple answers to any of these conundrums. The definition of homelessness depends heavily on how we define the ambiguous concept of 'home', and, in turn, the quantification of homelessness heavily depends on the manner in which it has been defined.

Similarly, one can *explain* homelessness in many different ways. Even if one can establish a clear relation between an issue like mental illness and homelessness, the causal nature of this relation can still be very open to debate and conjecture. Yet if we cannot agree on what causes homelessness in modern society, how can we possibly agree on solutions? After all, the heterogeneity of the homeless and their problems effectively precludes any single solution, and the effectiveness and impact of strategies and interventions can be hotly contested. None the less, the resolution of homelessness is important. As Tony Blair himself acknowledges, there really is no greater indication of social malaise in our wealthy society than the existence and persistence of homelessness as we begin the new century.

Issues to Consider

- What is homelessness?
- How much homelessness is there at the start of the twenty-first century?
- What are the most important causes of homelessness?
- How should the problem of homelessness be addressed?

Further Reading

The following books, which expand at length on some of the issues raised in this chapter, draw together a variety of relevant data and research findings. Hutson and Clapham (1999) is a very helpful text, pulling together the work of a number of experts to explore the problem of homelessness thoroughly. It includes original research, and diverse chapters on issues such as gender and homelessness, and European homelessness. Hutson and Liddiard (1994) look at homelessness as a social problem and explore the perspectives of different groups on the problem, including the mass media, homelessness agencies and young homeless people. Burrows et al. (1998) is a comprehensive study, which offers a wealth of data and is particularly good at considering policy responses to the problem of homelessness.

There is a variety of web sites concerned with different aspects of homelessness. The following are good places to start, and all of them offer links to relevant data and information on homelessness:

* Shelter: www.shelter.org.uk;
* Crisis: www.crisis.org.uk;
* Centrepoint: www.centrepoint.org.uk.

These bodies are all concerned with campaigning for the homeless, but other sites are more useful for accessing research and policy developments concerning homelessness. They include:

* Joseph Rowntree Foundation: www.jrf.org.uk;
* London Research Centre: www.london-research.gov.uk;
* Department of the Environment, Transport and the Regions: www.open.gov.uk/detr.

The 1998 report *Tackling Rough Sleeping* by the Social Exclusion Unit is also accessible online www.cabinet-office.gov.uk/seu/1998/rough/srhome.htm.

References

Anderson, I. 1999: Social housing or social exclusion? Non-access to housing for single homeless people. In S. Hutson and D. Clapham (eds), *Homelessness: Public Policies and Private Troubles*. London: Cassell.

Bines, W. 1998: The health of single homeless people. In R. Burrows, N. Pleace and D. Quilgars (eds), *Homelessness and Social Policy*. London: Routledge.

Bramley, G. 1988: The definition and measurement of homelessness. In G. Bramley, K. Doogan, P. Leather, A. Murie and E. Watson (eds), *Homelessness and the London Housing Market*, Occasional Paper no. 32, School for Advanced Urban Studies. Bristol: University of Bristol.

Burrows, R., Pleace, N. and Quilgars, D. (eds) 1998: *Homelessness and Social Policy*. London: Routledge.

Carlisle, J. 1998: The housing needs of ex-prisoners. In R. Burrows, N. Pleace and D. Quilgars (eds), *Homelessness and Social Policy*. London: Routledge.

Evans, A. 1999: Rationing device or passport to social housing? The operation of the homelessness legislation in Britain in the 1990s. In S. Hutson and D. Clapham (eds), *Homelessness: Public Policies and Private Troubles*. London: Cassell.

Franklin, B. 1999: More than community care: supporting the transition from homelessness to home. In S. Hutson and D. Clapham (ed.), *Homelessness: Public Policies and Private Troubles*. London: Cassell.

Hendessi, M. 1992: *4 in 10: Report on Young Women Who Become Homeless as a Result of Sexual Abuse*. London: CHAR.

Hutson, S. and Clapham, D. (eds) 1999: *Homelessness: Public Policies and Private Troubles*. London: Cassell.

Hutson, S. and Jenkins, R. 1989: *Taking the Strain: Families, Unemployment and the Transition to Adulthood*. Milton Keynes: Open University Press.

Hutson, S. and Liddiard, M. 1994: *Youth Homelessness: The Construction of a Social Issue*. London: Macmillan.

Liddiard, M. and Hutson, S. 1991: Homeless young people and runaways – agency definitions and processes. *Journal of Social Policy*, 20 (3), 365–88.

Liddiard, M. and Hutson, S. 1998: Youth homelessness, the press and public attitudes. *Youth and Policy*, 59, 57–69.

Lowe, S. 1998: Homelessness and the law. In R. Burrows, N. Pleace and D. Quilgars (eds), *Homelessness and Social Policy*. London: Routledge.

Oldman, C. 1998: Working together to help homeless people: an examination of inter-agency themes. In R. Burrows, N. Pleace and D. Quilgars (eds), *Homelessness and Social Policy*. London: Routledge.

Pleace, N., Burrows, R. and Quilgars, D. 1998: Homelessness in contemporary Britain: conceptualisation and measurement. In R. Burrows, N. Pleace and D. Quilgars (eds), *Homelessness and Social Policy*. London: Routledge.

Smith, J. 1999: Gender and homelessness. In S. Hutson and D. Clapham (eds), *Homelessness: Public Policies and Private Troubles*. London: Cassell.

Social Exclusion Unit 1998: *Tackling Rough Sleeping*. London: Stationery Office.

Somerville, P. 1999: The making and unmaking of homelessness legislation. In S. Hutson and D. Clapham (eds), *Homelessness: Public Policies and Private Troubles*. London: Cassell.

Watson, S. 1984. Definitions of homelessness: a feminist perspective. *Critical Social Policy*, 11, 60–73.

Chapter 9

Income and Wealth

Paul Spicker

Introduction

As preceding chapters in this section have indicated, awareness of the distributive implications of policy is central to the analysis of social problems and social policy. In the light of these discussions this chapter considers some of the concepts central to judgements about distribution:

- the meaning of income and wealth;
- the difficulties of measuring them;
- the distribution of resources;
- the effect of considering factors like household composition, gender, age or changes over time.

Resources and Inequality

Inequality in resources is important for social policy in three ways:

- *Poverty*   Inequality is intimately connected with poverty. People who do not have resources are poor, and poverty means that people are denied welfare.
- *Welfare*   Inequality in resources has important consequences for welfare in other senses. As later chapters show, inequalities in health consistently point to an 'inverse care law'; people with fewer resources have greater needs, but tend to receive less care for those needs. Inequalities in housing mean that people with fewer resources are more likely to become homeless, and are more likely to find themselves in inferior housing.

- *Social problems*   Some writers claim that inequality leads directly to social problems. Box, reviewing the evidence on crime, unemployment and inequality, argued that 'every study to date on income inequality and property offences or non-fatal violence shows that there is a statistical, maybe even a causal, relationship' (Box, 1987, p.87). The Rowntree Report on Income and Wealth (Joseph Rowntree Foundation 1995, p. 87) suggested that 'it is in the interests of all to remove the factors which are fostering the social diseases of drugs, crime, political extremism and social unrest'. (This argument has been criticized by Dennis (1997), who responds that crime has been steadily increasing for years. Inequality, however, has not consistently increased; it fell during the period 1961–77, and rose fairly sharply between 1982 and 1990. Crime increased throughout the period when inequality was falling. The position is not conclusive, because the definitions of crime are contested, and the pattern of inequality has changed.) The main argument for saying that inequality does create social problems is that it leads to economic marginalization. Economic marginalization, in turn, is strongly linked with both crime (Box, 1987) and family breakdown (Lampard, 1994).

Inequality and redistribution were for many years the key issues in British social policy: for much of the twentieth century, the policy of the Labour Party was to achieve greater equality through expenditure on public services (Le Grand, 1982). Concern with the distributive implications of policy was at its strongest in the 1970s, when the Labour government established a standing Royal Commission on the Distribution of Income and Wealth, but the Commission was abolished by the succeeding Conservative government, and the distributive implications of policy were subsequently considered much less frequently. Even so, the Conservative government continued to make distributive assessments: one of the strangest can be found in the Green Paper on the poll tax, in which the government seemed to have convinced itself that the tax would be relatively neutral in its effects on people on low incomes when compared with the preceding system (Cmnd. 9714, 1986, Annex F). The distributive implications of policy are still routinely considered in certain financial decisions, for example relating to personal taxation.

The emphasis on inequality in resources has diminished and for two main reasons. The first concerns ideology. Many right-wing critics take the view that inequality is not a matter of concern. Liberal individualists consider it irrelevant. Hayek (1976), for example, argued that 'social justice' is a mirage. Indeed for many Conservatives inequality is positively desirable; society works by putting people in different, complementary roles, and different roles imply different statuses and rewards (Charvet, 1983). The second relates to method. The analysis of the distribution of resources is complex, and most statements about the subject – including many in this chapter – rely on a number of disputable judgements. Information about income has tended to be more reliable than information about wealth, but both are uncertain, ill-defined and liable to sudden changes. This is why the discussion about inequality in health, for example, is usually related to social class, as Jones's chapter emphasizes, rather than to poverty and wealth.

Defining Resources

> ## Box 9.1:   Income, wealth and expenditure
>
> *Income* describes the flow of resources – what comes in. *Wealth* is a stock – the resources that a person holds. *Expenditure* surveys sometimes use expenditure as an indicator of what people are able to do with their resources.

The key concepts for understanding the distribution of resources are income, wealth and expenditure (see box 9.1). These are usually measured in terms of money. Money is a material resource in itself, as well as a unit of exchange. It is important for people's welfare, partly because some people find it a pleasant or useful thing to have in itself, partly because it represents security, but mainly because it can be used to buy things. From the point of view of welfare, however, what matters about resources is not really their monetary value, but what they imply for the way people live. Monetary value is important, because things that can be exchanged for money – such as bonds or share certificates – can also be exchanged for goods. But it is the ability to use goods that is really important: whether people can eat, whether they can afford somewhere to live and what its quality will be, whether they can obtain clothes, and so forth. Sometimes the monetary value of this use does not reflect its value for welfare. Someone who rents a house has much of the same use value as someone who has bought it, but the owner-occupier has a much more substantial financial asset. Titmuss (1968, pp. 22–3) made the case that social policy has to be concerned with 'command over resources', by which he meant not just the money people had, but the use they were able to make of resources. This is normally translated in studies into 'consumption', which is the process by which people use up goods and services (Gordon and Spicker, 1999).

The use of monetary values as a measure of resources has advantages and disadvantages. The main advantages are that money is measurable, widely understood and widely accepted. The main disadvantage is that money can come to dominate the debate, to such an extent that people forget what the real issues are. The figures for the distribution of wealth, for example, focus on 'marketable' wealth; the estimates in the UK are put together by the Inland Revenue, and they are strongly influenced by the question of what is taxable. The clothes that people wear are not 'marketable', but they are vitally important for welfare; the research for the book *Breadline Britain* (Gordon and Pantazis, 1997) found, for example, that 4 per cent of the population could not afford a warm water-proof coat.

The Distribution of Income and Wealth

Income

In most Western societies, the distribution of income has a shape similar to that of a *lognormal curve*. The normal curve, or bell curve, will be familiar to anyone who has done some basic statistics (although it is hardly ever found in real life): it looks like the curve on the left in figure 9.1. The height of the curve shows the number of cases at each point. An example of a lognormal curve is on the right. Lognormal distributions are widely used in this field, partly because they lend themselves to conventional statistical calculations, and partly because they seem to work, more or less (see Cowell, 1995).

Normal curve

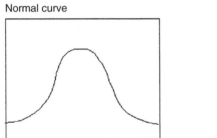

Lognormal curve

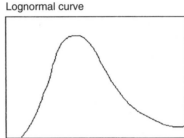

Figure 9.1 Normal and lognormal distributions

The distribution of income, like a lognormal curve, is very skewed: more people are near the bottom of the range than near the top. Most people have less than the average income, if by average we understand the arithmetic mean; it is more conventional to look at the median (or mid-point) income, which is lower than the mean but still higher than the mode (the top of the hump).

The idea that most people receive below average income takes a while to adjust to. Pen (1971, pp. 48–53) likened the distribution of income, famously, to a parade of dwarves and a few giants: if people had the same height as their income, and filed past us in order of their height, there would be a long, long procession of dwarves. If the parade is set to last an hour, we shall still be seeing dwarves after 45 minutes; people of average height appear only 12 minutes before the end. In the last few minutes, there are a few giants – lawyers 18 feet tall, some doctors 60 feet tall, and in the last few seconds some people as high as tower blocks. The last person is at least ten miles high.

The picture this conjures up is helpful, but it also leads to some misconceptions. Most people, including many who are very well off, assume that 'the rich' means someone else. As a general proposition, about a third of the population are likely to be on very low incomes, such as pensions and benefits: this varies from country to country, but a third is a useful generalization. That means that people who are earning are generally likely to find themselves in the top two-thirds, and that people who have average earnings (that is median earnings) are in the middle of that top two-thirds. Two middling earned incomes put people well into the top third; households with only a single earner, or two low wages, come in the next third. The top third, then, includes households with two teachers or two social workers, not just the super-rich.

Wealth

Table 9.1 The distribution of wealth in the UK, %

	1976	*1981*	*1986*	*1991*	*1994*	*1995*
Marketable wealth						
Percentage of wealth owned by						
most wealthy 1%	21	18	18	17	19	19
most wealthy 5%	38	36	36	35	39	38
most wealthy 10%	50	50	50	47	52	50
most wealthy 25%	71	73	73	71	74	73
most wealthy 50%	92	92	90	92	93	92
Total marketable wealth (£ billion)	280	565	955	1,711	1,950	2,033
Marketable wealth less value of dwellings						
Percentage of wealth owned by						
most wealthy 1%	29	26	25	29	29	27
most wealthy 5%	47	45	46	51	53	51
most wealthy 10%	57	56	58	64	66	64
most wealthy 25%	73	74	75	80	83	81
most wealthy 50%	88	87	89	93	94	93

Source: 'Social Trends 29', Office for National Statistics, 1999, © Crown Copyright 2000

Wealth is very unequally distributed (see table 9.1). In the UK 10 per cent of the population own half of all the wealth. Half the people own 92 per cent of the marketable wealth; the other half own only 8 per cent. These bald statements may seem shocking, but some reservations ought to be made about them.

The first is that the definition of wealth has an important effect on the figures that are returned. Currently the most important and influential wealth holdings in the UK are probably occupational pension funds, which have become the biggest bloc of shareholders on the stock market. They are owned (but not controlled) mainly by ordinary workers, whose interest lies in their pensions. If pension rights are included, the distribution of wealth looks a lot more equal.

The second is that formal ownership is not the same thing as command over resources. A council tenant who lives next door to neighbours who have bought their council house is not very much worse off than they are – they have similar property and similar use of resources – but one has no assets in housing, while the other does.

Third, 'marketable' wealth is not necessarily what is important. Fuel, clothing and food matter, but nothing in the figures about wealth says whether or not people will have access to them. Some 'asset-rich' pensioners have unsatisfactory lifestyles; some people with an enviable command over resources have no assets. In practice, then, income is usually considered a better indicator of welfare than wealth.

The distribution of wealth seems, at first blush, as if it should be at least as important as income. The amounts of money being considered are very large. An inheritance of £50,000 (close to the average value of a house in the UK) is not just the equivalent of three years' income; it might easily double a person's disposable income for the rest of his or her life. In practice, however, the oddities of measurement and the lack of clear links between wealth and consumption have tended to mean that statistics about income offer a better guide to command over resources. The vagueness of information about wealth and the difficulty of working out values also have an important implication for policy: income is much more likely to be the subject of regulation, and redistribution, than wealth.

Measuring Inequality

Measuring inequality is problematic. Box 9.2 outlines a simple numerical distribution of resources in two societies, each with four people. It is artificial, of

---

Box 9.2: Inequality in two societies

	Person 1	Person 2	Person 3	Person 4
Society 1	1	1	1	3
Society 2	1	2	3	4

---

course, to imagine a society with only four people, but it helps to bring the issues out; if you think of this as four divisions within a society, it will be clearer. Which society is more unequal? If the question is judged by relative privilege, or the concentration of resources, society 1 is more unequal. This is the kind of situation found in some less developed countries: most people live in relatively deprived conditions, and only a minority are engaged in the formal economic market.

The most commonly used measure of income inequality is the Gini coefficient, which is a measure of the concentration of resources. It is easiest to explain it graphically. The Lorenz curve is drawn by mapping the share of resources, going from the lowest to the highest. So, for example, if four people have £1, £2, £3 and £4 the cumulative share is 10 per cent for the lowest, 30 per cent for the lowest two, 60 per cent for three and 100 per cent for all. The line across the centre of the graph is the line of equality – where they would be if they had equal shares. (See figure 9.2.) The Gini coefficient is a measure of the area under the Lorenz curve. Technically it ranges from 0 to 1.1 is complete inequality (one person has all the income) and 0 is complete equality (everyone has the same).

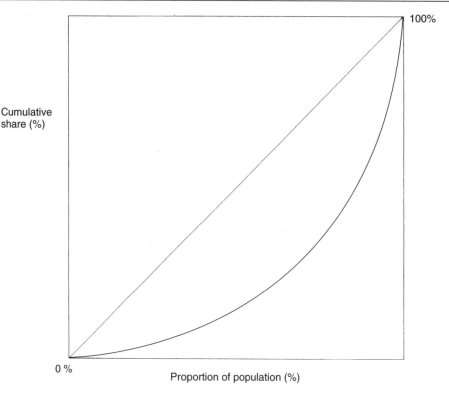

Figure 9.2 The Lorenz curve

It is much more common, however, to find the number printed as an index, between 0 and 100. Because the coefficient measures the concentration of income, a society like society 1 is considered much more unequal than one like society 2.

If, on the other hand, the judgement is made according to the dispersion of resources, society 2 is more unequal. The distance between the bottom and the top is greater, and the bottom half has a smaller share of resources than the bottom half in society 1. Economic distance is often used as a measure of poverty. O'Higgins and Jenkins (1990, p. 207) argue:

> there is an inescapable connection between poverty and inequality: certain degrees or dimensions of inequality . . . will lead to people being below the minimum standards acceptable in that society. It is this 'economic distance' aspect of inequality that is poverty. This does not mean that there will always be poverty when there is inequality: only if the inequality implies an economic distance beyond the critical level.

A commonly used measure is 50 per cent of the median income. At this level, no one in society 1 is poor, but person 1 in society 2 is poor – despite the fact that society 2 is richer than society 1.

Table 9.2 The distribution of income in six countries

Country	Share of income or consumption, %					Gini coefficient (measure of concentration of resources)
	lowest 20%	next 20%	middle 20%	next 20%	highest 20%	
Brazil (1995)	2.5	5.7	9.9	17.7	64.2	60.1
Malaysia (1989)	4.6	8.3	13.0	20.4	53.7	48.4
US (1994)	4.8	10.5	16.0	23.5	45.2	40.1
UK (1991)	7.4	12.0	17.0	23.0	41.0	33.7
Sweden (1992)	9.6	14.5	18.1	23.2	34.5	25.7
Slovak Republic (1992)	11.9	15.8	18.8	22.2	31.4	19.5

Sources: World Bank, 1999; Hills, 1995 (UK figures)

Table 9.2 gives figures for the distribution of income in six countries. The figures are drawn mainly from the World Bank's latest *World Development Report*. By contrast with the simplified figures used in the earlier abstract examples, the picture this kind of table draws is muddy, because the data sources cover different periods and they are not completely reliable.

The pattern of income distribution in different countries is very different, and few safe generalizations can be made. One interesting general proposition from development economics is the idea of the Kuznets inverted U-curve. Before development, resources tend to equality; as development progresses, they become more unequal. South American countries like Brazil are more unequal than many West African countries, though the African countries tend to be poorer. However, as development proceeds further and more people participate in the economic processes, the resources become less concentrated, so that the inequality is reduced. In recent years, an important question about this process has been raised: in the 1980s, a number of developed countries, including the UK, showed a trend towards increasing inequality. Atkinson argues that this reflects the complexity of income distributions. They are not set in concrete, and they are affected by many interacting factors (Atkinson, 1993).

A Fair Distribution?

Many discussions of inequality begin with the general presumption that people in the same circumstances should be treated equally, unless there are reasons to the contrary. This does not mean, however, that a fair distribution would be an equal one. The reward for work could also reasonably be affected by experience, qualifications, skills, effort and scarcity value. Many people are prepared to accept that the incomes of experienced workers should be higher than those of younger workers, in the expectation that as they gain experience, they will be rewarded in the same way. This alone implies substantial differences in

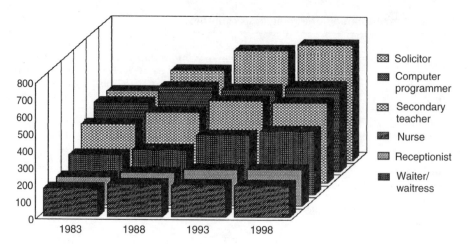

Source: 'Social Trends 29', Office for National Statistics, 1999, © Crown Copyright 2000

Figure 9.3   Relative incomes of people in selected occupations, Great Britain

income – and leads, besides, to gender disadvantage because women are likely to interrupt their work records.

The distribution of income is not 'fair': a great deal depends on luck, accidents of birth, changes in status and an eye to the main chance. The rewards that people receive for work often have little to do with effort, skill, training or the social utility of the work; over time, there have been considerable changes in the relative positions of bank clerks, teachers and secretaries, which have as much to do with convention and the role of women as they have to do with the demand for labour. Figure 9.3 shows changes in the relative positions of particular occupations.

Individuals and households

The conventional unit for the measurement of income, and so of inequality, is the household. Individual measures, like accounts based on tax returns, tend to be distorted, because people in a household share resources. At the same time, a concentration on households creates its own problems. The most important is the definition of the household. We may know roughly what a household is; but it is a difficult term to define, and the results of surveys are very sensitive to the definitions used.

Another important issue is the distribution of resources within households. The effect of inequality within a household is that individuals in it may have fewer resources than at first appears. Millar and Glendinning (1989) argue that, at the threshold of poverty, this could lead to a mis-classification and an underestimate of the number of people considered poor. Over time, this largely reasonable argument has been amplified into the much less well-founded argument

Table 9.3 People in households, by gender and income, UK 1996–7, %

Income group	Men	Women	Children	All
Bottom fifth	16	19	29	20
Next fifth	17	20	21	19
Middle fifth	21	21	20	21
Next fifth	23	21	18	21
Top fifth	23	19	13	19
All	100	100	100	100

Source: 'Social Trends 29' Office for National Statistics, 1999, © Crown Copyright 2000

that people might be poor in rich households. Payne (1991), for instance, writes about the 'poverty and deprivation women experience within affluent households'. The basic argument for this is that women may not have incomes in their own right; they do not have money. But those who live in affluent households, even if they do not have personal disposable incomes, still use furniture, fuel and household goods. Unless the women are locked away in a 'secret inner cabinet', like Mrs Rochester in *Jane Eyre*, they still have a considerable command over resources, and they cannot sensibly be compared to single parents on Income Support. Recent empirical evidence on the question does not support even the more moderate view; in general, women and men in household share resources fairly equally (Cantillon and Nolan, 1998).

It is true that women are more likely to be poor than men. This is partly because pensioners are more likely to be women (males tend to die earlier), partly because most single parents are women, and partly because women have lower pay, and lower associated benefit entitlements. This has been called the 'feminization of poverty', but the term feminization suggests that this is a new trend; it has long been true (Garfinkel and McLanahan, 1988; Lewis and Piachaud, 1992). Table 9.3 shows the gender balance of poorer households. There are more women than men: 39 per cent of women are in the lowest 40 per cent of households, compared with 33 per cent of men.

Much more striking, however, is the position of children; disproportionately more poor households have children than richer households, and more than half of all children are in the lowest 40 per cent of households (see too Rowlingson's chapter). This is a fairly recent trend; it reflects partly the growth of particular forms of deprivation (especially single parenthood), but also an improvement in the position of pensioners, which has taken many of them out of the lowest fifth.

Distribution over time

Income is only an indicator of command over resources, and taken at a particular moment it may not be reliable. Titmuss (1968) argued for a focus, not just on command over resources, but on 'command-over-resources-through-time'. It is difficult to gain a reliable sense of distribution over time, because people's incomes vary considerably. In the short term, people's circumstances may change: for example, they may change employment, become unemployed, work overtime, claim benefits or have changes in their rates of pay. In most cases, unemployed people do not remain unemployed indefinitely: many move in and out of jobs, especially if the jobs are low-paid and temporary. Single parents are not condemned to permanent poverty: many are able to start work when their children are old enough to go to school, or when they remarry into new circumstances. Jarvis and Jenkins (1998), using the British Household Panel Survey, found that in one year over one-quarter of their sample moved up or down by at least two decile groups (each decile group represents one-tenth of the income distribution). Of the remainder, about half stayed in the same decile, and half moved up or down one. In the long term, the general pattern tends to be that:

- children's resources depend on their parents' income;
- young single people's resources are likely to be low, but to increase rapidly;
- a single person who then shares a household with another has a large increase in family resources;
- a couple who have a child earn noticeably less because of the loss of the woman's income;
- the income of the couple is restored and then improved when the youngest child goes to school;
- the earnings of middle-class people increase as they get older, while those of working-class people tend to decline;
- income falls rapidly on retirement. (This does not mean that pensioners are necessarily poor; the fall is relative to the pensioner's previous income. The fall in income in the UK is considerable, but in France pensioners tend to be better off than average workers.)

If we look at the distribution of income according to age, younger and older people feature disproportionately in the lowest income groups (Goodman et al., 1997, p. 65). This means that changes in the demography of a population also have implications for the distribution of income. In the 1970s, most poor households in the UK were old people (Layard et al., 1978). By the 1990s, this was no longer true: part of the explanation was better pensions, but mostly it was because of the increasing numbers of people in other groups – particularly young single people forming independent households and single parents who had divorced (see figure 9.4).

Redistribution

Redistribution is conventionally described as 'horizontal' or 'vertical'. Vertical redistribution is redistribution between richer people – those higher up the income distribution – and poorer people, who are those lower down. In the rather emotive language conventionally used in this field, vertical redistribution

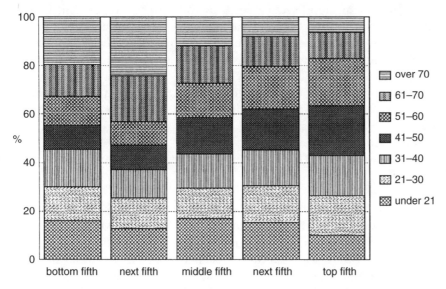

Source: 'Social Trends 29', Office for National Statistics, 1999, © Crown Copyright 2000

Figure 9.4 Age group by income quintile

is said to be *progressive* when it goes from rich to poor, and *regressive* when it goes from poor to rich. (The phrase 'from rich to poor' should not be confused with redistribution 'from the rich to the poor'. It is the same difference as that between going 'from north to south' and going 'from the north to the south'; the first is a direction, the second refers to specific locations.) A redistribution which does not change the distribution is *proportionate*.

Horizontal redistribution is redistribution from one sector of society to another – for example, from workers to old people, from people without children to people with children, from men to women, and so forth. Sometimes horizontal redistribution is also vertical; at times it has mixed effects, with some money going to better off people and some to worse off people. An example of this process is Child Benefit. Despite the frequent and repeated claims that it helps poor people, it is horizontal, not vertical, and it is likely to be regressive. There are four directions of movement:

- from people without children to people with children. Families without children include both younger people (who tend to earn less) and older earners (who tend to earn more).
- from people with small households to people with larger households (someone with three children receives more in child benefit that someone with one child). The families most vulnerable to low income are those with young children under 5 – partly because these families are likely to be younger, but mainly because very young children prevent one parent, usually the mother, from going out to work. Despite preconceptions to the contrary,

large families in the UK tend not to be on lower incomes. This is because large families tend to be older (it takes time to have children) and older workers tend to earn more. The main exception to this is large families whose children's ages prevent the mothers working for long periods – for example a family with children aged 15, 11, 7 and 3.

- from some people who are working to other people who are working. Child Benefit can in theory go to families on benefit, but the value is deducted directly from income support, which means it offers no net benefit to the poorest families.
- from men to women. This has been one of the main arguments in favour of Child Benefit.

Because small households tend to be on lower incomes than larger households, and because Child Benefit does not offer anything to families on Income Support, the pattern of redistribution is slightly regressive. This is not a comment about family allowances in general – it is specific to the system in the UK. By contrast, the complex system of family allowances in France is more likely to be progressive, because some of the benefits are means-tested, and so available only to families on low incomes; childcare is extensively available, which means that women can return to work, and some benefits are specifically concentrated on children under 3.

The strategy of equality

Tawney (1964, p. 122) made the case that public spending was the most effective way to redistribute resources. The aim, he wrote, is not to take money from one group of people to give it to another. 'Rather the aim of pooling surplus resources though taxation was to ensure access for all irrespective of their income, occupation or social position, to the conditions of civilisation which, in the absence of such measures, can only be enjoyed by the rich.' Le Grand (1982) has argued against this that universal social services are not available equally to all. The NHS gives most health care to middle-class people, as the Black report showed (see Department of Health and Social Security, 1980; Townsend et al., 1982; 1988). Education is regressive, partly because people are poorest when their children are young, but mainly because the middle classes gain most from education after the age of 16. Transport subsidies are worth most to people who travel the greatest distances, who tend to be middle-class. And housing subsidies tend to favour owner-occupiers, who are more likely to be wealthy; for Le Grand the 'strategy of equality' proposed by Tawney has failed:

Table 9.4 casts some doubt on this position. It needs, however, to be treated with some caution:

- The distribution of income by household depends a great deal on age and family structure. The lowest income groups contain mainly pensioners and

Table 9.4 Redistribution of income through taxes and benefits, UK, 1996–7, £ p.a.

Average per household	*Bottom fifth*	*Next fifth*	*Middle fifth*	*Next fifth*	*Top fifth*	*All house-holds*
Wages and salaries	1,300	4,450	11,100	19,190	31,780	13,560
Imputed income from benefits in kind	–	10	100	260	920	260
Self-employment income	420	670	1,340	1,830	6,460	2,140
Occupational pensions, annuities	280	850	1,380	1,770	2,600	1,380
Investment income	190	310	620	960	2,790	970
Other income	120	160	160	210	230	180
Total original income	2,310	6,450	14,710	24,220	44,780	18,490
Plus benefits in cash						
Contributory	1,990	2,340	1,840	1,130	720	1,600
Non-contributory	2,780	2,460	1,520	830	370	1,590
Gross income	7,080	11,250	18,070	26,180	45,870	21,690
Less income tax and NIC	320	960	2,570	4,690	9,880	3,680
Less local taxes (net)	400	490	610	710	840	610
Disposable income	6,360	9,810	14,890	20,770	35,150	17,400
Less Indirect taxes	1,930	2,470	3,420	4,280	5,390	3,500
Post-tax income	4,430	7,340	11,470	16,490	29,760	13,900
Plus benefits in kind						
Education	1,700	1,210	1,180	1,010	620	1,140
National Health Service	1,970	1,890	1,730	1,450	1,260	1,660
Housing subsidy	90	80	40	20	–	50
Travel subsidies	50	60	70	80	140	80
School meals and welfare milk	80	20	10	–	–	20
Final income	8,310	10,600	14,490	19,040	31,790	16,850

Source: 'Social Trends 29', Office for National Statistics, 1999 © Crown Copyright 2000

people on benefit. People who are earning are mainly found in the top 60 per cent. People in the lower half of earners tend to be those with an average wage, or two low wages; people in the upper half have either above average income or two incomes.

- The distribution of income shown here does not reveal the distribution of income by class. There may be class inequalities concealed by the broad averages.
- Income is only one of the criteria by which welfare is judged. Wealth is important; so is command over resources, which is the ability to draw on resources when in need.

Having said this, the figures in the table do seem to show that:

- the distribution of income is more equal than it is commonly thought to be;
- the social services do play a major part in redressing the balance;
- even where people in higher income groups receive more in cash terms from welfare services than people in lower income groups (as in health or education), the service is worth proportionately more to people on low incomes.

O'Higgins (1985) argues that, even if the allocation of benefits is not equal, universal benefits help to create equality by offering a basis of social protection for everyone.

Conclusion

Titmuss (1968, pp. 22–3) argued that distributive analysis was fundamental to an understanding of many social problems and policies; it is one of the central approaches which students of social policy need to consider. Although examining distributive effects calls for a distinct set of skills – much of the source material is drawn from economics – the kind of reasoning called for is fairly typical of much in the study of social policy. An understanding of process – the details of how systems work – can help to identify why and how certain outcomes are produced. Understanding process is not, however, essential; some studies, notably the Luxembourg Income Study, have used a 'black box' technique, making very effective international comparisons entirely on the basis of outcomes (Smeeding et al., 1990; Mitchell, 1991). Considering distributive issues begins, in most cases, with an examination of the effects of policy, rather than with its aims or methods.

Issues to Consider

- Does inequality of income matter more than inequality of wealth?
- Why do women have lower incomes than men?
- Which is fairest: taxes on income, taxes on wealth or taxes on expenditure?
- What are the distributive effects of pensions?
- Has the 'strategy of equality' failed?

Suggestions for Further Reading

The most extensive, accessible discussion of the distribution of income in the UK is provided by the Joseph Rowntree Foundation (1995) in its *Inquiry into Income and Wealth*, while Goodman et al. (1997) provide a more technical discussion of the issues. If you want to explore further, Pickvance (1999) offers an excellent introduction to the distributive implications of policy, while Wilkinson (1996) provides a challenging account of distributional issues in health care. Current data and coverage of ongoing debates on poverty and inequality generally can be accessed through a wide range of websites. The most useful are:

- Institute for Fiscal Studies: www1.ifs.org.uk – the IFS frequently considers the distributive impact of policy, placing press releases on the web;
- LSE Distributional Analysis Research Programme: www.sticerd.lse.ac. uk/publications/wspdps.asphttp://www.sticerd.lse.ac.uk/publications/darp.asp – this site offers downloadable pamphlets, varying from some very accessible 'think-pieces' to highly technical econometrics;
- Luxembourg Income Study: lissy.ceps.lu/access.htm – a major source of data on the distribution and redistribution of income in different countries;
- Department of Social Security: www.dss.gov.uk/asd/online.html – which provides summary information from the annual statistical series: this describes the position of households in the lowest parts of the income distribution;
- Office for National Statistics: www.ons.gov.uk.

References

Atkinson, A. 1993: *What is Happening to the Distribution of Income in the UK?* London: LSE/STICERD.

Box, S. 1987: *Recession, Crime and Punishment*. London: Macmillan.

Cantillon, S. and Nolan, B. 1998: Are married women more deprived than their husbands? *Journal of Social Policy*, 27(2), 151–72.

Charvet, J. 1983: The idea of equality as a substantive principle of society. In W. Letwin (ed.), *Against Equality*. London: Macmillan.

Cmnd. 9714, 1986: *Paying for Local Government*. London: HMSO.

Cowell, F. 1995: *Measuring Inequality*. Hemel Hempstead: Prentice-Hall.

Dennis, N. 1997: *The Invention of Permanent Poverty*. London: IEA Health and Welfare Unit.

Department of Health and Social Security 1980: *Report of the Working Group on Inequalities in Health (The Black Report)*. London: HMSO.

Garfinkel, I. and McLanahan, S. 1988: The feminisation of poverty. In D. Tomaskovic-Devey (ed.), *Poverty and Social Welfare in the United States*. Boulder, Colo.: Westview Press.

Goodman, A., Johnson, P. and Webb, S. 1997: *Inequality in the UK*. Oxford: Oxford University Press.

Gordon, D. and Pantazis, C. (eds) 1997: *Breadline Britain in the 1990s*. Aldershot: Avebury.

Gordon, D. and Spicker, P. (eds) 1999: *The International Glossary on Poverty*. London: Zed Books.

Hayek, F. 1976: *Law, Legislation and Liberty,* vol.2: *The Mirage of Social Justice.* London: Routledge & Kegan Paul.

Hills, J. 1995: *Joseph Rowntree Inquiry into Income and Wealth,* vol 2. York: Joseph Rowntree Foundation.

Jarvis, S. and Jenkins, S. 1998: Income and poverty dynamics in Great Britain. In L. Leisering and R. Walker (eds), *The Dynamics of Modern Society.* Bristol: Policy Press.

Joseph Rowntree Foundation 1995: *Inquiry into Income and Wealth,* vols 1 and 2. York: Joseph Rowntree Foundation.

Lampard, R. 1994: An examination of the relationship between marital dissolution and unemployment. In D. Gallie, C. Marsh and C. Vogler (eds), *Social Change and the Experience of Unemployment.* Oxford: Oxford University Press.

Layard, R., Piachaud, D. and Stewart, M. 1978: *The Causes of Poverty,* Royal Commission on the Distribution of Income and Wealth Background Paper no. 6. London: HMSO.

Le Grand, J. 1982: *The Strategy of Equality.* London: Allen & Unwin.

Lewis, J. and Piachaud, D. 1992: Women and poverty in the twentieth century. In C. Glendinning and J. Millar, *Women and Poverty in Britain in the 1990s.* London: Harvester Wheatsheaf.

Millar, J. and Glendinning, C. 1989: Gender and poverty. *Journal of Social Policy,* 18 (3), 363–81.

Mitchell, D. 1991: *Income Transfers in Ten Welfare States.* Aldershot: Avebury.

O'Higgins, M. 1985: Welfare, redistribution and inequality – disillusion, illusion and reality. In P. Bean, J. Ferris and D. Whynes (eds), *In Defence of Welfare.* London: Tavistock.

O'Higgins, M. and Jenkins, S. 1990: Poverty in the EC: 1975, 1980, 1985. In R. Teekens and B. van Praag (eds), *Analysing Poverty in the European Community,* Eurostat News Special Edition 1-1990. Luxembourg: European Communities.

Office for National Statistics 1999: *Social Trends 29.* London: ONS.

Payne, S. 1991: *Women, Health and Poverty.* London: Harvester Wheatsheaf.

Pen, I. 1971: *Income Distribution.* London: Allen Lane.

Pickvance, C. 1999: The impact of social policy. In J. Baldock, N. Manning, S. Miller and S. Vickerstaff (eds), *Social Policy.* Oxford: Oxford University Press.

Social Trends 1999: at www.ons.gov.uk.

Smeeding, T., O'Higgins, M. and Rainwater, L. 1990: *Poverty, Inequality and Income Distribution in Comparative Perspective.* Hemel Hempstead: Harvester Wheatsheaf.

Tawney, R. 1964. *Equality.* London: Unwin.

Titmuss, R. 1968: *Commitment to Welfare.* London: Allen & Unwin.

Townsend, P., Davidson, N. and Whitehead, M. 1982: *Inequalities in Health,* revised edn. Harmondsworth: Penguin.

Townsend, P., Davidson, N. and Whitehead, M. 1988: *Inequalities in Health,* revised edn. Harmondsworth: Penguin.

Wilkinson, R. 1996: *Unhealthy Societies: The Afflictions of Inequality.* London: Routledge.

World Bank 1999: *World Development Report 1998/99: Knowledge for Development.* Oxford: Oxford University Press.

Health

Chapter 10

Health Inequalities

Helen Jones

Introduction

Health is intimately related to our sense of well-being and the quality of our lives. Illness and early death not only affect individuals and families but also the whole of society not least in terms of economic costs, such as days lost at work and the funding of the NHS. Policies to reduce inequalities in health should, therefore, be a high priority. In order to develop appropriate and effective policies the causes of health inequalities need to be clearly identified. This chapter, reflecting the research and debate in the field, draws on British and comparative studies to discuss:

- class-related inequalities in health;
- gender inequalities;
- ethnic inequalities;
- spatial inequalities;
- the problematic and contested nature of much of the evidence on which debates about inequalities in health are based;
- the policy implications of health inequalities;
- the current government's strategy for combating health inequalities.

Health Inequalities and Socio-economic Circumstances

Since the mid-nineteenth century an accumulation of evidence has pointed to a relationship between death rates on the one hand and male occupations, overcrowding, poor areas and insanitary conditions on the other. Evidence has also grown of a link between high illness rates, high death rates and poverty (Macintyre, 1997). Since 1911 evidence of the relationship between social

Box 10.1: Occupations and social class

	Social class	Type of occupation
I	professional	doctors, accountants
II	managerial and technical	teachers, journalists
IIIN	non-manual skilled	clerks, shop assistants
IIIM	manual skilled	van drivers, cooks
IV	semi-skilled	farm workers, security guards
V	unskilled	labourers, cleaners

class (as defined by occupation) and death rates has been available from the decennial census. The definition of 'class', however, is complex and a matter of dispute (see Donnison's chapter). It can be defined according to a number of yardsticks, which may include occupation, income, level of education, type of home and now even car ownership. For the purposes of health analysis, class has traditionally been defined according to one indicator alone, that used by the Registrar-General – occupation. Until recently the Registrar-General divided occupations, and therefore classes, into five categories; the first two are middle class, the bottom three working class (see box 10.1).

Defining class by occupation is a crude way of conveying a complex set of social and economic circumstances, and the inadequacy of the definition is made worse by the fact that over the years certain occupations have been moved from one class to another. More importantly, married women automatically appear in the same classes as their husbands. The limitations of this classification notwithstanding, it is still widely used as a means of exploring differences in people's life chances and the incidence of ill-health.

The continuing significance of class-related inequalities in health have been extensively documented, most notably by two government-commissioned reports, the Black Report (Department of Health and Social Security, 1980) and the Acheson Report (Acheson, 1998). The former highlighted the close links between people's socio-economic characteristics and their standards of health and life expectancy. Eighteen years on, the latter provided convincing evidence not only of continuing disparities in health but of how these had become more marked. In terms of morbidity rates Acheson reported a steep class-related health gradient. In nearly every disease from stroke to lung cancer, including mental health, differences between individuals from the highest and lowest social groups were significant. For instance, the likelihood of having a long-standing illness among men aged 44–64 runs from 17 per cent among those in professional occupations to 48 per cent among the unskilled. Among women of the same age 25 per cent of those in professional employment and 45 per cent of unskilled workers reported a long-term illness.

Variations in mortality rates remained substantial. Death rates have fallen in the last two decades, the chances of dying before the age of retirement having fallen faster among the higher social classes. At the beginning of the 1970s, for instance, the mortality rate among men of working age in the lowest social class was twice as high as that among men in the highest social class. By the end of the century, reflecting the faster decline in mortality rates among upper social groups, it was three times higher. Like many earlier studies the Acheson report also pointed to other long-established inequalities in health standards, and it is to these that we now turn.

Gender and Health Inequalities

Throughout the twentieth century females generally outlived males. As well as differences in death rates, women and men have different experiences of illness and disability. Boys have more long-standing illness than girls until adolescence, when the pattern is reversed; boys are also more likely than girls to have a spell in hospital. Among adults (as Prior demonstrates later in this section), women experience worse mental health than men, but men suffer more from alcohol and drug dependency. Women also have higher rates of disability than men, especially as they get older (Acheson, 1998, pp. 100–10).

Differences exist between women and men in their day-to-day living. Women tend to eat more healthily than men and drink less alcohol, but the decline in men's smoking habits in recent years means that women and men now have roughly equal levels of tobacco addiction. Women tend to be involved in less physical activity than men, to be more socially isolated, to have greater unpaid caring responsibilities, to be in a less favourable position in the labour market (in terms of pay, autonomy and other benefits) and to be less likely to receive contributory benefits and occupational pensions (Acheson, 1998).

There is also evidence, going back many years, that women and men experience socio-economic circumstances and poverty differently. Studies since the 1930s have demonstrated that women bear the brunt of poverty, and that this in turn affects their health. Even within the same family, women – by prioritizing the needs of other family members, undertaking the day-to-day unpaid household tasks (including shopping on a low budget) and caring (including looking after others when they are ill), as well as, in some cases, paid work – endured the worst health (Jones, 1994). Research in the 1980s again brought to light the extent to which women suffer disproportionately from poverty (Glendinning and Millar, 1987). On the face of it then, women, though having a longer life expectancy than men, suffer more ill health during their lifetimes. While most studies recognize these differences, there is a profound disagreement about how the data should be interpreted; for instance:

- Women report more illness to GPs than men, but traditionally women have been responsible for taking their children to the GPs, thus gaining opportunities to voice their own health problems. Men in contrast have had to take time off work, and this deterrent may account for some of the differences between their health status and that of women.

- The Victorian images of women as frail and sickly and men as fit and hearty continue to affect women and men's willingness to recognize and admit to illness. Doctors appear more ready to diagnose women as ill, especially as mentally ill.
- Women's stresses and strains are possibly manifested more through illness, whereas men's come out in violence and drinking.

Some recent studies suggest that when reproduction-related reasons for women visiting doctors and obtaining health care are removed, gender differences in ill-health largely disappear. So, can we dismiss apparent differences between men's and women's standards of health? Not quite:

- It is wholly artificial to remove women's reproductive role from the picture. Although a number of women have criticized the increasing medicalization of women's natural functions, none the less women's reproductive organs are more complex than men's, and do create more health-related problems. There is no getting away from the fact that it is women who become pregnant, who run the risk of complications, who give birth and who have to suffer the consequences of unwanted pregnancies.
- Women are possibly 'iller' than men because they live more stressful lives. Many face the double burden of paid and unpaid work, while, as has already been suggested, there is evidence that they suffer a higher incidence of poverty; links between poverty and ill-health are well known.
- In the first half of the twentieth century health services and financial support during sickness were largely geared towards men; their provision in the second half of the century too has frequently been criticized as inappropriate for meeting women's needs, and this has affected their standard of health (Jones, 1994).

If the evidence suggested that there were no differences between women and men's experiences of health and illness, then the failure to measure women's health and illness, as distinct from men's, may not appear problematic. Hiding women in the male statistics, however, is misleading because it undervalues gender differences and, as we know that women's and men's experiences of health are not the same, it is important to measure them both as accurately as possible. In recent years feminist scholars have attempted to create more robust measures of women's socio-economic circumstances. These indicate that women in manual occupations, women living in rented accommodation and women with no access to a car suffer high mortality rates. When women suffer from a combination of these disadvantages, their death rate is 2 to 3 times higher than those for women in non-manual occupations and with access to a car (Graham 1990, p. 201). Women living in the most disadvantaged circumstances are also likely to behave in a less healthy way – in terms of diet, exercise, alcohol consumption and smoking – than women in more socially and economically advantaged situations.

Class Gap Widening, Gender Gap Closing

As mentioned earlier, in most cases mortality has declined faster among the better off than among the poorer sections of society, and thus class differentials remain at least as large as they were in the past (Dorling, 1999; see also the *Daily Telegraph* for 28 April 1999 and the *Guardian* for 2 December 1999). In the 1970s and 1980s worsening inequalities were the result not only of differential rates of improved health and longevity for all sections of the population, but also of an absolute increase in death rates for certain diseases among poorer people. In one area, the infant mortality rate (death in first year of life) differences declined, following a successful campaign to target the health needs of the poorest babies. This success provided evidence that it was possible to devise policies to reduce health inequalities.

Gender differences in life expectancy, so consistent throughout the century, are now plummeting. In 1987 there was a four-and-a-half-year gap in life expectancy between women and men; by 1999 women could expect to outlive men by only three years. So, over the decade a woman's life expectancy at the age of 35 has risen from 84 years and seven months to 88 years and one month, while a man aged 35 can now expect to live to the age of 85 years and one month, compared with the 1980s, when his life expectancy was only 80 years and one month. Men are catching up with women, probably as a result of the decline in smoking among men, better long-term care and improved medical technology, such as heart bypasses (see *The Times* for 25 July 1999).

Ethnicity and Health Inequalities

Even more problematic than class or gender differences are ethnic inequalities. There is no agreed definition of ethnicity, but it is commonly seen as composed of one's cultural identity, place of origin and, for some people, skin colour. There are three main problems in discussing ethnic inequalities in health:

- British information on mortality relates to immigrants to Britain rather than to ethnic origin (Acheson, 1998).
- The way people are assigned to a particular ethnic group is rather crude, and this often means that very specific statements are made based on general or woolly information, and that the particular experiences of numerous ethnic groups are lost in categories that are too broad. Until recently Irish people in Britain were subsumed under one miscellaneous category of 'white', yet, as Kelleher's chapter shows, they suffer systematically from some of the worst health conditions of any group in Britain (Harding and Maxwell, 1997).

- While there is no single influence on standards of health, and people cannot be analysed exclusively in terms of their class, their gender or their ethnicity, research into ethnicity has been conducted with only limited reference to class or gender. There is also less research on ethnicity and health than on class or gender and health, although in recent years more information has appeared (see, for instance, Ahmed, 1993; Nazroo, 1997).

Yet the evidence suggests that death rates from almost all causes, for all groups of immigrants with the exception of those from the Caribbean, is higher than average. It would be interesting to know whether those whose parents and grandparents emigrated to Britain continue to die younger than the average ethnic Briton. Overall, ethnic minority groups are more likely to describe their health as fair or poor than the majority of the population. Bangladeshis and Pakistanis have the highest rates of self-reported illness. Apart from Chinese and African Asians all ethnic groups consult their GPs more than white people. Among the latter, the Irish have the highest death and illness rates (Acheson, 1998, pp. 92–4).

Why do ethnic minority groups, including immigrants, have higher mortality and morbidity rates than white people and the indigenous population? The oldest explanation blames the genes of particular ethnic groups for poor health. This assumes that genetic diseases are the cause of the differences between ethnic groups, but there is no evidence to support this assumption, and while in highly specific and unusual cases there is a link between ethnicity and disease, it is too rare to act as an adequate explanation.

A second explanation assumes that the cultures of ethnic groups, for instance their diet, are the cause of differences. This assumes that if members of different ethnic minority groups changed their lifestyles to the lifestyle of the majority, then their standards of health would improve: the explanation and blame rest with the members of the ethnic minority groups themselves. Again, there is no strong evidence to support this view.

Third, it has been argued that the society in which ethnic minorities live makes them more prone to illness. This operates in two related ways. Racism exists throughout society, including the NHS, where it manifests itself in conscious and unconscious discrimination. Discrimination interacts with wider socio-economic inequalities. Many ethnic minorities have poorer health because they are among the poorer sections of society, in terms of income, education and total resources; discrimination and racism aggravate their poorer health. In addition, as Kelleher's discussion indicates, the experience of immigration can also affect people's health.

Spatial Inequalities

In Britain, people in the poorest areas have death rates which are – age for age – three times as high as those for people in the richest areas!

Wilkinson, 1998, p. 3

Class and ethnic inequalities, poverty and deprivation are reflected in inequalities in health between different areas: wealthier areas are healthier than poorer areas. Areas of different sizes have been analysed: Scotland is less healthy than England; Glasgow is the least healthy city, and Wokingham in Berkshire the most healthy town. Analyses by constituency and even by postcode show health inequalities (Wilkinson, 1996). Since the 1930s governments have, at different times, developed area-based anti-poverty policies; currently, for instance, the Health Action Zones initiative has been set up to develop policies for the least healthy areas. Area-based policies, however, are a blunt instrument for targeting the most needy: in poor areas there will be pockets of wealthier residents, while some poorer people will live in wealthy areas and miss out on such policies.

The UK's Experience Compared

Comparing inequalities in Britain over time and in different areas as well as with other Western countries demonstrates that existing patterns of socio-economic inequalities in health and illness are not inevitable. Also, by looking at other countries, Britain can pick up useful tips about the successes and failures of policies in tackling inequalities.

It is, however, very difficult to compare like with like, because countries collect their data differently. In Russia, for instance, a country with an appallingly high death rate, death certificates and census data are not linked. Much of the comparative information is partial and not very up to date. While numerous cross-national studies show links between socio-economic circumstances, class and deprivation on the one hand and health, illness and death on the other hand, definitions of many of these categories vary. Nevertheless, it is clear that inequalities in standards of health, linked to socio-economic circumstances, exist in all industrialized countries.

Class inequalities in long-term illnesses are less in England and Wales than in Sweden, and the inequalities in death rates for 35–44 year-olds are starker in Finland than in England and Wales. England and Wales experience greater inequalities in mortality rates than Denmark, Norway and Sweden, but smaller inequalities than Finland and much smaller than France. Patterns for women are not consistent between health indicators, but the biggest inequalities are in Italy, Spain, Canada and the USA. Self-reported illness among men is lowest in the UK, Norway, Sweden and Spain, intermediate in Denmark and Finland and highest in Italy, Germany, Canada and the USA (Macintyre, 1997, p. 735).

Wilkinson's arguments (1996) may help to explain why inequalities exist between apparently similar countries, as well as why they exist within countries. He suggests that standards of health in affluent societies are influenced less by people's absolute standards of living than by their standards of living relative to those of others in their society. Inequalities and hierarchies create psychosocial pressures which undermine rather than enhance standards of health.

Improvements in health will not therefore come from tinkering with a country's health-care system, but from reducing relative deprivation and promoting a more equitable distribution of resources. The reasons why health inequalities exist within countries, however, are contested. Six possible explanations are set out in the next section, followed by their policy implications.

Inequalities in Health Explained

Artefact   The methods employed to measure occupational class differences are unsound and have misleadingly inflated the extent of health inequalities. Changes in the classifications of occupations have altered over the years so that evidence of class-related trends is flawed. Information about the occupations of the deceased are taken from death certificates, which give only the most recent occupation. A married woman's certificate states only her husband's occupation, which in itself is misleading and even more so if she has been widowed for some time. Inaccurate information from death certificates is then put together with evidence from the decennial census of the numbers of people in each occupational class. Over the years membership of the Registrar-General's class V has shrunk and the other classes widened, as people have moved up the class scale, and the proportion of the middle class to the working class has grown. Those who argue that inequalities have not declined fail to take class mobility into account. Many calculations are based on the mortality rates of males aged between 15 and 64, so that boys, older men and all females are excluded, which means that calculations, interpretations and explanations are based on the health experience of only a fraction of the population.

Notwithstanding all these problems, which are real enough and should act as a warning to us to treat other arguments with some caution, there is a good deal of cumulative evidence that death rates, and indeed illness rates, are closely related to socio-economic circumstances, and that class position is still a potent indicator of life chances.

Natural/social selection   Unhealthy people fall down the socio-economic ladder; thus their health determines their socio-economic position, not vice versa. There is some evidence to suggest that in certain cases, such as schizophrenia, this explanation holds good, but it cannot be taken as a main explanation.

Health services   When the NHS was created in the UK it was assumed that a comprehensive service free at the point of use would improve the standard of health of the whole population, and especially that of the least well off. When this was found not to be the case research focused on the different uses made of the health service, the quality of treatment received and the attention health workers paid to patients of different social classes. Most of the research indicated that those people with a higher standard of living made most use of preventive services, such as screening programmes, antenatal care, vaccinations and family planning, and received more attentive service from staff. Similar differences have been found in other European countries. The number of variables we need to take into account when we explain these different rates, however, means that the use of health care is only one factor among many, and cannot on its own explain the differences in illness and death rates (Macintyre, 1989).

Behavioural/cultural   Culture, the attitudes and behaviour of individuals, families and groups, is often held to be responsible for inequalities in standards of health. Those who eat a healthy diet, take physical exercise and do not live risky lifestyles are healthier than those who eat unhealthily, fail to take enough exercise and run risks with their health. As a disproportionate amount of illness and early death is found in the lower socio-economic groups, it is argued that those with a lower standard of living behave in a more unhealthy way than the better off, either through a lack of awareness of healthy behaviour or through recklessness.

There are, however, various problems with this argument. First, it is not entirely clear what constitutes a 'healthy diet', as new food risks and scares continue to appear, and experts argue over the definition. While some groups may take less exercise through sports, they may exert more physical energy at work, or they may lack access to sports facilities. The extent to which people in poor material circumstances can improve their standards of health solely by changing their behaviour has been challenged by Blaxter (1990), who argues that unhealthy behaviour does not reinforce disadvantage as much as healthy behaviour increases advantages. Thus, those who already live the most materially privileged lives will benefit from a healthy lifestyle far more than those with the fewest material resources.

Materialist/structuralist   Some writers argue that inequalities in standards of health are the result of broader socio-economic divisions. Those lower down the class scale are exposed to worse hazards at work and have less control over their work; they are more subject to irregular employment and unemployment. They live in worse housing and in environments that are more polluted and physically unsafe. They have fewer personal resources to draw on to help them over periods of crisis. Daily life is more difficult and stressful and leads to poorer health.

The interplay between different factors   Health inequalities are not the result of a single cause but reflect the interaction of different influences. This argument has been put most cogently by Blackburn (1991), who argued that resources and behaviour interact and cannot be separated. Poorer people have fewer material resources and suffer more health hazards, which affect their physical health, and in turn their emotional health and behaviour. They experience more stressful life events, and a lack of physical resources makes them harder to resolve. Money brings choice and the means to resolve such pressures; people without the financial and emotional resources to deal with them are more likely to resort to unhealthy behaviour, such as smoking, alcohol and comfort food in order to cope. Physical resources and behaviour interact. For Blackburn behaviour does not take place in a social vacuum, and health differences require a multi-dimensional explanation. This explanation is also the view favoured by the Black Report into Inequalities in Health (Department of Health and Social Security, 1980; Townsend et al., 1982; 1988) and by the Acheson Inquiry into Health Inequalities (Acheson, 1998).

Policy Implications

As Box 10.2 indicates these differing approaches have varying implications for policy making.

Artefact   No action is necessary as the population's standard of living is improving, and inequalities are insignificant.

Natural/social selection   If those in poorest health sink to the bottom of the class pile, financial and social support should be given to them so that they can maintain their standard of living and social status. This approach has far-reaching consequences, because it entails not only financial and physical support for those with long-term illnesses and disabilities but also campaigns to change popular perceptions about various types of illness and disability which carry a social stigma.

Health services   All UK governments have supported the NHS, but they have all found it difficult to switch resources from richer to poorer regions, and from curative and high-technology medicine to public health, community care and preventive services.

Behavioural/cultural   If ill-health is the result of unhealthy behaviour, the answer is to develop health education programmes targeted at the people with the most unhealthy habits. This is harder to do than might seem, because it is usually the case that those with the poorest health are the least likely to respond to such campaigns, and those who are already healthy will adopt the latest government advice. Such a pattern of reaction has the effect of increasing inequalities rather than decreasing them. The other side of the coin is to reduce the volume of unhealthy propaganda that bombards us all every day, but with huge sums spent on advertising goods such as cigarettes, alcohol and sugary or fatty food and drink, this is a highly problematic process (see Huby's chapter).

Box 10.2: Explanations for health inequalities and policy implications

Explanation	*Policy implications*
1 Artefact	Do nothing.
2 Natural/social selection	Improve the employment opportunities and resources of those with long-standing illnesses.
3 Health services	Allocate more resources to the NHS; provide services more sensitive to the needs of the least healthy.
4 Behavioural/ cultural	Establish targeted health education programmes to change the attitudes and behaviour of the least healthy; clamp down on unhealthy advertising campaigns of food, drink and tobacco companies.
5 materialist/ structuralist	At its most extreme, overthrow the capitalist system; short of that, institute policies (education, housing, income maintenance, transport, environment and employment) to modify the economy and society, in order to promote the health of the most socially and economically disadvantaged.
6 The interplay between different factors	Enable individuals, families and communities to adopt more healthy lifestyles, supported by the policies under 3, 4 and 5.

Materialist/structuralist   Modifying the ill-effects of an unequal society has profound implications for government policies. It would involve a reallocation of resources and a more equitable distribution between individuals, communities and regions.

The interplay between different factors   This requires 'joined-up' government policies which direct health service, health education and material resources to the most deprived.

Policy Responses and Issues

Over the last two decades government responses to these different approaches and policy options have varied considerably. In very broad terms, however, Conservative governments have tended to view differences in health standards in individualistic, behavioural terms rather than in structural terms. Labour's stance, in contrast, has been more wide-ranging. These differences are well illustrated by the divergent fates of the Black and Acheson Reports. Commissioned by the Labour government, which then fell from power, the former was famously published in limited numbers on a public holiday and was then republished independently (Townsend et al., 1988). The government, however, continued to focus on its broader policy of raising health standards by reorganizing the NHS and by a stream of health education and promotion measures designed to persuade individuals to adopt healthier lifestyles. The issue of health inequalities failed to permeate central government and dropped off the political agenda (Acheson, 1998).

The Labour Party, in contrast, returned to office in 1997 with a commitment to tackle health inequalities (Labour Party, 1997, p. 21). It has focused attention on:

- public health;
- prevention;
- local initiatives, which include Health Action Zones: people living in these areas are among the most deprived and disadvantaged in the country and enjoy the worst health. The aim of Health Action Zones is to develop strategies in these areas to reduce inequalities in health over a seven-year period.
- new partnerships between the NHS, local governments, voluntary organizations and the business sector to improve health locally.

In addition all new government policies were to be subjected to new 'health impact assessments' and health was to be at the heart of policy making across government departments. Reducing health inequalities, however, is only one of the government's priorities; its other health policies include reducing waiting lists for hospital treatment and strengthening the relationship between the NHS and the private sector. These concerns may or may not be compatible with reducing inequalities, and it will be difficult to ensure that policies which improve standards of health overall also reduce inequalities. As the government does not have targets for reducing class inequalities in standards of health, there are no agreed goals against which we may judge the success of its policies.

Reducing health inequalities requires an integrated approach, as so many aspects of our lives affect our health, and this makes the problem more difficult to tackle. The Minister for Public Health supports small-scale healthy eating projects in deprived areas, but these efforts are dwarfed by the advantage that the better-off enjoy of supermarkets with a wide range of healthy, fresh, organic produce situated in relatively affluent areas, to which the poorest do not have easy access. A very large number of vested interests present arguments against the most radical policies; an early example of this came in the autumn of 1997, when the government agreed to exempt Formula 1 motor racing from the ban on tobacco advertising; a subsequent EU compromise means that the ban will be phased in over a number of years. The government is committed to a 'joined-up' approach, but there is a deep-seated Whitehall culture of developing policies in discrete departments, at times in rivalry with others.

Inequalities in health, which are a reflection of wider social and economic differences, are a significant problem, which cannot be solved alone by economic growth and rising standards of living. The fact that health differences fluctuate between countries and over time, however, indicates that a goal of reduced inequalities is achievable. Policies to achieve this goal are within the realms of political possibility, because they do not have to be pursued at the expense of other social goals: policies for education, employment, housing, the environment and transport are all part of a strategy to reduce inequalities in health. The social problems, which are reflected in health inequalities, and contribute to them, are now well recognized. Whereas at one time governments regarded health inequalities as unproblematic and not requiring a governmental response, the government now regards them as a social problem, for which it is developing a range of social policies. These policies need to be carefully monitored for their effectiveness, and to ensure that policy changes and a reduction in health inequalities match the government's rhetoric and promises.

Issues to Consider

- Why do inequalities in standards of health constitute a social problem?
- When developing their health policies should governments prioritize reducing inequalities in health or raising standards of health overall?
- What can be learnt from a comparative approach to studying health inequalities that can be used for framing health policies in Britain?
- What sort of yardsticks would you want to use for judging the success of health policies? What are the problems involved in assessing the yardsticks you have chosen?
- Are Labour's social policies likely to reduce inequalities in health?

Suggestions for Further Reading

The various editions of the Black Report (Department of Health and Social Security, 1980; Townsend et al. 1982; 1988) provide an essential starting point for a consideration of the problems of class and health. The Acheson Report (Acheson, 1998) should be consulted for a summary of more recent findings and concerns. Both are essential reading, as is Wilkinson's (1996) analysis. Jones (1994) discusses the issues at greater length and puts them in the context of the whole of the twentieth century. You will also find many of the issues raised in this chapter discussed at greater length in the special issue of *Social Science and Medicine* (1997). More detailed coverage of specific forms of inequality can be found in Nazroo (1997) and Roberts (1992). The British government website relating to health inequalities, www.ohn.gov.uk/inequ.htm, is also worth exploring for up-to-date coverage of current concerns and policy initiatives. Further data can be obtained from the Office for National Statistics website: www.ons.gov.uk.

References

Acheson, D. 1998: *Independent Inquiry into Inequalities in Health*. London: Stationery Office.

Ahmed, W. 1993: *'Race' and Health in Contemporary Britain*. Milton Keynes: Open University Press.

Blackburn, C. 1991: *Poverty and Health: Working with Families*. Milton Keynes: Open University Press.

Blaxter, M. 1990: *Health and Lifestyles*. London: Routledge.

Department of Health and Social Security 1980: *Report of the Working Group on Inequalities in Health (The Black Report)*. London: HMSO.

Dorling, D. 1999: *The Widening Gap*. Bristol: Bristol University and Townsend Centre for International Poverty Research.

Glendinning, C. and Millar, J. 1987: *Women and Poverty in Britain*. Brighton: Harvester Wheatsheaf.

Graham, H. 1990: Behaving well: women's health behaviour in context. In H. Roberts (ed.), *Women's Health Counts*. London: Routledge.

Harding, S. and Maxwell, R. 1997: Differences in mortality in migrants. In F. Drever and M. Whitehead (eds), *Health Inequalities*. London: Office for National Statistics.

Jones, H. 1994: *Health and Society in Twentieth-century Britain*. London: Longman.

Labour Party 1997: *New Labour: Because Britain Deserves Better*. London: Labour Party.

Macintyre, S. 1989: The role of health services in relation to inequalities in health in Europe. In J. Fox (ed.), *Health Inequalities in European Countries*. Aldershot: Gower.

Macintyre, S. 1997: The Black Report and beyond: what are the issues? *Social Science and Medicine*, 44 (6), 723–45.

Nazroo, J. 1997: *The Health of Britain's Ethnic Minorities*. London: Policy Studies Institute.

Roberts, H. (ed.) 1992: *Women's Health Matters*. London: Routledge.

Social Science and Medicine 1997, 44 (6), special issue.

Townsend, P., Davidson, N. and Whitehead, M. 1982: *Inequalities in Health*, revised edn. Harmondsworth: Penguin.

Townsend, P., Davidson, N. and Whitehead, M. 1988: *Inequalities in Health*, revised edn. Harmondsworth: Penguin.

Wilkinson, R. 1996: *Unhealthy Societies*. London: Routledge.

Wilkinson, R. 1998: Unhealthy societies: how inequality kills. *Sociology Review*, 7 (4), 2–5.

Chapter 11

Mental Disorder

Pauline Prior

Introduction

Words such as 'crazy', 'mad', 'a bit of a lunatic' are all part of our everyday vocabulary. We use them to describe our friends, when they are over-excited, and ourselves, when we fall in love. They conjure up a picture of behaviour that is not completely rational, not completely acceptable and, sometimes, illegal and slightly dangerous. What is interesting about these words is that they can be used either in an affectionate way – to describe our friends who are acting a little out of character – or in a pejorative way – to describe strangers who commit violent acts. The dual use of these words in our personal vocabularies is reflected in the media – headlines can range from 'crazy in love' to 'mad murderer' – and derives from the ambivalence with which society views this area of human life. In this chapter, I hope to introduce you to some of the principal issues of concern to policy makers in relation to this very complex area of life. We shall cover the following topics:

- changing approaches to mental disorder;
- the problem explained – the vulnerable population;
- society's response – mental health policies;
- a look into the future.

Changing Approaches to Mental Disorder

Language reveals a great deal about society's perception of and response to mental disorder, both of which are constantly changing. In the nineteenth century, it was referred to as madness, insanity or lunacy, the legislation was in the form of lunacy laws, and the service structure was composed of a network of publicly funded lunatic asylums and privately funded mad-houses. For most of the twentieth century, the language used has been that of medicine and health, madness being referred to as mental illness, the legislation formulated as mental health law, and the service structure composed of a network of health services (including hospitals and community services). As we begin a new century, the language is changing again, mainly arising from questions about the adequacy of the medical model either to describe or to deal with the range of problems related to mental health and its absence. The term 'mental disorder' is now used more widely than mental illness, mental health laws are under constant review, and the service structure includes not only health services, but employment and housing services, and a strongly anti-psychiatry consumer movement.

It is clear from this brief summary of the development of the social view of mental disorder that, in spite of changes to definitions and approaches, it has been recognized for a long time as a social problem requiring government intervention. This is because it clearly affects not only the individual but also the society in which he or she lives – the individual has to be protected from exploitation and unnecessary medical treatment, and society has to be protected from individuals who may be dangerous. Mental health laws throughout the world reflect these two concerns. People who are diagnosed as having a serious mental illness and are seen as being a risk either to themselves or to others can be admitted to hospital for treatment on a compulsory basis. This is considered being good not only for the individual who requires treatment but has not sought it on a voluntary basis (as is the case with most illnesses), but also for his or her family and friends and for the general public, who might be in danger from the individual (for the exact criteria for admission in England and Wales, see the Mental Health Act 1983; for a discussion on laws in Europe and the United States, see Prior, 1999, pp. 138–57).

In addition to enacting mental health legislation, which attempts to protect both the individual and society, all governments in the Western world provide services for people with mental disorders with similar aims in mind. Before the nineteenth century most people who showed any signs of mental disorder found themselves in the prison system. Later on, within the context of a growing belief that institutionalization was a way of dealing with the poor, the sick and the socially inadequate, a large number of publicly funded asylums opened to provide a more humane alternative to prison. Many of these establishments remained the main providers of services until the last quarter of the twentieth century. They were renamed and 'repackaged' as hospital services to be used in the same way as other hospital services. Now we have a situation in which many of these hospitals have closed, owing primarily to the anti-institution movement of the 1960s (Goffman, 1961; Szasz, 1961), and also to advances in medical treatment and to increasing pressures on health funding. The adequacy of current mental health services (community and hospital) is constantly being questioned and there is a growing demand for some reform of the law. In order to evaluate both the demands and the solutions, and explore some possible future trends, we shall look first at the size of this social problem and the shape and content of current responses.

The Problem Explained – the Vulnerable Population

The most comprehensive American study of mental health and mental disorder in the community in recent times – the *Epidemiologic Catchment Area Study (ECA)* – found that 32 per cent of all American adults had experienced one or more mental disorders at some time in their lives, and that 20 per cent had an active disorder – defined as having reported symptoms in the previous year (Robins and Regier, 1991). In other words, almost one in three people reported having had the experience, during their lifetime, of symptoms that corresponded to a psychiatric diagnosis, and one in five had experienced these symptoms recently. In England and Wales, one of the large-scale studies, which gives some indication of the size of the problem, is *The Health and Lifestyle Survey*, a longitudinal study carried out in the mid-1980s and repeated in the early 1990s. This study found that 30 per cent of women and 25 per cent of men had reported symptoms consistent with a minor psychiatric illness (Cox et al., 1993). These proportions were much higher than expected, and the authors suggest that the finding should be treated with caution. However, it does show clearly that a substantial proportion of the population report mental health problems.

Studies throughout the Western world, including those already mentioned in the United States and the United Kingdom, show clear differences in the experience of mental disorder by gender, ethnicity and income (Beiser and Edwards, 1994; Belle, 1990; Nazroo, 1997; Prior, 1999). In other words, inequalities in health show up in relation to mental health as they do in relation to physical health. The most obvious differences are gender differences. Traditionally, women have reported higher levels of mental disorder and have been greater users of mental health services than men (for discussions, see Busfield, 1996; Showalter, 1987). This has been explained theoretically in either of two ways – according to a social causation model or to a social construction model of human experience. (For a further discussion of these issues, see the chapters by Page and Clarke.) Those who explain the higher visibility of women in psychiatric statistics in terms of social causation accept that women have more mental health problems than men and attribute this to the fact that women have harder lives than men (associated with the female roles of wife and mother, which are seen as oppressive and limiting). Research based on this approach points to higher levels of mental illness among women with large families, with no employment outside the home, and on low incomes (see, for example, Bebbington et al., 1991; Belle, 1990). On the other hand, the social construction theorists argue that the higher visibility of women in psychiatric statistics is a reflection not of a higher level of mental disorder among women but rather of a greater vulnerability to psychiatric diagnosis and treatment. Research based on this approach suggests that stereotypical notions of female behaviour (such as irrationality, impulsiveness or high levels of emotion) are embedded in diagnostic labels and in assumptions underpinning research and service development (see, for example, Busfield 1996; Ussher, 1991).

Of particular interest in relation to gender differences in mental health statistics is that the trends seem to be changing. Men are becoming more visible in statistics on both the experience and treatment of mental disorder. This is particularly the case in the United States, but it is also showing up in the United Kingdom. For example, the American *ECA* was the first large-scale study to find a higher lifetime prevalence of mental disorder in men than in women – 36 per cent of men and 30 per cent of women reporting symptoms which had occurred at some time during their lives. There was nothing mysterious about this. For the first time disorders associated more often with men (substance dependence and personality disorder) were included in the calculations in addition to the traditional conditions more often associated with women (anxiety and depression). Similar patterns are beginning to be reported in the United Kingdom, as young men, in particular, seem to be increasingly vulnerable to substance dependence (alcohol and drugs) and to attempted suicide (see, for example, Payne, 1996; Prior, 1999). As discussed already in relation to women, the increasing visibility of men in psychiatric statistics can be explained in terms of social causation or by social construction theories. Put more simply, we can ask the questions:

Box 11.1

- Are men's lives becoming increasingly difficult, thus causing higher levels of stress leading to mental health problems?
- Or, on the other hand, are men more likely than before to be diagnosed mentally ill owing to changing definitions of mental disorder?

Similar questions can be asked about the two other main factors, which are highly correlated to statistics on mental health, ethnicity and social class. People from certain ethnic groups and from lower socio-economic backgrounds are more likely than others to feature in psychiatric statistics. For example, in the United Kingdom, higher rates of psychosis and admission to hospital treatment have been consistently found among people of Caribbean origin (Nazroo, 1997; see also the chapter by Kelleher). In the United States, higher levels of psychiatric hospital admission have been found among young black men, but these have not been reflected in higher rates of psychiatric morbidity (the experience of mental disorder) in the community. As far as social class and income are concerned, studies throughout the Western world have shown a consistent inverse relation between wealth and mental disorder – for example, people from lower socio-economic groups show higher levels of schizophrenia, depression and substance dependence (Belle, 1990; Ezzy, 1993; Robins and Regier, 1991).

The questions to be asked are those we have put already in relation to ethnicity:

> ## Box 11.2
> • Are these people experiencing higher levels of mental disorder because of the disadvantages and social exclusion that they suffer?
> • Or, alternatively, are they more prone to be diagnosed and treated for mental disorder because of their perceived risk to society?

The answer is not simple, as one would expect. However, the evidence emerging from large-scale research on the experience of mental disorder in the community (psychiatric morbidity studies) indicates that the trends are not necessarily reflected in patterns of service use (see, for example, Robins and Regier, 1991). For instance, not everyone who experiences depression or drug dependence goes to a doctor – some groups of people are more likely to go than others, women more than men, educated people more than uneducated people, old people more than young people. Then, of those who go to the doctor, not everyone is diagnosed as having a mental disorder or is offered a particular form of treatment such as hospitalization. For example, symptoms associated with depression or schizophrenia are more likely to be recognized than symptoms associated with drug or alcohol dependence, young men are more likely than young women to be offered hospital treatment, educated people are more likely to be offered talking therapies than uneducated people (Perkins and Moodley, 1993; Prior, 1999; Robins and Regier, 1991). This means that patterns of service-use tell us more about the social response to mental disorder – articulated by the medical and legal systems – than about the experience itself. In the next section we look at some of these responses.

Society's Response – Mental Health Policies

When we think of mental health services we think, first, of hospital beds and then of community care services. We may also mention employment and housing projects for people who have been discharged from hospitals. These are the traditional services, which are more or less available to people with mental health problems. Other less well-known services are now emerging from the growing consumer/user movement of people who see themselves as 'survivors' of the psychiatric system (see Barnes and Shardlow, 1997; Hatfield and Lefley, 1993; Ramon, 1996). These include self-help employment projects and advocacy services.

Hospital care

Until quite recently, most treatment for mental disorder took place within institutional settings, usually psychiatric facilities with roots in the public asylums and private madhouses of the nineteenth century. In a century characterized by the expansion of state institutions to control all forms of social deviance, the Western world prided itself on the architectural splendour of the 'palaces' built for the poor – workhouses, prisons and asylums. Many of these 'palaces' have now been taken out of commission as hospitals, but the fact remains that for almost two centuries they were the only response to the problem of mental disorder in society.

In England and Wales, the number of psychiatric beds reached a peak of 155,000 in 1955, after which time it decreased steadily; by 1993 it had dropped to approximately 50,000 beds. Similarly, in the United States, psychiatric beds in publicly funded hospitals reached a peak of 558,900 in 1955, after which they decreased steadily, reaching 71,619 in 1994 (for sources and further discussion about these trends, see Prior, 1999, pp. 116–37). The American statistics have to be treated with some caution, as there has been an expansion in psychiatric beds in the private sector as well as an absorption of psychiatric patients into other facilities, such as nursing homes and hospitals for war veterans. However, it does appear that, regardless of how the statistics are compiled, the reduction in publicly funded psychiatric beds has been substantial and highly significant during the second half of the twentieth century in most developed countries. Hospital treatment is now only one form of treatment for people with mental disorders, and for many it is not the treatment of choice.

Of course, it would be a mistake to think that hospital treatment was the treatment of choice for people when it was the only form of treatment. Most people, then and now, regard psychiatric hospital treatment as stigmatizing and upsetting (see Millet, 1991). Until the 1960s, most people were admitted to psychiatric hospital on a compulsory basis. However, since then mental health policies have been geared to making it easier for people to receive treatment on a voluntary basis, and compulsory admissions to hospital treatment now constitute only about 10 per cent of total admissions in most European countries (Jensen, 1995; Ramon, 1996).

The process of treating a person in a psychiatric hospital without consent is the main reason for the existence of mental health legislation. Depriving people of their liberty when they have not committed a crime is a very serious action, which has to be strictly regulated. Mental health laws in most countries define the criteria for admission and treatment as follows:

- The person has a mental disorder.
- The absence of treatment would lead to deterioration in the person's mental state.
- The person presents a serious danger to himself or herself or to others.

Countries' procedures for verifying that these criteria are present vary. Some involve the medical profession only, some the medical and legal professions, and some the medical and social work professions. The current law in England and Wales, the Mental Health Act 1983, authorizes the medical and social work professions to make the decisions surrounding this very difficult issue. However, this law is under review, and it may be that England and Wales will follow the trend in other European countries to expand the role of the judiciary (judges, magistrates or the court). Other aspects of the law are also under review, as there are calls from some sectors for the legal authorization of compulsory drug treatment in the community, and from others for greater legal protection for the majority of patients who are receiving hospital treatment on a voluntary basis.

Community care

The trend during the past three decades towards a policy of care in the community, for people who had till then been cared for in institutions, may have its roots in the anti-psychiatry movement of the 1960s, but it was made possible by the availability of new and effective therapeutic drugs and spurred on by the cost-cutting health policies of the 1980s and 1990s. It is now possible for people with mental health problems to live in their own homes and communities while availing themselves of mental health services, which include out-patient clinics and day hospitals, crisis support services, such as drop-in centres, and individual counselling and therapy. They should also be able to use supported housing and employment projects.

In theory, at least, this is possible. In practice, however, the situation is far from ideal for most people. In England and Wales, for example, according to a report of the Audit Commission in the mid-1980s, there were only 9,000 day-centre places available or 32 per cent of the target set out in the 1975 White Paper *Better Services for the Mentally Ill*, and 17,000 day-hospital places or 17 per cent of the target number (Audit Commission, 1986; DHSS, 1975). The traditional day hospital provides the transition between in-patient living and living in the community, while the traditional day centre, run by either a social services department or an independent organization, serves as a form of daily respite for carers and a social club for people with mental disorders. Neither of these facilities is particularly attractive to young adults, who want to be more integrated into the larger community of work and leisure. There is anecdotal evidence that community-based services have expanded since the NHS and Community Care Act 1990, but it is very difficult to get accurate information about these services because of the growing diversity of providers in the health arena (see Lewis and Glennerster, 1996). It is likely that the quality and extent of community care varies greatly from region to region, depending on the interest of local authorities and the funding available. Unfortunately, the promise that the money that had been devoted in the past to hospital services would be transferred to community services has not been realized.

The United Kingdom, however, is not alone in this. Italy, which was the first European country to introduce (in 1978) a radical law making admission to a psychiatric hospital illegal (law 180), has been criticized by many for failing to meet its promise of providing adequate care in the community (see Samele,

1999). The situation is similar in the United States, where relatives and friends of people with mental illnesses accuse the government of deliberately withdrawing from mental health services and pushing the burden of care onto them, especially for people with chronic mental health problems (Kuipers, 1993).

However, that is not to say that the situation is worse for everyone than it was fifty years ago. It is not. Many people who would have been confined to hospital in the past are living quite happily either independently or in sheltered housing and attending day centres or sheltered workshops. Though not fully integrated into society, these people manage to live lives of much higher quality than could be achieved in a hospital setting.

But they are the lucky minority. For a significant number of mentally ill people, community care has failed. The evidence for the failure comes from statistics on homeless people and on prisoners. Studies carried out on these two groups of people have consistently shown much higher rates of mental disorder among them compared with the general population. For example, in the United States, of the 2.5 million people who were homeless in 1983, approximately one-third were found to suffer from a serious mental disorder (see Dear and Wolch, 1987). Studies in prisons have shown that, though the incidence of major mental disorders (depression, schizophrenia) is not higher among prisoners, personality disorders, substance dependence, and neurotic disorders are much more common than in the general population (for a discussion and sources, see Prior, 1999, pp. 129 and 156–63). What is not clear is which comes first – the mental disorder or the imprisonment. In other words, are people with mental disorders more likely to commit a crime and be imprisoned, or does imprisonment lead to a higher level of mental disorder?

Self-help organizations

There has been a great expansion in recent years in the number and size of self-help organizations, including groups initiated by existing or former users of psychiatric services, their relatives and friends. Some of them are linked to formal mental health services; others are completely independent. Some of these organizations aim to help the individual sufferer find a solution to and move on from his or her mental health problem – one of the best known examples of this is the world-wide organization Alcoholics Anonymous (AA). Others aim to give support to people who accept their condition as chronic – for example the National Schizophrenia Fellowship (NSF) in the United Kingdom and the National Alliance for the Mentally Ill (NAMI) in the United States.

The number of organizations run by and for service users has increased steadily in Europe and North America, as mental health services have shrunk and as many people lose faith in the medical model of mental health care. The rise has also coincided with a greater awareness of basic human rights and of citizenship rights by people who had previously taken for granted their exclusion from many social and economic opportunities. The range of user groups is wide. Older organizations, such as the Finnish Mental Health Association, founded in 1897, provide services to support existing mental health services – day centres, housing projects, leisure projects, rehabilitation and education. Newer organizations are much more influenced by the civil rights movement, and are involved in promoting individual and group resistance to the status quo. This is carried out largely through advocacy schemes and lobbying tactics aimed at bringing about changes in policies or services that infringe basic human rights. An example of the very important work in this area is the support of people who wish to take cases to the European Court of Human Rights. Some of the successful cases have clarified the right of prisoners in the United Kingdom to adequate mental health services, their right to privacy and to protection from undue personal interference for all, and the right to marriage and parenthood for those who wish to choose it.

However, though successful in some areas of life, user organizations are disappointed by their inability to make much impact on changes in policy direction. For example, although they are increasingly being asked to sit on committees to give their opinions on mental health services to NHS trusts, there is little evidence that this feedback has made any impact on policy decisions (see Shaw, 1999). Perhaps in the future these organizations will become involved in more direct political lobbying for change.

A Look into the Future

From this brief sketch of mental disorder as a social problem and society's official response to it (in the form of law and services), we can see that the future for people with mental disorders is very uncertain. In the nineteenth century, the role of the government was clear – to protect this section of society from exploitation and harm by confining them to large institutions, a response that also pleased society at large because it also protected the public from any possible harm. In the first half of the twentieth century, medicine was hailed as the solution to all health problems, including those of the mind. The segregation of people with mental disorders did continue, but with a more scientific and humane approach. The adequacy of the institutional approach was questioned in the 1960s at a time when scientific advances in the development of drug treatments led to a transformation of care and treatment for people with mental disorders. Some could be cured and others contained – gone for ever were the florid symptoms of schizophrenia and mania.

With great optimism, people looked forward to an era of care in the community, an era during which people with mental disorders would be able to grasp the opportunities available to the wider society, while being supported by good quality care for their mental health problems. What has happened, however, is not quite as expected. Owing to the increasing cost of health services, most countries now devote a much smaller part of their health budgets to mental health services. As a result of this, the range of services available in the publicly funded sector are inadequate to meet the needs of people who are increasingly marginalized and stigmatized as they try to compete in the competitive world of advanced capitalism. As part of the growing underclass, people with mental disorders find themselves in other excluded populations – the unemployed, the homeless, the lawbreakers. Any violent acts committed by mentally ill people are widely publicized in the media and this leads to further exclusion and demands for tighter controls of their behaviour. Although the popular notion of a direct link between mental disorder and violent crime has not been supported by research, the tide of public opinion is moving steadily in that direction (for a discussion, see Monahan and Steadman, 1994).

Politicians are very sensitive to public opinion and are increasingly swayed by the growing public fear of this group of people. This is evidenced in changes in mental health laws, incorporating elements of more supervision for discharged patients and the introduction of compulsory treatment in the community. The move from a 'care' model of mental health policy to one of 'control' is clear, for example, in the White Paper on mental health issued by the Labour government in 1999 – promising a modernized mental health service that is 'safe, sound and supportive' (Department of Health, 1999). The emphasis is on lowering the risk to the public by ensuring that people who have mental disorders are supervised and obliged to follow their treatment regimes. The lack of commitment to an increase in resources to mental health services for the great majority of mentally ill people, who present no risk to the public, is of grave concern. We can only hope that this trend (towards a highly controlling model of mental health care) will not continue but, rather, that the lobby from the user movement and from mental health professionals for a range of services will lead to social inclusion rather than exclusion.

We have seen from our discussion of mental disorder and social responses to it that this is a social problem that changes shape and content from era to era and from place to place. In other words, the definition of the problem and how it should be tackled are both deeply rooted in the meaning assigned to mental disorder by society, and in the particular view of the government about its importance as an issue which should receive public funding. Policies aimed at protecting the public have higher priority than policies aimed at improving the quality of life for individuals. Lobbyists who use the words 'danger' and 'risk' are likely to get more political attention than those who focus on health and well-being. Ironically, when the institutional answer (which we now regard as inhumane) was an acceptable professional response to mental disorder, the use of public funding to provide these institutional services was not questioned. Now that treatment is no longer tied to institutions, the continued use of public funds for community-based health, education and employment services for people with mental health problems is constantly under threat. The current funding questions about these services are very like those about general health and social care services. Should the main provider of these services be the state? Should public funds be limited to selected services – those which address a clear risk to society at large?

The answers to these questions by each successive government will determine the size and direction of the mental health care system. Mental disorder as a social problem will not disappear, but our understanding of it will, undoubtedly, change as the century progresses. Whether people with mental disorders will be happy with this understanding and with the social response to it remains to be seen.

Issues to Consider

- Is it true that women are 'madder' than men?
- Are mentally ill people more dangerous than others?
- Should all services for people with mental disorders be within a country's health care system?
- Have mentally ill people the same human rights as others?
- Why do we need new mental health legislation in the UK?

Suggestions for Further Reading

A special issue of *Policy and Politics* (1999) contains an excellent sample of readings on the current debates by well-known contributors. Prior (1999) offers a more comprehensive survey, focusing particularly on the interaction between gender and mental disorder, while Nazroo (1997) explores the experiences of different minority groups. For an eminently readable account of the experience of mental disorder and its treatment, there is nothing better than Millet's autobiographical novel (1991). Two websites which are useful in themselves and offer links to other sites are the Department of Health's www.doh.gov.uk and the site for one of the largest mental health organizations in the United Kingdom, www.mind.org.uk.

References

Audit Commission 1986: *Making a Reality of Community Care: Report of the Audit Commission for Local Authorities (England and Wales)*. London: HMSO.

Barnes, M. and Shardlow, P. 1997: From passive recipient to active citizen: participation in mental health user groups. *Journal of Mental Health*, 6 (3), 289–300.

Bebbington, P., Dean, C., Der, G., Hurry, J. and Tennant, C. 1991: Gender, parity and the prevalence of minor affective disorder. *British Journal of Psychiatry*, 158, 40–5.

Beiser, M. and Edwards, R. 1994: Mental health of immigrants and refugees. *New Directions for Mental Health Services*, 61, 73–86.

Belle, D. 1990: Poverty and women's mental health. *American Psychologist*, 45 (3), 385–9.

Busfield, J. 1996: *Men, Women and Madness: Understanding Gender and Mental Disorder*. London: Macmillan.

Cox, B., Huppert, F. and Whichelow, M. (eds) 1993: *The Health and Lifestyle Survey: Seven Years On*. Aldershot: Avebury.

Dear, M. and Wolch, J. 1987: *Landscapes of Despair: From Deinstitutionalisation to Homelessness*. Bristol: Policy Press.

Department of Health and Social Security, 1975: *Better Services for the Mentally Ill*, White Paper, Cmnd. 6233. London: HMSO.

Department of Health, 1999: *Modernising Mental Health Services*. London: The Stationery Office.

Ezzy, D. 1993: Unemployment and mental health: a critical review. *Social Science and Medicine*, 37 (1), 41–52.

Goffman, E. 1961: *Asylums*. Harmondsworth: Penguin.

Hatfield, A. and Lefley, H. 1993: *Surviving Mental Illness: Stress, Coping and Adaptation*. New York: Guilford Press.

Jensen, K. 1995: *Mental Health Legislation in Europe*, paper presented at the World Congress on Mental Health in Dublin, Survey for the World Health Organization, Regional Office for Europe.

Kuipers, L. 1993: Family burden in schizophrenia (review and editorial). *Social Psychiatry and Psychiatric Epidemiology*, 28 (5), 207–10.

Lewis, J. and Glennerster, H. 1996: *Implementing the New Community Care*. Buckingham: Open University Press.

Manning, N. and Shaw, I. (eds) 1999: Mental health and social order, *Policy and Politics*. 27 (1, special issue), 1–120.

Millet, K. 1991: *The Loony Bin Trip*. New York: Virago Press.

Monahan, J. and Steadman, H. (eds) 1994: *Violence and Mental Disorder: Developments in Risk Assessment*. Chicago: University of Chicago Press.

Nazroo, J. 1997: *Ethnicity and Mental Health: Findings from a National Community Survey*. London: Policy Studies Institute.

Payne, S. 1996: Masculinity and the redundant male: explaining the increasing incarceration of young men. *Social and Legal Studies*, 5 (2), 159–78.

Perkins, R. and Moodley, P. 1993: Perception of problems in psychiatric inpatients: denial, race and service usage. *Social Psychiatry and Psychiatric Epidemiology*, 28, 189–93.

Prior, P. M. 1999: *Gender and Mental Health*. London: Macmillan.

Policy and Politics 1999: Mental Health and Social Order, 27 (1, special issue).

Ramon, S. 1996: *Mental Health in Europe*. London: Macmillan.

Robins, L. and Regier, D. (eds) 1991: *Psychiatric Disorders in America: The Epidemiologic Catchment Area Study*. New York: Free Press.

Samele, C. 1999: The evolution of Italian mental health care: advancement or inequality? *Policy and Politics*, 27 (1), 85–96.

Shaw, I. 1999: Evaluating quality in mental health services. *Policy and Politics*, 27 (1), 113–20.

Showalter, E. 1987: *The Female Malady: Women, Madness and English Culture 1830–1980*. London: Virago Press.

Szasz, T. 1961: *The Myth of Mental Illness*. New York: Harper & Row.

Ussher, J. 1991: *Women's Madness: Mysogyny or Mental Illness?* London: Harvester Wheatsheaf.

Chapter 12

Problematic Identities and Health

David Kelleher

Introduction

Health is important in everyone's life. It is important in the lives of individuals but, as in different ways the chapters by Jones and Prior show, it is also important for the state. As individuals many people invest time and money trying to stay healthy by exercising and eating healthy foods rather than unhealthy or fattening products. If they do not manage to exercise and eat healthily, many people at least read magazines about health – while they eat their chocolate! The British government spends a great deal of money on providing a health care system, about 7 per cent of GNP, although this is a smaller proportion than that of United States or most other European countries. This expenditure can be seen as part of the social wage or, alternatively, as an investment maintaining a healthy working population and reducing days lost through sickness. The health care system, as Parsons (1952) suggested, performs a social function and being ill can be seen as a form of deviancy.

Not everyone is able to stay healthy, however. People living in poverty and those who are elderly are particularly vulnerable to sickness, as are those who have a genetic susceptibility to a particular illness. Poverty may lead to people living in poor or damp housing, which may also be in areas where they and their children suffer the effects of environmental pollution. They may also work in situations damaging to their health or where accident levels are high. Some may also find it difficult to afford a healthy diet. But other less easily identifiable factors may affect people's health and can only be understood by considering other dimensions of their lives and broader divisions within society.

Building on Jones's and Prior's discussions, this chapter aims to illustrate these processes by focusing on the health experiences of one particular group, Irish immigrants in England. As Modood et al. (1994), among others, have shown, many members of immigrant groups face difficulties in sustaining a

coherent rather than a fragmented identity, with potentially adverse consequences for their health. On the surface it may be thought that immigrants from
the Irish Republic would, of all immigrant groups, be the least likely to experience dissonance or differential health patterns. Yet, as will be seen, the available evidence suggests otherwise. Drawing on this research this chapter aims
to cast further light on the structuring of health as a social problem through
exploring:

- the concept of identity;
- the difficulties faced by immigrant groups in establishing an identity which
  incorporates their past and present;
- whether the problematic nature of their identities partly explains the poor
  mental and physical health experienced by many immigrant groups;
- the implications for policy makers and service providers.

The Concept of Identity

Many factors shape identity. There are the obvious ones, such as one's occupation, one's stage in the life cycle, or one's biological sex, which is for most people
the basis of their first name, their gender and their sexual identity. Berger and
Kellner (1971) suggest that our marital status as a wife or husband may give
shape to our sense of self, as often at the start of a marriage there is a revalu-
ing of past friendships and an assessment of where we are now; similarly,
becoming a father or mother may be important to some and help them to
decide who they are. Bailey, in a study of women becoming mothers for the
first time, found that: 'Rather than encountering disjuncture, their experience of
self altered along a number of different dimensions. Hence the women seemed
to be experiencing a refraction of the self, in which their personality was felt
to be revealing hitherto concealed and compounded elements' (Bailey, 1999,
p. 339).

In the novel by Proust, *Remembrance of Things Past*, Charles Swann, the
central character, struggles to recover the meaning of his past life in order to
know who he is, pointing to the links between past and present in identities.
Giddens (1991, p. 54) similarly writes about identity being 'the ability to keep a
particular narrative going across time and space', while the philosopher, Taylor,
also suggests that: 'We grasp our lives in a narrative . . . In order to have a sense
of who we are, we have to have a notion of how we have become, and where
we are going' (Taylor, 1989, p. 47).

In the contemporary world ethnicity and culture are considered particularly
important elements in the construction of identity, and some would go as far as
saying that ethnic differences are essential differences rather than constructed
ones, and base their claims to being a separate nation on such a belief. Others
argue that all ethnicities are constructions. Identities are derived from the ways
in which one's culture is built around notions of difference from 'the Other',

often oppressor, group and the belief in an imagined community (Anderson, 1983). As Hall (1996) says, identities show whom we identify with.

In recent decades the Irish in England have been making a strong claim to be considered ethnically different from the English, arguing for an Irish category in the Census, a share of the resources set aside for ethnic minorities and culturally sensitive treatment from care agencies, including a recognition of the specific needs of Irish elders. Like other immigrant groups (Modood et al., 1994) they have also highlighted the need for cultural sensitivity in the diagnosis of medical conditions such as schizophrenia. There are other justifications for making this claim, however, which relate to the problematic nature of sustaining an Irish identity in England and the effect this may have on their physical and mental health, as I shall show later in this chapter.

Health and Identity

But first it is necessary to look at the possible role of health in the construction of identity. In modern society there is an expectation that we shall have good health, at least until we are elderly. To experience a chronic mental or physical illness such as epilepsy, diabetes or schizophrenia before that may mean that we cannot work or do the other things that we have taken for granted, and it may force us to change our view of ourselves and our sense of who we are, our identities. Some people say that chronic illness brings about a loss of identity (Charmaz, 1983). But it makes more sense to see it as the loss of one identity as many people with disabling conditions reconstruct themselves and emphasize different aspects of their being in another identity (Kelleher, 1994).

Moving from one's own country to another may bring many difficulties, particularly if one is moving from a rural community to an urban environment where one's neighbours are strangers one may see little of, where friendships have yet to be made. Hall (1996) suggests that globalization and migration have led to fragmented identities, making the joke that 'we construct our identities by looking at our routes', which is perhaps another way to say that people who migrate have to construct a new chapter in the narratives of their lives, as what they become is quite different in most cases from what they were 'back home'. Constructing a new identity is important says Bauman (1996); it is a way of fixing where we are at present and how we should live in a morally consistent way. Constructing a new identity does not mean, however, that we should shrug off the old us like a snake shedding its skin. As Rutherford (1990, p. 24) suggests, 'identity is never a static location, it contains traces of its past and what it is to become'.

The Experience of the Irish in England

Finding a place to live and finding a job are the first problems facing any immigrants, and although connections from back home may help them to get started, there quickly comes a time when they have to find things for themselves. For Irish working men the pub is often the place to find other Irish people who might help find a job and a place to stay; it is also a place where friendships and social support can start.

Other than in the pub, Irish club and church, Irish people may often find that their accent is noticed, and that those they meet or work with call them all 'Paddy'. They may often remain strangers in England and, although in many situations they may not be unwelcome, they may also experience the feeling of being in an alien and sometimes hostile country where they cannot be themselves (Cahill and Kelleher, 1999). Popular culture is saturated with jokes playing on stereotypes which portray Paddies as stupid and the English, by implication, as clever. As Hickman (1995) shows, this attitude towards the Catholic Irish in England is long-standing and deep-seated and is one of the ways in which the English define their difference from the Irish and in doing so remind them of their history of colonization.

More recently, over the period of the 'troubles', they have become used to being told when a bombing occurs in England that 'your lot are at it again', as though all Irish people support the bombings. In such a climate they get used to being stopped by police or port officials or held for a few hours under prevention of terrorism legislation. Indeed, although in the nineteenth century Irish people in England were active in political movements such as Chartism, in the current climate they have learned to keep their heads down and their thoughts to themselves. They become, as a number of writers (Greenslade et al., 1995) have suggested, 'invisible'. They are channelled into a limited range of jobs: on building sites, as barmen, the women recruited into nursing or service occupations, a lucky few making it into areas such as the media.

These limited employment opportunities are reflected in both their income levels and their housing, which is often of a poorer standard than that of the English. As many surveys and studies, such as the 1991 Census or the study by Owen (1995), show, the Irish, like other ethnic minorities, are more likely to be living in privately rented houses than in the usually better-quality houses of the public sector. They are also less likely than other groups to be owner-occupiers, while a high proportion of hostel dwellers are Irish people (Harrison and Carr-Hill, 1992). More recent studies paint a similar picture. Leonard's (1999) survey of Irish people in Coventry, for instance, found that 20 per cent of Irish households were of 'an unsatisfactory quality', with 18.8 per cent unfit by statutory standards.

These findings attest to the poor position of Irish people in England, a country to which they have been emigrating for over two hundred years. It suggests that the Irish are not well integrated into English society. The poor housing of the Irish in England is one of the factors relating to their health, as is their over representation in social classes 4 and 5, and in older age groups. It is also possible that, as the process of emigration to England is relatively easy in terms of distance and immigration procedures, many who are already in poor health emigrate. However, none of these factors completely explain the poor health status of Irish people in England. Nor do they fully account for the fact that, whereas usually the health of second-generation migrants tends to become similar to that of the host community, this does not seem to be the case for second-generation Irish immigrants (Harding and Balajaran, 1996).

The Health of the Irish

Just how poor the health of Irish immigrants is becomes apparent from official statistics and other surveys. As Kelleher and Hillier (1996, p. 105) note, the OPCS Mortality and Geography Review in the 1980s showed that mortality rates varied between country of birth groups, with significantly high levels at ages 20–69 in males from Ireland (SMR 128: SMR is the standardized mortality rate – the average death rate is 100, and groups that have a higher number therefore have a greater than average mortality rate). The findings are broadly similar for women; the highest mortality rates at ages 20–69 are among the Irish (SMR 120). In the age group 20–49 the rates were even higher, for both men and women, the SMR for men being 147 and for women 123.

Bracken et al. (1998), drawing on earlier studies, such as those of Haskey (1996) and Cochrane and Bal (1987; 1989), report that the mortality rates of Irish-born people exceed those of all residents of England and Wales by approximately 30 per cent for men and 20 per cent for women. They also repeat Pearson et al.'s (1991) assertion that Irish men are the only migrant group whose life expectancy worsens on emigration to England.

Bracken was mainly concerned with examining the mental health of Irish people. Although he relied mainly on old data, his findings were widely publicized and sufficiently startling to be mentioned in a debate in the Dail, the Irish parliament. The data on admissions to mental hospital showed that Irish men had a rate of 158 per 100,000 for schizophrenia and Irish women an even higher rate of 174. For people born in England the rates were 61 for men and 58 for women. The rates for depression were also high, particularly for Irish women, 410, compared with 166 for English women (which is itself worryingly high). The other high rate was for alcohol abuse, 332 for Irish men and 133 for Irish women; the comparable rates for English people are 38 for men and 18 for women. Bracken also drew attention to the high rates of suicide and attempted suicide (self-harm) among Irish people living in England, the rate for young Irish women (aged 20–29) being 167 per cent higher than that for young English women.

These statistics have their limitations, in that they are for hospital admissions and do not include those people being treated by a GP. The ways in which such data are collected also vary. Nevertheless, they indicate a serious mental health problem among the Irish in England. It might be expected, then, that Irish people would be targeted by health and social service providers, but this has not happened. As Doherty (1993) and Tilki (1996) demonstrate, despite the need for health and social care services that are culturally sensitive, there appears to be considerable resistance to ensuring such provision for Irish people.

As I indicated earlier, one of the striking and unusual aspects of the health of the Irish in England is that whereas the health of the children of immigrants usually becomes similar to that of the host population, second-generation Irish people also experience poor health. Indeed Harding and Balarajan's longitudinal mortality study (1996, p. 1389) concluded that the 'mortality of second generation Irish men and women was higher than that of all men and women and for most major causes of death'. Surprisingly, they found that these mortality rates were higher than those of the English in all social classes. Even those in social class 1 seemed to be affected either by something in the Irish culture or by something in the way Irish people experienced life in England.

It may be that the second-generation Irish have been socialized by Irish cultural beliefs and attitudes, as they are likely to have spent holidays as children in Ireland, learned Irish songs and ways of life from their parents and, very importantly, been brought up as Catholics and attended Catholic schools. But instead of pathologizing Irish culture in this way it seems more relevant, since the health of Irish people seems to decline when they come to England, to look for an explanation in their experiences in England. Hickman (1995) considers anti-Irishness has had a long history in England; writing in a Commission for Racial Equality report she states that: 'There is a widespread, and almost completely unquestioned acceptance of anti-Irish racism in British society. . . . The spontaneous responses of a majority of the sample . . . reveal a powerful sense of hurt and unjustified exclusion from an equal place in British society' (Hickman and Walter, 1997, p. 240). She goes on to suggest that for a migrant, and his or her descendants, having a varied existence and negotiating a variety of identities and stereotypical attitudes is a perennial experience (Hickman, 1995, p. 224), a point also emphasized in other studies; for instance Ullah's (1985, p. 310) survey of the attitudes and experiences of second-generation Irish secondary school pupils found that anti-Irish prejudice was 'widely experienced' and that 'questions related to identity formed a major issue' in their lives. One of the pupils he interviewed made the telling comment that 'I don't feel that Irish people are really disliked by the English, but they are laughed at' (Ullah, 1985, p. 311). This echoes the fairly mild view of anti-Irishness taken by Ryan (1990), who says that if the English do have a fault it is that they do not take the Irish seriously.

Material factors, such as poor housing and the difficulties of finding employment, and lifestyle factors, such as smoking and levels of alcohol consumption, help to explain poor health. But it remains now for us to consider whether a special factor, the identity dilemmas of first- and second-generation Irish people in England, may also help to explain it.

Problematic Identity and Health

If establishing identity is a way of knowing where we are and how to act, and if this is achieved by our being able to join our experiences of the present with those of the past to make a continuing narrative, it is possible to see how difficulties might arise for Irish people in England. Many come from families and communities in which control is exercised by tradition and religion, and, while a desire to escape and achieve greater freedom is often one of the motivating factors for emigrants, it is nevertheless difficult to achieve a balance which does not bring guilt with it. Considering how emigration has been viewed over the years by those who stay, Ryan takes the view that emigration was always seen by Irish people to be: 'from sinless Ireland to sinful England, so emigrants went away abundantly blessed but insufficiently prepared by parents, priests or politicians . . . For many emigrants, of course, the warnings and the dangers only served to make England appear more attractive' (Ryan, 1990, p. 67). He goes on to say that this was also 'part of the inability to see England or the English in realistic terms'. Another aspect of being Irish in England is that it is noticed and remarked on. This may lead immigrants either to play down their Irishness, and attempt to adopt an English way of speaking and seek to make English friends, or to accentuate it.

But taking on a clearly Irish identity in England has its problems, as English people tend, as has been seen, to have stereotypical views about Irish people, and the English in return are often seen by the Irish as 'the ould enemy', who had ruled Ireland, often brutally, for seven hundred years. Kelleher and Hillier (1996) note that Ireland had, until 1922, the status of an English colony and refer to Greenslade's work (1992), which suggests that colonized people and their ways of life were commonly considered inferior by the English. For Irish immigrants this view of themselves might be resistible in Ireland, but it was far more difficult when living in the land of the colonial oppressors. Greenslade uses this argument in his explanation of the high rates of mental illness which the Irish experience in England. Kelleher and Hillier (1996) add to this by using Antonovsky's (1960) concept of coherence, by which he described the problems of identity experienced by Jewish people in America, particularly at the times when some Jewish people (the Rosenbergs) were committing un-American activities by selling secrets to the Russians. At such a time he suggests, Jewish people in America struggled with their sense of identity and attempted to distance themselves from the Rosenbergs by saying that they were communists, not Jews. It may be that Irish people in England have had to struggle, over the past thirty years, to distance themselves from the 'troubles' and consequently struggle to achieve a coherent identity.

Explaining the Link Between Identity and Health

It is not difficult to see how all these factors may contribute to problems of identity and to high rates of mental illness. But although mental illness may lead to loss of employment and earned income and then to poor diet, it is quite a long chain of causation to account for the poor physical health of the Irish in England. Freund (1990), however, suggests a linkage between the emotions and illness, which is a useful line of enquiry. He argues that the emotional states experienced by those who feel themselves to be in inferior status positions, or positions in which they cannot express the emotions they feel, are subject to neural-hormonal activities; these change the levels of key hormones and produce physical states, such as increased blood pressure and cholesterol levels, as expressions of the emotional state they are experiencing. Attacking the mind/body division which is at the root of Western medicine, he argues that emotions are always in some way embodied. While accepting that diseases have biological components, Freund argues that they also have psychosocial dimensions, even though these may take years to have a noticeable effect. Thus, in a later discussion about the usefulness and limitations of the concept of stress, he suggests that the events which elicit the stress response in humans are not usually physical but more typically social and symbolic (Freund and McGuire, 1995).

Such considerations may not fully explain the poor health of Irish people in England, but they do point to the complex interplay between the experience of immigration and individual health. As I have suggested here, the lives of many immigrants may be lives of daily hassles about matters relating to a sense of identity and a feeling that they are different, not English. Irish people may look like English people, but they do not sound like them, and many want to retain their Irish identity. This life-long stress may increase the likelihood of mental and physical illness.

Conclusion

In the mean time, while the Irish in England go on experiencing poor health, welfare agencies need to be aware of similar pressures faced by other immigrant groups, including the increasing numbers of asylum seekers. It is not enough to have policies that are colour-blind; identities are shaped by more than colour and language. It is important to recognize the cultural differences of people and to recognize the constraints and dilemmas that immigrants experience in developing a coherent identity. If the health of the nation is to be improved, we must make an effort to understand how the everyday experiences of people from different ethnic minority groups influence their health.

Issues to Consider

- What do you think are the most important elements in your own identity?
- Have you ever been in situations relating to health or the provision of social services in which an important aspect of your identity (e.g. gender, ethnicity, class) has been challenged?
- How strong do you consider the link between problems of identity and health?
- What weaknesses do you see in the main argument presented in this chapter?
- How should policy makers respond to the evidence and arguments presented here?

Suggestions for Further Reading

Woodward (1997) provides a readable introduction to issues of identity and identity politics and a guide to the terms and concepts which are being developed to investigate them. Kelleher and Hillier (1996) offer a range of studies exploring how members of different ethnic groups perceive and manage their illnesses; they also discuss the concepts of ethnicity and culture, issues that are also explored in Song's (1997) study of the experiences of second-generation Chinese. Although they base their work on American research, Freund and McGuire (1995) provide a comprehensive sociological discussion of the factors linking material and economic factors to how health and illness are constructed. Apart from the websites cited in chapters 10 and 11, up-to-date coverage of current debates can be found in on-line journals, the most useful being *Social Science and Medicine*: www.elsevier.nl/locate/ssmabsonline; *Sociology of Health and Illness*: www.blackwellpublishers.co.uk.

References

Anderson, B. 1983: *Imagined Communities*. London: Verso.

Antonovsky, A. 1960: Identity, anxiety, and the Jew. In M. Stein, A. Vidich and D. M. White (eds), *Identity and Anxiety: Survival of the Person in Mass Society*. New York: Free Press.

Bailey, L. 1999: Motherhood. *Sociology*, 33 (2), 336–72.

Bauman, Z. 1996: From pilgrim to tourist – a short history of identity. In S. Hall and P. du Gay (eds), *Questions of Cultural Identity*. London: Sage.

Berger, B. and Kellner, H. 1971: Marriage and the construction of reality: an exercise in the microsociology of knowledge. In B. Cosin, I. Dale, G. Esland and D. Swift (eds), *School and Society*. London: Routledge & Kegan Paul.

Bracken, P., Greenslade, L., Griffin, B. and Smythe, M. 1998: Mental health and ethnicity: an Irish dimension. *British Journal of Psychiatry*, 172, 103–5.

Cahill, G. and Kelleher, D. 1999: The health of the Irish, paper presented to the British Sociological Association Medical Sociology Conference, September.

Charmaz, K. 1983: Loss of self: a fundamental form of suffering in the chronically ill. *Sociology of Health and Illness*, 5, 168–95.

Cochrane, R. and Bal, S. 1987: Migration and schizophrenia: an examination of five hypotheses. *Social Psychiatry*, 221, 181–91.

Cochrane, R. and Bal, S. 1989: Mental hospital admission rates of immigrants to England: a comparison of 1971 and 1981. *Social Psychiatry and Psychiatric Epidemiology*, 24, 2–11.

Doherty, K. 1993: The response of London Alcohol Services to the needs of Irish people with alcohol problems, dissertation, London: London Guildhall University.

Freund, P. 1990: The expressive body: a common ground for the sociology of emotions and health and illness. *Health and Illness*, 12 (4).

Freund, P. and McGuire, M. 1995: *Health, Illness and the Social Body*. Englewood Cliffs, NJ. London: Prentice-Hall.

Giddens, A. 1991: *The Consequences of Modernity*. Cambridge: Polity Press.

Greenslade, L. 1992: White skins, white masks: psychological distress amongst the Irish in Britain. In P. O'Sullivan (ed.), *The Irish in the New Communities* vol. 2. Leicester: Leicester University Press.

Greenslade, L., Pearson, M. and Madden, M. 1995: A good man's fault: alcohol and Irish people at home and abroad. *Alcohol and Alcoholism*, 30 (4).

Hall, S. 1996: Who needs identity? In S. Hall and P. du Gay (eds), *Questions of Cultural Identity*. London: Sage.

Harding, S. and Balajaran, R. 1996: Patterns of mortality in second generation Irish living in England and Wales: longitudinal study. *British Medical Journal*, 312, 1389–92.

Harrison, L. and Carr-Hill, R. 1992: *Alcohol and Disadvantage Amongst the Irish in England*. Hull: Department of Social Policy, University of Hull.

Haskey, J. 1996: Mortality among second generation Irish in England and Wales. *British Medical Journal*, 312, 1373–4.

Hickman, M. 1995: *Religion, Class and Identity*. Aldershot: Avebury.

Hickman, M. and Walter, M. 1997: *Discrimination and the Irish Community in Britain*. London: Commission for Racial Equality.

Kelleher, D. 1994: Self-help groups and their relationship to medicine. In J. Gabe, D. Kelleher and G. Williams (eds), *Challenging Medicine*. London: Routledge.

Kelleher, D. and Hillier, S. 1996: The health of the Irish in England. In D. Kelleher and S. Hillier, *Researching Cultural Differences in Health*. London: Routledge.

Leonard, M. 1999: *Exile Care Initiative*. Dublin: Rehab Care.

Modood, T., Beishon, T. and Virdee, S. 1994: *Changing Ethnic Identities*. London: Policy Studies Institute.

OPCS 1990: *Mortality and Geography: A Review in the Mid 1980s*, Series D.S. no. 9. London: HMSO.

Owen, D. 1995: *Irish-born People in Great Britain*. Warwick: Centre for Research in Ethnic Relations.

Parsons, T. 1952: *The Social System*. London: Routledge & Kegan Paul.

Pearson, M., Madden, M. and Greenslade, L. 1991: *Generations of an Invisible Minority*, Occasional Paper no. 2. Liverpool: Institute of Irish Studies.

Robins, K. 1996: Interrupting identities. In S. Hall and P. du Gay (eds), *Questions of Cultural Identity*. London: Sage.

Rutherford, J. 1990: A place called home: identity and the cultural politics of difference. In J. Rutherford (ed.), *Identity*. London: Lawrence & Wishart.

Ryan, L. 1990: Irish emigration to Britain since World War II. In R. Kearney (ed.), *Migrations: The Irish at Home and Abroad*. Dublin: Wolfhound Press.

Song, M. 1997: 'You're becoming more and more English': investigating Chinese siblings' cultural identities. *New Community*, 23 (3), 343–62.

Taylor, C. 1989: *Sources of the Self*. Cambridge: Cambridge University Press.

Tilki, M. 1996: The health of the Irish in Britain. *Federation of Irish Societies Bulletin*, 9, 11–14.

Ullah, P. 1985: Second generation Irish youth: identity and ethnicity. *New Community*, 310–20.

Woodward, K. 1997: *Identity and Difference*. London: Sage.

Community Problems

Chapter 13

The Problematic Community

Susanne MacGregor

Introduction

Community is a ubiquitous word in social policy. We have community policing, community development, community participation, punishment in the community, community care and community partnerships, to name but a few
instances. The word community has been said to be a 'weasel word' – useful precisely because its meaning is so unclear and attractive because it implies a nostalgic image of a time when conflict and difference were absent from social
relations. It is in this context that this chapter considers the issue of 'problematic communities', how they have been seen and the policy issues they pose. It
considers:

- how certain communities of poor people came to be treated as a social
  problem;
- the changes and consistencies in the way they have been perceived;
- how the problem has changed in the UK – over the past century, in the
  postwar years and, especially, in the last two decades of the twentieth
  century;
- the main explanations in the literature and the policy responses linked to
  these.

The word community has been popular in twentieth-century histories of the
UK, but social historians are vague about how much community or community
feeling actually existed. The word hints at an identification with a particular
neighbourhood or street, a sense of shared perspectives, and reciprocal dependency. We find the idea of a harmonious, traditional working-class community
(which some people think has decayed with deindustrialization) in two
separate discourses – a backward-looking romanticism and a forward-looking

socialism. But historical accounts show that, while there was some solidarity and mutual sympathy, there were also less attractive features, like the neglect of children, exhaustion and sickness, and the rejection of 'weird' people and outsiders. The truth is probably that there was always a mixture of good and bad, with different combinations at different times and in different places. Communities were often at their best when under threat – the most outstanding example being the 1940s experience of total war, with bombing raids and shared sufferings encouraging a spirit of cooperation and common concern.

Most people today do not live in ways that fit with the idealized image of community. They live in suburban settings, characterized by privatization and weak social ties with neighbours. The ideal of keeping yourself to yourself, having a quiet and peaceful life, is one held by many British people today. For some, the closest they get to a community is when watching television soaps such as EastEnders or Coronation Street. The car has made a big difference to community life, along with the increase in the number of married women who go out to do paid work. People do not live so close to their parents, and journeys to work have lengthened. There is less public life and less time to join in or even stop and chat.

The Policy Significance of Problematic Communities

The idea of a 'problematic community' is something of a contradiction in terms. If communities are thought to be good, how can there be problematic or bad communities? Problematic communities have often been seen as disorganized, disadvantaged or frightened. They can be portrayed as victims, as threats, or as activists. Certain communities, spaces or areas thought to pose problems for social control have become issues of policy significance. This may be because they appear to be falling apart. Or it may equally be because they are too united, standing apart from and opposing the values of mainstream society. When areas come to be seen as unsafe or dangerous and threaten to pollute or spread contagion to mainstream society, they become the focus of policy attention, and typically there are calls for 'something to be done'.

Concerns about pollution are found quintessentially in the ideas and myths surrounding drug-taking and drug-dealing (see the chapter by Gould) but also

---

Box 13.1: Giving a name to danger

In nearly every major First World metropolis, a particular urban district or township has 'made a name for itself' as that place where disorder, dereliction, and danger are said to be the normal order of the day. The South Bronx and Brownsville in New York City, Les Minguettes and Vaux-en-Velin near Lyons, London's Brixton and East End, Gutleutviertel in Hamburg, Rinkeby on the outskirts of Stockholm, and Neueu West in Rotterdam – the list gets longer by the year. (Wacquant, 1999, p. 122)

> ## Box 13.2: Problematic communities as a problem of 'people'
>
> This road is the king of all roads. I have been in practically all the slums in London: Notting Hill, Chelsea, Battersea, Fulham, Nine Elms, and the East End, but there is nothing so lively as this road. Thieves, Prostitutes, cripples, Blind People, Hawkers of all sorts of wares from boot laces to watches and chains are to be found in this road, Pugilists, Card Sharpers, Counter Jumpers, Purse Snatchers, street singers, and Gamblers of all kinds, and things they call men who live on the earnings of women, some of whom I saw outside the Town Hall with the unemployed last week. I could say a lot more about this road, but I think I have said enough to prove to you the class of people who inhabit it. Of course, there are a few who perhaps get an honest living, but they want a lot of picking out. (Sanitary inspector's report ISMB/PHC 1908–9, 4 January 1909, pp. 167–8, quoted in White, 1986, pp. 24–25).

in images of sexual practices which threaten to spread disease or disharmony to the rest of society. As the next two chapters also emphasize, communities may be considered dark and dangerous places. All the fears and discontents that lie in society are externalized onto these unfortunate places. By locating threats in them, attention is distracted from deep rifts in society at large. Defining 'the problem' as one of drugs similarly serves to place the blame on a simple external enemy, different and originating outside Britain, thus again diverting attention from the problems that lie in society as a whole.

Concepts of pathology, disorganization, anomie or deviance run through the main images of problematic communities. These assumptions have a long history, as box 13.2 suggests. The explanations focus on the different characteristics of the people who live in these areas, characteristics that are thought to be either inherent or the product of circumstance. What they usually fail to talk about, however, is the extent of the overlap between the behaviours that are deemed disreputable and the behaviours of the respectable groups. The deep denial of the extent of collusion is remarkable. In riots, it is often found that everyone joins in – the looting of shops becomes a collective festivity. But, less dramatically, everyday collusion occurs – who buy the videos, car radios and other goods stolen by criminals? Who, for instance, questions where the contents of car boot sales come from? Who are the clients of the prostitutes? Who buy drugs from drug dealers? The markets may be located in poor areas, but the customers often come from so-called respectable society.

And the gap in life experiences is not as great as the images make out. Divorced women plummet down the housing market; refugees escaping persecution drop from skilled and professional employment to life on a council estate; the children of respectable working people in deindustrialized areas cannot find

Box 13.3: Problematic communities: how the words and theories have changed and not changed

Late nineteenth century	Late twentieth century
Immigration from the countryside	Immigration from overseas
Irregular labour	Irregular labour
Prostitution	Prostitution
Drink	Drugs
Subsistence on charity	Welfare dependence
Agitation, demonstrations and riots	Riots
Ill-health due to a lack of ozone in the air	Ill health due to environmental pollution
Degeneration of the race	Low educational performance
Prejudice against the city	Postcode discrimination
Industrial restructuring leading to lack of work and low-wage economy	Industrial restructuring leading to lack of work and low-wage economy
Sneers at indiscriminate alms-givers and humanitarians	Sneers at liberals and *Guardian* readers
Concern about relations between casual residuum and respectable working class	Concern about relations between underclass and hard-working ordinary people
Crime and disorder	Crime and disorder
Impudent urchins with dirty brooms at every crossing	Squeegie beggars at traffic lights
Begging and homelessness	Begging and homelessness
Large families	Lone mothers
Slums	Council estates
Police go in twos; inhabitants violently hostile to strangers	Milkmen will not deliver; doctors will not visit
Thieves	Criminal records

work (a new generation develops who have never known regular work and, as Donnison also argues earlier in this book, have no expectation of improving their lives); chronic illness dramatically alters a household's income and lifestyle.

Some other themes constantly crop up in perceptions and explanations of problematic communities. Spatial segregation – geographical concentrations of rich and poor – has had an impact on local administration. The very local authorities trying to deal with the situation end up being blamed and accused of incompetence. The solution in the nineteenth century was to call for more involvement by 'men of property' in local administration; the modern equivalent is the call for more involvement from the business community. Quite commonly, effects have been felt in neighbouring communities, where people who are struggling to get by – the not quite poor – resent what they consider the preferential treatment of the very poor: special zones, positive discrimination, priority areas and so on can appear unfair. This is thought by some observers to have a demoralizing impact on the not quite poor. It is feared they may either turn their ire on the government or give up and join the ranks of the quite poor. The problem identified here is not one of poverty but of pauperism. The pauper is someone who gives up and becomes coarse, brutish, drunken and immoral – or, in contemporary terms, 'welfare dependent'. The solution is to do away with alms and welfare, and to encourage poor people to be more self-reliant. The most important policies, it is thought by those who take this view, are those which make work more attractive.

In the late twentieth century, there was a particular theme in the perceptions and explanations of problematic communities. What was considered initially a solution to the problem, council housing, came to be seen as the cause of the problem. Housing design and management and housing allocation policies have been identified as the key factors. Other broader social trends noted have been the spread of drugs and a 'crisis of masculinity' (Campbell, 1993).

Underlying these social developments is the deep beat of deindustrialization and the deincorporation of the working class. In spite of advances in technology and the standard of living, some commentators consider that in other ways the shape of society is changing back to that of the nineteenth century. The twentieth-century trend to incorporate the working class, through social democracy and the welfare state, was thrown into reverse in the 1980s by rising unemployment and a squeeze on public services. The re-emergence of long-term unemployment led to the deincorporation of increasing sections of the working class, 'who are being defined out of the edifice of citizenship' (Dahrendorf, 1985, p. 98; Bauman, 1998).

Bauman's analysis is that contemporary society has ceased to be a society of producers and become a society of consumers. Consumers are divided into two groups, 'satisfied consumers and flawed consumers', and the plight of the latter is used to frighten the former into satisfaction. The shift from a citizenship defined by the work ethic and a sense of duty to a citizenship based on shopping has undermined the effectiveness of the integrative processes of the old welfare state (Bauman, 1998). In this view, poor people have moved from being a 'reserve army of labour' and recast as 'flawed consumers' without a useful social function; poor communities are in an inferior category afflicted with faults common to them all and therefore presenting one 'social problem' (Bauman, 1998). Problematic communities of poor people unable to participate fully in consumer lifestyles become repressed communities, especially subjected to control and surveillance through the criminal justice, welfare and psychiatric systems.

So 'policing, crime and public order have turned full circle back to echo early Victorian conditions' (Reiner, 1990, p. 45). The trends towards lower crime and disorder and a greater acceptance of the police in the late nineteenth and early twentieth centuries depended on the historical process of working-class incorporation. Deincorporation explains rising crime. Relative deprivation also helps to explain crime, because for some people life is considered unjust and unfair. This erodes the social controls that might encourage conformity. Other factors cited as leading to a widening gap between poor communities and the rest of society are policing practice, immigration, racial tension, poverty and unemployment, the concentrations of disadvantage and deviance, and the flight of the middle class. In particular in the 1990s, attention focused on the situation of young people and lone parents; the two were linked, as inadequate parenting and ineffective neighbourhood control were considered part of the 'problem of youth'.

The Changing Scale and Incidence of Problematic Communities: Area-based Definitions

A note is needed about the nature of the evidence available on communities identified as problematic and on how this evidence has been collected and disseminated (see too the discussion by Clarke). Poor communities are subject to a greater surveillance than others, so the data may be distorted by the mechanisms of data collection. And the factors counted are often those assumed to be relevant explanatory factors, such as the proportion of ethnic minority households or the proportion of lone parent households. Other data, theoretically equally valid, may simply not be collected. Nowhere is this tendency more pronounced than in relation to crime statistics.

In recent decades, the rediscovery of poverty has had an area base. Problematic communities are at root poor communities, although there is more to the explanation than income alone. Economic and social change and the direction of social policy itself since the 1980s have produced winners and losers. There is a fear that some communities, the losers, are becoming dislocated from mainstream norms and values and pose a threat to law and order. In the UK, concern about the north–south divide has waxed and waned but has never completely disappeared, and there is strong evidence of a continuing divide. But there is also a spatial concentration of poverty within particular localities and districts of cities.

Evidence shows that geography matters. Indicators of poverty – such as unemployment, families with no car, rented housing, overcrowding, the lack of basic amenities, households with an elderly person, households with young children, large households, single-person households, lone-parent households – show concentrations of poverty in certain areas. Not having a car and housing tenure are key indicators.

In 1991, 74 per cent of 'concentrated poverty' wards were in northern Britain, compared with 80 per cent in 1981 (Green, 1996). A relative and an absolute increase in concentrated poverty wards in southern Britain was accounted for solely by their increased representation in large urban areas, especially in inner

London. In 1991, 55 per cent of wards in inner London were categorized as concentrated poverty areas, compared with 32 per cent in 1981 (Green, 1996). So large urban areas and older industrial areas are the context for concentrated poverty (see too Donnison's chapter). Labour market policy is a crucial influence because of the increasing salience of educational qualifications in the labour market, the spatial mismatch of job opportunities and the places where most disadvantaged people live, and the growth in no-earner households.

Problems are more likely to occur where people lack access to transport and employment. Problematic communities are more likely not to be owner-occupiers. The frequent turnover of residents undermines a community – length of residence is a mark of a neighbourhood's stability. It takes time for a sense of identity and pride and investment in a neighbourhood to develop, and for elders or leaders to emerge, who set the tone and intervene to protect it if things start to go wrong. The key to the strength of a community is whether people want to stay living there. If outsiders consider a community problematic, often its residents do too. Those who can leave.

The estates and areas defined as problematic have often suffered from a sense of physical and psychological isolation. A community may need to be identified as problematic before it can obtain selective, targeted funds for its renewal. Liverpool, for example, has been the target for almost every urban initiative since the 1960s. Criteria cited to justify its designation as a special area include its low GDP per person, its high levels of long-term unemployment, and the decline of its population. This need to attract special funding can lead to self-fulfilling prophecies and may be resented by local residents, who may find the concentration on gloom and doom depressing. Councils have to emphasize the problems, but this can add to the problem. Once a neighbourhood is defined as in decline, it is difficult to change its image: banks leave, people feel depressed and apathetic, they are rejected by outsiders, and young people in particular feel unwanted.

Power (1997) has shown that the problems of 'estates on the edge' are not separate from wider societal trends. The problems are more concentrated and more clearly defined only because they are area-based. Postwar housing policy meant that poor people ended up on large, unpopular modern estates. The isolation and concentrated poverty of these estates added to the stigma associated with them and preserved the processes of social segregation and discrimination they were originally meant to overturn. These estates were often located on the edges of cities, and poor transport connections added to the difficulties of finding employment and obtaining services.

Power identifies the underlying causes of social breakdown as a weakening of family ties, the speed of economic change and high levels of unemployment. Problems in these estates included physical decay, but also management problems, difficulties in letting property, rent collection and repair, and social and economic problems. Design and density interacted so that, for example, in flats designed as minimal boxes, there was no room for children to let off steam, so they had to play outside. As they became teenagers, the problems of controlling

Box 13.4: The metamorphosis of a community

A stable neighbourhood of families who care for their homes, mind each other's children, and confidently frown on unwanted intruders can change in a few years or even a few months to an inhospitable jungle. A piece of property is abandoned, weeds grow up, a window is smashed. Adults stop scolding rowdy children; the children emboldened become more rowdy. Families move out, unattached adults move in. Teenagers gather in front of the corner store. The merchant asks them to move; they refuse. Fights occur. Litter accumulates. People start drinking in front of the grocery; in time an inebriate slumps to the sidewalk and is allowed to sleep it off. (Wilson and Kelling, 1982, pp. 31–2)

youthful behaviour intensified. The design often meant that public spaces were not overlooked or supervised.

Problematic Communities in the Policy Literature: Explanations and Implications

The explanations for problematic communities fall broadly into two camps: those that find individuals responsible for the situation and those that blame the environment. Some argue that the innate pathology of the 'degenerates' who live in these areas accounts for the problems. Others see their difficult behaviour as a response to the situations they find themselves in, especially their rejection or neglect by conventional society.

Two theories in particular have influenced the assumptions on which policy responses have been based: the idea of a 'culture of poverty' and the idea of a 'cycle of decline'.

The culture of poverty thesis has had a powerful influence on policy and continues to do so. The founder of the notion, Lewis (1964), considered the culture of poverty to be the pragmatic reaction of poor people to their being marginalized in a class-stratified and individualistic society. The culture provides support to cope with feelings of helplessness and despair, as poor people realize that their achieving success in conventional terms is unlikely. Empirical studies have varied in their support for this thesis. While these attitudes are frequently found among poor people, ethnographic studies also record that many do accept the mainstream values of enterprise and achievement, although these may be pursued in illegal ways, such as through drug-dealing (Pearson, 1987). They also document resilience and self-help, and friendliness and liveliness, in poor communities (Cattell and Evans, 1999). But the notion of a culture of poverty is tenacious in government and influences many of New Labour's responses to what they see as a poverty of expectations in poor communities (and among the teachers and others who work in these areas).

Contained within these ideas is the notion of a cycle of decline. Poor families are caught in a vicious circle: they become trapped and are sucked further and further down. Ill health may lead to financial difficulties, children suffer from deprivation and they exhibit delinquency and an inability to adjust to adult life. They enter unstable marriages and show emotional problems and ill health, and the cycle repeats itself in the next generation.

The most frequently cited explanation of the cycle of decline is Wilson and Kelling's 'broken windows' thesis (1982). This explains how an area can be tipped into rapid decline; it is based on notions of social disorganization. Incivilities lead to fear, which leads to avoidance, withdrawal and flight from an area. Reduced informal social control results in more serious crime. Early aggressive policing of incivilities and other signs of crime is needed to stop the cycle of decline. This idea lies behind the 'zero tolerance' policing practices of New York and has been influential on recent British thinking too, for example influencing policies on anti-social neighbours.

Power (1997) has a rather different but related explanation for decline. She sees the pressures falling on three main areas – the buildings, the people and the services. When they compound each other, the near breakdown of communities can appear. Many estates are built of heavy, dominating, inhuman, ugly structures – the brutal modernism whose appeal few can now understand. Reluctance to admit that the design was a huge mistake meant that for a long time it was not blamed, and the responsibility for any problems was laid entirely at the door of the residents. But the residents did have a host of needs. They were generally poor, there was a high proportion of lone parent families, an absence of men in the community, large numbers of young people would congregate in communal areas, and tensions grew between the police and young people and others in the community. There was vandalism, graffiti, crime, the abuse of common areas, unneighbourly behaviour, welfare dependence, unemployment and drug-related problems.

The perception that there is a general problem with young people in contemporary society partly explains the definition of problematic communities as those with large concentrations of young people, especially those without education or jobs, who are disaffected and alienated. The failure of the principal institutions, especially the labour market and local schools, is thought to account for the behavioural problems found in some areas, which are related to but not entirely explained by poverty. Signs of wider personal and social malaise appear in all social classes, but when they occur in poor communities there are fewer resources available with which to intervene or offer help. Problems become entrenched, and secondary problems grow up round them.

Policy Responses to Problematic Communities

The story of policy development in this area in the mid- to late twentieth century is the story of a growing disbelief in traditional Fabian, welfare statist solutions and the search for alternatives (see Page's chapter). In this context, policy makers turned to the USA for ideas. They drew in particular on their War on Poverty and Urban Policy experiences. There was an increasing awareness of the role of racial tension and of the continuance of pools of poverty in a sea of increasing affluence.

The battle between universalist and selectivist ideas has been a constant one in the history of postwar social policy debate (MacGregor, 1981). The selectivist case is that public services should be available only to those who cannot afford to pay for them from their own or their families' resources. Universalists argue that a collective shared responsibility should make social welfare available by right and on the basis of need. They think that separate services for poor people will always be stigmatized and of poorer quality. As the selectivist arguments began to gain the upper hand in the 1980s, increasing attention was given to the need to distribute funds selectively – referred to initially as positive discrimination. Selective funds have become more and more influential, even though they remain small compared with general funds, because in a period of retrenchment and cuts they are a main source of new money. Through these devices, it is possible, therefore, to shape policies with quite small sums of money. New approaches, the use of new terminology and new ways of working can all be introduced through these new initiatives, and these have built up over time to make a dramatic difference to the shape and culture of public services.

So the policies I shall briefly review below (and summarize in Box 13.5) should be understood in the context of the long waves of social policy – the rise and fall of the welfare state. As the welfare state has unravelled and become less effective as a form of social control, we have seen an increasing proliferation of *ad hoc* initiatives to attempt to deal with fragmentation, disorder, disaffection and detachment – all indicators of the deincorporation of the working class. Why policy interventions have occurred at specific moments and why they have taken the form they have are best explained by the fear or actuality of riot and the slow rise of violent crime. Without these, neglect would be the more likely policy response.

A Review of Postwar Urban and Community Policies

In the middle years of the twentieth century, the new town concept aimed to produce balanced communities. The 1940s policies promoted social mixing as a desirable policy goal. Slum clearance aimed to improve the housing stock and particularly affected working-class communities – 'they broke us up and put us on the edge of town'.

The Urban Programme was announced on 5 May 1968, partly to quell fears encapsulated and exacerbated by Enoch Powell's infamous 'rivers of blood' speech (given in Birmingham on 21 April 1968). The link was thus closely established between urban deprivation and immigration/racial issues – an association that has dogged discussion since that time.

Box 13.5: A synopsis of key events and policy initiatives

1958	Notting Hill and Nottingham riots
1967	Plowden Report (on education)
From late 1960s	Educational Priority Areas
1968	Urban Programme
1968	Seebohm Report (on local authority and allied social services)
1969	Skeffington Report (on people and planning)
1969	Redcliffe Maud Commission (report on local government)
1969–78	Community development projects
1973	Urban Deprivation Unit (a think tank) established
1977	White Paper-Policy for the Inner Cities
1979	Priority Estates Project
Early 1980s	Inner city riots
1981	Scarman report on the Brixton disorders of 10–12 April
1981	Urban development corporations (continuing through 1980s)
1985	City action teams and task forces
1986	Abolition of metropolitan authorities
1986	Tackling Drugs Together
1988	Housing Act
1988	Action for Cities
1988	Safer Cities Programme
1990–1	City Challenge
1994	Single Regeneration Budget

In the 1970s, twelve Community Development Projects (CDPs) were launched. The CDPs aimed to provide low-cost, self-help models to regenerate localities facing economic decline. They concentrated on social problem groups in deprived areas. The aim was to reduce the extent to which children were removed from their families and put into care, presented for psychiatric treatment or were dependent on welfare benefits. But the target of intervention was not just the families or their children but the neighbourhoods in which they lived. The solution was thought to be the better coordination of services and the mobilization of self-help and mutual aid in the community – familiar themes today.

The inner city riots of the early 1980s are the key to explaining the pattern of policy development in that decade. Earlier inner-city policies were seen to have failed. The solution lay in creating an enterprise society. A contribution of Thatcherism was to add to the notions of the 'culture of poverty' the idea that this was compounded by 'welfare dependency'. The welfare state was itself an obstacle to individual initiative, and the market and the involvement of the private sector were judged the best solution to urban decay. Markets replaced politics, urban entrepreneurs mattered more than public servants, physical capital was targeted more than social capital, and the creation of wealth was considered more important than its redistribution. These years saw a proliferation of initiatives designed to give the private sector the lead. Regeneration was the goal – the regeneration not only of declining areas but of the whole society and culture. Property developers were given a pivotal role to play. Local government and local people living in the areas suffering from urban decline were marginalized. Ideas of 'trickle-down' dominated – poor and deprived communities would in time benefit from the wealth created by giving rich, enterprising people and organizations the leading role (MacGregor and Pimlott, 1990).

By the end of the 1980s, however, the government was being criticized for its lack of a coherent urban strategy, the exclusion of local government and the failure of local communities to benefit from urban regeneration initiatives (Hoggett, 1997). Increasing stress was placed on the role of communities in urban regeneration and the 1990s developments in City Challenge initiatives expressly aimed to involve local communities. City Challenge involved competition between local authorities for funds, and areas were selected because of high deprivation and indicators of high levels of crime. The two wings of concern thus came explicitly together – the rediscovery of the social was linked directly to the crime and disorder theme. Areas had also, however, to show some signs of potential and thus indicate that investment in them would be worthwhile. Key words used in winning bids were stakeholders, partnership, milestones, evaluation, business and community. This approach was continued with the Single Regeneration Budget (SRB) system, which also stressed the role of local communities in the development of strategies. The objectives set for the SRB indicate what were seen as the sources of problems in some communities. It was to:

- direct funds;
- enhance employment, education and skills, especially of young and disadvantaged people;
- sustain economic growth and improve the competitiveness of the local economy;
- improve housing – its physical condition – and offer greater choice and better management;
- support initiatives to benefit ethnic minorities;
- tackle crime and improve community safety;
- aim at environmental improvement and better design;
- enhance the quality of life, including through support for health, cultural and sport activities.

Safer Cities 1988 and the parallel developments in drugs prevention initiatives from the early 1990s also stressed, as Gould's chapter shows, the importance of adopting a multi-agency approach to the localized problems of drugs and crime. The emphasis was on lateral links, integrated service development, coordination and partnership – central characteristics of 1990s policy. Also the more moderated tones of 1990s policy statements reflect a strong injection of techniques drawn from human resource management – extending these approaches first from the private sector to the public sector and thence out to the community and the polity itself.

Riots and the growth of fear of crime are thus a key backcloth to late-twentieth-century developments in policy regarding problematic communities. The steady 'criminalization of social policy' in the past two decades (by which social control rather than social care becomes the dominant policy concern) is starkly exemplified in policy responses to problematic communities and those who live within them, especially the young (see Cook's chapter). But in response to the Scarman Report (Scarman, 1981) and the obvious failures of policing, the decade also saw the 'socialization of criminal justice policy' (the family, community and civil society being drawn into control and prevention initiatives rather than leaving everything to the police, courts and prisons). So there was a growing stress on the need for partnership between the police and local communities. Multi-agency working, linking the police, the health authorities, the local authorities, business and the voluntary sector, became established practice through schemes to prevent crime and deal with the drugs problem.

Recent policy has been shaped also by the dominant 'winners and losers' theme in broader social policies. Particularly notable after 1970 was the growth of influence of US thinking and a borrowing of policy approaches. But there has also been a considerable countervailing influence from continental Europe, i.e. from the European Union, especially through notions of social exclusion and partnership and with the specific injection of funds to areas identified as in special need because of their high rates of unemployment or poverty.

Policy Options for the Future: The Contemporary Mission of Social Inclusion

> In inner-city areas, outer-city estates and an increasing number of rural areas, excluded communities are teetering on the point of collapse, their resources of self-organisation and resistance overwhelmed by the sheer scale of economic and social change which they had endured.
>
> Hoggett, 1997, p. 12

The new term to define the old set of problems is social exclusion (see too Donnison's discussion and questions). Social exclusion refers to the problematic poor, the poor in problematic communities. In EU discourse, where the term originated, social exclusion refers to the denial of access to social rights such as employment, housing and health care. Policies built on these perceptions stress breaking down barriers to access, such as job opportunities, transport and childcare. It is also assumed in this discourse that if areas become progressively cut off from the mainstream they begin to develop alternative cultures, which can be a breeding ground for crime, disorder and deviance. Another assumption is that these conditions have proved resistant to traditional policy solutions, so something new must be tried. The language centres on gaps – the gap between the one-parent family and the two-income family, the gap between the inner city and the suburb, the gap between school failures and those who achieve ever more in the educational league tables.

An important influence on New Labour thinking has been an awareness of the distinction between work-poor and work-rich households and between the neighbourhoods where these are concentrated. Its policies are influenced by notions of social disintegration. Lack of control is at the root, its causes lying with broken families, ineffective or arbitrary discipline by parents (unclear boundaries being set), community disintegration and social disorder. The right response is to establish more effective control. Another problem is thought to be that with the proliferation of the agencies and professions involved – medicine, social work, criminal justice: architects, planners, community workers, housing officers, education authorities – agencies and authorities are often as much working against each other as working together. There were calls for better coordination. The 1990s reaction to the 1980s was to emphasize the importance of partnership and an awareness of people and of the social factor. Top–down, prescriptive programmes were thought to have little impact: economic regeneration without attention to social regeneration will do nothing to solve the problems of poor communities. The 1990s orthodoxy was to stress the need to link environmental improvements, economic regeneration and social regeneration, aiming at integrated and holistic local policy making. The multi-agency approach became the required solution to almost every problem. Joined-up policy and practice is expected.

Local partnerships should involve people working together to develop and implement local strategies – they might include public-sector agencies, employers, trade unions, voluntary organizations and community groups. The 1998 Social Exclusion Unit report *Bringing Britain Together: A New Deal For Communities* outlined the policy approach at the turn of the century. All bids for financial support would need to involve and engage the community – it was assumed they would not succeed unless they did so.

The thrust of the New Labour approach is to give as much support as possible to those people who are willing to be included. For those who refuse, the responses of the 1998 Crime and Disorder Act come into play. This requires local authorities and the police to develop community safety partnerships and to produce 'joint crime audits'. Anti-social behaviour orders have been created, providing a civil remedy to restrain anti-social behaviour by individuals or groups. Changes to the youth justice system were also introduced. Parenting orders may be served on the parents of young offenders and truants and the parents may be required to attend parental training in the form of counselling or guidance sessions.

The new 'third way' approach looks rather like a late-twentieth-century version of New Liberalism, the more hopeful philosophy that gained ground towards the end of the nineteenth century. Marshall, for example, debated 'whether progress may not go steadily if slowly, till the official distinction between working man and gentleman has passed away; till by occupation at least

---

Box 13.6: Some New Labour policy initiatives

To encourage labour-inclusion through an attachment to the world of work
    New Deal
    Working Families Tax Credit

To improve regeneration and conditions in poorer areas
    Regional Development Agencies (which administer the Single Regeneration Budget and are responsible for all European regeneration money)
    Health Action Zones
    Education Action Zones
    Employment Zones

To improve conditions in poor communities
    New Deal for Communities (which brings together investment in buildings and people; pilot projects in 17 cities designated as 'pathfinder areas' have been launched)
    Sure Start

To improve policy and the coordination of initiatives
    Social Exclusion Unit (which is directly responsible to the Cabinet and ensures that all policies that have a bearing on social exclusion, including urban renewal, are part of an integrated strategy, incorporating health, education and crime policy)
    Urban Task Force

---

every man is a gentleman' (1873, p. 18). The principal notions were progress, rationality, ethics and prudence. A moralized capitalism could develop the best in human society. With the decaying attraction of ideas of socialism, the wheel has come full circle. Those people who have been left behind in the general improvement in living standards, the excluded, are those thought to be socially maladjusted and lacking in skills – those who in the nineteenth century were seen to be of 'poor physique and weak character'. Thrift, sobriety and a place for cooperatives and friendly societies are again voiced as the way forward for poor communities. Through a variety of state-sponsored initiatives in education and training, in health and social security, a war is now being waged on the culture of poverty.

The story of this chapter has been of the continuance of old problems but also of the repeated invention of new terms to describe them. New terms imply that we have found a new explanation and that a new policy can solve the problem. Claims of newness and policy invention are the stuff of political life. A closer look, however, shows us a variation within a rather narrow range of policy options and much continuity over time. But there have been major disruptions and re-orientations of policy periodically, owing mainly to the need to respond to much larger forces emanating from outside the domestic polity, such as wars and global economic restructuring.

One question remains: how can we effect social control and bring about social cohesion in the absence of a welfare state? What mechanisms could adequately take its place? So far the alternatives appear ineffective – mere plasters which peel off quickly, revealing festering sores beneath. Why is it always so difficult for us to hear the message that what problematic neighbourhoods need is decent housing, basic social amenities, improved transport, some opportunity for

Issues to Consider

- Review the social geography of your local area. What evidence is there for a coincidence of spatial and social segregation? Which factors appear to account for these differences? Identify a range of residential areas in your locality. Conduct a pilot investigation talking to workers and agencies (from outside and inside these areas) about their images of these communities (e.g. the police, service personnel, news reporters, health and social services personnel, teachers, tenants associations, local councillors, leaders and members of different faith associations). How do images of areas differ? How can these differences between images be explained?
- Collect examples of media reports on 'problematic communities' (e.g. TV documentaries, national and local newspaper reports). Analyse the language used in these reports, the images and illustrations used and the nature of the evidence that appears in them. Do they appear to raise alarm about these areas? What kind of interventions do they seem to encourage?
- Outline one or more recent government initiatives which aim to help problematic communities. Evaluate their effects and benefits, including by talking to actual or potential users of their services.
- Select one report analysing the situation in 'problematic communities' (e.g. the Scarman report, the report of Social Exclusion Unit, one report from the Joseph Rowntree area regeneration programme). Critically review the main arguments presented, discuss the main assumptions, look carefully at the choice and presentation of evidence, and consider the policy recommendations that follow. What political forces are likely to influence the extent to which this report will be acted upon?
- Compare some books and reports written by journalists (e.g. Campbell (1993) and Davies (1998)) with some written by social scientists (e.g. Green (1996) and Power (1997)). Discuss the strengths and weaknesses of each approach.

entertainment and more jobs? Is it perhaps because if we are to meet these needs we should require a commitment to redistribution, which is presently off the political agenda?

Suggestions for Further Reading

Campbell (1993) describes social upheavals in Oxford, Cardiff, Tyneside and elsewhere from the perspectives of various people involved. One of her central themes is the contemporary crisis of masculinity. It argues that neither manners nor mothers are to blame but that there is an economic emergency in these areas. (See also MacGregor (1994) and Lewis's chapter.) Similarly, following the long-established genre of exploration of 'hidden Britain', Davies (1998) looks at 'the country of the poor', focusing especially on the lives of children and the damage inflicted on them by poverty. Power (1997) looks at the social consequences of mass housing in northern Europe, an issue also explored in a report from the OECD (1998), which represents the current orthodoxy on how to tackle this social problem. The issue of sink estates is also addressed in the SEU's report (Social Exclusion Unit, 1998), which both attempts to describe the problem and sets out a national strategy to address these issues. While not focusing particularly on distressed or problematic communities, the final report of the Urban Task Force (DETR, 1999) provides evidence on the wider context and on the need for policies addressing the concerns of distressed communities to be linked with broader proposals for urban renaissance. Silburn et al. (1999) focus on residents' perceptions of their neighbourhoods, their experience of living in these localities, their aspirations, the extent and strength of informal social networks and community groups, and the opportunities and difficulties faced by different ethnic groups.

Ongoing developments can be tracked through: Department of the Environment, Transport and the Regions: www.regeneration.detr.gov.uk; www.regen.net; Common Purpose (a charity aiming to bring together all those interested in urban renewal): www.commonpurpose.org.uk; Centre for Local Economic Strategies (the regeneration network): www.cles.org.uk. References on the changing welfare state can also be found through: www.dss.gov.uk and the Joseph Rowntree Foundation website: www.jrf.org.uk.

References

Bauman, Z. 1990: *Life in Fragments: Essays in Postmodern Morality*. Oxford: Blackwell.

Bauman, Z. 1998: *Work, Consumerism and the New Poor*. Buckingham: Open University Press.

Campbell, B. 1993: *Goliath. Britain's Dangerous Places*. London: Methuen.

Cattell, V. and Evans, M. 1999: *Neighbourhood Images in East London*. York: Joseph Rowntree Foundation.

Dahrendorf, R. 1985: *Law and Order*. London: Stevens.

Davies, N. 1998: *Dark Heart*. London: Vintage.

Department of the Environment, Transport and the Regions 1999: *Towards an Urban Renaissance*, Rogers Report (Urban Task Force). London: DETR.

Green, A. E. 1996: Aspects of the changing geography of poverty and wealth. In J. Hills (ed.), *New Inequalities.* Cambridge: Cambridge University Press.

Hoggett, P. (ed.) 1997: *Contested Communities*. Bristol: Policy Press.

Lewis, O. 1964: *The Children of Sanchez*. London: Penguin.

MacGregor, S. 1981: *The Politics of Poverty*. London: Longman.

MacGregor, S. 1994: Review of Goliath: Britain's dangerous places. *Renewal*, 2 (3), 81–4.

MacGregor, S. and Pimlott, B. (eds) 1990: *Tackling the Inner Cities*. Oxford: Clarendon Press.

Marshall, A. 1873: The future of the working classes, read to a conversazione of the Cambridge Reform Club, quoted in G. Stedman Jones, 1971. *Outcast London*. Oxford: Oxford University Press.

OECD 1998: *Integrating Distressed Urban Areas*. Paris: Organization for Economic Co-operation and Development.

Pearson, G. 1987: Social deprivation, unemployment and patterns of heroin use. In N. Dorn and N. South (eds), *A Land Fit for Heroin?* London: Macmillan.

Power, A. 1997: *Estates on the Edge*. London: Macmillan.

Reiner, R. 1990: Crime and policing. In S. MacGregor and B. Pimlott (eds), *Tackling the Inner Cities*. Oxford: Clarendon Press.

Scarman, Lord 1981: Brixton Disorder, 10–12 April 1981: Report of an Inquiry, Cmnd. 8427. London: HMSO.

Silburn, R., Lucas, D., Page, R. and Hanna, L. 1999: *Neighbourhood Images in Nottingham*. York: Joseph Rowntree Foundation.

Social Exclusion Unit 1998: Bringing Britain Together: A New Deal for Communities. London: Stationery Office. See too Social Exclusion Unit 1998: *Bringing People Together: A National Strategy for Neighbourhood Renewal*, Cmnd. 4045. London: Stationery Office.

Wacquant, L. 1999: The rise of advanced marginality: notes on its nature and implications. *Acta Sociologica*, 39 (2), 121–39.

White, J. 1986: *The Worst Street In North London*. London: Routledge & Kegan Paul.

Wilson, J. E. and Kelling, G. 1982: Broken windows. *Atlantic Monthly* (March), 31–2.

Chapter 14

Safe and Sound? Crime, Disorder and Community Safety Policies

Dee Cook

Introduction

As other chapters in this volume suggest, we live in an uncertain world with multiple social problems ranging from the personal (health risks, road and work accidents, job insecurity and poverty) to the global (risks of war, famine, pandemic disease, earthquakes and environmental pollution). Given this extensive catalogue of (post)modern problems, it is useful to ask the question: 'why do we worry so much about crime?'

Answers to this question are varied and often contradictory, including, on the one hand:

- because the media exaggerates our fears;
- because the government uses the issue of crime to divert our attention from more pressing social problems;

and, on the other hand:

- because, given our experience of crime and disorder, our fears are very real;
- because crime is spiralling out of control, and the police and the government are unable to tackle it.

Whichever perspective is adopted, there is little doubt that crime, disorder and the anxieties to which they give rise, were primary social concerns in the last quarter of the twentieth century. As other chapters show, these anxieties have also been reflected in the private as well as the public spheres, with mounting concerns about the role of the family, yet an awareness of its potential as a site of violence. The purpose of this chapter is to discuss the roots and context of concerns about crime, disorder and violence, and to examine ways in which recent government policy has been directed towards reducing crime and the fear of crime. It will proceed in three parts, which will:

- chart the development of public and policy responses to crime, and the fear of crime, over the past 25 years;
- analyse the assumptions underpinning the concept of community safety and its role in the reduction of crime and disorder;
- critically examine contemporary community safety policy and its implementation under New Labour.

Understanding Policy Responses to Crime

The legacy of the past 25 years

In terms of the government's economic and social policies, the years 1974–6 marked a significant break with what had gone before. In sharp contrast with the previous decade, Britain in the mid-1970s was beset by a deepening economic and industrial relations crisis coupled with a conservative backlash against what had come to be seen as the 'permissive' cultural climate of the 1960s. A vital component of this backlash was a powerful appeal for 'law and order', which served to bridge both sets of concerns – the economic and the social.

This fusion of economic and social concerns is particularly evident in the issues of crime and trade union power, which were frequently referred to within the same breath as, for example, in 1979 when Margaret Thatcher spoke of the 'vandals on the picket lines and muggers on the streets' (Hale, 1989). Appeals for law and order became unifying and populist themes which encapsulated a range of the social anxieties of the day: 'The Tory Party was able to present a coherent framework in which to tackle problems in both the economy and social life. The debate as they defined it had recurring themes: welfare scroungers, stand on your own two feet, the need to break the dependency culture, trades unions operating outside the law, moral decline, personal discipline and personal responsibility' (Hale, 1989, p. 344).

Law and order proved to be the decisive factor in the Conservative election victory in 1979, which brought Margaret Thatcher to power. In relation to this dominant agenda, 'the mugger on the street' had become a particularly powerful symbol of Britain's economic and social decline in the mid-1970s, although the word mugging and the moral panic it generated had been imported from the USA. Public fears about mugging in the UK were, therefore, largely shaped by the US experience and were distinctly racialized (Hall et al., 1978). The racialization of the law and order discourse continued into the 1980s as Britain witnessed a shift in concern from crime as such to wider social disorder following the riots (or disturbances or uprisings, depending on your perspective) in its cities during 1980–1 and 1985. Despite evidence to the contrary, the events in

Brixton (London), Handsworth (Birmingham), Toxteth (Liverpool) and Moss Side (Manchester) were defined as race riots, so the threat posed to social order was once again seen to be a racial one (Solomos, 1993, p. 129; and the chapter in this book by McLaughlin and Murji).

The policy responses to the law and order 'crisis' of the 1970s and 1980s were essentially punitive: the policies were primarily concerned to apprehend and punish offenders, rather than to rehabilitate them or prevent their offending. What crime prevention there was during the 1980s was *situational* rather than *social* – it involved locks, bolts and 'target hardening' and did not seek to address the social conditions which were regarded by many as the source of crime. The emphasis, then, was on crime as the product of individual 'wickedness', and there was little political truck with social explanations. For instance, the then Home Secretary Douglas Hurd's response to the 1985 disturbances in Handsworth was that the events marked 'not a cry for help, but a cry for loot'. Tabloid headlines including 'Hate of the Black Bomber' (the *Sun*), 'Bloodlust' (the *Daily Mail*) and 'War on the Streets' (the *Mirror*) similarly focused on the allegedly linked issues of race and criminality. The tabloid press ignored, however, the social problems of racism and the apparent breakdown of community policing in Handsworth, which many people felt to be at the heart of the problem.

Looking back at the list of social and economic problems, identified by Hale, which the Conservatives highlighted in 1979, we could, two decades on, ask the question 'what has changed?' Clearly, the perceived 'problem' of powerful trade unions is no longer on the political agenda, but the remaining concerns about welfare dependency and personal and moral responsibility are echoed in Tony Blair's New Labour agenda. Fears about the moral decline engendered by the 'permissive 60s' are now replaced by a 'moral crusade', which marches on into the twenty-first century.

The 1990s have witnessed a return to fears about crime – particularly about youth crime and 'anti-social behaviour' (Cook, 1997). Significantly, one of the most important mantras of the 1990s was Blair's promise (made in opposition) to be 'tough on crime and tough on the causes of crime'. The government's policy response to this promise is a community safety strategy, implemented at a local level, which adopts a twin-track approach – reducing the problems of crime and disorder, while addressing the perceived causes of crime within those localities. The community safety approach (discussed in detail below) also aims to tackle the problem of the insecurity and anxiety that crime engenders. To grasp the popular and political significance of this problem we need to try to unravel the complex issue of the fear of crime.

The fear of crime

As the brief historical outline above indicates, the past twenty-five years have been characterized by a series of moral panics and law and order campaigns about a range of issues: trade union 'vandals and militants'; mugging; street crime; 'race riots'; youth crime; anti-social behaviour. While criminal justice policy responses were primarily offender-focused, there has also been an increasing concern for victims of crime. In the 1970s the rhetorical question 'what about the victim?' was a rallying cry for those who advocated tougher punishments for offenders. But pioneering surveys of victims in the USA during the mid-1970s demonstrated a huge gap between official crime statistics and the higher levels of crime reported by the victims in the survey population.

The national British Crime Survey (BCS) was established in 1982 to address the problem of the 'hidden figure of crime', but it also sought to correct some other popular misconceptions about crime – notably to address the fear of crime. It attempted to allay public fears about violent crime by offering data which showed, for instance, that the statistical risks of becoming a victim of serious crime were low: an average person aged over 16 could expect a robbery once every 500 years, and an assault leading to injury once in 100 years. None the less, for some subgroups of the population the risks were far higher. Successive BCS reports have demonstrated that the risks of being a victim of crime are shaped by locality, lifestyle, age, gender and ethnicity (Mirrlees-Black et al., 1996). For example, they confirm that the risks of being a victim of 'contact crime' (including mugging, domestic violence and violence by strangers and acquaintances) are highest for men, those aged under 30, those living in inner-city areas and those living in privately rented accommodation.

None the less, according to the BCS it is frequently those who are least at risk of crime who are most anxious about it – notably older people and women. But the fear of crime is a complex phenomenon which cannot be merely labelled 'rational' or 'irrational', depending on the statistical risk. Such a rational calculation of the risk of crime therefore fails to address the deeper issue of anxiety. It may also fail to address other facets of those crimes, such as racial harassment and domestic violence, which remain 'hidden' even in victimization surveys. As we shall see below, community safety strategies have a remit to address precisely these hidden crimes by auditing and 'mapping' them within specific localities and generating action plans to reduce their incidence.

But it is worth sounding a note of caution on two grounds: first, many crimes remain hidden from victimization surveys and from view, and are not 'mappable' for the purposes of community safety strategy. For example, 'An accurate map of urban rape would highlight far more bedrooms than alleyways and parks' (Pain, 1997, p. 223). So we have a profound spatial paradox whereby women are most fearful of being victims of crime in lonely public spaces, yet most violent crime against women is domestic (see too Radford's chapter). Secondly, anxiety about crime is often firmly grounded in people's own experiences, whether direct or indirect: nationally based risk calculations thus fail to take into account the 'local crime climate' or the networked knowledge of local experiences, which profoundly shapes attitudes towards crime.

Any policy geared to tackling crime needs to address the anxiety to which it gives rise. Much anxiety is spatially experienced: people are fearful of particular places and neighbourhoods, and it is to this level of concern that community safety strategies are also addressed. As Smith noted in 1983, the principal effects of crime for a community are the fear, concern and suspicion it generates: 'The fears thus engendered are rooted in physical decay, institutional neglect and social disintegration; and they are manifest in the concerns about criminality that these factors either depict or encourage' (Smith, 1983, pp. 428, 432).

There is therefore a vicious circle (or spiral of decline) in which crime and environmental decay are seen to be mutually re-inforcing, as the one is cited as evidence of (and an explanation for) the other, very often in the context of 'sink' housing estates (see MacGregor's chapter). But, at the same time, crime and environmental decay are both seen to be associated with deeply rooted social and cultural changes – epitomized by the notion of the 'loss of community': 'With the collapse of local communities there is less stigma attached to criminality, the informal sanctions and expressions of disapproval which offenders fear are no longer there; and they have little reason to empathize with their victims. There are fewer inbuilt deterrents and greater incentives to criminal behaviour' (Hutton, quoted in Worrall, 1997, p. 49). However, for Hutton, community breakdown and crime are not the products of individual inadequacies, but the logical consequences of the economic and social policies of the past twenty years. These policies have resulted in what he considers an obsession with short-term profits, a lack of investment, unemployment, insecurity, impoverishment and social exclusion, particularly of the young. This view echoes earlier analyses in the USA, which similarly argued that urban communities blighted by such 'capital disinvestment' became associated with a 'recapitalization' around illegal activities – notably drugs and crime. Although, particularly for young people, crime may bring short-term gains, the long-term consequences are significantly diminished life-chances, and a spiral of decline prolonged into adulthood (Hagan, 1994, p. 93).

Assumptions Underpinning the Concept of Community Safety

What is community?

Community is a 'feel-good' word which 'evokes images of neighbourliness, mutual aid and a positive sense of belonging' (Worrall, 1997, p. 46). But, MacGregor's chapter also emphasizes that, beneath the feel-good factor, there is much debate over the uses and abuses of the term. The consequences of evoking the concept of community are not always positive and inclusive. For example, for those people who cannot gain access to the community 'club', it may be the source of racist, sexist or other forms of discrimination. Similarly, perhaps, 'communitarianism' may be used to justify the actions or reactions of those who feel 'betrayed' by the actions of criminals and who therefore close ranks against them. In both these cases, the use and implications of the term community may be exclusive not inclusive.

The term community is a deeply problematic one. Broadly, it may cover a *territory* (such as a neighbourhood) or comprise a set of people with a common interest or sense of identity (such as ethnic minority groups, the gay community or the deaf community). Beyond these different meanings, the term community may have very different implications where crime reduction is concerned. For example, according to the Home Office, a community may be:

- a *target* of crime (and so becomes the object of interventions to reduce crime);
- a *source* of crime (with significant numbers of that community being the subject of preventive and regulatory action);
- a *setting* within which crime reduction interventions are 'owned', planned and implemented;
- a source of *general capacity* to enhance trust, protect and empower residents (adapted from Ekblom, 1998, pp. 9–10).

Put simply, a community may be seen as a source of crime, or criminals may be seen as betrayers of community; the community may be a passive target of policy intervention, or actively engaged in policy making, to tackle crime.

Notwithstanding the contested definitions and different uses of the term, there remains, in the realm of crime reduction policy, a fundamental assumption – based on a nostalgic view of community – that 'more community equals less crime'. Harking back to an alleged golden age of community (with minimal crime), this view is appealing in theory, but is untenable in practice. Most low-crime areas in modern Britain are middle-class, suburban localities; they do not possess the features of mutual support, shared identity and 'connectedness' which are commonly associated with traditional notions of community. Paradoxically, then, community responses to crime (for instance, through residents' activism, Neighbourhood Watch and so on) 'are easiest to generate in exactly those [middle class] areas where they are least needed and hardest to establish in those where the need is greatest' (Crawford, 1998, p. 159).

What is community safety?

> Community safety is perhaps best *seen as an aspect of 'quality of life' in which people individually and collectively, are protected as far as possible from the hazards or threats that result from the criminal or anti-social behaviour of others, and are equipped or helped to cope with those they do experience. It should enable them to pursue, and obtain fullest benefits from, their social and economic lives without fear or hindrance from crime and disorder.* (Ekblom, 1998, p. 8, emphasis in original)

This extract, from a Home Office publication, indicates that within the context of community safety strategies, crime and disorder are conceived as essentially 'quality of life' problems. On the face of it, this marks a significant shift away from an individualized perspective to a 'socializing' of the problem of crime – tackling crime *and* its causes. But, as I shall go on to argue, the focus of the government's crime reduction strategy, based on the community safety approach, is far more geared to the former (tackling crime) than the latter (addressing its root causes).

In a briefing entitled *Reducing Crime and Tackling Its Causes* (Home Office, 1999) the Home Secretary announced the £250 million Crime Reduction Programme (CRP), which was (ambitiously) geared to securing a reversal in the long-term rise in crime and achieving a corresponding reduction in the fear of crime. The stated goals of the CRP are explicitly linked with broader social aims to 'add value to every aspect of life, enhance liberty and revitalise our communities.' (Home Office, 1999, p. 2). These goals tie in with the remit of the government's overarching Social Exclusion Unit (SEU), set up in 1997, to 'develop integrated and sustainable approaches to the problems of the worst housing estates, including crime, drugs, unemployment, community breakdown and bad schools etc.' (Social Exclusion Unit, 1998).

The first SEU report (1998), *Bringing Britain Together*, outlines the goals and plans of the 18 separate (but 'joined-up') policy action teams operating within the SEU framework. The four goals are to achieve:

- lower long-term unemployment;
- less crime;
- better health;
- better qualifications.

The SEU seeks to succeed, where other policy initiatives since the 1960s have failed, 'in setting in motion a virtuous circle of regeneration, with improvements in jobs, crime, education, health and housing all reinforcing each other.' (SEU, 1998, p. 9).

Box 14.1

Clearly the problem of crime is currently being set in the context of the broader problem of *social exclusion*. Consequently, the policy goals of both crime reduction and community regeneration are inextricably linked, as 'the fight against crime is at the centre of this Government's commitment to make Britain a better place to live'. (Home Office, 1999, p. 2). The fight against crime is currently being waged principally in local neighbourhoods, through the operation of community safety strategies.

Community Safety Policy under New Labour

Local solutions to local problems?

> At the heart of our strategy to build safer communities will be a network of local partnerships to reduce local crime and disorder. These statutory partnerships will bring together local authorities, the police and other statutory agencies. They will be required to examine local levels of crime and disorder, consult local people and then set targets to reduce crime and disorder which they identify. (Home Secretary Jack Straw, in a speech to the Magistrates' Association, 25 June 1998).

This speech captures the essence of community safety policy – seeing crime as a local problem requiring local solutions – and it crystallizes the policy's ingredients, which are:

- a multi-agency approach, involving all the relevant voluntary and statutory agencies (e.g. the local authority's chief executive, social services and health, education and criminal justice agencies);
- a joint leadership of multi-agency partnerships by the local authority and criminal justice agencies;
- conducting a local (borough-wide) crime audit, in consultation with the local community, to establish the extent of crime and disorder in the locality;
- setting targets and responsibilities for reducing crime and disorder in the form of a community safety plan (with deadlines and performance indicators).

Jack Straw saw the Crime and Disorder Act 1998 as setting the legislative framework within which local people could 'take control of the fight against crime and disorder in their area'. Although residents are often best placed to identify the problems which face them, and to suggest workable solutions, the extent to which community safety strategies implemented under the Act will facilitate such empowerment is open to debate. The requirement to consult the community may take a variety of forms: it may involve a purely token (*post factum*) consultation with a small number of community representatives. Or it may involve outreach work and qualitative research to identify the concerns of socially excluded groups.

As I have argued earlier, communities are not just places, but people with diverse sets of interests and identities. If genuine community safety strategies are to develop, there is a need to take into account the views of the community in both the spatial and normative senses of the term. Therefore, we need to pose the following questions when assessing the value and relevance of community safety strategies, in practice and at local level:

- Has the strategy obtained and voiced the views of 'hard to reach', marginalized and/or socially excluded groups?

- Who decides on the key priorities of the strategy?
- In whose interests are the strategy's targets set?

Put simply, often it is those who are already empowered (through active engagement with local politics and community activities) who are asked to help define the problem of crime and disorder. This, in turn, may distort the policy's priorities, as the views of, for example, minority ethnic groups, the disabled, lone mothers and members of the gay community may be unheard, despite their experiences of victimization and harassment. In the absence of alternative voices, community safety strategy may end up serving only established interest groups. An inadequate consultation thus restricts the scope of local community safety agendas, which go on to shape how targets to measure success are set: targets set may end up representing only those achievable tasks which dominant agencies feel can be tackled and measured in community safety plans. In such circumstances, it is probable that the managerial needs of the police and local authorities are more likely to be met than the safety needs of the local community.

In addition, the internal politics of partner agencies may well distort the collaborative ideal underpinning community safety. Sustained and positive collaborations depend first and foremost on equality between partners, whether they are voluntary, statutory or community based. Where the 'lead partners' (the police and local authority representatives) dominate the crime and disorder agenda and/or do not accord equal power and voice to their community partners, then the principles of consultation and empowerment are eroded and the community safety project may collapse. But this strategic project also requires political momentum (national and local) and adequate resourcing for its implementation. However, additional resources have not been provided by the government to local authorities or criminal justice agencies for the implementation of the Act. The government has argued that this crucial policy initiative will be financed retrospectively from the savings that will accrue from reducing crime and all its associated costs.

Box 14.2

At the root of community safety policy under New Labour is the impetus to *manage crime and disorder in its place*, within localities, and not to change the behaviour of those who commit crime. There is an imbalance, then, between the twin objectives of New Labour's crime reduction strategy – tackling crime and its causes. The causes of crime are not to be tackled so much as *managed*. There is far less concern about addressing the social and economic circumstances or behaviour of offenders, and there is far more concern to demonstrate that 'something is being done' about crime and disorder.

Joined-up criminal justice and social policies?

Any brief discussion of partnership working indicates the difficulties of joining up local multi-agency policies. In addition to the (often competing) politics of partner agencies, there are doubts about the seriousness of much partnership working: the partnerships are often either 'talking shops' or 'paper partnerships' that exist only to satisfy funding or other formal requirements (Crawford, 1998, p. 184). Given that the government's community safety strategy is premised on the effective working of partnerships between local community, statutory and voluntary agencies, such criticisms must be taken seriously. A range of other New Labour social policies are similarly predicated on a local partnership approach, including, for example, Education and Health Action Zones and the New Deal for Communities. Add to this list the local tapestry of Single Regeneration Budget (SRB) schemes in many deprived estates and localities, and the problem of strategic coordination and planning becomes even more acute (see too MacGregor's chapter). It is perhaps significant that the remit of one of the SEU's 18 action teams is 'joining it up locally', which aims to ensure that 'all these different initiatives should be dovetailed so as to make local planning to social exclusion the norm' (SEU, 1998, p. 76).

It could be argued that it is far too early to assess the success or otherwise of community safety policies. To be judged successful in their own terms, they will need to have:

- demonstrably reduced crime and disorder, measured locally;
- empowered local communities to find local solutions to local problems of crime and disorder;
- enabled communities to shape a better future for themselves;
- tackled the causes of crime (to the extent that it is defined as the product of social exclusion).

Measuring success depends on one's starting point: if crime audits are conducted on a 'quick, cheap and dirty' basis (to meet Home Office requirements and no more) then it is likely that the data could demonstrate reductions in the crimes targeted in community safety plans. To take a hypothetical example: if police statistics on recorded burglaries are accepted as robust audit data, if reducing burglary is, after consultation, deemed to be a local priority for community safety planning, if in subsequent years the number of recorded burglaries subsequently declines, then the community safety strategy which targeted this offence may be regarded, officially, a success. It would be very difficult to imagine a similarly simple and successful chain of events if the more challenging crimes of racial harassment and domestic violence were to be deemed the priorities.

Box 14.3

What of 'tackling the causes of crime'? In the current policy framework, tackling the causes of crime is considered part of the broader aim of tackling social exclusion. But it could be argued that the relation between the two is insufficiently conceptualized: until there is a clearer understanding (and clearer articulation) of the multiple causes of crime and the nature of their links with social exclusion, then it is impossible to achieve this goal. To put it simply, the scatter-gun approach to crime reduction implies that combating social exclusion will hit the causes of crime. But this is an act of faith rather than a sound basis for policy. For example, it is unclear how tackling social exclusion would reduce racially motivated crime, domestic violence or white-collar crimes such as embezzlement, fraud, pollution and tax evasion (see the chapter by Dean).

Moreover, it is unclear how the balance between combating social exclusion and combating crime will be struck: there is a danger that a range of social policies may be shackled to the goals of crime reduction (Crawford, 1998). The absence of the P word poverty in the lexis of New Labour, in favour of the 'softer' term social exclusion, may reveal a reluctance to tackle structural issues of poverty and the widening gap between rich and poor in contemporary Britain. There is ample evidence that it is the extent of social and economic inequality (rather than poverty or social exclusion, however measured) which is associated with increasing levels of crime, and that, therefore, tackling crime effectively will invariably mean reducing social inequalities. This is not an aim which New Labour currently espouses, as it promotes economic opportunity rather than redistribution.

In summary, the acid test of New Labour's crime reduction policy will be the extent to which it fulfils its stated aims to reduce crime and disorder, tackle the causes of crime, offer an enhanced sense of community safety, and reduce anxiety about crime. I should argue that, in practice, these aims are unlikely to be met unless we reconcile criminal justice policies with social *and* economic policies. The promise to 'tackle crime and the causes of crime' was a brilliant soundbite for Tony Blair to use while in opposition, but it requires a far greater synthesis between criminal justice, social and economic policies when in government.

Issues to Consider

- Examine the continuities and changes in the focus on law and order campaigns and 'moral panics' about crime and disorder over the past 25 years.
- How is the fear of crime and the experience of criminal victimization shaped by age, gender, race, lifestyle and locality?
- What kind of policies would best fulfil New Labour's promise to be 'tough on crime and tough on the causes of crime'? How can such policies – designed to address crime and its causes – be adequately reconciled?
- What are the strengths and weaknesses of a community safety approach to tackling crime and disorder?
- To what extent is it possible to produce and implement local solutions to the local problems of crime, the fear of crime, drugs and disorder?

Suggestions for Further Reading

Crawford (1998) and Cook (1997) provide lucid and comprehensive discussions of many of the issues discussed in this chapter. More extensive coverages of recent developments in criminal justice policy and policing and changing perceptions of community safety can also be found in Hudson (1993) and Marlow and Pitts (1998). The essays in Walker and Walker (1997) provide an illuminating survey of wider policy concerns and should be read alongside the studies recommended at the end of chapter 13. In addition to those mentioned in that chapter, websites useful for this topic are best accessed through www.open.gov.uk. This site provides a topic list and an alphabetical list of government departments and agencies including, for example, the Social Exclusion Unit, the Home Office Research and Statistics Directorate and the Department of Social Security. Further data can be obtained from the Office for National Statistics website: www.ons.gov.uk.

References

Cook, D. 1997: *Poverty, Crime and Punishment*. London: Child Poverty Action Group.
Crawford, A. 1998: *Crime Prevention and Community Safety*. London: Longman.
Ekblom, P. 1998: *The Crime and Disorder Act: Community Safety and the Reduction and Prevention of Crime*. Home Office Research and Statistics Directorate, August.
Hagan, J. 1994: *Crime and Disrepute*. London: Pine Forge Press.
Hale, C. 1989: Economy, crime and punishment. *Contemporary Crises*, 12 (4), 327–49.
Hall, S., Critcher, C., Jefferson, T., Clarke, J. and Roberts, B. 1978: *Policing the Crisis*. London: Macmillan.

Home Office 1999: *Reducing Crime and Tackling Its Causes: Briefing Note on the Crime Reduction Programme.* London: Home Office.

Hudson, A. 1993: *Penal Policy and Social Justice.* Basingstoke: Macmillan.

Marlow, A. and Pitts, J. (eds) 1998: *Planning Safer Communities.* Lyme Regis: Russell House Publishing.

Mirrlees-Black, C., Mayhew, P. and Percy, A. 1996: *The 1996 British Crime Survey, England and Wales,* Home Office Statistical Bulletin 19/96. London: Home Office.

Pain, R. 1997: Social geographies of women's fear of crime. *Transactions of the Institute of British Geographers,* new series, 22, 231–44.

Smith, S. 1983: Crime and the structure of social relations. *Transactions of the Institute of British Geographers,* new series, 9, 427–42.

Social Exclusion Unit 1998: *Bringing Britain Together: A National Strategy for Neighbourhood Renewal,* Cmnd. 4045. London: Stationery Office.

Solomos, J. 1993: Constructions of black criminality: racialisation and criminalisation in perspective. In D. Cook and B. Hudson (eds), *Racism and Criminology.* London: Sage.

Walker, A. and Walker, C. (eds) 1997: *Britain Divided: The Growth of Social Exclusion in the 1980s and 1990s.* London: Child Poverty Action Group.

Worrall, A. 1997: *Punishment in the Community: The Future of Criminal Justice.* London: Longman.

Chapter 15

Drugs and Drug Misuse

Arthur Gould

Any important disease whose causality is murky and for which treatment is ineffectual, tends to be awash with significance. First, the subjects of deepest dread (corruption, decay, pollution, anomie, and weakness) are identified with the disease. The disease itself becomes a metaphor

Sontag, 1991, p. 59

Introduction

Sontag was thinking primarily of diseases such as cancer and AIDS when she wrote the above, but it is just as applicable to the 'disease' of drug addiction. 'Addiction' is a disease whose 'cause' is murky and for which treatment is often 'ineffectual'. Our concern about drug problems is very much a consequence of our perception of drugs as addictive substances. We associate the growing use of illegal drugs with a cultural and moral decline that has led to the breakdown of family and community life. Drugs have become a metaphor for deeper fears and anxieties. Many people, spurred on by the moral panic created by politicians and the media, see drugs as the cause of other social problems, such as crime, unemployment and homelessness. Instead of seeking deeper explanations for the decline in communal life and community values, we make drug abuse act as a convenient scapegoat. In other words, drug misuse is considered a primary cause of other social problems. In this chapter, I shall argue that it would be more appropriate to see it as a *secondary* social problem – one that is a by-product of other social problems.

The chapter will begin by looking at how, historically, drugs came to be perceived as a problem and go on to examine some contemporary evidence on the scale of drug use and misuse. It continues with a consideration of the contentious concept of addiction. The relations between drug problems and other social problems – such as crime, homelessness and deprivation – is also explored. The chapter concludes with an outline of policy alternatives to prohibition: harm reduction, decriminalization and legalization. It therefore focuses on:

- the emergence of the drug problem;
- the scale of the drug problem;
- addiction;
- social problems and drugs;
- harm reduction in Britain;
- decriminalization and legalization.

The Emergence of the Drug Problem

Many of our illegal drugs – those that are controlled by the Misuse of Drugs Act of 1971 – have been, in one form or another, perfectly acceptable in other societies or at different times in our own society's past. Opium, the coca leaf, cannabis and peyote have had much the same status in those parts of the world where they have grown naturally as alcohol has had in Europe. Indeed, in nineteenth-century Britain, alcohol was considered a greater social evil than opium-based products such as laudanum, which could be bought over the counter from chemists and grocery stores (Berridge, 1989). Only in the twentieth century have drugs become the subject of international control. The International Convention of 1912, largely at the instigation of the USA, was the first attempt to control the drug trade. Control was a product of fears about the spread of foreign drugs, and must be seen as a product of Western, particularly US, imperialism. Musto in his history of American drug control cites frequent references to American anxieties about Mexicans and marijuana, Negroes and their use of cocaine, the Chinese and opium (Musto, 1987). Drugs were regarded as sexual stimulants – the cause of uninhibited sexual behaviour and crimes of rape. They were a threat to young Americans and the stability of American society.

Although the moral panic in Britain was not as marked as in the US, the British passed the Defence of the Realm Act in 1916 partly to prevent military personnel using drugs during World War I. This was followed by the Dangerous Drugs Act of 1920. British newspapers in the 1920s were obsessed by stories about innocent young white women being seduced by 'evil Orientals' with the aid of opium and cocaine (Kohn, 1992). Drug fears began to escalate in Britain from the 1950s with the arrival of immigrants from the Caribbean, India and Pakistan. Kohn cites one newspaper report that demonstrates the link very clearly: 'Thousands of these immigrants are pouring into Britain every year. A majority of them smoke hemp. They do not leave their vice at home – they bring it with them. And the blunt truth is that a number of them take a perverted pleasure from 'lighting up' a white girl. I know. I've watched it happen. And it's a horrible sight' (ibid, p. 181).

The drug problem, then, emerged only with the internationalization of trade in goods, services and labour. Fears about foreign drugs flooding into the country were associated with fears about immigration and 'alien' minorities. They were fears about the 'other'.

The Scale of the Drug Problem

For those people who fear the damage that drugs can do to a society, there is little distinction between drug use and drug misuse. An increase in occasional and recreational drug use can be regarded as problematic even when the individuals concerned do not experience any adverse consequences. In what follows, statistics about the prevalence of drug use will be cited, as they are often used to indicate the growing nature of drug problems. It must be remembered that drug use and misuse are not necessarily synonymous. However, the fact that use is frowned upon and possession of small amounts for personal use is a criminal offence does make even the most harmless use risky.

Every few years, the Institute for the Study of Drug Dependence produces a report on drug misuse in Britain that draws on a wide variety of sources and provides the most comprehensive overview of drug trends. The most recent report states that while only a quarter of those between 15 and 69 have used an illicit drug at some time in their lives, a half of all 16–19 year-olds have done so (ISDD, 1997, p. 31). Not only does reported use decline with age, but the percentage of users drops if you ask whether people have used drugs in the past year (10 per cent), or the past month (6 per cent). A worrying feature of recent research has been the reported incidence of drug use among children of school age. Various studies have thrown up figures of between 5 and 10 per cent.

Use is, as I have already indicated, not misuse. A frequently used indicator of misuse is the register of addicts maintained by the Home Office. Specialist doctors in Britain can provide people diagnosed as addicts with their drugs or a substitute for them, but they have to register each patient with the Home Office. Even as recently as 1977, this figure was only 2,000 (Plant, 1981). By 1987 it had risen to 11,000 and by 1996 37,000 (ISDD, 1997, p. 61). While in theory this could mean that a greater proportion of misusers visit their doctors and local drug services, it is widely accepted that misuse is growing in absolute terms.

Another indicator of growing use and possible misuse is the fact that the numbers of people found guilty of or cautioned for drug offences has been increasing year on year. In 1979 there were fewer than 15,000 but by 1995 there were almost 94,000 (ISDD, 1997, p. 78). The interesting constant about this particular statistic is that the drug concerned in 85 per cent of cases is cannabis. Now, while cannabis taken frequently and over a long period has, like any drug, damaging effects, it is widely accepted that it is one of the most harmless of drugs. Should its increased use therefore be regarded as a problem? Drug seizures by the police and customs has also grown considerably in the last twenty years. In 1977, they numbered 13,000. By 1995, this had reached almost 114,000 (ISDD, 1997, p. 76). Again around 85 per cent were for cannabis and related drugs.

Drug use and misuse have become much more widespread in the last few decades. Indeed, among particular groups within the population, the taking of drugs is the norm. A recent survey of those attending the 'dance drug scene' showed that 97 per cent had used drugs at some point in their lives (Release, 1997, p. 10). Moreover, 87 per cent were intending to use drugs on the evening when they were interviewed (p. 13).

A familiar theme in all these reports and surveys is that 'soft' drugs dominate, while 'hard' drugs are in a minority. Soft drugs are those considered least dangerous in terms of their toxicity or their addictive potential. The irony is that the fear of hard drugs has in practice led to a clamp down on soft drugs.

Addiction

The medical condemnation of drugs has, in part, to do with toxicity. Some drugs, even in small quantities, can damage the body or the brain. Taken to excess, they can lead to disability or death. But there are many toxic substances that are legally available and have not attracted stringent controls. It is the addictive potential of drugs that is used to justify their prohibition. Addiction implies that once a drug has been used the body demands more of it to achieve the original effect; this is called *tolerance*. Any attempt to stop using the drug results in *withdrawal* symptoms. The user is in danger of being controlled by the drug. Clearly, the argument that this powerful process occurs automatically is a strong justification for prohibition. Controls are necessary to protect vulnerable individuals. But when the concept of addiction is examined we find that medical people cannot agree on a definition; that many controlled drugs are not considered addictive, that addiction does not occur in most cases of drug-taking; and that many psychiatrists have thrown doubt on the validity of the concept, referring to the 'myth' of addiction and the 'myth' of alcoholism (Davies, 1992; Fingarette, 1989).

Addiction became so difficult to define that the World Health Organization abandoned the concept in 1964, in favour of the term drug dependence. Even this new formulation finished with the following statement: 'It is neither possible nor even desirable to delineate or define the term drug dependence independently of the agent involved. . . . It is the desire to . . . define a complex situation by a single term which has given rise to confusion in many cases' (cited in Krivanek, 1988, p. 52). It was the recognition that you cannot define what a drug does independently of the person taking it that led to the distinction between physical and psychological dependence. The former implies that drugs cause the body to become dependent, while the latter implies that an individual develops a compulsive desire to use them. In the one case drugs create the dependence, while in the other the source of the dependence lies within an individual's personal and social circumstances. Increasingly the trend is to emphasize psychological rather than physical dependence. Not only are cannabis and cocaine regarded as drugs which are not dependency creating, but even heroin does not create dependency in all users. Maris suggests that only 10 per cent of heroin users become dependent – exactly the same percentage as for alcohol (1996b, pp. 144–5). This would explain why large numbers of people use drugs but only a small minority become dependent, and why, of the 20 per cent of American soldiers who used heroin in Vietnam, only a small percentage were found to be using the drug after their return home (cited in Falk, 1994, p. 46).

The more the focus is on people becoming psychologically dependent, the more we are entitled to ask whether there is much difference between drug dependence and what psychiatrists call compulsive behaviour. Orford (1985) has described how people can develop excessive appetites for almost any substance or behaviour. They can become compulsive eaters, gamblers and shoppers. They can become addicted to computers, to sex and to fitness. The consequences of many of these compulsions can be as serious as those of drug dependency. People fixated by gambling can get into serious debt and lose their jobs, their families and their homes. Compulsive eaters and anorexics ruin their health and may die prematurely. We do not and cannot prohibit eating, shopping, sex and taking exercise. Why then do we prohibit the taking of drugs, some of which are not particularly toxic and none of which are addictive in themselves?

If the terms addiction and physical dependence are so unreliable why then do we use them? Davies (1992) has argued that the term addiction has become functional for both doctors and patients. The medical profession needed a justification for dealing with a particular set of symptoms. Addiction or dependence had therefore to be defined in terms of a specific disease. For the drug user, addiction can be seen as a form of 'learned helplessness' (Davies, 1992, p. 160). 'With respect to explanations for illicit drug use . . . the passive and helpless state implied by the term addiction derives from an 'implicit theory' which is primarily functional within a particular context, and . . . in other contexts people can and indeed do explain similar acts in terms which imply greater control and volition' (Davies, 1992, p. 157). In other words, it suits the purposes of both doctors and patients to use the term addiction to legitimize their relationship. Outside that context, 'addicts' admit to a much greater degree of control over their drug taking than they would be prepared to admit to their doctors.

Social Problems and Drugs

Addiction, however, is not the sole reason for condemning drug use. Whether or not drugs are addictive, excessive use causes concern about social and moral malaise. Drug taking is regarded as a cause of unemployment, homelessness, crime and prostitution. Drugs, it is argued, cause social misery for individuals, their families and their communities. This view was succinctly expressed by John Major when, as prime minister, he wrote in the introduction to a White Paper, *Tackling Drugs Together* (Home Office, 1995): 'Drugs are a menace to our society. They can wreck the lives of individuals and their families. They are a frequent cause of crime . . . Everyone's aim must be to put the drug barons out of business and protect our people from the misery and waste that drugs produce.'

The concern about a generation of young people using drugs as part of their normal existence also gives rise to fears of a counter culture. The drug culture in and around San Francisco in the 1960s rejected the work ethic and glorified religious ecstasy (Stevens, 1993) – qualities considered unlikely to lead to a disciplined work-force. The moral disapproval of drugs is in part a fear of what will happen to society if drug taking were to become the basis of the norms and values of a new generation. The problem with arguments of this kind is that they do not help us to understand why people use drugs excessively.

If we want to understand the relationships between drugs and other social problems we must consider more closely why people use them in the first place. We must also make a distinction between drug use and drug misuse. The stated reasons for taking different drugs are closely associated with the effects to which they give rise. Drugs are by definition mind-altering substances. They can stimulate (amphetamine, cocaine, ecstasy) or depress (heroin, barbiturates, benzodiazepines) mental and physical activity. They can also cause hallucinatory experiences (cannabis, LSD). People will take them to stay awake, to dull pain or to widen their sensory perception. At one level, drugs are taken for pleasure, for the pleasant feelings they give. At another level they may be taken to help cope with a difficult situation. Such use can be regarded unproblematic as long as the damage done to the users, their relationships and their economic security is minimal.

May it not be, therefore, that excessive use is associated with particularly stressful and anxiety-making situations? Some people use drugs excessively to cope with the despair created by unemployment. Having nothing to do promotes experimentation, and the daily routine of getting money for a fix provides a structure for existence (Pearson, 1987). Studies carried out in London, Glasgow and Manchester show the incidence of drug use to be much higher for homeless than for non-homeless youngsters (Flemen, 1997; Hammersley and Pearl, 1997; Klee and Reid, 1998). Young homeless people turn to drugs to help them cope with the bleakness of their situation.

> You get a good buzz off smack (heroin) at first, it helps you forget your situation. The same with the whizz (amphetamine) . . . it's such a high, you forget about your problems an' everything . . . same with anything, we sit around, have a smoke, everyone has a good laugh . . . and you forget. (Klee and Reid, 1998, p. 127)

> Just get totally wrecked so I don't think about it. (Klee and Reid, 1998, p. 127)

> I feel loads better when I'm stoned. I don't worry about money or getting a hostel . . . I think I'd get really depressed if I didn't stay out of it so much. When I use I don't start getting down about my situation. (Flemen, 1997, p. 22)

> I want to stop using but when I do, I start having bad dreams, then it all comes back and I start getting panic attacks, and get really depressed. I can't cope when I'm straight because there's too much in my head. (Flemen, 1997, p. 23)

Sargent's study of prostitutes (1992, p. 81) also suggests that their lives had been so stressful that they had used heroin to cope with:

> being expected to be grown up, taking charge of a family after the husband was arrested for murder, remaining economically independent . . . housework . . . childcare . . . socialising, preventing a nervous breakdown or the onset of depression . . . grief . . . parents quarrelling, alleviating loneliness and blocking out problems of various kinds.

About prostitution itself, one woman said, 'It's a vicious circle because to get money you have to go out and sell your body and to do that you have to be stoned' (Sargent, 1992, p. 144).

Even the argument that drug taking causes crime can be turned on its head. Hammersley has concluded that crime is a better explanation of opioid use than opioid use is of non-drug crimes (Hammersley et al., 1989). His conclusion is an important one. Since the drug trade by definition is illegal, many crimes are drug-related. But no drug can make someone engage in criminal behaviour. Bean and Wilkinson (1988) found that convicted drug users were engaged in crime long before they took drugs. All this suggests that people take drugs because it is part of the criminal scene and that they take drugs excessively because of the pressures and risks associated with criminal activity.

Even government documents admit that excessive drug use is a consequence of severe individual and social problems: 'Many explanations have been offered [for drug misuse]: personality defects, poor home background, peer group pressure, poor relationships, lack of self-esteem, youthful experimentation and rebellion' (Home Office, 1988, p. 4). Publicly, however, politicians continue to maintain the fiction that drugs cause social problems. The reason is clear. Drugs are what a Norwegian criminologist called 'The Good Enemy' (Christie, 1985). They provide a reason for many of the problems that politicians cannot or will not deal with. If addiction and dependence are functional for doctors and their patients (as was suggested above), may one not argue that they are functional for lawyers pleading on behalf of drug-taking offenders, for parents of drug-taking children and for politicians and the media seeking to find a scapegoat for society's ills?

This section has sought to show that people whose lives and personalities are secure may indulge in drug use that does not become problematic. Excessive use, which is likely to become problematic, is the result of very difficult and stressful situations.

Harm Reduction in Britain

This distinction between problematic and non-problematic use was first used officially by the Department of Health's Advisory Council on the Misuse of Drugs (ACMD) in its report into treatment and rehabilitation in 1982. While persisting with the generic term drug misusers, it said, 'The majority are relatively stable individuals who have more in common with the rest of the population than with any essentially pathological subgroup. However, for a minority, problem drug taking is sometimes one facet of a serious personality disorder or even of mental illness. There is no evidence of any uniform personality characteristic or illness' (ACMD, 1982, p. 31). The report went on to recommend the establishment of local drug advisory committees made up of representatives from health authorities, local government social services and other statutory and non-statutory agencies. They in turn would set up multi-disciplinary, community-based services to meet the particular problems of their areas. This change represented a departure from the clinics run by medical specialists for addicts (Stimson, 1987).

Under the auspices of the Thatcher government, the far-seeing Secretary of State for Health Norman Fowler set up the Central Funding Initiative (CFI) to finance a range of new community services throughout the UK. In her valuation of the project some years later, MacGregor claimed that the CFI's pump-priming £17.5 million had 'changed the landscape of drug services in England' (MacGregor et al., 1991, p. 6). Of the 323 services in England and Wales, 71 per cent had been established after 1984.

With only 2 per cent in the private sector, the other services were almost equally statutory and non-statutory. Almost half the statutory services were community drug teams and two-thirds of the non-statutory services were advice and counselling centres. MacGregor et al.'s other major finding was that there had been a 'general adoption of harm-minimisation strategies in drug agencies across the country' (1991, p. 8).

Harm minimization or reduction has had a long history in British drug policy. From the 1920s the 'British System' had evolved, whereby doctors could prescribe drugs to addicts who were their patients. The System worked well for many years but was strictly regulated in the 1970s after revelations that some doctors abused the system for profit. White (1999) has alleged that the curtailment of the British system of prescribing heroin to registered addicts was the result of deferring to US pressure. In the 1980s, the approach was revived in response to the emergence of AIDS. As HIV could be transmitted when intravenous drug-users shared needles, it was widely accepted that syringe exchange schemes should be established to encourage them to use clean equipment. Harm reduction meant much more than this. Advice centres assumed that drug users were rational beings who cared about their health. Recognizing that most drug users were unlikely to abstain from their habit immediately, the centres encouraged them to minimize the risks involved in their drug taking, and:

- not to inject, but to use other methods of administration;
- not to share needles;
- to use clean needles;
- to avoid drugs adulterated with other substances;
- not to mix different drugs;
- to reduce their intake.

This progressive approach from the 1980s still dominates most local practice. Unfortunately, during the 1990s national politicians felt the need to flex their muscles. Recent initiatives by both the Conservative and Labour governments reverted back to a more punitive approach and the need for an abstentionist strategy, while not rejecting harm reduction outright. The Conservatives raised the minimum fine for the possession of cannabis from £500 to £2,500. They also produced a White Paper which recommended improved coordination and effectiveness at every level and the establishment of local drug action teams consisting of senior representatives of the police, the probation service, the prison service, education, social services and health, together with coopted voluntary services (Home Office, 1995). In 1998 the Labour government produced a similar document with a similar title, having appointed a UK anti-drugs coordinator (the Drugs Czar) in 1997. Alongside the usual set of wishy-washy aims was a declared intention to transfer resources from law enforcement to preventive programmes. The former, together with reducing international supplies, had been swallowing up 75 per cent of the resources (*Druglink*, 1998, p. 5). Neither political party showed much willingness to deal with drug problems in a radical way.

Decriminalization and Legalization

The real stumbling block to a realistic national drug policy is the existence of the International Convention. Until the USA begins to recognize that drug taking is, for many people, normal, there is little likelihood that these agreements will be altered. Only the Dutch have taken on the challenge of finding a pragmatic solution to drug problems. They have done this by making a distinction between the markets for hard and soft drugs. The Dutch argue that by taking a more tolerant approach towards cannabis, users of soft drugs will not come into contact with the illicit market for hard drugs. They therefore permit the existence of coffee shops which sell small amounts of different kinds of cannabis. This policy to decriminalize cannabis, allied with a harm reduction approach to hard drugs, has been fairly successful. Certainly The Netherlands has no more serious problems than any other country, and thousands of cannabis users can enjoy their relatively harmless habit without fear of breaking the law. The problem the Dutch face is the large number of 'drug tourists', who come to Amsterdam simply because of the availability of cannabis. They have also incurred the hostility of neighbouring countries, which claim they suffer the adverse consequences of Dutch liberality. It is to the credit of the Dutch that in a recent review of their policy they did not give up their policy or its sensible rationale (Ministry of Health, Welfare and Sport, 1995).

One Dutch critic, however, has argued that The Netherlands has not gone far enough. In his view, there is no clear-cut distinction between soft and hard drugs, and the arguments in favour of the decriminalization of cannabis could equally be applied to heroin and cocaine (Maris, 1996a; 1996b). Supporters of legalisation would go a step yet further and argue that only by legalizing drugs can the problems with which they are associated be adequately dealt with. Space does not allow me to distinguish between the different legalization rationales. For a good introduction to the debate see Goode (1997), especially chapter 5. Legalizers claim that the prohibition of drugs has been just as counter-productive as the prohibition of alcohol in the USA in the 1920s (Nadelmann, 1991). They argue that prohibition provides the conditions in which organized crime and political corruption thrive; it does nothing to prevent people from using drugs and discourages them from seeking help when they need it; moreover, in an illegal drug market it is impossible to be sure what you are consuming. In other words many of our drug problems stem from prohibition rather than from the drugs themselves. Those who support legalization see no reason to think that consumption or misuse will increase uncontrollably once prohibition has been abolished.

Drug policy is an issue that cuts across political parties and the usual left/right distinctions. Libertarians, of the left and the right alike, attack prohibition as an unnecessary constraint on individual liberty. The previous Minister for Sport the Labour MP Tony Banks, once wrote in favour of the legalization of cannabis and one of William Hague's leading supporters wrote in favour of legalization generally. Supportive editorials have appeared in both the *New Statesman* (1993, p. 5) and *The Economist* (1989, p. 19). A campaign for the decriminalization of cannabis in the *Independent on Sunday* in 1998 drew considerable support from a wide range of people. Few researchers in the drugs field come out in its favour, however, perhaps because this may jeopardize their funding. But public opinion is changing. The British Social Attitudes Survey of 1995 showed that, whereas in 1983 only 12 per cent of people in the UK supported the legalization of cannabis, 20 per cent agreed in 1993 and 31 per cent in 1995 (Gould et al., 1996, p. 96). Only 1 per cent of the population, however, said that heroin should be made legal.

Conclusion

The prohibition of drugs has not managed to stop the escalation of either use or misuse. It is a policy strategy based upon a misguided notion of what drugs can do and a stereotypical view of the addict. Drug misuse should be seen as a secondary rather than a primary social problem, a symptom of other deeper social problems such as unemployment, homelessness, stress and alienation. The government should be addressing these, not pursuing the impossible goal of ridding society of drugs. While harm reduction approaches represent a more rational approach to the issue, its logic cannot be developed until we have a public and/or politicians willing to contemplate seriously the possibility of legalization. In a globalized world we have to accept that the vast movement of people, ideas and inventions that takes place means a commensurate change in cultural boundaries. This may be as true for drug taking as it is for other norms and values.

Issues to Consider

- What reasons would you advance for the continued prohibition of drugs such as cannabis, ecstasy, cocaine and heroin?
- How do we deal with forms of compulsive behaviour other than drug addiction? Can we apply this experience to those who misuse drugs?
- To what extent can unemployment in Britain be explained by drug misuse?
- Consider the damage done to individuals and society as a whole by alcohol and tobacco. What controls would be justified to reduce this damage?
- If cannabis were to be legalized, how would you seek to regulate its production, sale and consumption.

Suggestions for Further Reading

Gossop (1993) is one of the best textbooks on drug issues and provides more detailed coverage of many of the issues considered in this chapter. MacGregor (1989) and Coomber (1994) are both useful readers with a variety of articles on the relation between drugs and society. A recent and thorough discussion of the arguments for and against legalization can be found in Goode (1997), and up-to-date summaries of research and statistics can be obtained from a Drugscope publication, *Drug Misuse in Britain*, and through its website www.drugscope.org.uk. It is also worth consulting LOCATE, which provides free information for professionals on out-of-school drug education and prevention activities: www.hea.org.uk/locate.

References

ACMD 1982: *Treatment and Rehabilitation*. London: HMSO.
Bean, P. and Wilkinson, C. 1988: Drug taking, crime and the illicit supply system. *British Journal of Addiction*, 83, 533–9.
Berridge, V. 1989: Historical issues. In S. MacGregor (ed.), *Drugs and British Society*. London: Routledge.
Christie, N. 1985: *Den Goda Fienden: Narkotikapolitik i Norden*. Stockholm: Rabén & Sjögern.
Coomber, R. (ed.) 1994: *Drugs and Drug Use in Society*. Dartford: Greenwich University Press.

Davies, J. 1992: *The Myth of Addiction*. Reading: Harwood Academic Publishers.

Druglink 1998: Building a better strategy. 3 (3), 4–5.

The Economist 1989: Hooked on just saying no. 21 January.

Falk, J. 1994: Drug dependence: myth or motive. In R. Coomber (ed.), *Drugs and Drug Use in Society*. Dartford: Greenwich University Press.

Fingarette, H. 1989: *Heavy Drinking: The Myth of Alcoholism as a Disease*. London: University of California Press.

Flemen, K. 1997: *Smoke and Whispers: Drugs and Youth Homelessness in Central London*. London: Hungerford Drug Project.

Goode, E. 1997: *Between Politics and Reason: The Drug Legalisation Debate*. New York: St Martin's Press.

Gossop, M. 1993: *Living with Drugs*. Aldershot: Ashgate.

Gould, A., Shaw, A. and Ahrendt, D. 1996: Illegal drugs: liberal and restrictive attitudes. In R. Jowell et al. (eds) *British Social Attitudes: The 13th Report*. Aldershot: Dartmouth Publishing.

Hammersley, R. et al. 1989: The relationship between crime and opioid use. *British Journal of Addiction*, 84, 1029–43.

Hammersley, R. and Pearl, S. 1997: Show me the way to go home: young homeless people and drugs. *Druglink*, 12 (1), 11–13.

Home Office 1988: *Tackling Drug Misuse*. London: Home Office.

Home Office 1995: *Tackling Drugs Together*, Cmnd. 2678. London: HMSO.

ISDD 1997: *Drug Misuse in Britain 1996*. London: Institute for the Study of Drug Dependence.

Klee, H. and Reid, P. 1998: Drug use among the young homeless: coping through self-medication. *Health*, 2 (2), 115–34.

Kohn, M. 1992: *Dope Girls*. London: Lawrence & Wishart.

Krivanek, J. 1988: *Addictions*. London: Allen & Unwin.

MacGregor, S. (ed.) 1989: *Drugs and British Society*. London: Routledge.

MacGregor, S., Ettorre, B., Coomber, R., Crosier, A. and Lodge, H. 1991: *Drug Services in England and the Impact of the Central Funding Initiative*. London: Institute for the Study of Drug Dependence.

Maris, C. 1996a: Dutch weed and logic, part I: Inconsistencies in the Dutch Government's memorandum on drugs policy. *International Journal of Drug Policy*, 7 (2), 80–7.

Maris, C. 1996b: Dutch weed and logic, part II: The logic of the harm principle. *International Journal of Drug Policy*, 7 (3), 142–52.

Ministry of Health, Welfare and Sport 1995: *Drugs Policy in the Netherlands: Continuity and Change*. Amsterdam: Ministry of Health, Welfare and Sport.

Musto, D. 1987: *The American Disease: Origins of Narcotic Control*. Oxford: Oxford University Press.

Nadelmann, E. 1991: The case for legalisation. In J. Inciardi (ed.), *The Drug Legalisation Debate*. London: Sage.

New Statesman 1993: Legalise it. 12 November.

Orford, J. 1985: *Excessive Appetites: A Psychological View of Addictions*. London: John Wiley.

Pearson, G. 1987: Social deprivation, unemployment and patterns of heroin use. In N. Dorn and N. South (eds), *A Land Fit for Heroin: Drug Policies, Prevention and Practice*. Basingstoke: Macmillan.

Plant, M. 1981: *Drugs in Perspective*. London: Hodder & Stoughton.

Release 1991: *Drugs and the Law*. London: Release.

Release 1997: *Release Drugs and Dance Survey: An Insight into the Culture.* London: Release.

Sargent, M. 1992: *Women, Drugs and Policy in Sydney, London and Amsterdam.* Aldershot: Avebury.

Sontag, S. 1991: *Illness as Metaphor.* London: Penguin.

Stevens, J. 1993: *Storming Heaven: LSD and the American Dream.* London: Flamingo.

Stimson, G. 1987: British drug policies in the 1980s. *British Journal of Addiction*, 82, 477–88.

White, M. 1999: Lib Dem leader's drug call backed, *Guardian*, 16 August.

Part Three

Reporting Social Problems

Chapter 16

Press-ganged! Media Reporting of Social Work and Child Abuse

Bob Franklin and Nigel Parton

Introduction

The media are central to the process by which social issues become identified as social problems which society takes seriously and for which the state assumes responsibility. News media focus public attention on issues via an agenda-setting role, which prioritizes and frames problems as well as the ways in which policy responses are articulated and discussed. The media are central in identifying and defining social problems, influencing the policy process and influencing the way the public, professionals and users understand and experience welfare services: a point underlined in the next two chapters (Dean; McLaughlin and Murji). In this chapter we discuss these issues by analysing an area of social policy that has received considerable attention and debate over recent years and consequently provides an important case study: social work and child abuse. More specifically the chapter:

- examines recent reporting of social work and child abuse in British national daily and Sunday newspapers (tabloid and broadsheet);
- reviews a number of explanations for the unrelenting press criticism of social work that becomes evident;
- briefly explores the prospects for developing a news agenda which is more sympathetic to the professional practice of social work.

While it may be argued that we are confusing a social problem with a particular form of professional practice, as will quickly become apparent the two are inseparable – and, in fact, it is in part for this reason that they provide such a rich and fruitful focus for analysis. As a number of researchers have commented over the past twenty-five years, the media have played a central role in debates, developments and policies in relation to child abuse in Britain and abroad

(Gough, 1996; Nelson, 1984; Parton, 1985). It becomes readily apparent, however, that not only are news stories and inquiries into child abuse essentially concerned with social work, policy and practice but also, as we shall demonstrate, media reporting of social work is almost exclusively concerned with child abuse and other related areas of child welfare. As we shall also argue, however, this coverage is far from neutral or balanced. In this respect the media do not simply mediate; they actively contribute to and influence politics, policy and practice. The following recent example is illustrative.

The *Daily Express*'s headline on 24 June 1999 smacked more than a little of triumphalism. 'VICTORY' the paper announced, 'Couple who ran off with foster girls get custody.' The story below reported the court's 'controversial decision' to grant Jeff and Jenny Bramley legal custody of Jade and Hannah Bennett for a 'probationary period to prove they should have permanent care of the children' (*Daily Mail* 24 June 1999, p. 1). In August of the previous year, when Cambridgeshire Social Services decided the Bramleys were unsuitable to become adoptive parents, the couple had 'vanished with their foster children rather than hand them back to social workers'. But the tabloids now, as a year earlier, wished to vindicate the Bramleys. The *Daily Mail*, for example, carried the story on its front page and shared the *Express*'s self-congratulatory mood. Under the headline 'We Still Can't Call Jade and Hannah Our Own' the *Mail* revealed that the Bramleys were none the less 'celebrating last night after being told they could keep the little girls they could not bear to give up' (*Express* 24 June 1999, p. 1). The *Sun* was also celebrating. Sharing front page honours with 'Rory's Story' and a half-page picture of 'Rory Bremner and new fiancée Tessa', the saga of the Bramleys, 'who went on the run with their cherished foster daughters' and who 'were celebrating a huge victory over social workers last night', was captured by the headline 'THEY'RE OURS; Fugitive Pair Win Battle To Bring Up Girls' (*Sun* 24 June 1999, p. 1).

Throughout the drama, the press cast social services as the villains of the piece. It was reported as an example of politically correct social workers wishing to remove two children from what was presented in newspaper coverage as a self-evidently happy and loving family. By contrast, the Bramleys were the undoubted heroes of the drama. They had sacrificed their jobs and their home and made themselves fugitives to keep the children they loved. Press reports glamorized them as a couple who were only doing what any couple might do in similar circumstances; the Bramleys were presented as nothing less than a modern-day Bonnie and Clyde. Few newspapers expressed concerns about the schooling that Hannah and Jade were missing, the impact of four months' furtive retreat from society on two young children, or the reasons which had prompted Cambridgeshire Social Services' initial judgement that the Bramleys were unsuitable as adoptive parents. Mark Lawson was among a handful of journalists to introduce a sour note to this otherwise mellifluous discourse of press support, when he described Hannah and Jade as 'hostages': in the same newspaper, Polly Toynbee warned of 'the tidal wave of emotional and ideological reporting of the Bramley case' (*Guardian* 18 January 1999, p. 16).

Such highly critical press coverage misrepresents social work but has a number of additional damaging consequences. It:

- demoralizes social workers (Franklin and Parton, 1991, p. 12);
- creates difficulties for the recruitment of trainees into social work (Bernard, 1998, p. 2);
- influences the professional practice of social work (Parton, 1985, p. 12);
- undermines social workers' relations with their clients (Kitchen, 1980, p. 16);
- helps to shape the public esteem in which social workers are held (Aldridge, 1999, p. 90; Howarth, 1991, pp. 120–1);
- informs and influences the mood of public opinion (Kitzinger and Skidmore, 1995, pp. 10–11; Golding, 1991, p. 95), and ultimately influences social policy concerning social workers and their clients (Lyon and Parton, 1995), a process which has been termed 'legislation by tabloid' (Franklin and Lavery, 1989, p. 26).

In framing the story of the Bramleys' battle with Cambridge Social Services in ways which were hostile to social work, journalists tapped with great ease into more than 25 years of adverse press coverage dating back to the public inquiry into the death of Maria Colwell in 1973: Maria's death promptly became a 'media template' that influenced subsequent coverage of child abuse and social work. This template constitutes a 'rhetorical shorthand helping journalists and audiences to make sense of fresh news stories' as well as being 'instrumental in shaping narratives around particular social problems, guiding discussion not only about the past, but of the present and the future' (Kitzinger, 1999). It is in this context that we examine recent reporting of social problems, social work and child protection.

Reporting the Bad News: Press Coverage of Social Work and Child Protection

Our analysis draws on a study carried out by one of us (Franklin, 1998) concerning press coverage of social work for a twelve-month period prior to 30 June 1998. The data presented derive from an analysis of the coverage of social work and social services in national daily newspapers (the *Guardian*, the *Independent*, the *Daily Telegraph*, the *Daily Mail*, the *Mirror* and the *Sun*) and Sunday newspapers (the *Observer*, the *Mail on Sunday* and the *Sunday Mirror*) between 1 July 1997 and 30 June 1998. The research generated 1,958 published items measuring 97,932 column centimetres (ccm), of which 6,995 ccm were devoted exclusively to discussions of social work and social services. The initial study was funded by the journal *Community Care*. Each item of press coverage was assessed to establish whether the expressed attitude towards social work was 'beneficial', 'neutral' or 'adverse'. Reports were judged to be beneficial if they actively supported or endorsed social work, for example if social workers were praised for their caring nature. Text was designated neutral if it neither actively endorsed nor criticized social workers, for example if social workers were mentioned as being involved in a particular case without any judgement about the effect of their involvement. Finally, coverage was judged to be adverse when it actively criticized social work, for example a report about an abuse of trust by a social worker. This threefold classification revealed that coverage of social work was highly negative across virtually all newspapers (tabloids and broadsheets): the *Sunday Mirror* was the only paper to emerge with a positive appraisal of the profession overall (see table 16.1). The *Mail on Sunday*, the *Sun*, the *Daily Telegraph* and the *Daily Mail* were the most critical; approximately three-quarters of each newspaper's reports of social work was designated adverse. But the *Mail on Sunday* presented a very striking profile, 95 per cent of its reporting of social work rated as adverse, only 3.6 per cent neutral and a mere 1.2 per cent positive. By contrast, only 33 per cent of the reports in the *Guardian* and 14 per cent in the *Sunday Mirror* were adverse. Two further points emerge from table 16.1. First, and perhaps unsurprisingly, tabloid newspapers were considerably more critical in their reporting than the broadsheets; the degree of tabloid criticism of social work was quite remarkable. Secondly, while the broadsheets' coverage was more benign, it remained unequivocally critical. Even the *Guardian*, 'the social workers' friend', published adverse and benign reports in a ratio of more than 2:1.

Journalists routinely used a number of key 'messages' about social workers in their published reports. The 30 most frequently used words to describe the activities of social workers, from a list of 45, are detailed in table 16.2. The first 15 messages are all negative, with the possible exception of the 14th, which suggests social workers were 'under pressure', a phrase which may be read as supportive. There was no beneficial commentary in the reporting of the 15 most frequent messages. The five positive messages were well down the rankings: 'socially useful' (16th) 'caring' (21st), 'effective' (23rd), 'effectively using funds' (24th) 'supportive' (26th) and 'helpful' (27th). The 65 ccm of beneficial reporting was completely outweighed by the 973 ccm of adverse coverage; the good news about social work was lost under this deluge of bad news.

Newspaper reports during 1997–8 described social workers as 'bunglers', 'incompetent' (*Sun* 15 October 1997), 'blundering' (*Mail* 24 February 1998) and 'politically correct' (*Mail* 23 December 1997). They 'fail to intervene' (*Observer* 10 August 1997) or 'intervene ineffectually and help to create a costly dependency culture' (*Mail* 28 March 1998). They were 'slammed' for being 'too soft' (*Mirror* 5 June 1998). They were the 'faceless cohort of unjudgemental social workers' (*Telegraph* 13 August 1997). But they were also 'negligent' and 'take your kids away' (*Sun* 19 January 1998). They 'sexually abuse youngsters in their care' (*Mail* 5 December 1997), 'physically abuse clients' (*Independent* 30 October 1997) and refused to foster children with couples who were 'too old, too overweight or because they smoke' (*Mail* 13 April 1998). They 'suffer from the pernicious doctrine of political correctness' and 'consign black children to life in institutions in preference to life in a white home ... the philosophy which

Table 16.1 Newspapers' reporting of social work

Newspaper	Beneficial reports in ccm	Beneficial as % of total	Neutral reports in ccm	Neutral as % of total	Adverse reports in ccm	Adverse as % of total	Ratio of adverse to beneficial
Daily Mail	34	2.2	406	26.6	1,086	71.2	32:1
Sunday Mirror	19	32.8	31	53.5	8	13.7	Positive
Daily Telegraph	34	9.7	58	16.5	259	73.8	7.6:1
Guardian	97	14.4	354	52.7	221	32.9	2.3:1
Independent	44	14.5	107	35.3	152	50.2	3.5:1
Mail on Sunday	3	1.2	9	3.6	238	95.2	79:1
Mirror	12	5.1	75	32.1	147	62.8	12.3:1
Observer	10	6.8	50	33.7	88	59.5	8.8:1
Sun	7	4.5	32	20.5	117	75	16.7:1

Table 16.2 Newspapers' messages about social work

Messages about social workers	Beneficial reports in ccm	Neutral reports in ccm	Adverse reports in ccm	Total reports in ccm	As a % of all messages about social workers
Abusing trust	–	5	165	170	16.8
Negative	–	–	97	97	9.6
Incompetent	–	1	72	73	7.2
Negligent	–	1	63	64	6.3
Failed	–	1	62	63	6.2
Ineffective	–	–	56	56	5.5
Dismissed	–	5	48	53	5.2
Suspended	–	–	43	43	4.3
Misguided	–	–	40	40	3.9
Wasteful/extravagant	–	–	38	38	3.8
Bungling	–	–	36	36	3.6
Bogus social workers	–	24	1	25	2.5
Unregulated	–	9	14	23	2.3
Under pressure	–	18	1	19	1.9
Negative/stereotyped	–	12	7	19	1.9
Socially useful	10	6	–	16	1.6
Soft	–	2	13	15	1.5
Dishonest	–	5	8	13	1.3
Interfering	–	1	12	13	1.3
Lack of resources	–	7	6	13	1.3
Caring	9	3	–	12	1.2
Under-funded	6	2	3	11	1.1
Effective	11	–	–	11	1.1
Effective use of funding	10	–	–	10	1.0
Unsympathetic	–	–	8	8	0.8
Supportive	7	–	–	7	0.7
Helpful	7	–	–	7	0.7
Naïve	–	–	6	6	0.6
Left-wing	–	4	2	6	0.6
Positive	5	1	–	6	0.6

supported apartheid' (*Telegraph* 27 March 1998). They are the 'great blunder-buss (and blunder is usually the right word) of the social services' (*Mail on Sunday* 28 September 1997). In previous times, parents have only been able to 'watch in horror and disbelief as their weeping children were dragged from their beds and taken away by 'care' workers in frightening dawn raids' (*Mail on Sunday* 1 February 1998); in short, social services 'have taken over' (*Sun* 25 February 1998). But their work with children is 'haphazard and inconsistent'. It was 'often not possible to see why social services had intervened, what they hoped to achieve and how they would know whether the situation had improved or deteriorated' (*Independent* 25 June 1998). There was a 'culture of hopeless-ness in social services' (*Guardian* 12 June 1998). Professionally, 'social work methods are governed by a liberal and lenient philosophy which is quickly recognised by children as weakness' (*Mail* 28 September 1997). If social workers complained about such negative coverage, however, they were told to 'stop whingeing' and defining 'themselves as victims . . . rather than presenting rea-soned explanations for their actions' (*Guardian* 30 April 1998). It is perhaps unsurprising, in the context of this torrent of abusive press commentary, that a study of social workers' attitudes conducted by *Community Care* in May 1998 discovered that 90 per cent of respondents believe that media reporting of their work is inaccurate, generates public suspicions about social workers and 'makes their job harder' (Community Care, 1998).

If the most striking feature of the press reporting of social work is its highly critical nature, the second most evident feature of coverage is undoubtedly newspapers' preoccupation with social workers in their professional activities with children, a preoccupation that results in the near total exclusion of other aspects of social work from journalists' reports. Table 16.3 lists the 20 areas of activity for social workers (from a list of 66) most frequently mentioned in press reports.

Nine of the first ten activities identified by the press (child abuse, paedophiles, adoption, fostering, children's homes, problem children, child protection, chil-dren, and underage sex) directly concern children and constituted 67 per cent of all newspaper accounts of social work activities. If the substantial emphasis on children in items about training as well as reports discussing young people (ranked 15th), parenting (16th) abandoned babies (19th) and young offenders (20th) is recognized, the percentage of reports discussing children exceeds 71 per cent of all the reports. Table 16.3 also illustrates the almost complete absence of any substantive discussion of significant areas of social work practice, such as mental illness / mental health (3.3 per cent), work with older people (1.6 per cent), work with disabled people (ranked 38th with 0.3 per cent coverage), community care (39th, 0.3 per cent) learning difficulties (41st, 0.25 per cent), HIV (52nd, 1.5 per cent) and homelessness (62nd, 0.05 per cent). Finally, the table reveals the highly critical character of newspaper reporting of social work measured by the total volume of adverse (1,056 ccm) and beneficial (107 ccm) coverage – a ratio of 10:1. The ten most regularly cited social work activities attract even greater disapproval; 975 ccm of adverse coverage com-

Table 16.3 The main activities of social workers identified in newspaper coverage

Activity	Beneficial reports in ccm	Factual reports in ccm	Adverse reports in ccm	Total reports in ccm	As a % of total social work coverage
Child abuse	18	40	216	274	13.5
Paedophiles	6	16	222	244	12.2
Adoption	21	85	96	202	10
Fostering	–	73	115	188	9.3
Children's homes	–	9	145	154	7.6
Training	4	67	37	108	5.3
Problem children	–	50	28	78	3.9
Child protection	14	11	49	74	3.7
Children	19	39	12	70	3.5
Under-age sex	–	9	55	64	3.2
Mental illness	5	34	6	45	2.2
Health	4	13	22	39	1.9
Prison	3	28	4	35	1.7
Elderly people	3	16	14	33	1.6
Young people	2	13	18	33	1.6
Parenting	3	15	4	22	1.1
Mental health	1	19	1	21	1.1
Reform	4	8	6	18	0.9
Abandoned babies	–	17	–	17	0.8
Young offenders	–	11	6	17	0.8

pared with only 82 ccm of beneficial reporting, a ratio of 12:1. Reporting of certain activities is particularly negative. Child abuse, for example, suffers 79 per cent adverse coverage (only 7 per cent beneficial), while children's homes receive 94 per cent adverse (6 per cent beneficial), under-age sex 86 per cent adverse (14 per cent beneficial) and fostering 61 per cent adverse (zero beneficial).

This narrow press focus on social workers' professional involvement with children, combined with the highly critical character of much newspaper coverage, has generated two broad but seemingly contradictory stereotypes of social workers in press accounts: the social worker as wimp or bully (Franklin and Parton, 1991, pp. 13–24). Established during the high-profile press reporting of social work cases involving child deaths during the 1980s, these stereotypes continue to influence and shape much contemporary press coverage. Newspaper coverage of the Jasmine Beckford, Kimberly Carlile and Tyra Henry cases presented social workers as rather woolly-minded, indecisive, ineffectual and professionally incompetent people who were unwilling to intervene in the private realm of the family to protect children from a suspected abusing adult; to adopt the phraseology of the tabloids, social workers were 'too soft'. In a rather well-turned phrase, the *Daily Mail* described social workers as 'butterflies in a situation that demanded hawks' (20 December 1987).

Journalists repeatedly use telling phrases to establish this stereotype in readers' minds. For example, social workers have been denounced as 'official do-gooders with no experience of the world' (*Sun* 29 March 1985), 'naïve, bungling, easily fobbed-off, easily hoodwinked' (*Express* 29 March 1985), 'incompetent and insufficiently professional' (*Daily Telegraph* 18 December 1987) and having 'laid back attitudes' (*Mirror* 19 December 1987).

But the wimp is more than a pathetic figure: newspapers occasionally misrepresent this alleged professional incompetence as a crime no less damnable than the initial act of abuse. In some press accounts the social worker may be reported as a greater threat to children than the abuser. Reporting the death of Jasmine Beckford, the *Sun* claimed 'Brent Council had blood on their hands.' The paper published a photograph of Maurice Beckford and the social worker in the case under the headline 'They Killed the Child I Adored' (*Sun* 29 March 1985). The *Mirror's* coverage of the Carlile case alleged 'a bungling social worker was blamed yesterday for the death of four year old Kimberley Carlile' (*Mirror* 12 December 1987). The papers' suggestion is that of all the professionals who may be involved in a particular case (teachers, parents, foster parents, health visitors, the police, youth workers, medical practitioners) it is the social worker who must shoulder the burden of responsibility for what has happened. The unspoken assumption is that somehow social workers have it in their power to prevent a particular tragedy but choose not to do so (Skidmore, 1995, p. 88).

A second, equally pejorative stereotype emerged with the Cleveland case. Social workers ceased to be wimps incapable of intervening to protect children and metamorphosed into bullies. They became the representatives of an unwarrantedly interventionist state who, with little concern for civil liberties, interfere in the private realm of family life. Journalists operationalized a distinctive cluster of negative phrases to flesh out this alternative stereotype. Social workers became 'authoritarian bureaucrats' who 'speak in a chilly jargon' (*The Times* 17 June 1987) and 'seize sleeping children in the middle of the night' (*Sunday Telegraph* 10 July 1988). They are 'child stealers' (*Today* 29 March 1991) engaged in 'legalised kidnap and baby snatching' (*Mail on Sunday* 7 April 1991). Synthesizing the wimp and bully stereotypes, the *Sunday People* derided social workers as being 'like the SAS in cardies and Hush Puppies' (10 March 1991).

These two polemical images of social workers impale them uncomfortably on the horns of a representational dilemma: denounced as wimps if they fail to intervene but decried as bullies if they intervene too much. To cite a conclusion that has become a cliché, social workers are 'damned if they do and damned if they don't'. But how may these two contradictory images be reconciled? Their essential unity lies in the suggestion that during the 1980s social workers became a powerful symbol for state welfare. The ascendant New Right castigated state welfare for being on the one hand inefficient and incapable of meeting the demands placed upon it, but on the other allegedly repressive and illiberal. As a metaphor for the public sector, social work assumed in caricature form what the New Right considered its worst features. In this process, social work comes to be defined on a spectrum whose parameters are authoritarianism and ineffectiveness. This account explains the considerably warmer mood of press reports about social work conducted in the voluntary rather than statutory sector. Howarth, for example, recalls the very different coverage she received when she was Director of Social Services during the Beckford case, compared with her work at ChildLine. The *Star*, which had been highly critical during the Beckford case, carried Howarth's photograph following her appointment to ChildLine below the headline 'The Caring Social Worker They Called a Monster' (Howarth, 1991, p. 123).

These two stereotypes persist in contemporary press coverage. The wimp was evident in the *Daily Star*'s story about gullible social workers' alleged 'feather bedding' of a young offender who lived alone because he was too violent to share accommodation with other young people (9 December 1997). The story also provided some newspapers with an opportunity to explore another favourite theme: society is too soft on young offenders. Headlined 'Scandal of Teenage Yob's £100,000 luxury jailhouse', the *Star* related the story of Robbie 'a 15 year old thief who is living like a king', who has 'six social workers acting as his round-the-clock servants . . . a car with a chauffeur; drugs and sex nights; free holidays and stereos'. The picture of the house where Robbie lives is captioned 'Thugs retreat: the luxury three bedroomed detached house where 15 year old Robbie rules the roost'.

The bully also continues to stalk the corridors of social services, but the alleged authoritarianism of social workers has become closely tied to 'political correctness' in press accounts. The *Daily Mail*, for example, had a headline 'Crackdown on the PC Adoption Police' and quoted an unnamed government source, who claimed 'we are pretty fed up with those politically correct social workers. Many couples have faced the humiliation of being told that they are too old, the wrong race or even too fat to adopt children.' Kent County Council was damned by the *Mail* for approving an adoption agency which tried to bar any prospective parent who was 'over 37, overweight, who smoked or who had unprotected sex' (28 December 1996, p. 27). To illustrate at least one such case, the *Guardian* obligingly carried the story of Julie and Stuart Meadwell, who 'had their dreams of adopting a child ended by a letter from . . . social services . . . informing them that Mr Meadwell is too fat' (6 December 1997).

Explaining the Press Coverage of Social Work and Child Abuse

Three broad explanations for the negative coverage of social services are available in the literature. The first focuses on the nature of social services and social work, the second on the changing context in which social services are provided, the third aspects of newspapers' news-gathering and reporting regimes.

First, social work is judged to be an essentially conflictual and 'messy' business (Franklin and Parton, 1991, pp. 33–9). Conflictual, because social work involves mediating between the interests of the individual client, society and the state as well as balancing the potentially oppositional aspirations of different clients. Messy, because professional judgements draw on a wide range of personal understanding, practical experience and knowledge of social science. This hardly constitutes rocket science and the 'information base' for decisions as well as the eventual outcomes may be hotly contested, with no agreed yard-sticks with which to adjudicate in disputes. In brief, social work contains a substantial potential for criticism when it is conducted as 'well as might be expected'. For a journalist seeking a story it offers 'rich pickings' (Franklin and Parton, 1991, p. 39).

Secondly, the economic, political and ideological context for social services altered radically during the 1970s and 1980s, and in a direction that was unfavourable. The postwar commitment to the collective provision of welfare goods and services, funded by direct taxation, began to change under the pressure of sustained economic recession, the growing number of people requiring welfare services and the emergence of the New Right in British political life. A new consensus superseded the old collectivist assumptions. A political agenda committed to 'rolling back the frontiers of the state', created an 'enabling' state and identified the market as the central mechanism for the allocation of goods and services. Individuals exercised freedom of choice, beyond the reach of the 'nanny state' and were expected to assume personal responsibility for many aspects of their welfare previously considered within the state's remit. Established within one ideological setting, but obliged to operate within another, many aspects of social services seemed anachronistic and received critical appraisal. A number of newspapers are undoubtedly ideologically hostile to social work and opposed to the emphasis that social services place on collective (rather than individual) and public (rather than private) solutions to social problems. Social work, with its professional emphasis on altruism, collective responsibility and the universality of services, is subject to persistent editorial challenge from certain newspapers, which argue that such values are inappropriate in the context of cuts in public (especially local authority) expenditure, the emphasis on individual responsibility, and initiatives such as care in the community. Such newspapers' address readers who are 'middle England', a notoriously conservative constituency. These changes and concerns have continued with the election of the New Labour government in May 1997 (Jordan, 1998).

Thirdly, certain aspects of the organisational structures and operational philosophies of newspapers are identified as central to explanations of coverage: there are four suggestions. First, news values – those aspects of a story which journalists believe make it newsworthy – tend to emphasize bad rather than good news; as one journalist noted 'bad news is to journalism what dung is to rhubarb' (Jacks, 1986, p. 1). A story about child abuse and social workers reflects such news values;

> Child abuse makes good copy. There is the trial which involves hundreds of column inches devoted to details of the child's grisly end. This allows for both public conscience and appetite for horror to be satisfied at the same time. Then there is the ritual purification: the inquiry into what went wrong and the execution of the guilty parties – the social workers. (Hills, 1980, p. 19)

The bad news and moral panic offered by high profile 'crisis' cases makes better reading than stories of day-to-day successful child protection work. Journalists can also claim to be market-led, doing nothing more contentious than providing their readers with the sorts of story they demand.

Secondly, certain aspects of journalists' news gathering routines provide insights into coverage. Journalists reporting social work tend to be generalist rather than specialist reporters. An analysis of the stories published in 1997–8 revealed that 784 bylined journalists published stories during the year, but only nine journalists wrote more than ten articles during the period. For the great majority (518) social services journalism was a one-off experience: a further 128 published two articles each during the year. In brief, the greater part of social services journalism is written by generalist reporters who lack the range and depth of expertise necessary to provide detailed and specialist coverage. This means that the majority of reporters covering social services issues bring general news values emphasizing sensationalism and drama to their reports. The consequences of this 'cult of the generalist' are exacerbated by the 'pack mentality' of journalists. A particular news line or news 'peg' emerges which proves popular, and, when the journalists covering a particular story are overwhelmingly general reporters, the prospects for in-depth coverage are slight (Skidmore, 1995, p. 89). Journalists, moreover, rely heavily on cuttings to influence their coverage, and in this way particular angles on stories become consolidated and repeated: what Skidmore calls 'history repeats itself' (Skidmore, 1995, p. 90).

Thirdly, journalists privilege the accounts of certain news sources. Deacon's (1999, pp. 51–68) study of the media's reporting of charities and the voluntary sector reveals how particular news sources are routinely contacted by journalists for comment and opinion because they are authoritative and constitute 'primary definers'. One study, which conducted extensive interviews with journalists, discovered that they believed that the media strategy of a well-organized pressure group such as PAIN (Parents Against Injustice) can be highly influential in shaping media coverage of events such as child abuse in the Orkneys, especially when a local authority has adopted a 'trench mentality' towards the media while they are given unlimited access to the parents' viewpoint. The coverage of the Orkneys child abuse case reported the parents twice as often as social services; it is rare for children to find a voice in coverage (Kitzinger and Skidmore, 1995).

Finally, news about social services is allegedly 'gendered news' or 'male news' (Skidmore, 1995; Aldridge, 1994). Women journalists in one study alleged that their male colleagues were less interested in reporting social services and much less likely than women to believe that child abuse occurred. Skidmore (1995, p. 95) cites a woman journalist who recalled that she had 'never known the whole office to be so divided along gender lines as over that issue – it was totally, you know [makes parting motion with hands] men and women'. Social services, moreover, remains 'women's work': more than 85 per cent of social services staff are women and almost 75 per cent of social workers are women (Aldridge, 1994, p. 195). Aldridge argues that in a society where to be female 'continues to be a source of disadvantage' this social demography of social services must offer at least a partial explanation of hostile coverage. Following Cleveland, Nava (1988, p. 105) was more explicit in her analysis. Negative reporting focused on the two women in the case: 'Feminism' she alleged, 'became the folk devil' to be denounced.

Changing the Bad News?

The sustained media criticism of social work has generated a predictable response from social workers and social services departments, who have increasingly developed media strategies both for coping defensively with persistent media hostility and, more proactively, for promoting more positive and sympathetic images of the social work profession. The degree of commitment to such strategies varies considerably, but since 1987 a number of local authorities have followed the lead of Bradford Metropolitan District Council and appointed a pubic relations officer with a specific brief to promote and protect the public image of social services. The incumbent's initial observation concerning 'the reluctance of the statutory sector to grasp the public relations nettle' seems curiously anachronistic a decade later (Walder, 1991, p. 208). Social work organizations' involvement with the media and in public relations is currently burgeoning. A number of how-to-do-it practical guides have been published; they offer guidance to social work organizations seeking to establish media relations strategies (see, for example, Neate and Philpot, 1997).

The conventional wisdom suggests that the most significant element in any strategy is the need to plan for a crisis – perhaps the death of a child in care, with all the attendant front-page headlines and accusations. The *telos* of such crisis planning is little more than an exercise in limiting press damage, but it is judged to be important to organize a crisis team, to identify potential points of crisis, to ensure that sufficient resources are available to deal with the crisis and to agree in advance on the lines of response to possible press claims. The crisis team in Glasgow, for example, was triggered by a front-page story in the *Glasgow Herald*, which reported the contentious claim by the then Director of Social Services, that ecstasy was no more dangerous than aspirin (Neate and Philpot, 1997, pp. 31–4).

But social workers' involvement in the media and public relations is not confined to reacting to crises in press coverage. Media strategies emphasize a more positive and promotional role for social work agencies, which requires a close day-to-day involvement with the news media in an effort to manage the news reporting of social work, especially in the field of child protection. A promotional media strategy can:

- identify and target the most appropriate and sympathetic news media;
- select the most significant messages which need to be conveyed and keep stressing them in press releases and at press briefings and conferences;
- identify the target audiences for the 'good news' messages;

- recruit articulate and experienced spokespeople to liaise with the news media;
- develop close links with supportive journalists;
- develop an understanding of journalists' working routines, especially the pressure imposed by their publishing deadlines;
- encourage the training of staff in relevant media skills, such as drafting press releases or communicating clearly without recourse to jargon;
- develop cooperative links with other social services departments, voluntary organizations and children's charities to facilitate better-resourced and more broadly based campaigns.

Finally, social work organizations can complain to the Press Complaints Commission (PCC), the newspaper industry's self-regulatory body, whenever newspapers' coverage breaches its code of practice.

These media and public relations strategies may well prove effective at the margins of newspapers' coverage of social work. They will undoubtedly generate more 'good news' stories in certain newspapers, especially local newspapers; their shortage of financial and journalistic resources combined with their willingness to follow through and publish press releases from local public relations and news sources provides genuine prospects for news management opportunities and improved press coverage (Franklin, 1998, p. 26). But in national newspaper markets there are more powerful factors operating, which social work's media strategy will not offset so readily. National newspapers are market-driven and ideologically antipathetic to many of the values that permeate social work and social services. Newspapers' search for readers, advertising revenues and ultimately profits, in an increasingly and intensely competitive market, triggers a journalistic appetite for dramatic, if not sensational 'bad news' and human-interest stories. Allegations about the 'dumbing down' of the news media, moreover, suggest that newspapers reporting social problems are increasingly likely to emphasize the confrontational, negative and sensational aspects of stories rather than strive for a balanced and informed coverage (Franklin, 1999, p. 8).

Hostile coverage, moreover, reflects some newspapers' opposition to social work, which will not be offset by the provision of press releases about the more positive aspects of professional practice. Newspapers' criticisms are not the consequence of an information deficit, but reflect, as we have argued, a deep-rooted ideological opposition to social work and social services. In the process the way child abuse is debated, understood and responded to is similarly distorted by a failure to engage seriously with the most appropriate ways that policy and practice might develop. There is an evident failure to recognize the complexities involved. Roy Greenslade, a former tabloid newspaper editor, reviewed press coverage of child abuse, and concluded that, when there was little that could be presented as sensational or generate moral indignation, 'the ill-treatment of children is considered inside tabloids as not merely serious and boring – like politics and news from abroad – but a turn-off. It does not add sales and it might alienate readers' (*Observer* 27 October 1996).

Issues to Consider

- How would you describe the way social work is portrayed in the media, and how would you explain this portrayal?
- Why are the media so significant in contemporary society for our understanding of social problems?
- Do the media influence social problems? If so, how?
- To what extent is it possible for a social services department to construct an effective defensive media strategy when a major child protection story, such as Cleveland, is reported extensively in the national tabloid press? Outline the main elements of such a strategy.
- Select a social policy story that has recently received considerable press coverage. Does newspaper reporting clarify or misrepresent the particular events and the broader policy context?

Suggestions for Further Reading

Aldridge (1994) provides a detailed critical analysis of the way social work was portrayed in the media – particularly the press – until the early 1990s. This issue and the broader concerns generated by the media's coverage of social policy are also explored in Franklin (1999). This provides a radical collection of chapters by academics, journalists and broadcasters that examines various influences on the making and implementation of policy. A number of chapters are explicitly concerned with social work and different aspects of child abuse, issues that are also addressed in Franklin and Parton (1991). Gough's (1996) short paper presents a thorough and critical review of the literature on the relation between the media and child abuse. Parton (1985) offers a critical explanation of the way the issue of child physical abuse was brought to public and political attention in the 1970s and discusses the key role played in this process by the media. Skidmore (1995) provides an interesting case study of the way child sexual abuse is reported in the media. A discussion and history of the Bramley case can be found at www.newsunlimited.co.uk/bramley; more broadly the National Children's Bureau: www.ncb.org.uk is an excellent place to start for anyone interested in the issue of children and social policy, including child abuse. The National Institute of Social Work site: www.nisw.org.uk is also worth consulting. It includes two e-mail discussion lists about social work and social services: uksocwork@nisw.org.uk and intsocwork@nisw.org.uk.

References

Aldridge, M. 1994: *Making Social Work News*. London: Routledge.
Aldridge, M. 1999: Poor relations: state social work and the press in the UK. In B. Franklin (ed.), *Social Policy, the Media and Misrepresentation*. London: Routledge.

Bernard, J. 1998: Problems for social work recruitment. *Times Higher Education Supplement*, 7 August, 2.

Community Care 1998: Survey of social workers attitudes. *Community Care*, 1 May, 6.

Deacon, D. 1999: Charitable images: the construction of voluntary sector news. In B. Franklin (ed.), *Social Policy, the Media and Misrepresentation*. London: Routledge.

Franklin, B. 1998: *Hard Pressed: National Newspaper Reporting of Social Work and Social Services*. London: Reed Business Publications.

Franklin, B. 1999: Misleading messages: the media and social policy. In B. Franklin (ed.), *Social Policy, the Media and Misrepresentation*. London: Routledge.

Franklin, B. and Lavery, G. 1989: Legislation by tabloid. *Community Care*, 24 March, 26–9.

Franklin, B. and Parton, N. (eds), 1991: *Social Work, the Media and Public Relations*. London: Routledge.

Golding, P. 1991: Do-gooders on display; social work, public attitudes and the mass media. In B. Franklin and N. Parton (eds), *Social Work, the Media and Public Relations*. London: Routledge.

Gough, D. 1996: The literature on child abuse and the media. *Child Abuse Review*, 5 (5), 363–76.

Hills, A. 1980: How the press sees you. *Social Work Today*, 20 May, 19–20.

Howarth, V. 1991: Social work and the media: pitfalls and possibilities. In B. Franklin and N. Parton (eds), *Social Work, the Media and Public Relations*. London: Routledge.

Jacks, I. 1986: Professional journalism. *UK Press Gazette*, 10 February, 1.

Jordan, B. 1998: *The New Politics of Welfare*. London: Sage.

Kitchen, M. 1980: What the client thinks of you. *Social Work Today*, June, 14–19.

Kitzinger, J. 1999: Media templates: patterns of association and the (re)construction of meaning over time. *Media Culture and Society*, November.

Kitzinger, J. and Skidmore, P. 1995: *Child Sexual Abuse and the Media*, summary report to the ESRC Award no. R000233675, available from Glasgow Media Group, University of Glasgow.

Lyon, C. and Parton, N. 1995: Children's rights and the Children Act 1989. In B. Franklin (ed.), *The Handbook of Children's Rights: Comparative Policy and Practice*. London: Routledge.

Nava, M. 1988: Cleveland and the press: outrage and anxiety in the reporting of child sex abuse. *Feminist Review*, 28, 103–22.

Neate, P. and Philpot, T. 1997: *The Media and the Message*. London: Reed Business Information.

Nelson, B. 1984: *Making an Issue of Child Abuse*. Chicago: University of Chicago Press.

Parton, N. 1985: *The Politics of Child Abuse*. London: Macmillan.

Skidmore, P. 1995: Telling tales: media power, ideology and the reporting of child sexual abuse in Britain. In D. Kidd-Hewitt and R. Osborne (eds), *Crime and the Media: The Post-Modern Spectacle*. London: Pluto.

Walder, L. 1991: Public relations and social services: a view from the statutory sector. In B. Franklin and N. Parton (eds), *Social Work, the Media and Public Relations*. London: Routledge.

Chapter 17

Defrauding the Community?
The Abuse of Welfare

Hartley Dean

Introduction

We have already seen in the chapter by Franklin and Parton the role the media can play in the process of problem 'identification' and policy formation. It is an issue that recurs in this chapter, which is primarily concerned with the problem of social security benefit fraud and, especially, with individual rather than organized benefit fraud. The chapter will:

- locate benefit fraud in relation to other fraudulent or unofficial activities;
- identify three different senses in which benefit fraud may be regarded as a 'social problem';
- consider how benefit fraud has been uniquely constituted – through the mass media and by politicians – as a very particular problem;
- discuss the measurement and extent of fraud in the British social security system;
- provide an account of the policies that recent governments have adopted to combat fraud;
- draw on recent research findings to discuss the advantages and disadvantages of different policy approaches to benefit fraud.

The Significance of Fiddling

According to criminological evidence, most of us at some time add to our incomes in ways which are illegal. We 'fiddle' the state or our employers to obtain petty cash savings or rewards in kind by means that we do not consider criminal, yet which we know to be, technically at least, unlawful (Mars, 1994). The colloquial English euphemism, fiddling, trivializes the theft or fraud that may be involved and, in the mind of the perpetrator, distinguishes such 'excusable' activity from 'real' or 'serious' dishonesty. To recognize this tendency – whether in ourselves or in others – is not to condone the dishonesty involved: rather it should sensitize us to the different ways in which illegalities can be socially constructed. While some kinds of illegality are widely tolerated as fiddling, others can attract a disproportionate degree of popular opprobrium. Few people would hesitate to condemn organized social security fraud, any more than they would hesitate to condemn robbery; yet people's attitudes to social security fiddling may differ from their attitudes to the fiddling of personal expense claims or tax returns, although the two offences are ostensibly equally serious.

Other kinds of fiddling

Although we shall focus on social security fraud, there are other kinds of fiddling that affect the welfare state. For example, it is estimated that prescription fraud costs the National Health Service some £150 million per year, while £600 million per year is lost to the criminal legal aid budget through false claims (see the *Guardian*, 14 August 1999 and 5 February 1999). However, the biggest single loss to the Exchequer is suffered through tax evasion. The Treasury's own estimate of tax avoided – by way of income tax, duties, national insurance contributions and other taxes – amounted to a staggering £100 billion in 1997–8 (Atkinson, 1999). There is of course a fine distinction to be drawn between tax that is avoided by 'creative accountancy' and that which is dishonestly evaded by concealment or mis-statement. None the less, as we shall see, even the most extravagant estimate of the losses incurred through social security fraud amounts to (only) £7 billion per year (Department of Social Security, 1998b). Despite this disparity, public and official attitudes to tax evasion are consistently more lenient than attitudes to social security fraud (Cook, 1989; 1997). The government's approach to the prosecution of offenders is less aggressive, even though the financial returns obtainable from enforcement activity against tax payers are far greater than those obtainable from fraudulent benefit claimants (see table 17.1).

Tax evasion is partly associated with working practices whereby employees receive perks, tips or other rewards which, though sanctioned by their employers, are not declared for tax purposes. However, there are other fiddles that may be conducted at the employers' expense, such as the falsification of expenses claims, the pilfering of supplies and scams based on the short-changing or overcharging of customers or the overloading or underdropping of delivered goods (Mars, 1994). Where the employer is a government department, a local authority or a public agency, then the losses incurred from workplace crime may be borne indirectly by the tax payer, and the Audit Commission (1998) has suggested that the incidence of management fraud within local authorities has been increasing as senior staff enjoy unfettered access to computerized accounting systems.

Table 17.1 Prosecutions and revenue recovery by the Department of Social Security and the Inland Revenue, 1991/2–1995/6

Year	DSS prosecutions of fraudulent claimants	Imputed benefit savings from counter-fraud measures (£ millions)	Inland Revenue prosecutions of fraudulent tax payers	Actual yield from compliance meaures (£ millions)
1991/2	4,379	446	249	4,905
1992/3	5,239	558	217	4,575
1993/4	7,645	654	216	4,697
1994/5	9,546	717	216	6,118
1995/6	10,677	1,222	357	5,242

Source: Cook, 1997, tables 5.1 and 5.2

Beyond the sphere of public services and private employers lies the informal or 'hidden' economy, in which a range of unregistered production and services occurs (Gershuny, 1978; Jordan, 1996). The effect of global economic trends in countries like Britain has been to accelerate the fragmentation of labour markets, to expand the scope of casual labour and to promote the growth of peripheral and unregulated economic activities. Some semi-official estimates have placed the level of such activity at about 8 to 10 per cent of Britain's GDP, but recent research suggests it may be twice this (Hetherington, 1999). By its nature this sector of the economy is not susceptible to scrutiny. It encompasses some organized criminal enterprises, but also the fiddling of individuals, some of whom are entirely dependent on illicit earnings in the informal sector, some moonlighting from jobs in the formal economy, others fraudulently claiming social security benefits.

Policy and social security

Why should the activities of social security claimants who conceal or misrepresent their circumstances in order to obtain benefits to which they are not legally entitled represent a *social* rather than an *administrative* problem?

First, and most obviously, fraud entails a significant loss of revenue. The government claims that social security fraud 'is stealing billions of pounds from the public' and 'takes money which could otherwise be spent on those genuinely in need' (Department of Social Security, 1998b, p. 1). As we have seen, the same and more can be said about tax evasion, but as the annual social security budget for the UK has reached £100 billion, the haemorrhage of funds through fraud still has to be taken seriously. Whether indeed the money that is lost would otherwise be used to enhance the benefits system and whether those who make fraudulent claims are not sometimes themselves in genuine need remain moot points.

Box 17.1: What kind of a problem?

Social security benefit fraud entails or represents:
- an avoidable loss of public revenues;
- a loss of trust in the welfare state;
- the unwelcome side-effects of labour market 'flexibilization'.

Secondly, fraud is a problem if it means that people are losing faith in the social security system. The government has acknowledged this point when it says that fraud 'strikes at the root of public support of our welfare system' (Department of Social Security, 1998b). However, fraud may not only represent a cause *of*, it may be caused *by*, a failure of popular support. Perhaps the major challenge facing the welfare state relates to its perceived capacity to support its citizens in handling the risks of everyday life (Taylor-Gooby et al., 1999). In other words, people have to trust the welfare state, and there is evidence that some of those who commit benefit fraud do so because they no longer trust, but feel betrayed by the social security system. When benefit levels are eroded and conditions of entitlement become stricter people may not believe the state is affording them the security to which they are entitled (Dean and Melrose, 1996; 1997).

Thirdly, fraud is a problem because it is an intractable manifestation of 'flexibilized' or 'hypercasualized' labour markets (Jordan and Redley, 1994; Evason and Woods, 1995; Cook, 1998). To an extent it is a byproduct of the kind of global process outlined above, about which national governments are increasingly powerless to do anything (e.g. Esping-Andersen, 1996). Governments have little choice but to contain public spending, and, though they may invest in education and training, the shaping of labour markets will be determined not by policy, but by the market. If this were true (but see Hirst and Thompson, 1996), benefit fraud is in one sense an inevitable consequence of a wider problem, while in another it represents the means by which a government – however unwillingly – may covertly subsidize peripheral employment in the informal economy.

Constituting the Problem

Dealing with potentially fraudulent claims upon the public purse has been a problem since the days of the Poor Laws. It has been argued that mechanisms for distinguishing between the genuine and the fraudulent – or the deserving and the undeserving – continue to lie at the heart of social security rules and decision making, particularly in relation to means-tested benefits (Dean, 1991). Part of the stigma that attaches to the process of means-testing stems from the implicit suspicion to which claimants are subject. The association between fraud and the act of claiming benefits has been sustained by interventions in the mass media and is clearly evident within public opinion.

A media-inspired panic

Just as public fears about crime can be as much of a problem as the prevalence of crime itself (see Cook's chapter), so popular beliefs about benefit fraud can be as much of a problem as the actual scale of fraud. A social problem in this sense can be promoted or manufactured by the mass media. Manning (1985) has argued that there are three distinct interpretations of the role that journalists and the popular media can play in relation to public opinion: they can inform and educate it, they can reflect and reinforce it, or they can politically manipulate it.

In a classic study Golding and Middleton (1982) charted the rise from the 1970s of 'scroungerphobia'. They demonstrated the pivotal role of the popular press and broadcasting media in fuelling resentment, not just about fraud, but about the supposed abuse of the welfare system at a time when its sustainability was being brought seriously into question. By raising the profile of a couple of celebrated cases of benefit fraud and providing distorted accounts of the lifestyles achieved by a handful of benefit claimants, newspapers such as the *Daily Mail* succeeded in portraying the majority of claimants as idle and feckless scroungers who were preying on an overly bureaucratic and incompetent benefits system. This was a process partly instigated and later perpetuated by the intervention of politicians. Initially right-wing back-bench MPs bombarded the press with stories of benefit fraud, but, later, government ministers (from both parties) were to use the media to demonstrate the vigour of their response to fraud and so maintain the impression that fraud was rife and that all claimants were potentially suspect.

During the 1980s the media were invited, for example, to observe and report elaborate 'sting'-style operations intended to catch benefit cheats (Smith, 1985), while in the 1990s Peter Lilley, the Conservative Social Security Secretary, attracted publicity for a succession of annual party conference speeches featuring the innovations by which he planned to tackle social security fraud. By and large, therefore, the role of the media has been to manipulate rather than educate public opinion, or at best to reflect and nourish a popular perception that tends to equate benefit fraud with the abuse of welfare, abuse with scrounging, and scrounging with the claiming of benefit entitlements in general. A recent study that monitored the national press's coverage of news stories relating to poverty revealed that, in a year when high unemployment and redundancies dominated such news, this by no means eclipsed the attention that stories of welfare scrounging and benefit fraud continued to attract, especially – in proportional terms – in tabloid newspapers (see table 17.2).

Public attitudes

Popular opinion is a complex phenomenon, and although the mass media help set the climate in which opinions are formed they represent only one of several influences (Dean with Melrose, 1999). Public opinion surveys reveal that

Table 17.2 National news items relating to poverty, January–December 1996

Subject of item	All papers		Tabloids		Broadsheets	
	number of items	as % of all items	number of items	as % of all items	number of items	as % of all items
Unemployment/redundancy	1,145	55.8	381	52.6	764	57.5
Welfare scrounging/fraud	218	10.6	115	15.9	103	7.8
Low pay/poor wages	188	9.2	64	8.8	124	9.3
Experiences/lifestyles of the poor	169	8.2	62	8.6	108	8.1
Homelessness/house repossessions	154	7.5	45	6.2	109	8.2
Others	179	8.7	59	8.1	120	9.0
Totals	2,053		726		1,328	

Source: Dean with Melrose, 1999: table A.5a

people's attitudes to the welfare state are curiously ambivalent. By and large people support the existence of the welfare state – because they may need it – but they are suspicious of it. That suspicion is reflected in beliefs that 'most people on the dole are fiddling in one way or another' (fairly consistently subscribed to by around one-third of respondents in the annual British Social Attitudes Survey) or that 'large numbers of people are claiming benefits falsely' (subscribed to by about two-thirds of respondents) (see Jowell et al., 1997; and previous BSA reports).

The Scale of Fraud

In fact, the true scale of benefit fraud cannot be accurately measured. The Department of Social Security has publicly conceded that, while it may estimate the financial losses arising from *detected* fraud, it can never estimate the incidence of *actual* fraud (Social Security Committee, 1991, p. 25). More recently the government has acknowledged that 'We will never know exactly how much fraud there is in social security' (Department of Social Security, 1998b, p. 2). Despite this, governments continue to compile and the media to publish estimates of the amount of money that is lost through benefit fraud.

Suspect methodologies

There are two major problems with such estimates. One is overestimation: 'fraud officers, like fighter pilots, are apparently liable to take an over-optimistic view of their successes' (Smith, 1985, p. 116). The other relates to methods of calculation.

Overestimation occurs because the only data available are based not on objective scientific inquiry, but on the reports of benefit fraud investigators whose

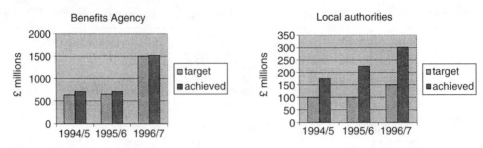

Source: Sainsbury, 1998, figures 1 and 2

Figure 17.1   The benefit savings achieved by the Benefits Agency and local authorities against annual targets, 1994/5–1996/7

terms of engagement subject them to certain incentives. When additional personnel were assigned to counter-fraud work in the 1980s at a time of staff cuts in government departments, they were under intense pressure to justify themselves by the benefit savings they generated (Smith, 1985). In the 1990s, the Benefits Agency, the Employment Service and local authorities (which administer housing benefits) were all set specific targets for the amount of benefit savings generated through the detection and prosecution of fraud. The achievement of targets is rewarded in the case of senior staff in government agencies through performance-related pay and in the case of local authorities 'through increases in central government subsidy' (Sainsbury, 1998). The Benefits Agency has progressively increased the amount of savings it generates in response to every increase in the targets set for it, while local authorities have increased their savings far in excess of their targets (see figure 17.1). Concern has been expressed – by welfare groups, civil service unions and official watchdogs – that such incentives may lead on the one hand to heavy-handed methods in relation to claimants merely suspected of fraud, and on the other to what the National Audit Office (1997) called 'possible sharp practice' in the recording of savings.

   The benefit savings that are officially recorded as having been made when fraudulent claims are detected and disallowed are calculated by multiplying the weekly sum that is no longer being paid by an arbitrary multiplier – currently 32 – to reflect the period of time that the offending claimant might have remained on benefit. Not only, depending on the circumstances, may this entail an erroneous assumption, but also it takes no account of what the claimant's entitlement would be if he or she were now to reclaim it legitimately. As a result, as one commentator has put it, 'it is difficult to lend any credence at all to official measures' (Sainsbury, 1998, p. 6).

Putting benefit fraud in perspective

Official estimates of fraud have lately been placed on a slightly more systematic basis than hitherto by the conduct of 'Benefit Reviews' (Social Security Benefits

Agency, 1995; 1996). These involved concerted exercises by fraud investigators resulting, initially, in an estimate that 5.2 per cent of income support claims reviewed were fraudulent, while a further 4.6 per cent were suspected to be fraudulent. Based on projections from these reviews, the total estimated loss of revenue through income support and unemployment benefit fraud was estimated at £1.4 billion and through housing benefit fraud at £900 million. However, a repeat exercise in 1997 suggested that losses through income support fraud might have risen to £1.77 billion, despite the resources devoted to combating it. By the time the New Labour government published its Green Paper on benefit fraud it was being claimed that 'a conservative estimate of fraud is £2bn a year; but the figure could be much higher, around £7bn *if all suspicions of fraud were well founded*' (Department of Social Security, 1998b, p. 12, emphasis added).

Taking all kinds of benefit into account, therefore, the government believes that fraud amounts to about 7 per cent of the social security budget, although it does not have firm evidence. This is by no means inconsiderable, but in the broad context of the massive challenges faced by our social security system some readers may question whether the government is being just a little alarmist when it insists that benefit fraud is one of the existing system's 'three key problems' (Department of Social Security, 1998a, p. 1).

Policy Responses

As I have already indicated, the current preoccupation with benefit fraud can be traced back to the economic upheavals of the early 1970s, when a Conservative Secretary of State, Keith Joseph appointed a committee to investigate the 'abuse of social security benefits' (Fisher Committee, 1973). This was followed in the late 1970s by the creation by a Labour Secretary of State, Stan Orme, of a departmental coordinating committee that developed a 'fraud action plan' (Smith, 1985).

The Conservatives (1979–97)

The Conservative government commissioned a further report (Rayner Committee, 1981) on the payment of benefits to unemployed people, which alleged that 8 per cent of unemployed claimants were in fact working. At the same time the government appointed more than a thousand additional benefit fraud investigators and introduced Specialist Claims Control teams, which toured local social security offices to conduct targeted investigations on groups of claimants suspected of fraud, including unemployed people believed to have marketable skills and lone parents believed to be cohabiting (Smith, 1985). This drive against fraud subsumed a range of established enforcement activity – against, for example, child maintenance defaulters and voluntary unemployment cases – involving 'abuses' that were not fraudulent in any legal sense.

During the 1990s even greater numbers of staff were engaged on counter-fraud work. Telephone hotlines were established at national and local levels to encourage members of the public to report suspected cases of benefit fraud. Preparations were begun for the introduction of fraud-proof swipe card technology to replace existing benefit payment methods. The activities of Specialist Claims Control investigators were superseded on the one hand by the introduction of intensively publicized 'spotlight' campaigns in local areas and on the other by the creation, for example, of a well resourced Organised Fraud Investigation Team in London. The Benefits Integrity Project was introduced in order to spot-check the entitlement of disabled people to received disability benefits. The Social Security Administration (Fraud) Act of 1997 provided additional powers to various official agencies in order to further the investigation of fraud, and it created new offences and penalties for offending benefit claimants. The government established a Benefit Fraud Inspectorate to inspect Benefits Agency Offices and local authorities (Sainsbury, 1998).

New Labour (1997–)

Even before the 1997 general election, a media-conscious Labour Party began to assert its credentials in the press as a party that would give a high priority to combating benefit fraud. On assuming office as Prime Minister, Tony Blair appointed Frank Field, an outspoken believer that the existing social security system perversely encouraged fraudulent behaviour (Field, 1995), as Minister of Welfare Reform. Field resigned some 15 months later, having failed to achieve reforms on the scale he wanted, but perhaps the biggest mark he left on government policy was a commitment – supposedly greater even than its predecessors – to contain benefit fraud. This was signalled in two Green Papers (Department of Social Security, 1998a; 1998b), published while Field was still in post. The first, a wide ranging statement of New Labour's vision for a welfare state that promotes 'opportunity not dependence', made it clear that 'rooting out fraud' was a priority. The second contained an outline of the government's strategy to this end.

That strategy professes four aims:

- to develop an anti-fraud culture among staff and the public and to deter fraud;
- to design and operate policies and systems that minimize fraud;
- to create an environment in which the work against fraud can flourish;
- to develop a highly skilled anti-fraud profession (Department of Social Security, 1998b, p. 3).

Unlike previous initiatives, the document draws attention to the activities of fraudulent employers, landlords and organized criminals, and not just of individual claimants. The premise on which it is proposed that a professionalized anti-fraud machinery should be built is expressed in terms of 'the need to stay ahead of the game as patterns of fraud and attacks by fraudsters change' (Department of Social Security, 1998b, p. 53). This may well have been framed with the predations of organized criminals in mind, but the implications may yet be disturbing if it is implied that beating fraud requires a battle of wits between staff and claimants generally. This would not necessarily be conducive to repairing the trust and good faith upon which an effective, fraud-free benefit system depends.

In the event, in spite of the strident tone of the Green Paper, the government has lately dismantled some elements of the anti-fraud measures introduced by the Conservatives: the Organised Fraud Investigation Team has been disbanded, because it proved ineffectual, the development of benefit swipe cards has been abandoned because of prohibitive costs, and, in the face of concerted opposition from the disability lobby, the Benefits Integrity Project is to be set aside as part of a wider package of benefit reforms affecting disabled people. The government's latest pronouncements appear to be reaching towards a balance between the punishment and the prevention of fraud (Department of Social Security, 1999).

Policy Options

Bearing in mind the three senses in which benefit fraud is a 'problem' (see box 17.1), we can see that there are three possible approaches to remedying it (see box 17.2). It is possible to assess these options in relation to evidence from qualitative studies of the attitudes and perceptions of people who engage in benefit fraud (Dean and Melrose, 1996, 1997; Dean, 1998; Rowlingson et al., 1997; Rowlingson and Whyley, 1998).

Box 17.2: Alternative approaches to combating social security benefit fraud

Approaches	Counter-indications
1 Increased deterrence	This may reduce people's trust in the welfare state in general and the take-up of benefit entitlements in particular.
2 Decreased incentives	To be effective, this would require increased public revenues.
3 Alternative opportunities	Effectiveness would depend on the substantive nature of the opportunities opened up to benefit claimants.

Increasing deterrence

First, the government can continue to get even tougher on benefit fraud. It can increase the degree of surveillance to which claimants are subject, and it can increase the penalties which those who are caught committing fraud will attract. Such an ambition is reflected in some aspects of the Green Paper, and Field (1998) himself insisted that he wanted there to be 'no no-go areas for the prosecution of benefit fraud'.

However, the evidence suggests that fraudulent claimants are not easily deterred. Certainly, the risk of detection weighs more on claimants' minds than the fear of harsh penalties, and the shame of being caught is enough to deter some. It must be recognized that many, if not most, people who are claiming fraudulently already endure a considerable degree of anxiety in connection with what they are doing: for them, the trials and anxieties associated with living on an inadequate income and of meeting their responsibilities to their dependants simply outweigh the fear of detection and prosecution. A 'get tough' strategy would serve further to heighten such levels of anxiety. It is possible that the odds of detection and punishment would eventually become unacceptable for some, but most would probably endure the risk in the hope that they might yet escape undetected.

Such a strategy would have other implications. The stigmatizing effect which anti-fraud measures can have on all claimants has been recognized as one of the main factors accounting for the low take-up rates universally associated with means-tested benefits (van Oorschot, 1995). A tough anti-fraud policy that exposes all claimants to surveillance and suspicion may in fact militate against the objective of ensuring that 'those who are eligible claim and receive their entitlement' (Department of Social Security, 1998b, p. 1). By undermining people's trust and sense of entitlement, it may deter legitimate claims as much as fraudulent ones.

Decreasing incentives

Secondly, the government could seek ways to reduce the incentives people have to defraud the system. This would mean, on the one hand, addressing some of the perverse incentives that arise from the rules of the system. On the other hand, it might also mean increasing the levels of benefit available to claimants so that they would have less incentive to increase their income fraudulently. The first of these objectives is part of the approach outlined in the Green Paper: the second is not on the political agenda.

It is possible to design benefits systems so that they are simpler and more transparent – so that people do not either unwittingly or out of frustration claim things to which they are not entitled. It is also possible to design means-tested systems which do not punish claimants for variations in their circumstances, which can offer variable amounts of weekly benefit as casual earnings or other irregular sources of income fluctuate, which allow a claimant to re-establish a claim immediately if a temporary source of alternative income should cease. Such changes remove a claimant's temptation to withhold or misrepresent information about his or her circumstances, but they are not achieved without cost. Simplifying a complex benefits system cannot usually be achieved without either creating both winners and losers or increasing expenditure on the system as a whole. Making a means-tested system ultra-sensitive to the changing needs of claimants is administratively expensive. It is also possible to provide more generous income disregards for people on means-tested benefits (allowing them to retain more of their income from other sources without losing benefits), which again removes the incentive for claimants to under-declare their income, although this too increases the cost of benefits.

Beyond these objectives, it is of course possible to make the benefit system more generous, in particular to provide more benefits through insurance-based or universal schemes without the necessity for a means test. Such schemes are less prone to fraud, but they require higher levels of public funding. The evidence suggests that any attempt to make the benefit system less forbidding, more comprehensible and better adapted to people's day-to-day lives would do much to restore or to build a sense of trust between citizens and the welfare state, and, for most claimants, this would reduce the likelihood of their committing fraud. None the less, without some significant enhancement in the standards of living that are sustainable on benefits a risk of fraud will remain. There will always be a small minority of unprincipled people against which any social security system will have to protect itself, but the likelihood is that a strategy that seeks to establish a more universal and comprehensive welfare state would best succeed in minimizing fraud.

Providing alternative opportunities

The evidence finally suggests that most people who commit benefit fraud are not street-wise, venal and calculating, but are muddling by in the hope that something better will turn up. They are more like Mr Micawber than Mr Fagin. They are not indulging some alternative lifestyle choice but would value above all a 'proper' job with 'decent' pay and status. The problem for many is that the 'flexible' labour market simply cannot fulfil their expectations.

The New Labour government claims to be pursuing a 'third way' between the parsimonious economic liberalism of the New Right and the overgenerous social democracy of the Old Left, and one would expect it similarly to steer a path somewhere between increasing deterrence and decreasing incentives so far as combating benefit fraud is concerned. At the heart of the government's welfare reforms lies the New Deal strategy, premised on the idea that people in receipt of social security benefits should be given opportunities to get legitimate jobs, if necessary by increasing their employability. If this were to succeed in providing meaningful choices for claimants, it would of itself reduce benefit fraud. However, can such a policy counteract the unwelcome effects of labour-market 'flexibilization'?

Tony Blair claims that New Labour wants 'to rebuild the system around work and security' (Department of Social Security, 1998a, p. iii). There are opposing views about what this might entail. An optimistic view (e.g. Giddens, 1998) would be that it is possible to invest in the employability of claimants, and that this, by stimulating labour markets, will generate the opportunities for participation and a route out of dependence on benefits. A more pessimistic view (e.g. Jessop, 1994) is that the logic of 'flexibilized' labour markets requires the government to coerce claimants into low-paid, insecure and uncongenial jobs. The success of the government's drive to root out fraud may depend more than anything else on who is right.

Conclusion

Benefit fraud is undeniably an abuse of welfare. There is a risk, however, that a politically inspired and media-led preoccupation with fraud may have counter-productive effects, by reconstituting the problem as a pretext or as a means to undermine the security that the benefit system is supposed to offer. This could represent an even greater abuse of welfare.

> ## Issues to Consider
> - Why are attitudes to benefit fraud so different from attitudes to tax evasion?
> - Do the press and broadcasting media make any difference to the way people think about the significance of benefit fraud and the importance of the welfare state?
> - Why is it so difficult to estimate or measure the extent of social security fraud?
> - Which would be the more effective way of restoring the confidence of genuine social security claimants: simplifying the claims process or getting tough with fraudsters?
> - Why might benefit fraud be such an issue for New Labour?

Suggestions for Further Reading

There is no single text that deals with the issue of social security benefit fraud. However, several studies provide useful background to the debates and accounts of recent research. Golding and Middleton (1982) provide essential background reading on the role the media has played in highlighting fraud. Mars (1994) provides a theoretical and highly readable exposition of the related issue of workplace fraud. Though dated now, Cook (1989) provides a seminal account of the very different ways in which benefit fraud and tax evasion are treated. The principal sources for recent research are perhaps Dean and Melrose (1996), Evason and Woods (1995) and Rowlingson et al.'s (1997) Department of Social Security commissioned report. A very useful collection of short articles is contained in a special edition of the journal *Benefits* (1998), 'The Politics of Fraud'. At the time of writing, the most significant source relating to government policy is the 1998 Green Paper *Beating Fraud is Everyone's Business* (Department of Social Security, 1998b), while for the latest official data, refer to the DSS website – www.dss.gov.uk – which frequently features press releases and other reports.

References

Atkinson, D. 1999: Tax evasion: the pie in the sky nightmare. *Guardian*, 4 February.

Audit Commission 1998: *Protecting the Public Purse*. Abingdon: Audit Commission Publications.

Benefits 1998: The Politics of Fraud, 21, January special issue.

Cook, D. 1989: *Rich Law, Poor Law*. Milton Keynes: Open University Press.

Cook, D. 1997: *Poverty, Crime and Punishment*. London: Child Poverty Action Group.

Cook, D. 1998: Between a rock and a hard place: the realities of working 'on the side'. *Benefits*, 21, 11–15.

Dean, H. 1991: *Social Security and Social Control*. London: Routledge.

Dean, H. 1998: Benefit fraud and citizenship. In P. Taylor-Gooby (ed.), *Choice and Public Policy*. Basingstoke: Macmillan.

Dean, H. and Melrose, M. 1996: Unravelling citizenship: the significance of social security benefit fraud. *Critical Social Policy*, 16 (3), 3–31.

Dean, H. and Melrose, M. 1997: Manageable discord: fraud and resistance in the social security system. *Social Policy and Administration*, 31 (2), 103–18.

Dean, H. with Melrose, M. 1999: *Poverty, Riches and Social Citizenship*. Basingstoke: Macmillan.

Department of Social Security 1998a: *New Ambitions for Our Country: A New Contract for Welfare*, Cmnd. 3805. London: Stationery Office.

Department of Social Security 1998b: *Beating Fraud is Everyone's Business: Securing the Future*, Cmnd. 4012. London: Stationery Office.

Department of Social Security 1999: *A New Contract for Welfare: Safeguarding Social Security*, Cmnd. 4276. London: Stationery Office.

Esping-Andersen, G. (ed.) 1996: *Welfare States in Transition*. London: Sage.

Evason, E. and Woods, R. 1995: Poverty, de-regulation of the labour market and benefit fraud. *Social Policy and Administration*, 29 (1), 40–54.

Field, F. 1995: *Making Welfare Work*. London: Institute of Community Studies.

Field, F. 1998: Speech to a meeting of fraud experts at the Department of Social Security. London, 3 June.

Fisher Committee 1973: *Report of the Committee on Abuse of Social Security Benefits*, Cmnd. 5228. London: HMSO.

Gershuny, J. 1978: *After Industrial Society*. London: Macmillan.

Giddens, A. 1998: *The Third Way*. Cambridge: Polity Press.

Golding, P. and Middleton, S. 1982: *Images of Welfare: Press and Public Attitudes to Poverty*. Oxford: Martin Robertson.

Hetherington, P. 1999: Black economy booms as crooks eye nice little earner. *Guardian*, 5 July.

Hirst, P. and Thompson, G. 1996: *Globalisation in Question*. Cambridge: Polity Press.

Jessop, B. 1994: The transition to post-Fordism and the Schumpeterian workfare state. In R. Burrows and B. Loader (eds), *Towards a Post-Fordist Welfare State?* London: Routledge.

Jordan, B. 1996: *A Theory of Poverty and Social Exclusion*. Cambridge: Polity Press.

Jordan, B. and Redley, P. 1994: Polarisation, underclass and the welfare state. *Work, Employment and Society*, 8 (2), 153–76.

Jowell, R., Curtice, J., Park, A., Brook, L. and Thompson, K. (eds) 1997: *British Social Attitudes: The 14th Report*. Aldershot: Dartmouth.

Manning, N. 1985: Constructing social problems. In N. Manning (ed.), *Social Problems and Welfare Ideology*. Aldershot: Gower.

Mars, G. 1994: *Cheats at Work: An Anthropology of Workplace Crime*. Aldershot: Dartmouth.

National Audit Office 1997: *Measures to Combat Housing Benefit Fraud*, HC 164. London: Stationery Office.

Rayner Committee 1981: *Payment of Benefits to Unemployed People*. London: Department of Employment / Department of Health and Social Security.

Rowlingson, K. and Whyley, C. 1998: The right amount to the right people? Reducing fraud, error and non-take-up of benefit. *Benefits*, 21, 7–10.

Rowlingson, K., Whyley, C., Newburn, T. and Berthoud, R. 1997: *Social Security Fraud: The Role of Penalties*. London: Stationery Office.

Sainsbury, R. 1998: Putting fraud into perspective. *Benefits*, 21, 2–6.

Smith, R. 1985: Who's fiddling? Fraud and abuse. In S. Ward (ed.), *DHSS in Crisis: Social Security – Under Pressure and Under Review*. London: Child Poverty Action Group.

Social Security Benefits Agency 1995: *Benefit Review (Income Support and Unemployment Benefit)*. Leeds: BA Security.

Social Security Benefits Agency 1996: *Housing Benefit Review*. Leeds: BA Security.

Social Security Committee 1991: *The Organisation and Administration of the Department of Social Security*. Minutes of Evidence, 25 June, HC 1990–91, 550-i. London: HMSO.

Taylor-Gooby, P., Dean, H., Munro, M. and Parker, G. 1999: Risk and the welfare state. *British Journal of Sociology*, 50 (2), 177–94.

van Oorschot, W. 1995: *Realising Rights*. Aldershot: Avebury.

Chapter 18

Ways of Seeing: The News Media and Racist Violence

Eugene McLaughlin and Karim Murji

Introduction

Racist violence is a serious social problem by any standards, affecting the lives of thousands of people on a daily basis. However, it was not until the publication of the report into the murder of Stephen Lawrence in 1999 that it was widely recognized as a social problem that required urgent action. This chapter considers the ways in which the news media selects, defines and influences particular forms of seeing or understanding the problem of racial violence. To do so we examine how and why:

- 'black crime' has been constructed as a social problem;
- racist violence has been traditionally denied the status of a social problem;
- the Stephen Lawrence Family Campaign finally led to the official recognition of racist violence as a social problem.

Two linked points should be noted at the outset. First, 'race' is commonly used to refer to people of African, Caribbean and Asian origins. However, the narrow focus on all those 'visible' ethnic minorities who are 'not white' is questionable and itself a problem, especially when 'whiteness' and the ethnic *majority* are rarely considered. Race does not have a pre-given meaning but is produced only through representation in specific contexts. Second, by looking at the news media it would be possible for us to focus on any one of a number of areas in which highly problematical perspectives on race have been articulated, such as representations of families and kinship and black masculinity. As the chapters by Franklin and Parton, and Dean also demonstrate, when discussing the role of the news media in the construction of social problems, the process of looking at one thing or issue is, simultaneously, a way of *not* looking at or 'seeing' something else, a point that we regard as fundamental for understanding what follows.

Reporting Crime

The importance of the news media in framing the public's understanding of social problems is widely recognized. Research in many countries confirms that crime reports are among the most headline-catching of news commodities. It also suggests that there is broad correspondence between the images of criminality articulated in the news media and the interpretations and 'orders of meaning' postulated by the police. There are at least two explanations for this.

First, the police are the primary definers of law and order issues for journalists and programme makers. Although many criminal justice professionals and pressure groups can provide expert commentary on crime matters, it is only the police 'who proclaim a professional expertise in the "war against crime" ', based on daily personal experience (Hall et al., 1978, p. 68). This exclusive and particular 'double expertise' seems to give the police especially authoritative credence in the hierarchy of credibility. Hence, it seems natural that crime journalists both take their lead from and foreground the views of the most accessible and visible part of the criminal justice system. This makes police accounts of 'what happened' and 'what is significant' seem the obvious starting points for any crime story.

Second, studies of the news making process have illustrated just how dependent journalists are on the police as a routine and predictable source of 'newsworthy' stories. Reporters are nearly always in an uneven negotiating position when dealing with the police. Indeed journalistic careers are advanced by receiving 'scoops' and 'leaks' and harmed by being left out in the cold. The resulting dependency can promote a partisanship that makes objective reporting of the problem of crime virtually impossible (Schlesinger and Tumber, 1994).

The Construction of a Social Problem: 'Black Crime'

Research during the early 1970s indicated that 'the Press has continued to project an image of Britain as a white society in which the coloured population is seen as some kind of aberration, a problem, or just an oddity, rather than "belonging" to the society' (Hartman and Husband, 1974, p. 145). Crime and criminality came to be the central motif that constructed black people as a 'problem presence' and as signifying that they were not really British. Hall et al. (1978) and Gilroy (1987), among others, extensively discuss this period of the racialization of British society, and we just want to highlight some key points. As the headlines in box 18.1 indicate, in the early to mid-1970s newspapers began to carry stories about 'mugging', a frightening new form of hit-and-run street crime that had been imported from the United States.

Using a social constructionist approach to social problems (see Clarke's chapter), Hall argued that the news media was actively involved in the orchestration of a moral panic:

Box 18.1

- 'Muggers murder for 20p' (*Daily Mirror* 19 October 1972)
- 'You and the Muggers' (*Sunday Mirror* 22 October 1972)
- 'London – the Violent Truth' (*Evening News* 31 January 1975)
- 'Murder and Mugger Land' (*Daily Express* 6 October 1975)
- 'Race to Blame for Mugging Says Powell' (*Daily Telegraph* 13 April 1976)
- 'A Mugging Every Hour in London' (*Evening Standard* 18 October 1976)

The image is already familiar – the mugger is callous, violent; he attacks the weak and vulnerable, robs for kicks rather than gain. Naturally certain features which fall outside this image don't get reported. Now, the general public is sensitised to 'mugging' via this image, and they then express fears about 'mugging' – perhaps in letters to the press. Judges who are deciding on a sentence refer to this 'public anxiety'. The sentences get longer. This, in itself, is newsworthy, it becomes a news story, and it refocuses public attention. This is an amplification spiral, and the media don't stand outside this spiral. They form part of it. (Hall, 1975)

Significantly, police forces released reconstructed, racially coded crime statistics to journalists which suggested that the perpetrators of mugging (a term which has no legal definition or status and which, in practice, cuts across the legal categories of theft and robbery) were disproportionately young males of West Indian origin, and the victims often white, female and elderly.

For all practical purposes, the terms mugging and black crime are now virtually synonymous. In the first mugging panic . . . though mugging was continually shadowed by the theme of race and crime, this link was rarely made explicit. This is no longer the case. The two are indissolubly linked: each term references the other in both the official and public consciousness. (Hall et al., 1978, p. 217)

Gilroy (1987) has added to this by analysing discourses on race, crime and nation. Perceptions of the 'weakness' of black culture and family life, sometimes 'explained' by the absence of a father or authority figure, or more crudely, by a lack of respect for the law and English traditions of civility, served to define black people as 'lesser breeds without the law', as 'the other' who stand outside what it means to be English or British. Hence, there are several overlapping layers in which people, places, culture and nation are tied together in diverse ways to mark out the boundaries of inclusion and exclusion.

'Race' or 'blackness' became a medium through which fears and anxieties about crime were focused and given a recognisable shape: 'Race' has come to provide the objective correlation of crises – the arena in which complex fears, tensions and

> ## Box 18.2
>
> The intensive news coverage of mugging as a particular form of racialized crime:
>
> - exaggerated the seriousness of the crime;
> - accentuated the 'otherness' of young black men as 'a race apart';
> - suggested that the problem of racial violence in Britain was one of black-on-white street crime;
> - generated demands for firm police action.

anxieties, generated by the impact of the totality of the crisis as a whole on the whole society, can be most conveniently and explicitly projected, and as the euphemistic phrase runs 'worked through'. (Hall et al., 1978, p. 33)

Demands for something to be done were accentuated in media coverage of anti-mugging policing initiatives, such as intensive stop-and-search operations, the deployment of special units and the use of tough prison sentences as a deterrent. The selective nature of media coverage meant that considerably less coverage, and credibility, was given to community representatives who:

- protested about the ways in which mugging had become a means for the blanket criminalization of all young black men;
- warned that institutionally racist policing and socio-economic disadvantage would provoke serious disorder on the streets of Britain's inner cities.

The riots or uprisings of 1980 and 1981 therefore seemed to come as a shock to the media, the police and the government. Although the outbreak of violent public disorder reinforced the news media's images of black criminality, a judicial inquiry that emphasized the role of racial discrimination helped to rebalance the debate. Lord Scarman's report into Brixton also acknowledged that there was a problem of racially discriminatory policing and emphasized that the principal issue was rebuilding public confidence in the police, particularly in black neighbourhoods. Scarman recommended a range of what were, for police officers, controversial proposals to improve police recruitment, training procedures and disciplinary arrangements. Improvements to the democratic accountability and local operational practices of the Metropolitan Police were also advocated (Scarman, 1981).

Within weeks of the release of the report certain crime reporters were being given off-the-record briefings by police officers to the effect that London was experiencing a dramatic increase in muggings as a consequence of the

> ## Box 18.3
>
> - 'More and more muggings but the Yard fights back' (*Daily Mail* 21 January 1982)
> - 'Menace of the Muggers: The Sun Joins Police on Patrol in Britain's Dangerous Streets' (*Sun* 18 February 1982)
> - 'Prisoners Behind Their Own Curtains' (*Daily Mail* 5 March 1982)
> - 'On Britain's Most Brutal Streets' (*Daily Express* 9 March 1982)
> - 'Black crime: the alarming figures' (*Daily Mail* 11 March 1982)
> - 'Black muggers blamed by the Yard' (*Sun* 11 March 1982)
> - 'Yard reveals race link in street crime explosion' (*Daily Express* 11 March 1982)
> - 'London's Streets of Fear' (*Daily Mirror* 11 March 1982)

'Scarmanisation' of policing (Sim, 1983). A series of exclusives about a rising tide of black criminality appeared (see box 18.3). The manner in which the Metropolitan Police selectively leaked the 1982 crime statistics and fed them to specific newspapers served to further:

- criminalize black people, especially young black men, and to blame them for violent crime in the inner city;
- racially code certain areas of British cities as lawless, threatening, criminal sanctuaries;
- justify and legitimate a police crackdown.

'Common-sense' associations between race, crime and specific places intensified in the aftermath of the news media coverage of large-scale riots in London and Birmingham in 1985. Broadwater Farm Estate, in particular, was constructed in both official and press reports as an 'estate of fear', where black criminals terrorized their law-abiding elderly white neighbours and defied police authority (Gifford, 1986). Right-wing press coverage – and the accompanying visual images – of the trial and conviction of Winston Silcott, one of the men convicted of the murder of PC Keith Blakelock during the Broadwater Farm riots, was saturated with racist meanings. 'Once the Tottenham Three had been convicted, the media described Winston as an "animal", a "wild killer ape", practising "the evil eye", having a "dreadful Black visage" . . . The aim can only be to make Winston an "untouchable", cutting him off from all social sustenance and support' (Legal Action For Women, 1998, p. 16).

In 1991, as a result of the exertions of the Winston Silcott Defence Campaign, the convictions were overturned as 'unsafe and unsatisfactory'. In August 1994 the *Daily Mail* launched a bitter attack on the decision to award Winston Silcott £10,000 compensation for wrongful conviction. During the 1990s the unfinished

---

Box 18.4

- 'Most muggers are black says top cop' (*Sun* 7 July 1995)
- 'Condon tackles black muggers' (*The Times* 7 July 1995)
- 'Met chief breaks taboo to reveal that most muggers are black' (*Daily Telegraph* 7 July 1995)
- 'Condon acts on black crime' (*Daily Express* 7 July 1995)
- 'Mugging: is it a black and white issue?' (*Independent* 8 July 1995)
- 'Fury at black crime claim' (*Guardian* 8 July 1995)
- 'Seeing crime in black and white' (*Observer* 9 July 1995)
- 'Black muggers: is Condon right?' (*Daily Telegraph* 9 July 1995)

---

debate about race and crime and mugging in particular continued to flash across the front pages of the newspapers (see box 18.4):

Denying a Social Problem: Racial Violence

An excess of media coverage played a critical role in the racialization of street crime, but at the same time the extent and seriousness of racially motivated attacks on black communities was being systematically played down or given limited coverage. A succession of reports published in the 1970s documented dramatic increases in levels of racial harassment and violence in certain parts of London. They expressed concern about the inadequate, or simply racist, non-response of the police, particularly their refusal to recognize the racist motivation for some attacks (for a review see Hesse et al., 1992; Bowling, 1998).

In February 1981, one month after the death of 13 young black people in a suspicious house fire in New Cross (south London) had sparked a wave of community protest, the cross-party Joint Committee Against Racialism presented the Home Secretary with an extensive dossier of incidents of racial violence that it had documented during the previous eighteen months. The Conservative government agreed to carry out a study on racial attacks, and the resulting report proved to be a significant moment in the history of policy responses to racial violence in the UK (Home Office, 1981).

First, it confirmed what black community groups had been claiming about victimization rates. On the basis of cases reported to the police, the report estimated that approximately 7,000 incidents were occurring each year in which there was strong, or at least some, indication of racial motive. It noted that 'the incidence of victimisation was much higher' for the ethnic minority population, particularly Asians, than for white people. Indeed the report found that the victimization rates for Asians were 50 times, and for blacks 36 times, higher than for white people (Home Office, 1981). The report acknowledged that there was 'a tendency

Box 18.5

When right-wing newspapers did report incidents, coverage tended to:

- report only the most conspicuous and horrific cases;
- view incidents of racial harassment as random in nature;
- reject the classification of incidents as racially motivated unless there was evidence of organized involvement by racist and fascist groups;
- deplore, but view as 'natural' and inevitable, white resentment that their localities were being 'invaded' or 'swamped' by ethnic minorities;
- deny that there was a history of deep-seated racism in Britain;
- emphasize the traditions of tolerance that are the hallmark of British society;
- blame misguided government immigration policies for fostering rather than ameliorating racial tensions;
- invoke the idea that mugging could be defined as a form of racial violence;
- play down allegations of an ineffective or inadequate police response;
- highlight the involvement of anti-racist groups and the 'race relations industry' in exploiting incidents and manipulating victims to foment minority conflict and discontent with British society.

on the part of the police to under-estimate the significance of racialist attacks for those attacked or threatened' (Home Office, 1981, para. 76).

Second, the report represented an official recognition, in theory at least, that racial attacks should be regarded a serious social problem: 'Hitherto, as the problem did not officially exist there had been no police, central or local government policies aimed at tackling the problem. There had been neither government-funded research nor even an official definition of the problem; no information about its nature or prevalence was published' (Bowling, 1998, p. 200).

A succession of local and national initiatives were launched throughout the 1980s to formulate an effective response to racial violence (Hesse et al., 1992; Bowling, 1998). However, the harrowing evidence presented in various official reports was not reflected in news media coverage. The lack of reporting of racial violence applied even to cases of serious assault, arson and murder (Gordon and Rosenberg, 1989; Van Dijk, 1991).

The nature of the de-racializing response from right-wing newspapers cannot be separated from the fact that throughout the 1980s and early 1990s they were engaged in an extensive backlash against so-called 'loony left' local authorities, particularly for seeking to advance anti-racist policies. Gordon's (1990) analysis of media coverage shows that anti-racist initiatives were defined as either an interference with individual 'freedom of speech' or a form of 'reverse racism' against white people – or both. Furthermore, reflecting the 'hierarchy of credibility' we discussed previously, many journalists and reporters were emphasizing the perspective not of the victims nor of pressure groups who complained of lack of police protection but of police officers who continued to view racist violence as minor neighbourhood disputes. In this context, and despite various Home Office reports and national and local initiatives, the problem of racist violence failed to achieve national prominence.

'An Extraordinary Situation . . . Demanded an Extraordinary Response': The Stephen Lawrence Case

On 22 April 1993 eighteen-year-old Stephen Lawrence was murdered by a group of white youths in Eltham, South London. There appeared to be nothing that made this event particularly newsworthy for the media. The murder was reported in local newspapers and featured on regional television and radio news bulletins the next day. The national press picked up the story on 24 April, but it was not front-page news. However, it went on to become one of the defining cases of the 1990s, transforming a violent local incident of apparently limited newsworthiness into an issue of public importance. In examining how and why this occurred, we also want to draw attention to those aspects that are concealed by dominant readings of the role of the news media in this case. Just as we have, albeit briefly, mentioned the social context in which mugging and racist violence were, or were not, defined as social problems, we think there is a need to draw attention to a number of complex interrelated developments in British society in the 1990s:

- The changing socio-economic position of blacks in Britain, including the consolidation of a black middle class.
- The working through of various race relations initiatives.
- An increase in the number of black people in the media, who helped to shape a more sophisticated news coverage of race issues and facilitated the increasing prominence of black perspectives within mainstream media coverage.
- A blurring of the boundaries of the conventional coverage of race as a social problem; thus, in the early 1990s the *Daily Mail* 'discovered' that 'Asian values' were close to those of the traditional English middle class, in terms of self-reliance and the importance of the family.
- The changing nature of the politics of race in the UK and the increased willingness of the main political parties to acknowledge that equality and fair treatment extended to ethnic minorities.
- Shifts in the relationship between sections of the news media and the police with some journalists taking a more critical stance in their reporting of policing controversies.

- Emerging campaigns to categorize racist violence as a specific crime in the context of the resurgence of extreme- and far-right groups across the European Union and the emergence of the British National Party in the UK.
- Intense media panic about a crime wave carried out by teenagers from a white 'underclass' who had no respect for the law.
- Changes in the news media's discussion of law and order politics, the perspectives of a variety of media-literate civil liberties, crime victims and anti-racist pressure groups being increasingly included in crime reports.
- Formal police acceptance that tackling racist violence would be a priority.

None the less, it is important to acknowledge that the Stephen Lawrence Family Campaign waged a long struggle for adequate news media coverage, for a proper police investigation and, subsequently, for the establishment of a judicial inquiry.

While the case has been widely defined as a turning point in the politics of race in Britain, we think that observing the process by which the case was eventually taken up by the news media and the content of that coverage suggests that the extent to which racist violence is regarded as a persistent, constitutive feature of everyday life in Britain is still open to question (McLaughlin and Murji, 1999). We can illustrate this argument by examining a BBC programme entitled 'Why Stephen?', presented by the respected journalist Charles Wheeler (broadcast by BBC2 on 13 February 1999). Wheeler set out to explore why and how the case of Stephen Lawrence achieved such prominence, when very similar cases, such as the racist murder of Rolan Adams by five white youths in 1991, did not. In the course of the programme, a number of crucial differences between the two cases were identified. First, from the outset the Metropolitan Police accepted that the murder of Stephen Lawrence was racist in intent. In the case of Rolan Adams the police declared that the murder was the result of a territorial dispute between rival gangs. Second, on 6 May 1993 Nelson Mandela, the President of South Africa, met Doreen and Neville Lawrence and publicly endorsed their campaign for justice. This both widened the parameters of news coverage, so that it was no longer just a local crime story, and contrasted the respectable figure of Mandela with the 'disreputable' Reverend Al Sharpton, who had played an active role in the Rolan Adams campaign. Third, despite some initially unfavourable coverage focusing on the role of the Anti-Racist Alliance, the Stephen Lawrence Family Campaign successfully resisted the accusation of being a front for extremist anti-racist groups. Because of the 'inflammatory' comments of Sharpton, the Rolan Adams campaign was ignored or condemned by the news media. And this leads us to the final difference between the two campaigns. Through the dramatic intervention of the *Daily Mail*, the Stephen Lawrence Family Campaign managed to make the murder relevant not just to one place in South London but, beyond that, to the concerns of the imaginary community of 'middle England'.

The *Daily Mail*'s advocacy of the case deserves recognition, not least because the paper had acquired the label of a home for a 'respectable' racism:

> I can remember journalists commenting on their surprise when the Daily Mail named the five suspected killers of black schoolboy Stephen Lawrence as being guilty. When one asked why they were surprised few had the guts to say what they all thought. Namely that Stephen Lawrence was black and why would a newspaper like the Daily Mail do anything to support a 'black case'. It's what most black people thought too, but the difference is that they would have no problem in openly articulating that view. As the 'victims' the black community has no difficulty in seeing how natural media reporting operates. (Pope, 1999, p. 59)

The newspaper's initial interest in the case was almost non-existent. Indeed, eighteen days after the murder it carried a story attacking the family campaign for allowing itself to be hijacked by anti-racist militants. However, on 14 February 1997 it ignored legal and ethical guidelines and controversially printed the names and the photographs of the five white suspects under the front-page banner headline: 'Murderers: The Mail Accuses These Men of Killing. If We Are Wrong Let Them Sue Us'. As part of its crusade on behalf of the Lawrence family, between 14 February 1997 and the publication of the official report into the murder on 24 February 1999 this newspaper published approximately 530 stories referring to the murder: we offer a small selection of the titles in box 18.6.

Why did the *Daily Mail* become actively involved in a campaign for racial justice? The dominant explanation is that the newspaper changed its editorial line when it became known that Neville Lawrence, Stephen's father, had once worked as a plasterer and decorator for Paul Dacre, the paper's editor. However, those people closely associated with the Stephen Lawrence Family Campaign argue that a conscious effort was made to make the case 'play' to 'middle England', emphasizing that Stephen Lawrence could have been the son of every reader of a paper such as the *Daily Mail*, and that any of them could be in the same position as his parents. A more cynical accounts articulated by rival newspapers suggests that the campaign was initiated in order to raise circulation. Although there is some truth in each of these accounts, we believe that it is more fruitful to view the paper's dramatic U-turn in terms of 'crisis management'.

> The Mail thought long and hard before deciding to name Gary Dobson, Neil Acourt, Jamie Acourt, Luke Knight and David Norris as the murderers. In no way does this newspaper want to set itself up as an unofficial adjunct to the judicial system. It would have been easier to stay silent. But this was an extraordinary situation and demanded an extraordinary response. The Lawrence case threatens to damage race relations and the reputation of British justice. (*Daily Mail*, editorial 15 February 1999)

The implication was that the newspaper would be colluding with this outrageous state of affairs if it stayed silent. (See also box 18.7.)

There is no doubt that the vanguard role played by the *Daily Mail*, Britain's leading mid-market tabloid, heightened the public profile of the Stephen

Box 18.6

- 'Murderers: The Mail Accuses These Men of Killing. If We Are Wrong Let Them Sue Us' (14 February 1997)
- 'Lawrence Killers: The Video of Hate' (15 February 1997)
- 'Now They Must Give Evidence' (1 August 1997)
- 'Lawrence Gang Face Jail Threat' (9 October 1997)
- 'Lawrence: The Damning Facts' (16 December 1997)
- 'Lawrence: Amazing Trial of Blunders by the Police' (25 March 1998)
- 'Don't Forget Where the Guilt Really Lies' (2 October 1998)
- 'Judge Accuses 'Racist' Police' (16 February 1999)
- 'Lawrence: Why We Stand Firm' (20 February 1999)

Box 18.7

The most significant factors in the *Daily Mail*'s decision to become involved seem to have been that:

- Stephen Lawrence was a model teenager with a promising future. He did not have a criminal record and was not in a street gang. Instead, he was a hardworking A-level student who had been brutally murdered in an unprovoked racist attack.
- Doreen and Neville Lawrence were ordinary, decent and dignified parents, who were not political and had worked hard to bring up their children to be ambitious and law abiding.
- The murder did not occur on the mean streets of the inner city but in law-abiding suburbia.
- The police and the criminal justice system had done everything possible to bring the killers to justice.
- The inquest jury had returned a verdict of unlawful killing 'in a completely unprovoked racist attack by five white youths'.
- A videotape provided 'proof' that the prime suspects were violent, arrogant, contemptuous, racist young men, who had outwitted the criminal justice system and were using the law to get away with murder.

Lawrence murder. These representations of the case played no small part in enabling the Lawrence family to press the Home Office to establish a judicial inquiry. During the inquiry, media coverage of the case intensified because the proceedings produced dramatic news events. Allegations of police incompetence, racism and corruption not only flashed across the front pages of news-

Box 18.8

- 'Riddled with racism: damning report on the Met which could change the race laws in Britain' (*Daily Record*)
- 'The legacy of Stephen: Radical measures to root out racism' (*Daily Mail*)
- 'Campaign to Banish Racism' (*The Times*)
- 'A Family Tragedy, A Police Force Shamed and a Nation Shamed' (*Independent*)
- 'Never Again' (*Express*)
- 'Now Change Must Come' (*The Voice*)
- 'The Lawrence Report: A Victim of Incompetence and Racism' (*Evening Standard*)
- 'Nail Them: Mirror Offers £50,000 to Catch Lawrence Killers' (*Mirror*)
- 'Stephen Lawrence's Legacy: Confronting Racist Britain' (*Guardian*)
- 'Straw's War on Racism' (*Sun*)
- 'We must change as a nation' (*Daily Telegraph*)

papers, news broadcasts and documentaries, but also were detailed in a prime-time docu-drama and a popular play. With the publication of the report into the murder in February 1999, the issues of racist violence and institutional racism were headlined by the news media and finally achieved recognition as social problems deserving urgent government action (Macpherson, 1999). Virtually every newspaper carried extensive coverage of the report's findings and recommendations as well as editorial supporting the Home Secretary's commitment to make the Stephen Lawrence case a defining moment in British race relations (see box 18.8).

Conclusion

The significance of the prolonged campaign that led to the inquiry into the murder of Stephen Lawrence cannot be overstated. Dominant representations of black people as 'problems' for white British society have been successfully challenged. Racist violence has been defined as a government priority, with an action plan setting out how the recommendations of the Macpherson report will be implemented. The Metropolitan Police version of what happened was rejected by the judicial inquiry, and police forces have been required to commit resources to tackling all forms of racially motivated crime and disorder. Of equal importance, incidents of racist violence have acquired significant and sustained news media coverage, several newspapers running their own anti-racist-violence campaigns. Within the broader historical narrative of the news media coverage of race discussed in this chapter, these are noteworthy changes and should not be underestimated. However, a central thread of our argument has been that news media definitions of social problems are context-specific, and that attention to some ways of seeing what a problem is simultaneously overlooks other problems or other ways of seeing them. Consequently, social policy analysts should look for what has been ignored or downplayed in the news media in order to construct the widely accepted narrative that racist violence is regarded as a social problem.

For example, important aspects of the *Daily Mail*'s representational and associative strategies in the Stephen Lawrence case deserve closer reading. We believe that the newspaper's decision to champion the Lawrence family can be seen as part of a complex and volatile reworking of the coverage of race relations in the British news media. In its own important way, the discursive changes deployed by the *Daily Mail* acknowledged that blackness and British-ness were not necessarily incompatible. Black Britons were no longer homogeneously the 'alien other' or quintessentially 'different' because of their 'non-whiteness'. Rather the *Daily Mail*, in accepting the family values and inte-gratedness of Doreen and Neville Lawrence was redefining the conventional vocabulary of race as a social problem. Its depiction of Stephen Lawrence broke out of the long-established framing of young black men as criminals and muggers and the case of this particular young black man moved from being just another crime statistic to become one of the most powerful images of Britain in the 1990s.

However, the *Daily Mail*'s construction of the case is beset with problems and contradictions, which need to be acknowledged. First the identification of the five suspects and their families as uneducated, unemployed and criminal constructs racism as a problem 'out there' and thereby distanced from civilized 'middle England'. This cut-and-dried image of the prime suspects built on and strengthened an already constructed discourse that blamed many of Britain's social problems on the, paradoxically, *nouveau riche* but culturally and morally impoverished 'white' underclass of hidden Britain, obsessed with designer clothes, lacking the work ethic and respect for authority, and having criminal associations. Hence, racism is treated as exceptional rather than routine or commonplace. Second, the *Daily Mail*'s acceptance of Doreen and Neville Lawrence as 'just like us' glosses over uncomfortable facts that do not fit the preferred narrative of the newspaper. In its embrace of the attempts of the Stephen Lawrence Family Campaign to invest the campaign with universal human interest and the moral claim to 'sameness', a process of de-racination occurs, that is race is made to matter less and to some extent is even written out of the script. This process manifests itself in several ways. The most famous photograph of Stephen Lawrence in a striped top appears to feature him making a clenched fist salute. However, in the 'locking' of this iconographical representation this is rarely, if ever, noted. While we have no way of knowing that it was intended as a 'Black power' salute or street wise gesture, the fact that it can have these associations clearly makes it uncomfortable for sections of the news media. Similarly, because the *Daily Mail* initially believed that the Metropolitan Police and the criminal justice system were beyond reproach, some extremely critical remarks about racism and the police made by Doreen Lawrence in particular were disregarded. The radical edges did not fit in with the ways in which the newspaper wanted to represent the Stephen Lawrence case; yet they are evident for all to see.

The suppression of race manifests itself in other ways. Victims of racist violence who do not fit the narrative of the authentic victim and the idealized image established in the course of the Stephen Lawrence case will have had to fight vigorous battles to prevent exclusion or marginalization by a hostile or suspicious news media. For example, on the night of his murder Stephen was with a friend, Duwayne Brooks. The fact that the police were unable to see the latter as a victim and that this was probably due to their stereotypical images of young black men has been noted in the Macpherson report and elsewhere. Duwayne is often written out of the Stephen Lawrence story, because the news media find it difficult to locate his ragamuffin image and his angry denunciation of his treatment by the police within the favoured narrative.

One final point needs to be noted. Older, more straightforwardly xenophobic and racist discourses are still in play. As the ambivalent reporting of violent attacks on asylum seekers indicates these have the ability to subsume and subordinate anti-racist discourses. Consequently, those studying news media coverage of racist violence since the Stephen Lawrence case will have to pay careful attention to representational practices and signifying systems which are not settled but inconsistent and contradictory.

Issues to Consider

- Why do the police occupy such a pivotal role in crime reporting?
- How was mugging constructed as a racialized social problem?
- What discourses have been used to deny racist violence the status of a social problem?
- What did the *Daily Mail*'s involvement in the Stephen Lawrence case signify?
- What evidence is there that the Stephen Lawrence case represents a watershed in the reporting of racist violence?

Suggestions for Further Reading

Schlesinger and Tumber (1994) provide the most detailed analysis of the complexities of crime reporting in the UK. Hall et al. (1978) and Gilroy (1987) provide the framework for understanding the role of the news media in the construction of mugging as a pressing social problem during the 1970s and 1980s.

The campaign to force racist violence onto the political agenda during the 1980s and 1990s is comprehensively covered by Bowling (1998). An overview of the news media's initial response to the Stephen Lawrence report is provided by McLaughlin and Murji (1999). A more general introduction to the many debates about the role of the media in policy formation and the relationship between the media and the public perception of social problems can be found in Liddiard (1999).

References

Bowling, B. 1998: *Violent Racism*. Oxford: Clarendon Press.

Gifford, Lord 1986: *The Broadwater Farm Inquiry*. London: Karia Press.

Gilroy, P. 1987: *There Ain't No Black in the Union Jack*. London: Hutchinson.

Gordon, P. 1990: A dirty war. In W. Ball and J. Solomos (eds), *Racism and Local Politics*. Basingstoke: Macmillan.

Gordon, P. and Rosenberg, D. 1989: *Daily Racism: The Press and Black People in Britain*. London: Runnymede Trust.

Hall, S. 1975: Mugging: a case study in the media. *Listener*, 1 May.

Hall, S., Critcher, C., Jefferson, T., Clarke, J. and Roberts, B. 1978: *Policing the Crisis*. London: Macmillan.

Hartman, P. and Husband, C. 1974: *Racism and the Mass Media*. London: Davis-Poynter.

Hesse, B. et al. 1992: *Beneath the Surface*. Aldershot: Gower.

Home Office 1981: *Racial Attacks*. London: Home Office.

Legal Action For Women 1998: *A Chronology of Injustice: The Case for Winston Silcott's Conviction to Be Overturned*. London: Crossroads Books.

Liddiard, M. 1999: Arts and culture policy. In J. Baldock et al. (eds), *Social Policy*. Oxford: Oxford University Press.

McLaughlin, E. and Murji, K. 1999: 'After the Stephen Lawrence report'. *Critical Social Policy*, 19 (3), 371–85.

Macpherson, W. 1999: *The Stephen Lawrence Inquiry*, Cmnd. 4262. London: Stationery Office.

Pope, S. 1999: The ignorance of Middle England. *British Journalism Review*, 10 (1), 56–60.

Scarman, Lord 1981: *The Brixton Disorders, 10–12 April 1981*, Cmnd. 8427. London: HMSO.

Schlesinger, P. and Tumber, H. 1994: *Reporting Crime: The Media Politics of Criminal Justice*. Oxford: Clarendon Press.

Sim, J. 1983: Scarman: the police counter-attack. In *The Socialist Register 1982*. London: Merlin Press.

Van Dijk, T. 1991: *Racism and the Press*. London: Routledge.

Part Four

Consumer Protection in Social Policy

Chapter 19

Protecting the 'Vulnerable': Welfare and Consumer Protection

Margaret May

Introduction

This chapter is concerned with an issue that is attracting increasing attention from policy analysts. As will emerge from the discussion this is primarily a reflection of the growing concern about the implications of attempts to restructure welfare in the UK along market-based lines. Over the past two decades this has put individuals under increasing pressure to protect themselves against many life-cycle risks. Yet demographic trends and changes in both the labour market and the family have meant that these contingencies and people's abilities to meet them are themselves changing. It is in this context that this chapter considers consumer protection as a key social problem in social policy. Focusing on the issues faced by both those who use state welfare services and purchasers and consumers of commercial welfare, it surveys:

- traditional conceptions of the individual consumer and consumer protection in social policy;
- the re-emergence of consumer protection as a social problem in social policy;
- current issues.

Traditional Approaches

For much of the past century perceptions of social problems within social policy were heavily shaped by Fabian thinking. With their reformist, technocratic leanings, the early Fabians perceived social problems in predominantly 'realist' terms, as the outcome of unregulated market forces (see the chapters by Clarke and Page). From this perspective, commercially based welfare was intrinsically incapable of stemming such problems or meeting the manifold needs thrown up by industrial urbanism. Their scale and incidence was also beyond the capacity of voluntary agencies. Only services that were publicly funded and delivered, equitable, and accessible could meet these common contingencies and protect individuals against the vagaries of the market.

The state's provision of services was viewed not only as the means of countering the inherent uncertainties and inequities of market exchanges; it also offered a way to protect welfare consumers against the questionable practices and power of non-statutory service providers. For Fabian writers throughout the first half of the century the greatest need for protection lay in commercial welfare, but their concern also extended to voluntary agencies, particularly the services provided by charitable and philanthropic organizations. This partly reflected a belief that voluntary endeavour was inherently incapable of meeting the scale of need revealed by contemporary social surveys. It also sprang, however, from a more deep-seated objection to charity as a mode of social distribution and welfare delivery. All too often access and entitlement to the support provided by voluntary agencies seemed to be determined by the private, unchallengeable decisions of committees and trustees or delegated to particular individuals. Unaccountable to the wider society and frequently drawn from a narrow self-selecting social segment, their highly discretionary procedures offered little redress for claimants and lent themselves to potentially capricious, personal judgements of need or treatment.

These criticisms were not confined to philanthropic bodies; the practices of mutual aid agencies were also questioned. It was, however, commercial provision, particularly the insurance products providing protection in the event of illness or bereavement and for retirement, that were the focus of Fabian disquiet. As was repeatedly emphasized by social investigators between the two world wars, prospective consumers varied not only in their ability to buy welfare benefits and services, but also in the purchasing power and choice they could exercise. Where profit-making opportunities were slim, as with many occupational groups and working-class areas, consumer choice was likely to be minimal. As importantly, many consumers lacked the specialist information necessary to assess their own needs or discriminate between competing products, while the advice proffered by welfare service providers was often misleading and unreliable. That provided by sales personnel, particularly those selling insurance cover, was governed more by their commission or job requirements than by customers' needs. Purchasing costs as compared with the benefits were often glossed over or hidden in the small print, and, as many early-twentieth-century studies showed, the chances of redress for dissatisfied or ill-advised consumers were minimal (May and Brunsdon, 1999).

Equally critically, attempts to tighten regulation, especially of the insurance industry, had been heavily diluted by powerful parliamentary lobbying. Potentially, those who felt they had been misled could also seek redress through the courts. This, however, was both an expensive and a protracted process, governed primarily by the common-law rules of contract. Based on cases decided by the superior courts during the nineteenth century, these rested on the notions of the freedom and equality of contracts. In essence the courts operated on the presumption that consumers were free and informed agents, able to manage their own affairs and operate in the market on an equal footing with sole traders and large businesses alike. Though by the early twentieth century, insurance providers were subject to regulation, it was minimal and designed primarily to protect shareholders rather than regulate sales practices. Despite the manifest asymmetries of information and power in welfare (and other) markets, more fundamental attempts to protect ordinary consumers had made little headway in the face of both business and legal opposition. Self-protection through the application of the maxim *caveat emptor* (let the buyer beware) remained the basis of legal decision making, the courts effectively maintaining what a recent commentator describes as the 'juristic equivalent of laissez-faire economics' (Harris, 1997, p. 67).

Concerns about the difficulties consumers faced when exercising an informed choice in welfare markets and the limitation of the legal system contributed to the growing pressure for a more interventionist state, which culminated in the welfare legislation of the 1940s. Though its roots were manifold (see the chapter by Page), the organizational architecture of the welfare state owed much to the writings of early Fabians such as the Webbs. Their critique of the market and individual consumers' weak position within it was paralleled by a corresponding faith in public services upheld not only on universalist, redistributive grounds but as offering an inbuilt form of consumer protection.

To begin with, these services were to be structured on formalistic, bureaucratic lines. As such they were presumed to guarantee standard, uniform modes of service and transparent, impartial decision making by personnel subject to clear hierarchies of accountability. Consumer interests would also be safeguarded by the employment of specialist professional staff equipped to assess a user's needs and dispense the most appropriate treatment. Bound by professional codes of ethics, rather than by financial incentives, such experts promised impartial, scientifically based, user-centred services and, in effect, 'a court of appeal against profit' (Hobsbawm, cited in Lee and Raban, 1988, p. 25). This blend of professional expertise and bureaucratic rigour was held to ensure due care for all users and particularly for the most vulnerable, children subject to neglect or abuse, the frail elderly, people with disabilities and those with mental health care problems.

For its proponents, this 'bureau-professional' format (Parry and Parry, 1979; Clarke and Langan, 1993) also secured a particular ethos, that of a 'public service'. Committed to promoting the general good and the best interest of users, this orientation was assured by the processes of democratic representation to which public servants were ultimately accountable. Viewed in this essentially benign light, the only safeguards required were against unintended maladministration and professional misconduct. The former was ensured through a system of tribunals, the latter through the sureties against malpractice offered by professional associations' regulation of their members' conduct.

The expansion of state welfare, moreover, meant that broader regulatory changes to protect individual welfare purchasers appeared less necessary. Apart from the introduction of means-tested legal aid in 1949, little attempt was made to extend their opportunities for legal redress or to overhaul the regulation of private welfare provision, which remained subject to an essentially liberal regime. Indeed it was widely assumed that the minority who continued to buy education, health care or housing were capable of managing their own affairs or seeking advice when they needed it. Those who invested in private insurance or long-term savings were similarly deemed to be in a position different from that of the mass of working-class consumers, a view implicit in the Beveridge Report (Cmnd. 6404, 1942).

The Re-emergence of Consumer Protection as a Social Problem in Social Policy

In the immediate postwar decades, this notion of consumer protection embedded in the structures of bureau-professionalism gained cross-party support. It was seen as one of the hallmarks of state welfare, which, it was widely assumed, had supplanted other forms of provision and the need for further protection. In retrospect, however, it is clear that the Fabian template was based on a particular, fundamentally paternalist concept of the welfare consumer, which by the 1970s was increasingly out of tune with the expectations of a more affluent society. Its premises were also subject to a barrage of criticism from differing points on the political compass, which, in varying ways, questioned the nature of the protection offered by public service professionals and administrators.

One key strand in this process was the emergence of 'consumerism' as a social movement. The 1960s saw a proliferation of pressure groups claiming to represent the common interests of consumers against what were seen to be the manipulations of increasingly large corporations, compared with whom individual purchaser's power was minimal. Modelled on similar developments in the USA, these groupings captured anxieties about both the growth of powerful multiples and the standard and reliability of service offered by retailers and manufacturers generally. Much of their lobbying focused on the new consumer goods markets and hire-purchase facilities that had developed since the war and the related rise in high-pressure advertising and selling techniques. But it also drew attention to the incomprehensibility of the information provided by the companies selling health and welfare insurance, the prevalence of hidden charges and 'small print clauses', and the aggressive sales practices of their agents.

Though not directly enhancing protection for private welfare purchasers, their campaigning inspired a rash of measures regulating consumer credit, increasing the responsibilities of retailers and manufacturers and widening the scope for legal redress. The Office of Fair Trading (OFT) was established in 1973 to oversee their implementation and improve information for consumers. Organized consumer pressure combined with this legislation also stimulated an upsurge in self-regulation in the form of codes of practice developed by trade and industry associations. Furthermore it appears to have contributed to a growing awareness of the commercial value of a loyal customer base as distinct from the high-volume sales approach adopted by many companies during the immediate postwar boom. By the 1980s, as national and international competition intensified in the wake of successive oil crises, the responsive, customer-focused provision of goods and services became a central tenet of management manuals. At its heart lay a recognition of one of the principal features of the consumer pressure groups formed in the 1960s and 1970s, one typified by the Consumers' Association. From its foundation in 1957 the Association campaigned both for tighter regulation and for transparent information projecting an image of the consumer as needing protection, but in an enabling rather than a paternalist way.

Consumerist pressure on these lines was not confined to the private sector. It spread to state services, in which the professionalized nature of welfare provision began to appear overly autocratic. In one sense, the professionalized welfare state (Perkin, 1989; Marquand, 1990) had emerged in response to the undeniably low levels of working class literacy and general standards of education in early-twentieth-century Britain. It embodied the Fabians' reformist belief in the power of empirical research combined with professional expertise in identifying and responding to social problems (see too the discussion by Page). It also reflected the authority patterns of a still highly deferential, class-divided society and the extent to which, despite its egalitarian aspirations, the Fabian tradition was rooted in a deep mistrust of ordinary people's capacity to 'govern themselves' (N. and J. Mackenzie, cited in Lee and Raban, 1988, p. 25). Whether in education, income support, health, housing or social care, welfare consumers were considered to lack the competences to determine their own needs: left to themselves they were liable to opt for instant or inappropriate remedies. As the lexicon of 'recipient', 'tenant', 'client' and 'patient' denoted, state welfare was envisaged as a form of 'enlightened paternalism' (Mishra, 1989, p. 134), safeguarding the potentially misguided welfare consumer.

From a user's perspective bureau-professionalism was frequently experienced as authoritarian, patronizing and insensitive to varying individual needs (Barnes, 1997). Far from offering consumer-oriented services, state bureaucracies appeared to operate according to procedures designed to suit themselves, which often masked highly arbitrary and intrusive modes of delivery. Professional interventions too were attacked for cultivating a passive, unilateral, submissive relationship that gave little credence to users' views or requirements (Powell, 1997).

Users' dissatisfaction was mirrored in a growing disillusion with professional practices expressed by a new generation of Fabian and other researchers who began to question the reverence previously granted to the caring professions.

Their concerns rested particularly on findings which suggested that the professionalized welfare state operated in ways that enabled articulate, well-informed, middle-class users to negotiate the 'best deals' (Le Grand, 1982). As a wealth of studies demonstrated it was also riven with patriarchal, ethnocentric assumptions and driven more by the status-enhancing concerns of practitioners than by those of users (Clarke, 1993). Effective consumer protection required a different strategy, combining the regulation of state provision with responsive, participative modes of delivery.

Though designed to reform rather than undermine public services, this questioning of their administrative base fed into the very different critique advanced by neo-liberal writers. Popularized from the 1970s in a stream of publications, this rested on a converse belief in the supremacy of the market, the pivotal role of consumers within it and the detrimental effects of public service monopolies. Drawing on the work of Hayek and other Austrian School economists, the market was presented as the most efficient and creative means of generating prosperity and allocating scare resources. Market mechanisms, it was argued, also provided the most effective means of assuring the interests of consumers. Indeed, competitive market systems were geared to satisfying consumers' needs and maintaining their loyalty. Consumers rather than providers were held to be in control. They signalled their preferences about the types and quantities of the products they required, and providers responded by supplying the amounts that consumers' purchasing indicated they would buy.

For neo-liberals, the major justification for market-based welfare lay in this notion of consumer sovereignty and the freedoms it generates. In cataloguing the ways in which state welfare prevented individuals from exercising these freedoms and making their own welfare arrangements, they also challenged the notion of a disinterested, vocationally inspired, public service. Public choice theorists in particular argued that far from serving the public interest, state agencies served the sectional self-interests of service providers. Shielded from competition, they had exploited their monopoly status for their own benefit, creating large, inefficient empires run according to their own convenience rather than that of users.

'Consumer-citizenship'

The corollary, taken up by the Conservative governments of the 1980s and early 1990s, was to emancipate the consumer by restoring market-based welfare. Where this could not be achieved directly by dismantling state services, consumers were to be empowered by reproducing market conditions in public services. To this end, successive governments introduced a stream of measures aimed at realigning the user–provider relationship and the basis of consumer protection in state services. Though developed incrementally and unevenly across different service areas, these hinged on five developments, summarized in box 19.1.

Box 19.1: Consumer empowerment in state welfare

- Increased choice
- Clearer information
- Improved complaints and redress procedures
- New forms of quality assurance
- Tighter regulation

In attempting to expand consumer choice they adopted a two-fold strategy. In some areas, such as council housing and education, the choices available were widened through the introduction of opting-out arrangements. More generally, provision was recast on competitive, businesslike lines with purchasing separated from provision. Purchasers were charged with securing both value for money and more responsive modes of delivery; this gave competing statutory providers the incentive to diversify and develop a wider range of services. To further extend choice some suppliers, particularly in social care, were also exposed to external competition from voluntary and commercial enterprises.

Apart from nursery vouchers, however, state welfare consumers gained only an indirect say in this new order. Ironically, purchasing remained with the much maligned professional staff. Under care management, GP fundholding and related initiatives, they became responsible for procuring services on behalf of users, subject though to increasing pressure to involve them in the purchasing process. First, in a bid to enable potential users to establish their own needs and shop around for possible solutions, statutory providers were required to increase the flow and quality of their promotional literature. They were also subject to a new system of league tables and performance indicators, again aimed to help individuals make decisions.

Empowerment through increased information was supported by the introduction of new consultative arrangements; this forced purchasers in the key areas of health, housing and social care to involve users and potential consumers in planning, delivering and evaluating the services. In a parallel move, providers were also expected to publicize clear, user-friendly details of their complaints procedures, supported by appropriate forms of redress. Given that the 'right to complain' was one of the few entitlements consumers had, this was considered a critical development serving to pinpoint areas for improvement and assuring accountability to users (Department of Health, 1991).

Protection as well as more responsive provision was thus to be secured by actively engaging users in decision making and quality control. It was further guaranteed by the introduction of a raft of new quality assurance procedures throughout the welfare system. These ranged from service-level agreements and contractual arrangements in health, social care and housing, to the national curriculum in schools, and new performance and response rate targets for processing benefits, to attempts to develop national benchmarks and performance criteria for key service areas (Audit Commission, 1992). Professional discretion was also constrained by strengthened audit, inspection and regulation systems.

These measures, which were also meant to foster a more cost-conscious, efficient statutory provision of services, were promoted through legislation and ministerial rulings throughout the 1980s and early 1990s. But the underlying approach to consumer protection was most clearly articulated in the Major government's 1991 White Paper on the *Citizen's Charter* (Prime Minister, 1991). This brought together the various mechanisms devised to empower state welfare users and enable them to determine and protect their own interests by exercising pressure akin to that of private sector customers. In particular, they were to be 'told what service standards are and be able to act when services are unacceptable' (p. 14). This requirement was explicated in service-specific charters, advising users what they should expect in terms of quality, value for money, progress-chasing (including audit and inspection) and complaints and redress procedures. By 1996, 42 charters setting out the minimum standards for the main public services had been published, supported by over 100,000 local charters and the Charter Mark scheme launched in 1992 (Prime Minister, 1996). Together they recast state welfare users in a neo-liberal mould as responsible, self-managing 'consumer-citizens' (Le Grand, 1991), capable of expressing their own needs and pressing for responsive provision, rather than dependent on the stewardship of welfare professionals.

The charter programme centred on encouraging statutory providers to invest in the customer-care practices that seemed to ensure satisfaction in the private sector. It offered no new substantive rights; nor were the standards laid out in the charters legally enforceable. Securing them depended on consumers' pressure and vigilant inspection. For many critics these were an inadequate base on which to improve services and restore public confidence in statutory welfare.

Charter standards, it was claimed, were undemanding and, in some instances, pitched lower than normal service levels. The information provided was poor and insufficient for consumers to exercise choice or make their views known; consultation arrangements, particularly in health and social care, appeared tokenist rather than genuinely participative (Barnes, 1997).

For its architects, however, the programme was part of a wider agenda, aimed to enhance choice by giving the users of state welfare not only a voice, but also the ability to 'exit' (Hirschmann, 1970) and take their custom elsewhere. To facilitate this, the Thatcher and Major governments introduced a variety of incentives prompting people to switch to private sector services and encouraging the latter to expand. In marked contrast to statutory providers of welfare, these suppliers were promised less regulation and a flow of new customers partly subsidized by the state. Private schools remained outside the national curriculum and inspection system; the 1986 Financial Services Act sustained a liberal regulatory regime; mortgages and house sales were left to voluntary codes of practice supervised by trade associations. Meanwhile, a swathe of initiatives including discounted council house sales, tax relief on pensions and long-term savings products such as PEPs and TESSAs and the privatization of some services encouraged individuals to provide for themselves.

Like the citizen's charters, the resulting surge in do-it-yourself welfare (Klein and Millar, 1995) was hailed by the government and its neo-liberal supporters as signifying increased choice and consumer driven provision. It presupposed, however, a financially literate, risk-aware citizenry exercising extensive consumer sovereignty and operating on the rational, self-interested, calculative base enshrined in classical economic thinking. It became clear that many consumers lacked the necessary purchasing skills and acumen. As the experiences of those left with negative equity following the collapse of the 1980s housing boom showed, in the face of the sales pitch and marketing ploys available to corporate suppliers their sovereignty was also illusory.

The gap between the rhetoric and reality of consumer power was most strikingly revealed by the private pensions scheme introduced under the 1986 Social Security Act. It transpired that poorly supervised, commission-hungry sales personnel persuaded people to opt out of SERPS or secure occupational programmes into inappropriate private pension schemes offering lower returns for higher charges. Revelations of the scale of this mis-selling forced the Major government to tighten the regulation of the financial services industry and, belatedly, to implement a system of compensation. This was subsequently revamped by the Blair government, which also adopted a policy of naming, shaming and fining companies that were slow to arrange redress for the people involved. But the scandal threw into sharp relief the difference between the protection offered to the users of state welfare through the Conservative government's various reforms and that afforded to private purchasers. It also reopened the debate about the need for and provenance of consumer protection in welfare services generally.

New Issues: New Directions?

Pressure for more extensive safeguards gained momentum as Labour returned to power and continued during its first years in office. Concern over the sales of private pensions continued to attract widespread publicity and spilt over into new revelations of the possible mis-selling of free-standing additional voluntary contribution pension schemes. Public confidence was further shaken by reports showing that the payout from endowment mortgages, again heavily promoted by commission-driven staff, was unlikely to cover the costs faced by a significant proportion of house purchasers (*Guardian* 9 October 1999). As house prices rose mortgage providers were also once again accused of sanctioning packages insufficiently related to their purchasers' ability to pay (Hunter, 2000).

The Blair administration also faced renewed anxiety over the safeguards provided within state welfare. Most disturbingly, a succession of inquiries into abuse in children's homes in North Wales and elsewhere and into the maltreatment of elderly people in state-run care homes pointed incontrovertibly to serious deficiencies in the protection offered to the most vulnerable user groups. Pressure for stronger regulation also surfaced in reports from OFSTED, the Audit Commission, the Social Service Inspectorate and other quality assurance agencies set up by Labours' predecessors, all of which indicated the continued need for a more responsive provision of services. Meanwhile, faith in the efficacy of professional self-regulation was shaken by a separate series of scandals, including the case of Harold Shipman and other medical practitioners.

Labour's response was foreshadowed in its version of the citizen's charter. Unlike its counterpart this dealt with the needs of consumers in both public and private sector transactions. To safeguard their dealings with companies, public bodies and central and local governments, they were to be given nine rights: choice, quality, safety, equal treatment, swift and fair redress, citizen's action, voice, knowledge and advocacy (Labour Party, 1991). Though these have not yet materialized in legislation, the government has adopted a stance very different from that of its predecessors based on the indirect application of these precepts.

Its broad strategy appears to rest on four premises outlined in box 19.2:

Box 19.2

- stronger quality assurance and control in state welfare services;
- a stricter regulation of private welfare provision;
- an education and advice programme designed to enhance consumer literacy;
- ensuring competition.

In terms of the first premise, New Labour has built on and extended the measures introduced by the Thatcher and Major governments, particularly in education. Its approach centres on more rigorous surveillance of service providers, the establishment of national performance frameworks or benchmarks and sanctions for 'poor' performers. These apply across the welfare spectrum but include new systems for overseeing services for 'looked after children' and those in care homes and a plethora of helplines. The system of league tables for different services has been refined, and providers who fail to meet appropriate standards face the prospect of being replaced by private-sector managers. These developments span the main service areas and, through the Best Value programme (introduced nationally in early 2000), all areas of local government. Moreover, the government's attempt to secure more flexible, user-responsive inputs from care practitioners has extended to professional associations, particularly in medical care, which are similarly being expected to manage their performance more tightly.

More rigorous standards in their dealings with consumers are also being imposed on private welfare suppliers, particularly in financial services. Here again, the government is moving on so many fronts that only a brief indication of its strategy is possible. The Financial Services and Markets Act heralds sweeping regulatory changes, while a new umbrella, the Financial Services Agency (FSA), has become responsible for the previously separate regulation of different financial products. Set up in 1999, its remit included stronger protection for consumers as well as a more direct oversight of the industry. The regulation of mortgages has been tightened, and consumers have been offered further protection through 'CAT' mortgages (i.e. with clear specifications on charges, access and terms). Private pension schemes have been overhauled, the stakeholder pension system has been developed for those on low incomes, and Individual Savings Accounts (brought in to replace PEPs and TESSAs) have become subject to new kite-mark standards.

Alongside overseeing these and other financial services, the FSA has taken on an educational role. This involves producing and disseminating information to aid personal financial decision making and various forms of what is best described as 'awareness training'. Thus its consumer education department is to publish information tables on pensions, insurance and other welfare products to help 'the vulnerable and inexperienced' make sense of what is on offer (Selva, 2000). It is also supporting the introduction from September 2000 of personal finance lessons as part of the national curriculum for children aged between 5 and 16. Introducing it within the Personal Social and Health Education (PSHE) curriculum (it is hence not a statutory requirement), the FSA nonetheless anticipates its high take up. In the longer run there is considerable pressure for compulsory provision alongside an expanded network of consumer advice centres and helplines. These are believed to be a prerequisite for developing discerning, financially responsible consumers. As the government has made clear, however, the best safeguard is a highly competitive market in which quality is assured through consumers' ability to shop around. To this end, it has established stronger controls of firms under the 1998 Competition Act aimed to penalize and prevent anti-competitive activities.

Many of these developments are still at an embryonic stage, but Labour's four-pronged approach is already attracting opprobrium. Much of this has been directed at the business aspects of the FSA and the Financial Services and Markets Act, which have been heavily criticized for imposing unnecessary costs on Britain's crucial industrial sector and threatening its global competitiveness. Critics have also expressed concern about the heavy burden of individual consumer protection and the impediments to innovation and flexibility implicit in the tighter policing of private- and public-sector performance.

Other writers feel that the government has not gone far enough and that its wider welfare agenda demands a more fundamental, rights-based approach. This partly stems from concerns about the importation of commercially generated forms of quality assurance to state welfare services with little regard for the complexities of specifying and measuring 'quality' in the latter (Flynn, 1997). It also reflects concern about the possible implications of the government's drive to boost consumer literacy. Given its wider emphasis on the duties and responsibilities of citizens, it is feared that this carries the danger of pushing the onus of protection back onto the individual. Behind these criticisms lie more fundamental reservations about the extent to which 'self-provisioning' remains as central to the remodelling of state welfare under Labour as it was under its predecessors.

Although committed to improving health and education, Labour envisages an 'opportunity state' in which work pays and individuals acquire the resources to channel into long-term and contingency savings. Its active labour market and New Deal policies and support for lifelong learning are, like the minimum wage and the working families tax credit, geared to this end. Pressure to 'self-provide' is also visible in the continuing brake on benefit entitlements and the changed basis of student finance, while the much-vaunted stakeholder pensions and tax exempt savings accounts point to the government's interest in promoting individual asset-building. Implicit in these policies is an acceptance of a widening role for private providers, especially in the area of social security and with it a 'strategic shift' away from the thinking which underlay the social legislation of the 1940s (Glennerster, 1999, p. 31). Whatever their views on the wider questions posed by this policy switch, many commentators feel that what Glennerster (1999, p. 31) describes as 'harnessing' the market 'for social purposes' requires further safeguards for individual consumers.

A more proactive approach, it is argued, is required if Labour is to successfully pursue an asset-building policy (Kelly, 2000) and encourage personal investment, particularly given the advent of the 'electronic economy'. On the surface 'wired welfare' has given consumers new powers to make more personalized arrangements and manage their own welfare. They can shop around and select from a wealth of offers from established and new suppliers selling everything from mortgages and houses to pensions, life-insurance and other savings products, to education (and educational qualifications) and personal counselling. 'Cyber-medicine' too potentially undermines professional dominance, enabling individuals to access information on diagnoses and potential treatments directly. Products and advice alike, moreover, are increasingly available across a global market.

But in facilitating direct access to a wealth of options, the Internet brings its own information risks as, relatedly, do the new medical technologies. Advances in genetic testing, for instance, potentially enable insurers to adjust their risk-ratings for income protection, health, life and other forms of insurance and annuity payments according to an individual's family background and makeup. At the time of writing this was subject to a voluntary code whereby such testing is not required by insurers and individuals can choose whether or not to take such tests. Testing has been heavily criticized for threatening to create an uninsurable 'genetic underclass'. A report into its feasibility undertaken by the Department of Health's genetics and insurance committee was due in late 2000.

Whatever the outcome of the looming debate over genetic testing and kindred developments in medical science, it raises new questions about the need for and nature of individual consumer protection. Further questions arise about the government's approach to consumer protection in the area of personal finance and commercial welfare more generally. As indicated in this chapter, the notion of the consumer and hence of consumer protection in welfare markets has been discussed in homogeneous terms. A number of studies have emphasized that this is a highly questionable presumption. In practice, people with disabilities, members of different ethnic groups and those on low incomes, particularly women, are poorly protected and experience various forms of financial exclusion (Kempson and Whyley, 1999; Pahl, 1999).

These findings have been confirmed in a recent review of financial services by the Office of Fair Trading, which concluded that regulation had 'failed to reflect the interests of vulnerable consumers'. In a radical attempt to reconfigure consumer protection along more differentiated lines it proposed that government regulations and those responsible for self-regulation 'should take far more account of consumers' relative incomes' (Office of Fair Trading, 1999, p. 3). Possible ways of implementing this proposal have already been developed (Cowell and Gardiner, 2000).

Whether this 'fundamental departure from current practice' (OFT, 1999, p. 3) will materialize remains to be seen. For some analysts, however, it represents yet another attempt to accommodate to rather than challenge the unequal structures of capitalist society, a criticism they would apply to consumer protection in general. For others it opens up questions about the ways in which concerns about safeguarding individual service users and purchasers deflects attention from consideration of the role of democratic processes in ensuring accountable, consumer-driven services and broader citizenship entitlements. Focusing on consumers' education and procedural justice may also mask more fundamental issues of substantive justice.

These questions are likely to feature increasingly in social policy debates about the nature of consumer protection as a social problem and possible responses to it. In the mean time it would appear that, whether one is using state services or purchasing commercial welfare, one should follow the advice of the Molony Committee on Consumer Protection: 'The consumer's first safeguard must always be an alert and questioning attitude' (Molony Committee, 1962).

Issues to Consider

- Why has consumer protection emerged as a social problem in social policy?
- Is consumer protection different for statutory welfare services and commercial and voluntary services?
- Is it possible to have common standards of provision in welfare service?
- How effective is education as a form of consumer protection?
- How effectively do regulatory measures and bodies protect the users and consumers of welfare services?

Suggestions for Further Reading

Useful guides to the debates within economics about consumer power and protection in welfare markets can be found in Barr (1993) and Glennerster (1997). Clarke (1993) provides a stimulating account of the emergence of user movements and related critiques of state welfare services, while Beresford's (1997) review of the neglect of users' perspectives within social policy raises equally fundamental issues. Current information can be tracked through the many publications of the Office of Fair Trading www.oft.gov.uk and of the Financial Services Agency. The Consumers' Association website Which.Support.@which.co.uk is also worth consulting.

References

Audit Commission 1992: *Citizen's Charter Indicators: Charting a Course*. London: HMSO.

Barnes, M. 1997: *Care, Communities and Citizens*. Harlow: Addison, Wesley, Longman.

Barr, N. 1993: *The Economics of the Welfare State*, 2nd edn. London: Weidenfeld & Nicolson.

Beresford, P. 1997: The last social division? Revisiting the relationship between social policy, its producers and consumers. In M. May, E. Brunsdon and G. Craig (eds), *Social Policy Review*, 9.

Clarke, J. 1993: *A Crisis in Care? Challenges to Social Work*. London: Sage.

Clarke, J. and Langan, M, 1993: Restructuring welfare: the British welfare regime in the 1980s. In A. Cochrane and J. Clarke (eds), *Comparing Welfare States: Britain in International Perspective.* London: Sage.

Cmnd. 6404 1942: *Report of the Committee on Social Insurance and Allied services*, the Beveridge Report. London: HMSO.

Cowell, F. A. and Gardiner, K. 2000: *Welfare Weights*. London: Office of Fair Trading.

Department of Health 1991: *Inspection for Quality: Guidance on Practice for Inspection Units in Social Services Departments and Other Agencies: Principles, Issues and Recommendations*. London: HMSO.

Flynn, N. 1997: *Public Sector Management*, 3rd edn. London: Prentice-Hall.

Glennerster, H. 1997: *Paying for Welfare Towards 2000*, 3rd edn. Hemel Hempstead: Prentice-Hall.

Glennerster, H. 1999: A third way? In H. Dean and R. Woods (eds), *Social Policy Review*, 11.

Harris, P. 1997: *An Introduction to Law*, 5th edn. London: Weidenfeld & Nicolson.

Hirschmann, A. 1970: *Exit, Voice and Loyalty: Responses to Decline in Firms, Organisations and States*. Cambridge, Mass.: Harvard University Press.

Hunter, T. 2000: The great endowment deception. *Sunday Telegraph*, 23 January.

Kelly, G. 2000: Ownership for all. *Progress*, Spring.

Kempson, E. and Whyley, C. 1999: *Kept Out or Opted Out? Understanding and Combating Financial Exclusion*. Bristol: Policy Press.

Klein, R. and Millar, J. 1995: Do-it-yourself social policy: searching for a new paradigm? *Social Policy and Administration*, 29 (4), 303–16.

Labour Party 1991: *Citizen's Charter: Labour's Deal for Consumers and Citizens*. London: Labour Party.

Lee, P. and Raban, C. 1988: *Welfare Theory and Social Policy: Reform or Revolution*. London: Sage.

Le Grand, J. 1982: *The Strategy of Inequality*. London: Allen & Unwin.

Le Grand, J. 1991: Quasi-markets and social policy. *Economic Journal*, 101, 1256–67.

Manning, N. 1985: *Social Problems and Welfare Ideology*. Aldershot: Gower.

Marquand, D. 1990: Smashing times. *New Society* and *New Statesman*, 27 July.

May, M. and Brunsdon, E. 1999: Commercial and occupational welfare. In R. Page and R. Silburn (eds), *British Social Welfare in the Twentieth Century*. London: Macmillan.

Mishra, R. 1989: *The Welfare State in Crisis*. Brighton: Wheatsheaf.

Molony Committee 1962: *Final Report of the Committee on Consumer Protection*, Cmnd. 1781. London: HMSO.

Office of Fair Trading 1999: *Vulnerable Consumers and Financial Services: The Report of the Director General's Inquiry*. London: OFT.

Pahl, J. 1999: *Invisible Money Family Finances in the Electronic Economy*. Bristol: Policy Press.

Parry, N. and Parry, J. 1979: Social work, professionalism and the state. In N. Parry, M. Rustin and C. Satyamurti (eds), *Social Work, Welfare and the State*. London: Edward Arnold.

Perkin, H. 1989: *The Rise of Professional Society England Since 1880*. London: Routledge.

Powell, F. 1997: The new poor law. In M. Mullard and S. Lee (eds), *The Politics of Social Policy in Europe*. Cheltenham: Edward Elgar.

Prime Minister 1991: *Citizen's Charter: Raising the Standard*, Cmnd. 1599. London: HMSO.

Prime Minister 1996: *Citizen's Charter: Five Years On*, Cmnd. 2101. London: HMSO.

Selva, M. 2000: FSA widens 'educating public' role. *Daily Telegraph*, 21 January.

Chapter 20

Food and the Environment

Meg Huby

Introduction

Social policy has traditionally been mainly concerned with social security, housing, health, education and personal social services. It is only recently that the questions of equity, responsibility and accountability raised by environmental problems in general, and by food in particular, have been recognized as having an important influence on the potential for social development. Nevertheless, food is not a new problem in British social policy. The importance of a diet adequate to sustain physical well-being was recognized in studies of poverty at the turn of the nineteenth century. A hundred years later, amid the complex and often subtle arguments about definitions of poverty and deprivation, there is no dispute about the role of food as a basic human need.

However, the problem food presents for social policy has changed enormously, at least in richer industrialized countries. While the availability of, and access to, adequate quantities of food are still matters of vital concern in many parts of the world, at the end of the twentieth century Britain has food in abundance. But patterns of food consumption, distribution, processing and production are leading to growing social problems which merit the attention of social policy analysts.

This chapter argues the case for establishing food-related problems firmly on the social policy agenda:

- systems of food production directly affect rural employment and living standards and have effects on the environment and on human health;
- patterns of food processing and distribution are both products and causes of changing demands for different types of food;
- demand is driven by social and economic conditions and changing lifestyles, but also by interests within the food industry;

- the unequal distribution of resources underlies patterns of food consumption and their implications for health and well-being.

The Nature of the Problem

Most of us in Britain today eat more than we need simply to keep us alive. But our health is affected by *what* we eat and can also depend on our attitudes to food. Physical health and dental problems can result from eating too much of certain kinds of food. Coronary heart disease, for example, has been associated with high fat intake, and dental caries with sugary foods. On the other hand, some problems are related to a lack of fibre, vitamins or minerals caused by a diet that is too restricted. The desire to lose weight, for example, often leads teenage girls to reduce their milk intake; public health experts are currently concerned because milk is an important source of calcium, thought to be a key nutrient for reducing the risks of osteoporosis in later life.

Both physical and mental health are threatened by eating disorders such as anorexia and bulimia, while obesity, often caused by overeating, has been linked to an increased incidence of conditions such as diabetes and arthritis. Patterns of food consumption, then, have clear implications for public health care, health promotion and education policy.

Social policy is deeply concerned with the ways in which an inequitable distribution of resources affects welfare (see the chapters by Donnison and Spicker). This topic also pervades the question of how much control people have over what they eat. In poorer households the choice of food is known to be constrained by income. Larger shops and supermarkets offering lower prices are often situated in out-of-town retail parks, difficult to get to for people without cars.

Rich and poor alike are disempowered in the face of conflicting advice about food-related health risks. The last decade has seen a number of food scares characterized by scientific uncertainty about the causal links between food and health. Risks related to salmonella in eggs, listeria in soft cheeses and cook-chill meals and bovine spongiform encephalopathy (BSE) in beef have all been interpreted differently by different experts and at different points in time. This tends to foster either feelings of acute anxiety about food, or disillusionment about and mistrust of the government's advice and policy.

Some heath risks are associated with the intensified production systems of primary food in agriculture, livestock farming and fisheries. Changing farming methods have also had impacts on rural employment and income security in addition to their, often devastating, effects on the countryside. Damage to landscapes and wildlife is a problem in its own right, but it has social relevance in that it affects the opportunities which people have for many leisure pursuits and limits the intellectual, sensual and spiritual pleasures offered by diverse natural environments.

The wider environmental impacts of the food industry are associated with the large-scale processing, packaging, transport and storage of food, and these compound the direct effects of food consumption and production on social conditions. The pollution of land, air and water by fertilizers, pesticides, pharmaceuticals, chemical additives, refrigerants and motor vehicle emissions, together with the generation of huge quantities of solid waste, have indirect implications for social life and development in the longer term and on a scale that transcends national boundaries.

While the food industry in Britain presents direct problems for public health, education, social security, employment, social empowerment and well-being, the indirect effects of the environmental problems it causes are less obvious. To understand the crucial importance of the environment to social policy it is useful to recognize that the people benefiting most from environmentally damaging activities are not usually the people who would benefit most from policies to alleviate them. The latter tend to be people living on low incomes and those for whom age, disability, gender or race means that they lack the means, resources or power to avoid or ameliorate the effects of living in a degraded environment. The benefits of the food industry in Britain today accrue largely to big businesses and to better-off consumers. But social inequalities result in a varied distribution of direct and indirect costs, making food a major and growing cause for social concern.

The Changing Nature of the Food Industry

Explaining why food has attained problem status is complicated by the relation between food supply and demand. If the food industry simply provided what consumers demanded to meet their nutritional needs, many of today's problems would probably not exist. But changing social and economic conditions have elevated food from a basic subsistence need to a commodity imbued with many social meanings. In addition to its nutritional value, food has come to be valued for its taste, its visual attractiveness, convenience and its meaning as an indicator of lifestyle. Joffe (1991) traces the development of food production in Britain over time. He highlights the change from postwar policies designed to maximize production to satisfy the needs of a growing population to production which meets the demands of consumers who want and expect variety and choice in the food they buy.

> Expectations and demands are fuelled by the way in which food is advertised and marketed; the rapid increase in advertising in particular during the last few decades reflects changes in the nature of the food industry. Food is now big business and in 1996 five retail chains accounted for around two thirds of all food bought in Britain. (Lang, 1996)

With production and distribution located in the private sector, control of the food industry is left largely to the market, but the separation of consumption from the production of food has become so pronounced that consumers have little power to influence its supply. Large companies are able to develop the foods that bring them most profit and then create the demand for them through advertising, cashing in on the increasing power of the mass media, particularly television. In the UK in 1996 an average of 17 advertisements an hour were shown on children's television, ten of these advertising food. And 95 per cent of UK food advertisements were for products high in fat, sugar or salt (Consumers International, 1996). It may be argued that food supply now dictates demand.

Changes in Methods of Primary Production

The concentration of control over the food industry in large companies, often transnational corporations (TNCs), has also had impacts on what farmers produce. The dominance of TNCs such as Coca-Cola, McDonalds and Nestlé gives them power over world commodity prices, influencing the prices that British farmers are paid for their produce. But market prices are distorted by state support for agriculture and by the European Common Agricultural Policy (CAP). Before 1992 the price support system of the CAP encouraged monocultural agriculture. Most profits were made by larger landowners using capital-intensive modern systems in large fields. At the same time, market prices held at artificially high levels constituted an implicit tax on food, which was paid by consumers (Renwick and Hubbard, 1994).

CAP reforms in the mid-1990s reduced subsidies and introduced direct payments to farmers for actions that would protect and enhance the environment. Costs were shifted from consumers to taxpayers, with distributional consequences for different income groups. In a minor way these changes were progressive and did have some beneficial effects on the countryside, but they still failed to address the plight of smaller farmers.

Pressures on farmers to constantly produce 'more for less' are on the whole still operating to encourage increasing intensification in both agriculture and livestock production. Retailers' demands for fresh fruit and vegetables of uniform size and unblemished appearance put pressures on growers to standardize, use increasing levels of chemical fertilizers, pesticides and herbicides and reduce natural genetic diversity. The wide-ranging environmental impacts of these changes are discussed, together with their effects on social well-being, in Huby (1998).

Increased mechanization and the amalgamation of many small farms to achieve economies of scale have led to a decline in employment. Between 1993 and 1998 employment in the agricultural sector fell by 17 per cent, while over the same period in the food wholesale and retail trades it rose by 15 per cent (Office for National Statistics, 1999). Farm incomes are also falling, with concomitant effects on rural communities. Recent responses by the government include consultation on early retirement plans for beef and sheep farmers – plans which have implications for pensions and social security.

The economic disaster facing many small farmers stems from the falling demand for their products, itself related to changing farming methods. The spread of salmonella in eggs, with its devastating effects on poultry farmers, is thought to have been accelerated by the overuse of antibiotics in animal feed, leading to the development of resistant strains of bacteria. The crisis over BSE exploded in 1996, when the Spongiform Encephalopathy Advisory Committee (SEAC) announced that ten human deaths from a variant of Creutzfeldt-Jakob disease (CJD) could possibly be linked to BSE-infected beef. The spread of BSE has been blamed on the increased use, in intensive beef production, of commercial concentrate feed containing ruminant-derived meat and bonemeal.

Intensified methods of agriculture rely on the use of chemicals to increase crop yields per acre. Pesticide and herbicide residues in or on food and in the atmosphere can have direct effects on health and have been associated with many cases of cancer, immune deficiencies, lung and nerve damage, asthma and hay fever. In 1996 it was estimated that £1 billion of capital investment was needed to remove pesticides from drinking water in England and Wales (Taylor, 1996).

Some effects of pesticides are less direct but no less important. Methyl bromide, for example, is one of a group of chemicals known to deplete the ozone layer and is thus responsible for increasing risks of skin cancers and glaucoma caused by exposure to the UV radiation in sunlight. Death rates from malignant melanoma have increased by 53 per cent in Britain over the last 20 years. But methyl bromide is still in common use as a soil pesticide for growing strawberries and salad vegetables.

Ironically, if the genetically modified (GM) maize at the centre of Britain's current political food furore is approved for use in agriculture in the UK, herbicide use could increase. The idea behind modification is that herbicides can be applied with less discrimination on crops resistant to their toxic effects. Interestingly, Monsanto, the US-based chemical company playing a leading role in developing GM crops resistant to the herbicide Roundup, also produces Roundup. The herbicide currently accounts for 40 per cent of Monsanto's operating profits.

The Royal Society (1998) notes some potential benefits of the use of GM organisms in food production. But it recognizes that legitimate safety concerns have not yet been resolved. Dangers posed by GM organisms all relate to uncertainties about their potential to affect the environment and human health. There are risks that herbicide-resistant genes could transfer to wild species, creating 'superweeds', that the increased use of herbicides will lead to a loss of biodiversity, and that there may be unforeseen effects on herbivores and animals higher up the food chain. Threats to human health include the higher allergenic potential which may characterize transgenic plants, and the possible transfer of antibiotic-resistant genes, used as markers, into gut bacteria, increasing the potential for the development of antibiotic-resistant, disease-causing strains.

GM soya, maize and oilseed rape are used as ingredients in thousands of food products, but, as yet, there is no clear regulatory system governing their labelling. Whether or not concern about risks is justified, the story of GM food demonstrates the corporate power of large companies and the erosion of consumers' 'right to know' about the food they are eating.

Changes in Food Processing

To increase profits, the food industry now processes food in a remarkable variety of ways. Its expansion has been achieved by increasing the range of food products such as snacks, sweets, precooked and frozen meals, sold on the basis of their novelty, packaging and appeals to lifestyle and convenience. Some 80 per cent of British food is processed, and one-third of meals are 'pre-prepared' (Lang, 1996).

During treatment, the same basic foods can be artificially coloured and flavoured to give us products that look and taste different. The effect on health of chemical food additives has long been the subject of scrutiny, and additives must now be included on food labels, supposedly to increase consumer choice. But labels do not always tell the whole story. The artificial sweetener aspartame, for example, has been approved by committees on the safety of food additives in the UK, in Europe and, internationally, in the Food and Agriculture Organization (FAO) and the World Health Organization (WHO). Yet controversy still remains about the possible toxic effects of aspartame on the nervous system.

There is no real consensus in the food industry and among governmental and interested non-governmental organizations (NGOs) about the safety of certain methods of preserving food. Irradiation, for example, was approved by the government in 1991, in the face of strong public opposition. By 1997, none of the leading supermarkets were *knowingly* stocking irradiated food, but in 1996 the Ministry of Agriculture, Fisheries and Food (MAFF) acknowledged that some of it was being imported to Britain with labelling that was misleading – or absent altogether. Current concerns about the dangers of PVC packaging were sparked initially in 1996 by the discovery of phthalates (used as softeners in PVC production) in baby milk at levels high enough to trigger oestrogenic effects. But disagreement still persists among retailers, PVC manufacturers and environmental groups about how to set standards to reduce the risks of PVC packaging to health and the environment.

Changing Patterns of Food Distribution

The need to treat food so that it retains its freshness for longer partly stems from the increased time which most food now needs to reach the consumer after leaving the factory. In 1979 and in 1993 the same amount of food was transported in Britain, but in 1993 it travelled 50 per cent further (Lang, 1997a). The ability to make food available at long distances from its point of production has some advantages for consumers, many of whom are now offered a much wider choice. Supply is no longer restricted to goods produced locally or limited to particular seasons of the year.

However, food transport demands an increasing use of fossil fuels in engines and refrigerated vehicles. Together with the additional fuel used for farm machines, the increased energy requirements of the food industry have major implications for the environmental damage associated with greenhouse gas production. The potential for social problems to arise as global warming leads to climate change is enormous. Changing climate patterns affect, for example, the range and distribution of the insect vectors of numerous human pathogens, and this increases the potential for outbreaks of infection in new areas. There is already evidence that conditions in Britain are suitable for the survival of malaria-carrying mosquitoes, and in September 1999 the entire city of New York was sprayed with insecticide to eradicate mosquitoes carrying the tropical St Louis encephalitis virus.

Although the processing and transporting of food carries costs for health and the environment, these are not borne to any great extent by the food industry. Instead, profits in the industry are enhanced by vastly expanding markets. Economies of scale and extended shelf life do allow some foods to be produced more cheaply, and some consumers benefit from wider choice and lower prices. These benefits are, however, unevenly distributed.

Recent years have seen a decline in the number of local retail outlets situated centrally in residential communities and a rapid growth in large supermarkets able to supply a huge range of food products. Five supermarket chains now account for about two-thirds of all the food bought in Britain, but their branches are predominantly located in retail parks outside towns. The same food can cost up to 60 per cent more in small local stores than in supermarkets. But people with either financial or practical problems that limit their mobility may be excluded from the benefits offered by greater variety and cheaper prices. These people are most often those who live in rural areas, have lower incomes, are disabled or elderly or are parents with young children – the very groups with which social policy is most often concerned. 'Changes in food retailing have created new mechanisms for the social exclusion of the poor' (Lang, 1997b).

Changing Patterns of Consumption

The growth of income inequalities in Britain since the late 1970s is mirrored by inequalities in the kinds of food people eat. Fresh fruit, vegetables and food rich in fibre constitute the healthiest kind of diet, but it is fatty, sugary and salty foods which often provide the cheapest way to get adequate energy. In 1999, elderly people living alone and relying on state retirement pensions still find it difficult to afford, buy and prepare acceptable food of appropriate nutritional quality (Lyon and Colquhoun, 1999). 'The 20 per cent of Income Support claimants with compulsory deductions for rent or fuel have very restricted spending on food, and their resulting diets are far below reference values for intakes of iron, calcium, dietary fibre and vitamin C' (Acheson, 1998, p. 63).

Gaining access to a healthy diet is strongly influenced by one's disposable income, facilities, skills and knowledge (see also the chapter by Jones). Lang (1997b), however, in reviewing the links between diet and low income, stresses that the problem is more often one of affordability than one of lack of concern or information. The 1996 Health Education Monitoring Survey found that 29 per cent of respondents with annual incomes of £20,000 or more agreed or strongly agreed that eating healthy food is expensive. This figure rose to 51 per cent of people with incomes under £5,000 (Hansbro and Bridgwood, 1997). 'People on low incomes share the rest of the population's desire to eat healthily' (Lang, 1997b, p. 218).

Linked to affordability are the demands placed on working mothers in low-income households. The gendered distribution of household labour can mean that feeding a family after a working day is made easier by using processed or frozen foods and snack food that needs little preparation or cooking. The pressures of tight budgets and heavy demands on time are exacerbated by the ways in which convenience foods and snacks are advertised to appeal to children and to women playing dual roles as earners and nurturers.

The kinds of precooked food bought by richer people are more expensive and more likely to be chosen for taste and status than for affordability. For the rich, eating, and particularly eating in restaurants, has grown in popularity as a leisure activity. Fatty and sugary foods are more likely to be chosen for pleasure than for price. Dietary deficiency problems are rare among people with middle or high incomes, but diet accounts for about a quarter of all cancer deaths in Britain. Coronary heart disease and obesity are common problems; England has one of the worst rates of coronary heart disease in Europe. Of women in social class V (unskilled) 25 per cent are obese, but so are 14 per cent of those in social class I (professional). The rates of obesity in children are increasing across all social classes (Department of Health, 1999).

Regardless of income and class, our choice of food is increasingly dominated by advertising and marketing. On the one hand, we are encouraged to buy snacks and rich luxury foods and to indulge our tastes, tastes which, it could be argued, have been developed by the food industry itself. On the other hand, we are bombarded with images and messages emphasizing the desirability of being slim. Slimness is sold as being healthy and sexually alluring but is, of course, closely related to eating habits. In the face of such contradictions there is little wonder that eating disorders like anorexia and bulimia are increasingly common, especially among young women and teenage girls.

Changes in social and economic conditions and changing lifestyles over the past twenty years have had huge impacts on patterns of food consumption. But the extent to which consumer demand for certain types of food has led to changing patterns of production, processing and distribution is far from clear. It can be argued that it is the food industry itself, incorporating a wide range of policy areas, which has been the driver of change.

Recent Policy Responses to the Problem

Given the range of social and environmental problems associated with food production and consumption, it is perhaps not surprising to find that policies to deal with food-related problems have so far been fragmentary. Postwar British policy centred on production, with MAFF clearly identified as the key player responsible for the intensification and industrialization of agriculture and for creating and implementing regulations. By the 1980s, however, the food industry was dominated by commercial interests. The state's role seemed to be to facilitate further expansion, and the industry was largely left to regulate itself.

The mid-1980s saw a burgeoning of public interest in environmental issues, stimulated by the activities of NGOs and pressure groups and intensified by the growing influence of European environmental policy. The food scares which attracted so much media attention brought together the interests of environmental, health, education and welfare groups, giving them an increasingly important role in shaping government policy and crossing the divide between MAFF and the DHSS. The National Food Alliance, representing over 50 public organizations, was established to promote food policies and practices to enhance public health, to protect living and working environments and to enrich society. The government was at last forced to pay attention to the social and environmental aspects of food production.

The government's policy to address problems arising from the effects of a poor diet on health at first placed responsibility squarely on the shoulders of individuals, with the notorious Look After Your Health campaign. Blame was placed on ignorance and unhealthy lifestyles, and the links between low income and diet, which research had consistently shown to be crucial for health, were ignored. But public pressure continued to grow, with a coalition of medical bodies, civil servants and NGOs pressing for change, and it was the publication of the Health of the Nation White Paper in 1992 that marked an important change in government policy. Food was finally recognized as a problem for public health, and a Nutrition Taskforce was established within the Department of Health (DoH) to work on the subjects of school meals, catering education and the relation between diet and income.

The 1980 Education Act removed from schools the obligation to provide meals for all children and abolished prevailing nutritional standards. Thanks to campaigning by organizations such as the Child Poverty Action Group (CPAG), new nutritional guidelines for school meals were published in 1997, but they are implemented only on a voluntary basis. There has been little progress to date on CPAG's campaign for the wider extension of entitlement to free school meals. Cooking is still not part of the school curriculum, although the 1993 Get

Cooking! campaign to help people become less dependent on the food industry's products was supported by both the DoH and MAFF.

The 1990s have seen other small but significant developments involving cooperation between various government departments, NGOs and parts of the food industry, but there has been little in the way of real progress to develop any comprehensive food policy. In 1994, for example, a House of Commons Select Committee on the Environment reported some consensus on the need to reduce the use of motorized transport for shopping and to reinvigorate local shop culture (House of Commons Select Committee on the Environment, 1994). But the 1998 White Paper on transport (Department of the Environment, Transport and the Regions, 1998) does little to address the issue in practical terms, and out-of-town shopping centres continue to grow in number.

The current controversy over the field trials of GM crops in Britain illustrates the extent to which food has become a political issue. There is no place in the regulatory system for formal public consultation, but consumers are exerting some influence. Following customer surveys, Tesco has stated that it will try to ensure that its own-brand products will be free from GM ingredients. After a 50 per cent drop in the sales of its main soya product Beanfeast, Unilever announced a commitment to remove GM ingredients from all its UK products 'wherever practicable'. These moves have been hailed as a triumph for public concern in influencing the food industry through the supermarkets. Indeed, the latter appear to have responded to the problem more positively than the government. But the industry's commitments have been given 'for the time being' and it remains to be seen whether they will hold good after the media's interest in GM foods declines.

In some instances the development of government policy on food is succeeding in bringing a wider range of interest groups to the negotiating table. The debate about the water quality standards needed to meet the 1979 Directive on shellfish waters is bringing together not only representatives of the EU, the Department of the Environment, Transport and the Regions (DETR), MAFF and the Environment Agency (EA), but also health experts, supermarkets and the shellfish industry. But a fragmentation of interests still prevails in many areas. Recent moves to introduce a tax on pesticides, supported by environmental organizations, are meeting with strong opposition from the agrochemical industry and farmers, supported by MAFF. The water companies, which are required by EU directives to improve the treatment of sewage, charge fish processors for cleaning up trade effluent. But in July 1999 the House of Commons and the Scottish Parliament were told that increases in charges to meet environmental standards are likely to lead to widespread plant closures and thousands of job losses in the industry (Environmental Data Services, 1999).

Plans to establish a new Food Standards Agency (FSA), introduced in January 1998, have not yet come to fruition. The FSA, regarded by many as the most significant development in food policy since 1945, is intended to 'protect public health from risks which may arise in connection with the consumption of food (including risks caused by the way in which it is produced or supplied) and otherwise to protect the interests of consumers in relation to food' (Ministry of Agriculture, Fisheries and Food, 1999). The responsibility for food safety is to be moved from MAFF to the DoH, but the FSA will need to work closely with MAFF, the DETR and the EA where food safety and environmental concerns overlap. A cooperation between local authorities, members of the public and the food industry will also be needed. The draft Bill suggests that the costs of establishing the agency will be met by a levy on food retailers and caterers; but if these costs are passed on to consumers there may be severe implications for food affordability in low-income groups.

Options for the Future

The systems for the production, distribution and consumption of food in Britain today pose problems of environmental deterioration, instability of income and employment, food poverty and widening inequalities in health. Control over what people eat has shifted away from consumers and is now vested largely in the food industry. If these problems are to be resolved, it is essential to recognise that food is a matter for both social and environmental concern. Policy goals are needed that take into account the wide range of stakeholders in the food economy in ensuring a healthy and secure food supply. Consumer rights need to be protected in policy-making processes that are transparent and fair and which involve consumers themselves.

The development of policies on production currently depends on decisions taken in Europe and on the national policies of MAFF and the DETR. Health interests are not yet adequately represented and the relations between the social, environmental and economic goals of the government still lead to apparently contradictory policy directions. The newly established Pesticides Forum, for example, has the objective of minimizing the impact of pesticides on human and environmental health. But the government has failed to discourage the development of GM crops, specifically designed to allow the easier use of the pesticides produced and sold by their developers.

Threats to the survival of British farming are currently enjoying a high media profile. Rural employment in agriculture is unlikely to expand under intensive farming systems, but it could be encouraged by moves away from mass production towards small-scale farms growing food on principles of environmental stewardship. Agricultural wages, like those of many workers in the food-processing, small-scale retailing and catering sectors, are low. Subsidies negotiated through MAFF, the Department of Trade and Industry (DTI) and the Department for Education and Employment (DE&E) to stabilize employment and incomes could pay dividends in improved food quality and public and environmental health.

Of course any such subsidies would need funding from taxation. The problem is how to do this without compounding the inequities in food consumption that are embedded in the social constructs of gender, race and class. Lang (1997b) recognizes the crucial importance of alleviating food poverty by improving incomes at the bottom end of the scale, particularly for people relying on social security benefits. He challenges the government to pay heed to the results of research estimating the costs of diets which are 'modest but adequate' (Bradshaw, 1993) and to take account of these when setting benefit levels.

Healthy eating depends not only on the affordability and availability of food and an understanding of what constitutes a healthy diet but also on personal tastes and preferences. These are influenced by early eating habits and there is a good case for investment in developing comprehensive school health programmes, integrating school meals services with education on nutrition, health and practical cooking skills.

Increased regulation and control over advertising, food retailing and labelling are options which the government could use to influence consumers directly, relying on individual choice to improve the health of people and the environment. Government policy shapes the context in which decisions about food are made. But worries about food have recently been fuelled by changing and sometimes conflicting advice given by the government and media scientists. The 'food credibility gap' is in urgent need of attention. The new FSA could have a role to play, but its success depends on the extent to which it succeeds in bringing together for debate the diverse interests of the public and the private and voluntary sectors to enable a shift of power and control to consumers of all social strata.

The dominance of TNCs in the food industry gives them a degree of power which may appear insurmountable. Yet it can be argued that in the face of such power it is even more imperative that national governments take strong action to protect and promote the public interest. In addition to reforming agricultural policy, they could apply tighter regulations to food production and processing and direct research funds away from intensive agriculture towards the development of organic and environmentally sound systems at a more local level. Taxes and subsidies could be designed to encourage food manufacturers to reformulate their products, presenting people with better choices about what they eat.

Lang (1997a) proposes some general objectives for British food policy. These include goals to enhance public health and well-being and to protect the natural environment. But he also stresses the need to reduce the trade gap and to ensure that inequalities between rich and poor are reduced both within and between countries. This chapter has limited its focus to food production and consumption in Britain, but the argument that food is a social problem applies equally to an international context. The challenge for the future is to find policies that help to democratize the food economy on a local, national and international scale.

Issues to Consider

- How can the intensification of agriculture lead to social policy problems through its effects on health, employment and the countryside?
- A huge range of food products is now available all the year round in British supermarkets. What are the social and environmental implications of this apparent increase in 'consumer choice'?
- How may the growing availability of processed food be related to the number of women with families entering the labour market?
- What obstacles lie in the way of policies that aim to improve public health by encouraging healthier eating habits?
- Can inequalities in food consumption be explained in terms of the social constructs of class, gender and ethnicity?

Suggestions for Further Reading

The emergence of food – and environmental issues in general – as a social problem and the challenges presented to social policy analysis are explored more fully in Huby (1998). This study considers how access to food varies between different groups of people and how this has different impacts on the environment, which, in turn, have the capacity to influence social well-being and development. Yearley (1992) provides an accessible introduction to the major changes that have taken place in the food industry in the latter half of the twentieth century, both in what is eaten and how it is produced. Joffe (1991) clearly explains how food has come to present problems of quality rather than of quantity in much of the industrialized Western world. Lang (1997a;b) argues convincingly for the need to reform food policy in the UK, taking account of social and environmental as well as agricultural and economic considerations. The related issues of consumer protection can be followed through the websites of a number of environmental groups, the best starting point being that of the Office for National Statistics: www.ons.gov.uk; the Department of Health: www.doh.gov.uk; the World Health Organization: www.who.org; Friends of the Earth: www.foe.org.

References

Acheson, D. 1998: *Independent Inquiry into Inequalities in Health*. London: Stationery Office.

Bradshaw, J. 1993: *Household Budgets and Living Standards*. York: Joseph Rowntree Foundation.

Consumers International 1996: *A Spoonful of Sugar: Television Food Advertising Aimed at Children: An International Survey*. London: Consumers International.

Department of the Environment, Transport and the Regions 1998: *A New Deal for Transport: Better for Everyone: The Government's White Paper on the Future of Transport*, Cmnd. 3950. London: Stationery Office.

Department of Health 1999: *Saving Lives: Our Healthier Nation*, Cmnd. 4386. London: Stationery Office.

Environmental Data Services 1999: *Report 294*. London: Environmental Data Services.

Hansbro, J. and Bridgwood, A. 1997: *Health in England 1996*, Office for National Statistics and the Health Education Authority. London: Stationery Office.

House of Commons Select Committee on the Environment 1994: *Shopping Centres and Their Future*, fourth report, Session 1993–94. London: HMSO.

Huby, M. 1998: *Social Policy and the Environment*. Buckingham: Open University Press.

Joffe, M. 1991: Food as a social policy issue. In N. Manning (ed.), *Social Policy Review 1990–91*. Harlow: Longman.

Lang, T. 1996: The challenge for food culture: healing the madness, 1996 Schumacher Lecture, 19 October. Bristol: Colston Hall.

Lang, T. 1997a: Food policy for the 21st century: can it be both radical and reasonable? Discussion paper 4. Centre for Food Policy, Thames Valley University.

Lang, T. 1997b: Dividing up the cake: food as social exclusion. In A. Walker and C. Walker (eds), *Britain Divided: The Growth of Social Exclusion in the 1980s and 1990s*. London: Child Poverty Action Group.

Lyon, P. and Colquhoun, A. 1999: Home, hearth and table: a centennial review of the nutritional circumstances of older people living alone. *Ageing and Society*, 19 (1), 53–67.

Ministry of Agriculture, Fisheries and Food 1999: *The Food Standards Agency: Consultation on Draft Legislation*, Cmnd. 4249. London: Stationery Office.

Office for National Statistics 1999: *Annual Abstract of Statistics 1999 Edition*. London: Stationery Office.

Renwick, A. W. and Hubbard, L. J. 1994: Distributional aspects of the UK costs of the Common Agricultural Policy. *Food Policy*, 19 (5), 459–68.

Royal Society 1998: *Statement on Genetically Modified Plants for Food Use*. London: Royal Society.

Taylor, M. 1996: Public health and water quality. In C. Hewitt, C. Hogg, M. Leicester and H. Rosenthal (eds), *Health and the Environment*. London: Socialist Health Association and Socialist Environment and Resources Association.

Yearley, S. 1992: *The Green Case: A Sociology of Environmental Issues, Arguments and Politics*. London: Routledge.

Index